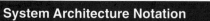
System Architecture Notation

Components

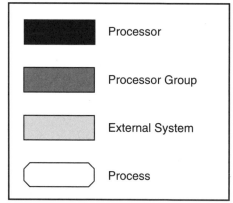

Processor

Processor Group

External System

Process

Connections

☐ Bridge

Primary Network

— Backup Network

Process Notation

Influences

Generates or Produces

Time

Human Agent

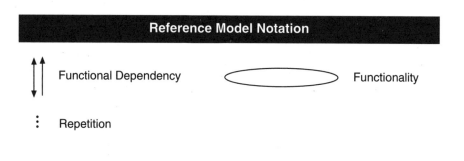

Reference Model Notation

Functional Dependency

Functionality

Repetition

Software Architecture in Practice

Len Bass
Paul Clements
Rick Kazman

 **ADDISON-WESLEY**

An imprint of Addison Wesley Longman, Inc.

Reading, Massachusetts • Harlow, England • Menlo Park, California
Berkeley, California • Don Mills, Ontario • Sydney
Bonn • Amsterdam • Tokyo • Mexico City

Software Engineering Institute

The SEI Series in Software Engineering

Many of the designations used by manufacturers and sellers to distinguish their products are claimed as trademarks. Where those designations appear in this book and Addison-Wesley was aware of a trademark claim, the designations have been printed in initial caps or all caps.

The authors and publishers have taken care in the preparation of this book, but make no expressed or implied warranty of any kind and assume no responsibility for errors or omissions. No liability is assumed for incidental or consequential damages in connection with or arising out of the use of the information or programs contained herein.

The publisher offers discounts on this book when ordered in quantity for special sales. For more information, please contact:

Corporate & Professional Publishing Group
Addison Wesley Longman, Inc.
One Jacob Way
Reading, Massachusetts 01867

Library of Congress Cataloging-in-Publication Data

Bass, Len.
 Software architecture in practice / by Len Bass, Paul Clements,
 Rick Kazman.
  p.   cm.
 Includes bibliographical references and index.
 ISBN 0-201-19930-0
 1. Computer software.   2. Computer architecture.   3. System
design.   I. Clements, Paul.   II. Kazman, Rick.
III. Title.
QA76.754.B37   1998
005.1--DC21   97-13979
                                                CIP

Text printed on recycled and acid-free paper.

ISBN 0201199300

6 7 8 9 1011 MA   02 01 00 99

6th Printing August 1999

Contents

Preface

Software architecture is an important field of study that is becoming more important and more talked about with every passing day. But, to our knowledge, there exists little practical guidance on how to manage software architecture within a real software development organization from a technical or from a managerial perspective. This book has emerged from our belief that the coupling of the software architecture of a system and its business and organizational context has not been well explored.

Our experience with designing and reviewing large and complex software-intensive systems has led us to recognize the role of business and organization in the design of the system and also in its ultimate success or failure. Systems are built to satisfy an organization's requirements (or assumed requirements in the case of shrink-wrapped products), and these requirements determine the extent to which a system must meet performance targets, be highly available, interoperate with other systems, or be designed for long lifetimes. These properties of a system are constrained by the system's software architecture; or, to put it another way, the desire to achieve these properties influences the design choices made by a software architect.

In this book we demonstrate this coupling through the use of case studies drawn from real systems, including the following:

- In Chapter 7, we show how the desire to quickly and easily share documents within an organization, with a minimum of centralized control, led to the software architecture of the World Wide Web.

- In Chapter 11, we discuss how the extreme safety requirements of air traffic control led one company to build a system around an architecture for achieving ultrahigh availability.

- In Chapter 14, we describe how the distribution of the subsystems of a flight simulator to different remotely located developers led to an architecture geared to enable the easy integration of these subsystems.

- In Chapter 16, we explain how the need to satisfy simultaneous product deliveries led (in fact, forced) one company to adopt an architecture that enabled the company to economically build a set of complex, related software systems as a product line.

These and other case studies show how the architectures flow from requirements of organizations and their business models, from the experience of the organization's architects, and from the prevailing design climate.

In addition, we discuss how architectures themselves can be powerful vehicles for influencing all of the preceding. A successful product or set of products can influence how other products are built; certainly, the case study of the software underlying the World Wide Web is a good example of this. Before this system existed, there was far less network awareness; less thought was given to accessibility of data; and security was the concern of only a few organizations, typically financial institutions and government agencies.

This book is aimed at the software professional—the person designing and implementing large software-intensive systems—and at the managers of software professionals. It does not contain, for example, detailed financial justification for using a software architecture, for doing early architectural analyses, or for investing in a product line approach to building software. We provide only anecdotal evidence to support the claims that these pay off, although we passionately believe they do.

A software architecture is the development product that gives the highest return on investment with respect to quality, schedule, and cost. This is because an architecture appears early in a product's lifetime. Getting it right sets the stage for everything to come in the system's life: development, integration, testing, and modification. Getting it wrong means that the fabric of the system is wrong, and it cannot be fixed by weaving in a few new threads or pulling out a few existing ones, which often causes the entire fabric to unravel. Also, analyzing architectures is inexpensive, compared with other development activities. Thus, architectures give a high return on investment partially because decisions made for the architecture have substantial downstream consequences and because checking and fixing an architecture is relatively inexpensive.

We also believe that reusable components are best achieved within an architectural context. But components are not the only artifacts that can be reused. Reuse of an architecture leads to the creation of families of similar systems, which in turn leads to new organizational structures and new business opportunities.

A large percentage of this book is devoted to presenting real architectures that were designed to solve real problems in real organizations. We chose the case studies to illustrate the types of choices that architects must make to achieve their quality goals and to show how organizational goals affect the final systems.

In addition to the case studies, this book offers a set of techniques for designing, building, and evaluating software architectures. We look at techniques for understanding quality requirements in the context of an architecture and for building architectures that meet these quality requirements. We look at architecture description languages as a means of describing and validating software architectures. We look at techniques for analyzing and evaluating an architecture's fitness for its purpose. Each of these techniques is derived from our experience, and the experience of our colleagues at the Software Engineering Institute, with a variety of software systems. These systems range up to millions of lines of code and are large-team, multiyear development efforts.

We have also provided a visual language for describing software architectures that contains enough expressiveness to describe both procedural and object-oriented systems and enough generality to describe systems at any granularity: a division of functionality, a set of software structures, a set of hardware structures, or any combination of these. Although a visual notation is not, in itself, documentation of an architecture, it is an integral part of such a documentation. One of our complaints with the state-of-the-practice in architecture today is the vagueness of architectural descriptions. We hope that the visual language described here is a contribution to the field, aimed at increasing the effectiveness of architectural documentation.

The book targets software professionals, or students who have knowledge and experience in software engineering, and we anticipate the following three classes of readers:

1. Practicing software engineers who wish to understand both the technical basis of software architecture and the business and organizational forces that are acting on them

2. Technical managers who wish to understand how software architecture can help them to supervise the construction of systems more effectively and improve their organizations

3. Students in computer science or software engineering who might use this book as supplemental reading in a first or second software engineering course

Although business issues are discussed throughout the book (for example, how an architecture affects an organization's ability to compete in a market or how the architecture underlying a product family affects time to market), we present this material without going into the business issues in great depth and without using business jargon. We are, after all, software engineers. The technical sections are presented in more depth. These sections represent current work in the field of software architecture—the point where research meets practice; they are the philosophical foundations of the book. The case studies illustrate these technical foundations and show how they are realized in practice. However, we have written the case studies in such a way that expertise in the application domain from which each case study was drawn is not required. You will not need to be a pilot to understand either the air traffic control system or the flight simulation case studies. However, you will need to have a reasonable background in computer science, software engineering, or a related discipline to benefit from the lessons of the case studies.

One final note on the organization of the book. *Software Architecture in Practice* is not intended to be a prescriptive method for architectural design. In fact, we believe that it is impossible to satisfactorily create such a prescriptive design method. Any design involves trade-offs: Modifiability affects performance, security affects modifiability, scalability affects reliability, and everything affects cost. Any prescriptive method implicitly or explicitly assumes that some of these qualities are more important than others and guides users toward the maximization of that goal. Our feeling is that although such an approach may be appropriate in a specific domain, it cannot possibly work in general. Quality requirements are different from organization to organization and from year to year.

By way of contrast, we offer a toolbox approach to design. We believe that different architectural tools and techniques are appropriate for different situations and different quality goals. No single technique will ever suffice. So, we present a number of different architectural tools (layering, multiple views, patterns, blackboards, and so forth) and techniques (analysis methods, integration strategies, engineering principles) and illustrate their usage in different business and technical contexts.

Not surprisingly, most of the case studies use a mix of tools and techniques because they were chosen to illustrate how software architecture was the foundation for a successful system. These systems were successful precisely because they chose the right tools and implemented them using the right techniques. Anything less would not have resulted in a successful system, as we hope to persuade you in the coming pages.

Reader's Guide

The book is divided into four parts, roughly following a life-cycle perspective, what we call the *architecture business cycle* of how architectures fit into a business. They are as follows:

1. Envisioning Architecture: Chapters 1 through 3
2. Creating and Analyzing an Architecture: Chapters 4 through 11
3. Moving from Architectures to Systems: Chapters 12 through 14
4. Reusing Architectures: Chapters 15 through 19

The case studies are in Chapters 3, 7, 8, 11, 14, 16, and 18 and are clearly noted in the chapter titles. The material covered in the chapters and parts is summarized here.

PART ONE ENVISIONING ARCHITECTURE

Chapter 1 – The Architecture Business Cycle. The theme that weaves throughout this book is that architectures do not exist by themselves but are part of a cycle. Architecture is a means toward an end. It is influenced by the functional and quality goals of both the customer and the developing organization. It is also influenced by the architect's background and experiences and by the technical environment. Architecture, in turn, influences the system being developed, but it is potentially a core asset that influences the developing organization. The system also has an effect on the developing organization, the architecture, and potentially, the technical environment. This affects the future goals for the system and its organization. The influences and feedback loops that surround an architecture form the architecture business cycle (ABC).

Chapter 2 – What Is Software Architecture? An architecture is a description of system structures, of which there are several (data flow, modular, process, and so on). Architecture is the first artifact that can be analyzed to determine how well its quality attributes are being achieved, and it also serves as the project blueprint. An architecture is also a description of the relationships among components and connectors. These are the things we mean when we use the word *architecture*.

Chapter 3 – A-7E: A Case Study in Utilizing Architectural Structures.   The A-7E Avionics System was a project that paid special attention to the engineering and specification of three distinct architectural structures to achieve developmental simplicity and future modifiability. The chapter shows how the structures were designed and documented.

PART TWO   CREATING AND ANALYZING AN ARCHITECTURE

Chapter 4 – Quality Attributes.   An objective for all architectures is the desire to achieve particular software qualities. This chapter discusses software qualities and their implications. Some qualities can be achieved through architectural means, others are only partially dependent on the architecture; and still others have no dependence on the architecture. The chapter discusses the software qualities in terms that tie them to software architecture.

Chapter 5 – Moving From Qualities to Architecture: Architectural Styles. Once the desired qualities of a system are known, the problem of designing an architecture to achieve these qualities still remains. This chapter discusses the relationships among organization goals, system quality attributes, and architectural structures. The chapter describes a number of techniques used to achieve run- and development-time qualities.

Chapter 6 – Unit Operations.   Unit operations are a set of design operations that an architect can use to transform one architecture into another. We present the unit operations and then show how they have been applied in the historical evolution of user-interface reference models, which have been evolving since the early 1980s. We trace this evolution to understand it in terms of the unit operations.

Chapter 7 – The World Wide Web: A Case Study in Interoperability.   The World Wide Web was created out of a single organization's desire to exchange information about its researchers but has far outgrown these original goals. This chapter describes the architecture of the software underlying the Web; how this architecture has changed to allow the growth of the Web; and how this growth, in turn, has greatly influenced the organizations that use it.

Chapter 8 – CORBA: A Case Study of an Industry Standard Computing Infrastructure.   The Object Management Group was created to address the goal of interoperability of products created by independent software vendors. Specifically the Common Object Request Broker Architecture (CORBA) is an architecture to achieve this goal. This chapter describes the business climate in which the Object Management Group was created and how the various architectures, standards, and reference models they have designed (including CORBA and object management architecture) reflect those goals.

Chapter 9 – Analyzing Development Qualities at the Architectural Level: The Software Architecture Analysis Method. It is possible to evaluate an architecture to see if it allows certain system quality attributes to be achieved. This chapter presents a method for performing this evaluation with respect to the quality attribute of modifiability. We present the method using several examples to clarify its steps.

Chapter 10 – Architecture Reviews. Reviewing a system at the architectural level is more than an examination of the system. Timing the review, having contracts, specifying inputs and outputs, and using the correct process all are important in carrying out a review. This chapter presents a summary of the "best industry practice" for carrying out architecture reviews.

Chapter 11 – Air Traffic Control: A Case Study in Designing for High Availability. A system designed for air traffic control had the quality goal of being almost continually available. This goal caused a number of design decisions, which are discussed in this chapter. In addition to illustrating architectural choices motivated by quality goals, such as high availability and performance, the chapter also discusses an evaluation of the architecture.

PART THREE   MOVING FROM ARCHITECTURES TO SYSTEMS

Chapter 12 – Architecture Description Languages. Architectures are typically represented informally. In the past few years, architecture description languages have emerged as a way of formally representing architectures. Many such languages are being developed at research organizations, and a few are commercially available, but they will become increasingly important in the future. This chapter discusses how to evaluate the suitability of architecture description languages and gives an example that shows the benefits of using one.

Chapter 13 – Architecture-Based Development. An architecture provides a blueprint for a system, but the system must still be constructed from this blueprint. The process of moving from an architecture to an executable system deals with the creation of the work breakdown structure and its relationship to the architecture, the use of the architecture as a basis for creating a limited version of the system, the use of patterns within an architectural structure, the incorporation of reused components into the system, and the conformance of the final system to the architecture.

Chapter 14 – Flight Simulation: A Case Study in Architecture for Integrability. This chapter describes an architecture for flight simulation. It shows how careful attention to the software architecture in a complex domain enabled the construction of a set of large systems that met their stringent functional and fidelity requirements could be understood by a variety of software engineers, were easy to integrate, and were amenable to downstream modifications.

PART FOUR   REUSING ARCHITECTURES

Chapter 15 – Product Lines: Reusing Architectural Assets Within an Organization. Architectures are the basis for different types of reuse. Components developed to conform to a particular architecture can be reused, as can the architecture itself. This chapter discusses both component-based development and the development of product lines.

Chapter 16 – CelsiusTech: A Case Study in Product Line Development. CelsiusTech is an organization that successfully implemented a product line based on an architecture. This chapter describes the architecture of the product line and shows why this architecture was crucial to success. Without this approach CelsiusTech would not have been able to build these systems—it simply did not have adequate personnel. The product line approach brought consequent changes to the organizational structure and the manner in which it solicits and contracts for business.

Chapter 17 – Communitywide Reuse of Architectural Assets. Customers who develop systems based on software products are interested in having the software producers adhere to standards. This chapter discusses both the customer's perspective on using systems conforming to standards and the standards process itself.

Chapter 18 – The Meteorological Anchor Desk System: A Case Study in Building a Web-Based System from Off-the-Shelf Components. This chapter describes a system that was quickly and inexpensively implemented and fielded using World Wide Web and CORBA technology. A major consideration in the fielding of the system was the involvement of the end users in the decisions about which functionality should be implemented next in the sequence and how that functionality should appear to the user.

Chapter 19 – Software Architecture in the Future. We look at the architecture business cycle again and identify open problems associated with software architecture that require more research.

VISUAL NOTATION

Throughout this book we use the following visual notation for presenting software and system architectures. The notation is meant to be a *visual language* and as such has an internal logic that is meant to parallel the software-design process. As we move through the software-design process, we start with a vague definition of functionality and gradually make design decisions that make this more concrete, finally resulting in a fielded system. We visually mirror this process by moving from rounded to square corners. We show functions in a functional partitioning as ovals, software components as rounded rectangles, processes as rectangles with the corners cut off, and hardware components as rectangles.

In addition, the visual notation consistently indicates *data* via dotted lines and *control* via solid lines. We use dotted and solid lines to depict both components and connectors. For example, a computational component, such as a procedure, is depicted as a rounded rectangle because it is software. But this rounded rectangle is described by a *pair* of lines, one solid and one dotted, indicating that a procedure contains both *data* and *control* elements. By contrast, a passive data component, such as a file, is described by a single dotted line, indicating that a file contains only data. Similarly, data connections, such as socket connections, are shown as *dotted lines*, whereas control connections, such as process spawning, are shown as *solid lines*.

The visual notation for software architectures is shown in Figure G.1. Our notation for system architectures, in addition to using the node shapes just mentioned—*rectangle* for processors and *rectangle with cut-off corners* for processes—also defines processor groups (processors tightly grouped together for reasons of fault tolerance or performance) and hardware connections: network connections and bridges (see Figure G.2). System architectures are not the main focus of this book, but at times we need to show the allocation of software to hardware to understand a software architectural design decision. Finally, Figure G.3 presents notations for processes and reference models. We use a variety of arrows to suggest that processes are a sequence of steps that occur through time. Reference models (Figure G.4) represent the functions realized by a software architecture, along with their partitioning. These functions are shown with *rounded* corners, indicating their more abstract nature.

CASE STUDY ORGANIZATION

Different readers of the book will want to "mine" different information from this book and will read the book at various levels of detail. To address this need, we have organized the case studies in a consistent fashion around the following sections:

- A brief description of the study, the problems it was solving, and what points about software architecture it illustrates
- A description of how the ABC is realized (or partially realized) in this study
- The requirements and qualities that propelled the design
- The architectural approach: a brief discussion of the techniques that were brought to bear to address requirements and quality goals
- The architectural solution: a detailed discussion of the architectural solution, comprising the bulk of many of the case studies
- A summary of the important points made in the chapter

Software Components

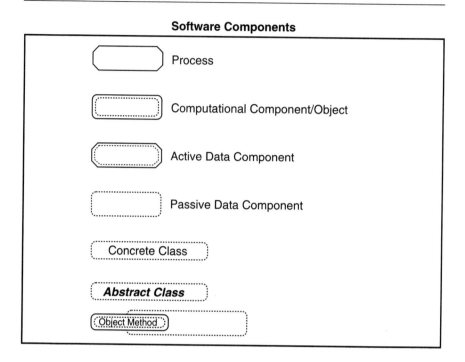

Process
Computational Component/Object
Active Data Component
Passive Data Component
Concrete Class
Abstract Class
Object Method

Software Connections

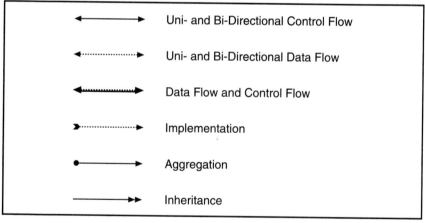

Uni- and Bi-Directional Control Flow
Uni- and Bi-Directional Data Flow
Data Flow and Control Flow
Implementation
Aggregation
Inheritance

FIGURE G.1   Software architecture visual notation key.

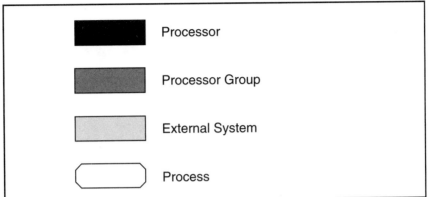

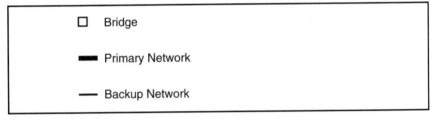

FIGURE G.2 System architecture visual notation key.

The architectural solution contains most of the detail in the case studies. If you are interested only in the technical and business environment and a high-level description of the architectural approach, you can get the gist of a case study by reading the brief description, its requirements and quality goals, and its architectural approach sections. If you are looking for a fuller discussion, you can also read the architectural solution section.

THREADS THROUGHOUT THE BOOK

Although the ABC is the primary theme of this book, there are other conceptual threads that run throughout. A reader interested in pursuing a particular aspect of architecture may wish to concentrate on the chapters that discuss one or more of the following threads:

- Where architectures come from—Chapters 1, 2, and 4
- Development of the architecture and the resulting system—Chapters 5, 6, 9, 10, 12, and 13

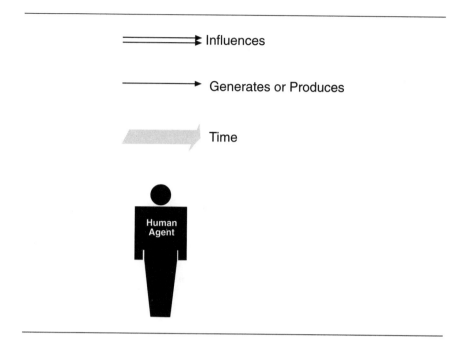

FIGURE G.3   Process visual notation key.

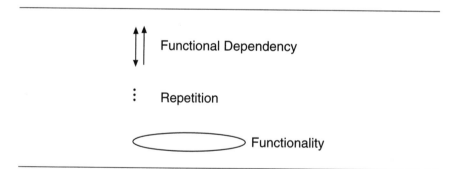

FIGURE G.4   Reference model visual notation key.

- How qualities derive from architecture—Chapters 4, 5, 6, 9, and 10, plus the case studies
- Case studies of qualities deriving from architecture—Chapters 3, 7, 8, 11, 14, 16, and 18
- Architecture as a reusable asset—Chapters 15, 16, and 17
- Component-based systems and commercial infrastructures—Chapters 7, 8, 15, 17, and 18

- Business issues—Chapters 1, 4, 8, 15, 16, and 18
- Architectures for real-time systems—Chapters 3, 11, 14, and 16

SIDEBARS

At various locations throughout the book we have included short, signed, visually separated sidebars written by one of us. These are intended to give background or perspective that is outside the normal flow of the text.

Acknowledgments

We would like to thank a large number of people without whom this book would not have been a success. First of all, we must thank the coauthors of individual chapters in this book: Gregory Abowd, Lisa Brownsword, Jeromy Carrière, Linda Northrop, Patricia Oberndorf, Mary Shaw, Rob Veltre, Kurt Wallnau, Nelson Weiderman, and Amy Moormann Zaremski.

We would also like to make a special mention of the people at the Software Engineering Institute who helped to make this book happen through their support and encouragement: Linda Northrop, Sholom Cohen, Lisa Lane, Bill Pollack, Barbara Tomchik, and Barbara White.

Our many reviewers, both known and anonymous, deserve a substantial portion of the credit for the quality of this book. Their comments spurred us on to improve it and make it more readable and more consistent. So, we want to acknowledge our debt of gratitude to Felix Bachmann, John L. Bennett, Sonia Bot, Lisa Brownsword, Bob Ellison, Jorge Diaz-Herrera, Larry Howard, Richard Juren, Phillippe Kruchten, Chung-Horng Lung, Joaquin Miller, Linda Northrop, David Notkin, Patricia Oberndorf, Jan Pachl, Lui Sha, Nelson Weiderman, and Amy Moormann Zaremski.

We also wish to thank Commander Rob Madson of the U.S. Navy for providing production support, and Peter Gordon of Addison-Wesley, who kept us grounded in reality.

And finally we thank our families for their endurance and good humor throughout this process.

PART ONE

ENVISIONING ARCHITECTURE

Where do architectures come from? They spring from the minds of architects, of course, but how? What must go *into* the mind of an architect for an architecture to come *out*? For that matter, what *is* a software architecture? Is it the same as design? If so, what's the fuss? If it is different, how so and why is it important?

In Part One of this book, we focus on the forces and influences that are at work as the architect begins the task of creating—*envisioning*—the central artifact of a system whose influences persist for longer than the lifetime of the system. Whereas we often think of the task of design as taking the right steps to ensure that the system will perform as expected—produce the correct answer or provide the expected functionality—architecture is additionally concerned with much longer-range issues. The architect is faced with a swarm of competing if not conflicting influences and demands, surprisingly few of which are concerned with getting the system to work correctly. The organizational and technical environment brings to bear a weighty set of sometimes implicit demands, and in practice these are as important as any of the explicit requirements for the software even though they are almost never written down.

Also surprising are the ways in which the architecture produces a deep influence on the organization that spawned it. It is decidedly not the case that the organization produces the architecture, ties it to the system for which it was developed, and locks it away in that compartment. Instead, architectures and their organizations dance an intricate waltz of influence and counterinfluence, helping each other to grow, evolve, and take on larger roles.

The architecture business cycle (ABC) is the name we give to this waltz, and it is the theme of this book and the focus of Chapter 1. Chapter 2 lays the foundations for the study of software architecture, defines it, places it in the context of software engineering, and provides some conceptual tools for its consideration. Chief among the concepts is the notion that architectures consist of separate coordinated structures and that each of these structures provides an engineering leverage point in the development of the system.

Chapter 3 is the first case study in the book. It illustrates how a particular architecture solved the unique set of requirements faced by its architect—in this case, a real-time embedded avionics system whose focus was on long-term modifiability—but also brings home the conceptual points made earlier. Three separate architectural structures—module, uses, and process structures—came together to provide the architectural solution for this system.

With this introduction, we begin our tour of the architecture business cycle.

1

The Architecture
Business Cycle

> *Simply stated, competitive success flows to the company that*
> *manages to establish proprietary architectural control over a*
> *broad, fast-moving, competitive space.*
> — C. Morris and C. Ferguson [Morris 93]

For decades, software designers have been taught to build systems based exclusively on statements of the technical requirements. Conceptually, the requirements document gets tossed over the wall into the designer's cubicle, and the designer must come forth with a satisfactory design: Requirements beget design, which begets system (see following sidebar). Of course, modern software-development methods recognize the naivete of this model and provide all sorts of feedback loops from designer to analyst. But they still make the implicit assumption that design is a product of the system's technical requirements, period.

Architecture has emerged as a crucial part of the design process and is the subject of this book. For the moment, we can consider a software architecture to be the realization of early design decisions made regarding decomposing the system into parts. Chapter 2 will provide our working definitions and distinguish between architecture and other forms of design. For reasons we shall see throughout, architecture serves as an important communication, reasoning, analysis, and growth tool for systems. But until now, architectural design has been discussed in the same light: If you know the requirements for a system, you can build the architecture for it.

This is short-sighted and fails to tell the whole story. What do you suppose would happen if two different architects, working in two different organizations, were given the same requirements specification for a system? Do you think it more likely that they would produce the same architecture or different ones?

The answer is that, in general, they will produce different ones. This immediately belies the notion that requirements determine architecture. Other factors are at work, and to fail to recognize those factors is to continue working in the dark.

The Swedish Ship *Vasa*

In the 1620s, Sweden and Poland were at war and the king of Sweden determined to put a swift end to it. Gustavus Adolphus commissioned a new warship, the likes of which had never been seen before. The *Vasa* shown in Figure 1.1 was to be the world's most formidable instrument of war: 70 meters long, able to carry 300 soldiers, and with an astonishing 64 heavy guns mounted on two gun decks. The king, seeking to add overwhelming firepower to his navy to strike a decisive blow and shorten the war, insisted on stretching the *Vasa*'s armaments to the limits. Her architect, Henrik Hybertsson, was a seasoned Dutch shipbuilder with an impeccable reputation, but the *Vasa* was beyond even his broad experience. Two-gun-deck ships were rare, and none had been built of the *Vasa*'s size and armament.

Like all architects of systems that push the envelope of experience, Hybertsson had to balance many concerns. Swift time to deployment was critical, but then so were performance, functionality, safety, reliability, and cost. He was also responsible to a variety of stakeholders. First of all, in this case, the customer really was king. But Hybertsson also was responsible to the crew that would sail his creation. Also like all architects, Hybertsson brought his experience with him to the task. In this case, his experience told him to design the *Vasa* as though it were a single-gun-deck ship and then extrapolate, which was in accordance with the technical environment of the day. Faced with perhaps an impossible task, Hybertsson had the good sense to die about a year before the ship was finished.

The project was completed to his specifications, however, and on Sunday morning, August 10, 1628, the mighty ship was ready. She set her sails, waddled

FIGURE 1.1   The warship *Vasa*.   Used with permission of *Vasa* museum, Stockholm, Sweden.

out into Stockholm's deep-water harbor, fired her guns in salute, and promptly rolled over. Water poured in through the open gun ports, and the *Vasa* plummeted. A few minutes later her first and only voyage ended 30 meters beneath the surface. Dozens among her 150-man crew drowned.

Inquiries followed, which concluded that the ship was well built but "badly proportioned." In other words, its architecture was flawed. Today we know that Hybertsson did a poor job of balancing all of the conflicting constraints levied on him. In particular, he did a poor job of customer management (not that anyone could have fared better) and acquiesced in the face of impossible requirements.

The story of the *Vasa*, although 370 years old, well illustrates the architecture business cycle: Enterprise goals beget requirements, which beget an architecture, which begets a system. The architecture flows from the architect's experience and the technical environment of the day. Hybertsson suffered from the fact that neither of those were up to the task before him.

In this book, we'll provide three things that Hybertsson could have used:

1. Case studies of successful architectures crafted to satisfy demanding requirements, so as to help set the technical playing field of the day

2. Methods to assess an architecture before any system is built from it, so as to mitigate the risks associated with launching unprecedented designs

3. Techniques for incremental architecture-based development, so as to uncover design flaws before it is too late to correct them.

Our goal is to give architects another way out of their design dilemmas than the one that befell the ill-fated Dutch ship designer. Death before deployment is not nearly so admired these days.

— PCC

The focusing question is this: What is the relationship of a system's software architecture to the environment in which the system will be constructed and will exist? The answer to this question is the organizing motif of this book. Software architecture is a result of *technical, business,* and *social* influences. The existence of the software architecture in turn affects the technical, business, and social environments that subsequently influence future architectures. We call this cycle of influences, from the environment to the architecture and back to the environment, the *architecture business cycle* (ABC).

This chapter introduces the ABC in detail and sets the stage for the remainder of the book. The major sections of the book tour the cycle by examining how

- Organizational goals influence requirements
- Requirements lead to an architecture
- Architectures yield systems
- Systems suggest future new organizational capabilities and requirements

We begin building the ABC by identifying the influences to and from architectures.

1.1   Where Do Architectures Come From?

In this section, we discuss the forward portion of the ABC: the influences on the architect.

ARCHITECTURES ARE INFLUENCED BY SYSTEM STAKEHOLDERS

Software architecture concerns the structures of large software systems. The architectural view of a system is an abstract view that distills away details of implementation, algorithm, and data representation and concentrates on the behavior and interaction of "black-box" components. A software architecture is developed as the first step toward designing a system that has a collection of desired properties. We will discuss the term *software architecture* in detail in Chapter 2. For now we will provide, without comment, the following definition:

> The software architecture of a program or computing system is the structure or structures of the system, which comprise software components, the externally visible properties of those components, and the relationships among them.

Many people and organizations are interested in the construction of a software system. We call these *stakeholders*: The customer, the end users, the developer, the developer's organization, and those who maintain the system are a few examples. These stakeholders have different concerns that they wish the system to guarantee or optimize. The concerns may include things as diverse as providing a certain behavior at runtime, performing well on a particular piece of hardware, being easy to customize, achieving a short time to market or low cost of development, or gainfully employing programmers who have a particular specialty. Figure 1.2 shows the architect receiving "suggestions" from the stakeholders.

The software architecture of a system is the earliest artifact that enables the priorities among competing concerns to be analyzed, and it is the artifact that manifests the concerns as system qualities. The trade-offs between performance and security, between maintainability and reliability, and between the cost of the current development effort and the cost of future developments are all manifested in the architecture. The system's response to these qualities is the result of structural trade-offs made and probably not documented by the original designers. Properties can be listed and discussed, of course, in an artifact such as a requirements document. However, if all properties were equally easy to achieve, the analysis of trade-offs and setting of priorities would be a simple task. It is not. The relative costs of different concerns, and the architectural alternatives that support these concerns, become more concrete when design begins.

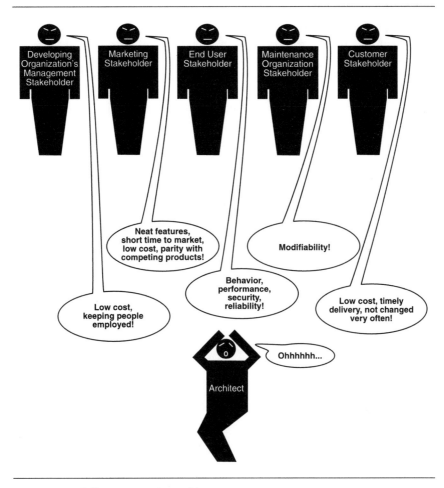

FIGURE 1.2 Influences on the architect.

ARCHITECTURES ARE INFLUENCED BY TECHNICAL AND ORGANIZATIONAL FACTORS

An architecture is the summary result of a set of business and technical decisions. There are many influences at work in the design of an architecture, and the realization of these influences will change depending on the environment in which the architecture is required to perform. An architect designing a system for which the hard real-time deadlines are believed to be tight will make one set of design choices; the same architect, designing a similar system in which the deadlines can be easily satisfied, will make different choices. And the same architect, designing a non-real-time system, is likely to make quite different choices still. Even with the same requirements, hardware, support software, and human resources available, an architect designing a system today is likely to design a different system than might have been designed five years ago.

In any development effort, the requirements make explicit some of the desired properties of the final system. Not all requirements are concerned directly with the properties of the final system; a development process or the use of a particular tool may be mandated by the requirements. But the requirements specification only begins to tell the story. Failure to satisfy other constraints may render the system just as worthless as if it functioned poorly.

The underlying problem is that each of the different stakeholders has different concerns and goals, and some of them may be contradictory. In addition to requirements, an architecture is influenced by the structure or nature of the development organization. Does the organization have an abundance of idle programmers skilled in client-server communications? If so, a client-server architecture might be an approach that would be supported by management.

Some of the stakeholder influences are represented in Figure 1.3. Architects are influenced by the requirements for the product, the structure and goals of the developing organization, the available technical environment, and their own background and experience.

These influences are described in detail in the following sections.

Customers and End Users.   The software engineering literature makes a clean distinction between the customer and the end user. The customer pays for the development or purchase of a system and specifies the requirements that ensure suitability to the end user. The end users use it. In reality the customer is more concerned with cost, even to the point of compromising usability. Another reality is that there are many different categories of end users: those who provide input

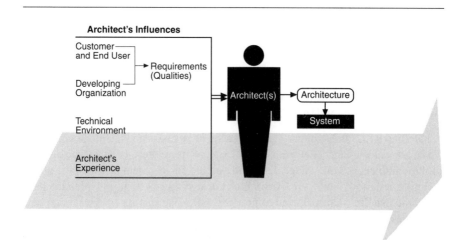

FIGURE 1.3   Influences on the architecture.

to the system, system administrators, and those who receive output from the system. Having an acceptable system involves behavior as well as other properties such as performance, reliability, availability, platform compatibility, memory utilization, network usage, security, modifiability, and interoperability with other systems. All of these properties and others affect the way in which the delivered system is viewed by its eventual recipient. Some properties, such as modifiability, may become apparent to the customer only over time.

Sometimes the customer's requirements are affected by the availability of a system or an architecture. Shrink-wrapped software has clearly affected people's requirements by providing solutions that are not tailored to their precise needs but which are inexpensive and (in the best of all possible worlds) of high quality. Product lines have the same effect on customers who cannot be so flexible with their requirements. In Chapter 16 we will show how the existence of a product-line architecture caused customers to happily compromise their requirements because they could get high-quality software that fit their basic needs quickly, reliably, and at relatively low cost.

Developing Organization.   The developing organization and the customer may or may not be the same. In either case, the interests of the developing organization are different from those of the customer. There are three different classes of influences that come from the role of the developing organization: immediate business, long-term business, and organizational structure.

A business may have an immediate business investment in certain assets such as an investment in existing architectures and the products based on them. The foundation of a development project may be that the proposed system is the next in a sequence of similar systems, and the cost estimates assume a high degree of asset reuse. Or, an organization may wish to make a long-term business investment in an infrastructure to pursue strategic goals and may view the proposed system as one means of financing and extending that infrastructure.

Finally, the organizational structure can shape the software architecture. In the case study in Chapter 14, the development of some of the subsystems was subcontracted because the subcontractors provided specialized expertise. This was made possible by a division of functionality in the architecture that allowed isolation of the specialities.

Conversely, the division of functionality in the architecture for a large system may affect the structure of the organization. In the case study in Chapter 16, separate groups were responsible for building and maintaining individual portions of the organization's architecture for a family of products. So, in any design undertaken by the organization at large, these groups have a strong voice in the system's decomposition, pressuring for the continued existence of those portions.

Background and Experience of the Architects.   If the architects for a system have had good results using a particular architectural approach such as distributed objects or implicit invocation, chances are that their first inclination will be to try that same approach again on a new development effort. Conversely, if a prior experience was disastrous, the architects may be reluctant to try this approach again. architectural choices may also come from an architect's education and training, exposure to successful architectural styles, or exposure to systems that have worked particularly poorly or particularly well. The architects may also wish to experiment with an architectural style or technique learned from reading a book (such as this one) or taking a course.

Technical Environment.   A special case of the architect's background and experience is reflected by the *technical environment*. The technical environment that is current when an architecture is designed will influence that architecture. The environment might include industry standard practices or software engineering techniques prevalent in the architect's professional community. It is a brave architect who, in today's environment, does not develop, or at least consider, an object-oriented design.

RAMIFICATIONS OF THE INFLUENCES ON AN ARCHITECT

Almost never are the properties required by the business and enterprise goals consciously understood, let alone fully articulated. Indeed, even customer requirements are seldom documented completely. However, it is important for architects to know and understand the kinds of constraints on the project as early as possible. Therefore, *architects must identify and actively engage the stakeholders to solicit their needs and expectations*. Without such active engagement, the stakeholders will, at some point, engage the architects to explain why each proposed architecture is unacceptable, thus delaying the project and idling workers. Early engagement allows the architects to understand the constraints of the task, to manage expectations, and to negotiate priorities.

It is important that the architects understand the nature, source, and priority of these constraints. This places the architects in a better position to make trade-offs when conflicts among competing constraints arise, as they inevitably will. Architecture reviews (Chapters 9 and 10) and iterative prototyping (Chapter 18) are two means for achieving early engagement of the system's stakeholders.

It should be apparent that the architects need more than just technical skills. Continual explanations to one stakeholder or another will be required to explain the chosen priorities of different properties and why particular stakeholders are not having all of their expectations satisfied. Thus, for an effective architect, diplomacy, negotiation, and communication skills are essential.

THE ARCHITECTURE AFFECTS THE FACTORS THAT INFLUENCED IT

The main message of this book is that the relationships among business goals, product requirements, practitioners' experience, architectures, and fielded systems form a cycle with feedback loops that a business can manage. A business

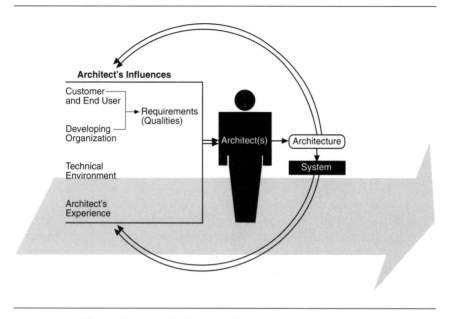

FIGURE 1.4   The architecture business cycle.

manages this cycle to manage growth, to expand its enterprise area, and to take advantage of previous investments in architecture and system building. Figure 1.4 shows these feedback loops. Some of the feedback comes from the architecture itself and some comes from the system built from the architecture.

Here is how the cycle works:

1. The architecture affects the structure of the developing organization. An architecture prescribes a structure for a system; in particular, as we shall see, an architecture prescribes the units of software that must be integrated to form the system. These units correspond to work assignments, and these work assignments form the basis for the development project's structure. Teams are formed for each software unit; the development, test, and integration activities all revolve around the units. Schedules and budgets allocate resources in chunks corresponding to the units. If a company becomes adept at building families of similar systems, it will tend to invest in each of the teams by nurturing each area of expertise. Teams become engraved in the organization's structure. This is feedback from the architecture to the developing organization.

2. The architecture can affect the enterprise goals of the developing organization. A successful system can enable a company to establish a foothold in a particular market area. The system can provide opportunities for the efficient production and deployment of similar systems. Often, the architecture itself is a primary factor in this efficiency and acts as a core asset of invested capital. The enterprise may adjust its goals to take advantage of its newfound expertise to plumb the market. This is feedback from the system to the developing organization.

3. The architecture can affect the customer requirements for the next system by presenting the customer with the opportunity to receive an upgraded system (based on the same architecture) in a manner that is more reliable, timely, and economical than if the subsequent system were to be built from scratch. The customer may be willing to relax some requirements to gain these economies.

4. The process of building this system will affect the architect's experience for subsequent systems by having added to the corporate experience base. A system that was successfully built around a tool bus or an object request broker or encapsulated finite-state machines will engender future similar systems that are built the same way. On the other hand, architectures that failed are not likely to be chosen again in the near future.

5. A few systems will influence and actually change the software engineering culture, the technical environment in which system builders operate and learn. The first relational databases, compiler generators, and table-driven operating systems had this effect in the 1960s and early 1970s. The first spreadsheets and windowing systems had this effect in the 1980s. CORBA, Java, and the World Wide Web may be the examples for the 1990s, as we will suggest in Chapters 7 and 8. When such pathfinder systems are constructed, subsequent systems are affected by their legacy.

These and other feedback mechanisms form what we call the ABC. The representation of the ABC shown in Figure 1.4 depicts the influences of the culture and business of the development organization on the software architecture. That architecture is, in turn, a primary determinant of the properties of the developed system or systems. But the ABC is also based on a recognition that shrewd organizations can take advantage of the organizational, enterprise, and experiential effects of developing an architecture and can use those effects to position their business strategically for future projects (see following sidebar).

1.2 Software Processes and the Architecture Business Cycle

Most human endeavors can be organized, ritualized, and managed. *Software process* is the term given to the organization, ritualization, and management of software-development activities. There are a collection of activities—processes—that are undertaken to move from one activity in the ABC to the next. These activities usually start with one group of artifacts and transform them into some other group of artifacts: Specifications are transformed into a design, a design is transformed into an implementation, etc. The results of these transformations must be validated, and this validation, in turn, introduces additional activities.

Some of the activities (both creational and validational) are *intuitive* activities, such as the transformation that turns a statement of requirements, enterprise goals, and available development environment into an architecture. By *intuitive,* we mean that there are few analytic tools to aid with this feat of alchemy that we call design, which is primarily done by intuition, pattern matching, experience, rules of thumb, and ad hoc reasoning. Procedures to support intuitive activities include negotiating decisions, keeping track of rationales for decisions, representing the results of the intuitive activities, and reviewing the results of these activities.

Architecture, Schmarchitecture—Is Microsoft a Counterexample?

Microsoft is arguably the most successful, most profitable company ever. But it is a common impression in the software engineering community that Microsoft doesn't do architecture, that it doesn't follow the best software engineering practices. If this is true, why should you read this book? After all, if Microsoft doesn't care about architecture, and it has done all right despite this, why should *you* care about architecture?

The answer to this question has several parts. First, Microsoft *does* care about software engineering and software architecture. Some of the software engineering practices that it uses contribute significantly to its success (although much of its success can be attributed to other factors, such as canny marketing, a fanatically motivated workforce, and a short time to market). Second, there are things that Microsoft doesn't care about, but which *your* organization might care about, such as integrability with other vendors' products, high reliability, real-time performance, and so forth, that might cause you to adopt practices that differ from Microsoft's.

Finally, there are some causes for concern regarding Microsoft's historic inattention to architecture; consider the following analysis of its development process [Cusumano 97]:

> The company now needs to pay more attention to, for example, product architecture, defect prevention mechanisms, and some more conventional engineering practices, such as a more formal design and code reviews. New product areas also pose new challenges for its development methods . . . These new products . . . require more advance planning and product architectural design than Microsoft usually does to minimize problems in development, testing, and operation.

Microsoft does many things correctly. It has a feature-oriented design and a feature-oriented culture that emphasize frequent "sanity checks" with users, rigorous usability testing, an agile development process that encourages designers and coders to use their ingenuity and contribute new ideas, and a "hold everything" attitude to testing—a programmer who has been found responsible for a bug does nothing else until that bug is fixed. In addition, because designers and coders have a common site and a common programming language, they can communicate easily and frequently with each other.

Microsoft doesn't care about all qualities of a system. Its product reliability is not ideal. It doesn't worry much about integrability. It doesn't need to. Its products typically only need to integrate with a specific subset of its other products, and this can be negotiated in the hallway. Its products do not, in general, integrate with the products of competitors. If your products are driven by reliability, high performance, or high-availability requirements, you will need to adopt additional architecture practices, such as those recommended in the rest of this book.

Having said all this, Microsoft *does* care about the structure of the system that it builds and it uses many of the techniques that we will be espousing throughout this book. In particular, Microsoft

- Modularizes its design
- Builds a skeletal system first and then progressively adds features (so that it has a working version of the product early in its life cycle)
- Matches the structure of the system to the structure of the development/ maintenance organization

— RNK

Since most of software architecture creation falls into this category, *a software architect must have considerable organizational talents and negotiating skills* in addition to comprehensive technical and domain knowledge.

Because the transformations implied by the ABC are largely intuitive, there must be a collection of management and review activities, activities intended to help participants understand and control the intuitive processes in software development to support these transformations. We will be explicit about the architecture-based aspects of software process in Chapters 9 and 10, where we describe review processes specifically designed to verify that a software architecture achieves the desired system qualities. This form of review is not currently addressed in the software process literature.

ARCHITECTURE-BASED PROCESS STEPS

What activities are involved in creating a software architecture, using that architecture to realize a design, and then implementing or managing the evolution of a target system or application? These activities are as follows:

- Creating the business case for the system
- Understanding the requirements
- Creating or selecting the architecture
- Representing and communicating the architecture
- Analyzing or evaluating the architecture
- Implementing the system based on the architecture
- Ensuring that the implementation conforms to the architecture

As indicated in the structure of the ABC, these activities have comprehensive feedback relationships with each other. We will briefly introduce each activity in the following subsections.

Creating the Business Case for the System. Creating a business case is broader than simply assessing the market need for a system. It is an important step in creating and constraining any future requirements. How much should the product cost? What is its targeted market? What is its targeted time to market? Will it need to interface with other systems? Are there system limitations that it must work within?

These are all questions that must involve the system's architects. They cannot be decided solely by an architect, but if an architect is not consulted in the creation of the business case, it may be impossible to the achieve those business goals.

Understanding the Requirements. There are a variety of techniques for eliciting requirements from the end users and the customers. For example, object-oriented analysis uses scenarios, or "use cases" to embody requirements. Safety-critical systems use more rigorous approaches, such as finite-state-machine models or formal specification languages.

One fundamental decision with respect to the system being built is the extent to which it is a variation on other systems that have been constructed. Since it is a rare system these days that is not similar to other systems, requirements elicitation techniques extensively involve understanding the characteristics of these prior systems. The technique used to capture these similarities is called *domain analysis*. A domain model—the product of a domain analysis—will identify the commonalities and variations among different instantiations of similar systems, whether fielded together or sequentially.

Another technique that helps understand requirements is the creation of prototypes. Prototypes may help to model desired behavior, design the user interface, or analyze resource utilization. This helps to make the system "real" in the eyes of its stakeholders and can quickly catalyze decisions on the system's design and the design of its user interface.

Regardless of the technique used to elicit the requirements, the desired qualities of the system to be constructed determine the shape of its architecture. Less obvious is how to mediate between conflicting requirements and how to master the fine balancing act of creating an architecture that satisfies the priorities in the stakeholders' requirements. Prototyping helps with this; other techniques for achieving this balance are discussed in Chapters 5 and 6, where we consider how to derive an architecture from a set of desired system qualities.

Creating or Selecting the Architecture. Brooks argues forcefully and eloquently that conceptual integrity is the key to sound system design and that conceptual integrity can only be had by a small number of minds coming together to design the system's architecture [Brooks 95]. We discuss in Chapters 5 and 13 how some of the techniques used to create an architecture, such as the use of architectural styles and pattern-based simplicity, allow a design to be more easily comprehended by other designers.

We do not prescribe a method for creating an architecture. We believe that prescriptive methods always emphasize some qualities over others, and this emphasis is made implicitly. If the qualities implicitly promoted by the method do not match the system's requirements, the method is actually deleterious. What we offer instead is a technique whereby designs are generated in a less rigorous fashion but are analyzed rigorously for fitness with respect to requirements.

In any design process there will be multiple candidate designs considered. Some will be rejected immediately. Others will contend for primacy. Choosing among these competing designs in a rational way is one of the architects' greatest challenges. Chapters 9 and 10 describe methods for making such choices.

Representing and Communicating the Architecture.   For the architecture to be effective as the backbone of the project's design, it must be communicated clearly and unambiguously to all of the stakeholders who have an interest in it. Developers must understand the work assignments it requires of them, testers must understand the task structure it imposes on them, management must understand the scheduling implications it suggests, etc. Toward this end, the representation medium should be informative, unambiguous, and readable by many people with varied backgrounds.

The architects themselves must make sure that the architecture will meet the behavioral, performance, and quality requirements of the systems to be built from the architecture. Therefore, there is an advantage if the representation medium can serve as input to formal analysis techniques such as model building, simulation, verification, or even rapid prototyping.

Architectures can be represented or specified using a formal language called an architecture description language (ADL). ADLs are emerging as an important new technological trend to support architecture-based development and will be discussed in Chapter 12.

Analyzing or Evaluating the Architecture.   ADLs provide valuable analytical capabilities but tend to concentrate on the runtime properties of the system— its performance, its behavior, its communication patterns, and the like. Less widespread are analysis techniques to evaluate the nonruntime quality attributes that an architecture imparts to a system. Chief among these is maintainability, the ability to support change. Maintainability has many facets: Portability, reusability, adaptability, etc., are all special instances of a system's ability to support change. A consensus is emerging on the value of scenario-based evaluation to judge an architecture with respect to nonruntime quality attributes.

The most mature methodological approach is found in the software architecture analysis method of Chapter 9; however, other scenario-based techniques for evaluating architectures that are less structured but share the same goals and concerns can be found. We present these in Chapter 10.

Implementing Based on the Architecture and Ensuring Conformance.
This activity is concerned with keeping the developers faithful to the structures and interaction protocols constrained by the architecture. Having an explicit and well-communicated architecture is the first step toward ensuring architectural

conformance. Having an environment or infrastructure that actively assists developers in creating and maintaining the architecture (as opposed to just the code) is better. This means that we need tools for architecture development to complement our existing ones for code development.

Finally, when an architecture is created and used, it goes into a maintenance phase. Constant vigilance is required to ensure that the architecture remains faithful to its representation during this phase. Although work in this area is comparatively immature, there has been intense activity in recent years. Chapter 13 will present the current state of architecture-based development and architectural conformance.

1.3   What Makes a "Good" Architecture?

If it is true that, given the same technical requirements for a system, two different architects in different organizations will produce different architectures, how can we determine if either one of them is the *right* one?

There is no such thing as an inherently good or bad architecture. Architectures are either more or less fit for some stated purpose. A distributed three-tier client-server architecture may be just the ticket for a large enterprise's financial management system but sheer lunacy for an avionics application. An architecture carefully crafted to achieve high modifiability doesn't make sense for a throwaway prototype. One of the messages of this book is that architectures can in fact be evaluated—one of the great benefits of paying attention to them—but only in the context of specific goals.

Nevertheless, there are rules of thumb that should be followed when designing an architecture. Failure to apply any of these does not automatically mean that the architecture will be fatally flawed, but it should at least serve as a warning sign that should be investigated.

We divide our observations into two clusters: process recommendations and product (or structural) recommendations.

Our process recommendations (most of which are elaborated in Chapters 9 and 10) are as follows:

- The architecture should be the product of a single architect or a small group of architects with an identified leader.
- The architect (or architecture team) should have the technical requirements for the system and an articulated, prioritized list of qualitative properties (such as portability) that the architecture is expected to satisfy.
- The architecture should be well documented, using an agreed-on notation that all stakeholders can understand with a minimum of effort.
- The architecture should be circulated to the system's stakeholders, who should be actively involved in its review.

- The architecture should be analyzed for applicable quantitative measures (such as maximum throughput) and formally reviewed for qualitative properties (such as modifiability) before it is too late to make changes to it.

- The architecture should lend itself to implementation via the creation of a "skeletal" system in which the communication paths are exercised but which at first has minimal functionality. This skeletal system can then be used to "grow" the system incrementally, easing the integration and testing efforts (see Section 13.2).

- The architecture should result in a specific (and small) set of resource contention areas, the resolution of which are clearly specified, circulated, and maintained. For example, if network utilization is an area of concern, the architects should produce (and enforce) for each team guidelines that will result in a minimum of network traffic. If performance is a concern, the architects should produce (and enforce) time budgets for the major threads.

Our structural rules of thumb are as follows:

- The architecture should feature well-defined modules whose functional responsibilities are allocated on the principles of information hiding and separation of concerns. Each module should have a well-defined interface that encapsulates or "hides" changeable aspects (such as implementation strategies and data-structure choices) from other software that uses its facilities.

- The modules should reflect a separation of concerns that allows their respective development teams to work largely independently of each other.

- The information-hiding modules should include those that encapsulate idiosyncrasies of the computing infrastructure, thus insulating the bulk of the software from change should the platform change.

- The architecture should never depend upon a particular version of a commercial product or tool. If it depends upon a particular commercial product, it should be structured such that changing to a different product is straightforward and inexpensive.

- Modules that produce data should be separate from modules that consume data. This tends to increase modifiability because changes are often confined to either the production or consumption side of data. If new data are added, both sides will have to change, but the separation allows for a staged (incremental) upgrade.

- For parallel-processing systems, the architecture should feature well-defined processes or tasks that do not necessarily mirror the module structure. That is, processes may thread through more than one module; a module may include procedures that are invoked as part of more than one process (see Chapters 2 and 3).

- Every task or process should be written so that its assignment to a specific processor can be easily changed, perhaps even at runtime.

- The architecture should feature a small number of simple interaction patterns. That is, the system should do the same things in the same way throughout (see Section 13.3 and Chapter 14). This will aid in understandability, reduce development time, increase reliability, and enhance modifiability. It will also show conceptual integrity in the architecture, which while not measurable, leads to smooth development.

As you examine the case studies in this book, each of which successfully solves a challenging architectural problem, it is useful to see how many of them followed each of these rules of thumb. This set of rules is neither complete nor absolute but can serve as a guidepost for an architect beginning to make progress on an architectural design problem.

1.4 Summary

In this chapter, we have shown that architecture is more than the result of the technical requirements for a system. It is equally the result of nontechnical factors: the architect's background, the environment, and the sponsoring organization's business goals. The architecture in turn influences the environment that spawned it by adding its presence to the technical environment and by giving the business new marketing possibilities. We introduced the ABC as the motif for the book, but the reader should be aware that the ABC as described here will be extended in later chapters.

We also touched upon process issues, mainly to make the point that most of the activities in moving through the architecture business cycle are intuitive, not analytic.

Finally, we posited a set of rules of thumb that generally lead to successful architectures and should be ignored only at the architect's peril.

Next, we turn our attention to software architecture, per se.

1.5 Discussion Questions

1. How does the nature of your enterprise affect the architectures that it develops? How do the architectures affect the nature of the enterprise?

2. What kind of business goals drive (or have driven) the creation of the software architectures of your enterprise?

3. Who are the stakeholders that exert the most influence over the architecture of systems in your organization? What are their goals? Do the goals ever conflict?

2

What Is Software Architecture?

with Linda Northrop

> *If a project has not achieved a system architecture, including its rationale,
> the project should not proceed to full-scale system development.
> Specifying the architecture as a deliverable enables its use
> throughout the development and maintenance process.*
> — Barry Boehm [Boehm 95]

In the previous chapter, we explained that architecture plays a pivotal role in allowing an organization to meet its business goals. Architecture commands a price (the cost of its careful development), but it repays that price handsomely by enabling the organization to achieve its goals and expand its software capabilities. Architecture is an asset that holds tangible value to the developing organization beyond the project for which it was created.

In this chapter we will focus on architecture strictly from a software engineering point of view. That is, we will explore the value that a software architecture brings to a development project in addition to the value returned to the enterprise in the ways described in Chapter 1.

2.1 What Software Architecture Is and What It Isn't

Figure 2.1, taken from a system description for an underwater acoustic simulation, purports to describe the top-level architecture and is precisely the kind of

Note: Linda Northrop is a program manager at the Software Engineering Institute, Carnegie Mellon University.

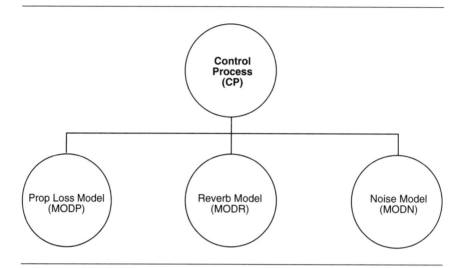

FIGURE 2.1   Typical, but uninformative, presentation of a top-level architecture.

diagram most often displayed to help explain an architecture. Exactly what can we tell from this diagram?

- The system consists of four components.
- Three of the components might have more in common with each other— Prop Loss Model (MODP), Reverb Model (MODR), and Noise Model (MODN) than with the fourth—Control Process (CP)—because they are positioned next to each other.
- All of the components apparently have some sort of relationship with each other, since the diagram is fully connected.

Is this an architecture? Assuming (as many definitions do) that architecture consists of components (of which we have four) and connections among them (also present), this diagram seems to suffice. However, even if we accept the most primitive definition, what can we *not* tell from the diagram?

- *What is the nature of the components?*   What is the significance of their separation? Do the components run on separate processors? Do they run at separate times? Do the components consist of processes, programs, or both? Do the components represent ways in which the project labor will be divided, or do they convey a sense of runtime separation? Are they modules, objects, tasks, functions, processes, distributed programs, or something else?
- *What is the significance of the links?*   Do the links mean that the components communicate with each other, control each other, send data to each other, use each other, invoke each other, synchronize with each other, or some combination of these or other relations? What are the mechanisms for the communication?

- *What is the significance of the layout?*   Why is CP on a separate level? Does it call the other three components, and are the others not allowed to call it? Or was there simply not room enough to put all four components on the same row in the diagram?
- *How does the architecture operate at runtime?*   How do data and control flow through the system?

We *must* raise these questions, because unless we know precisely what the components are and how they cooperate to accomplish the purpose of the system, diagrams such as these are not much help and should be regarded warily.

This diagram does not show a software architecture, at least not in any useful way. We now define what *does* constitute a software architecture:

> The software architecture of a program or computing system is the structure or structures of the system, which comprise software components, the externally visible properties of those components, and the relationships among them.

"Externally visible" properties refers to those assumptions other components can make of a component, such as its provided services, performance characteristics, fault handling, shared resource usage, and so on. The intent of this definition is that a software architecture must abstract away some information from the system (otherwise there is no point looking at the architecture; we are simply viewing the entire system) and yet provide enough information to be a basis for analysis, decision making, and hence risk reduction. Let us look at some of the implications of this definition in more detail.

First, *architecture defines components.* The architecture embodies information about how the components interact with each other. This means that architecture specifically *omits* certain information about components that does not pertain to their interaction. Thus, an architecture is foremost an *abstraction* of a system that suppresses details of components that do not affect how they use, are used by, relate to, or interact with other components. In systems that use information hiding as the design criteria, components react with each other by means of interfaces that partition details about a component into public and private parts. Architecture is on the public side of this division; private details of components— details having to do solely with internal implementation—are not architectural.

Second, the definition makes clear that *systems can comprise more than one structure* and that no one structure holds the irrefutable claim to being *the* architecture. For example, large projects are usually partitioned into components that are used as work assignments for programming teams. Let us call those components *modules.* A module will comprise programs and data that software in other modules can call or access and programs and data that are private. Modules may be subdivided for assignment to subteams. This is one kind of structure often used to describe a system. Suppose the system is to be built as a set of parallel processes. The set of processes that will exist at runtime, the programs in the various modules that are strung together sequentially to form each process, and the synchronization relations among the processes form another kind of structure often used to describe a system. Are any of these structures alone *the* architecture? No, although they all convey architectural information. The architecture consists of these structures and possibly others. This example shows that since architecture can comprise more than one kind of structure, there is more than one kind of component (e.g., modules and processes), more than one kind of interaction among components (e.g., subdivision and synchronization), and even more than one context (e.g., development time versus runtime). By intention, the definition does not specify what architectural components and relationships are. Is a software component an object? A process? A library? A database? A commercial product? It can be any of these things and more.

Third, the definition implies that *every software system has an architecture* because every system can be shown to be composed of components and relations among them. In the most trivial case, a system is itself a component. While an architecture composed of a single component is not interesting and probably not useful, it is nevertheless by our definition an architecture. Even though every system has an architecture, it does not necessarily follow that the architecture is known to anyone. Perhaps all of the people who designed the system are long gone, the source code has been lost (or was never delivered), and all we have is the executing binary code. This reveals the difference between the architecture of a system and the description or specification of that architecture. Unfortunately, an architecture can exist independently of its description or specification, which raises the importance of *architecture representation*.

Fourth, *the behavior of each component is part of the architecture* insofar as that behavior can be observed or discerned from the point of view of another component. This behavior is what allows components to interact with each other, which is clearly part of the architecture. Hence, most of the box-and-line drawings that are passed off as architectures are in fact not architectures at all. They are simply box-and-line drawings. When looking at the names of the boxes (database, graphical user interface, executive, etc.), a reader may well imagine the functionality and behavior of the corresponding components. This mental image approaches an architecture, but it springs from the imagination of the observer's mind and relies on information that is not present. This does not mean that the exact behavior and performance of every component must be documented in all circumstances; but to the extent that a component's behavior influences how another component must be written to interact with it or influences the acceptability of the system as a whole, this behavior should be part of an interface specification for that component.

The definition allows *the architecture for a system to be a good one or a bad one,* meaning that the architecture will allow or prevent the system from meeting its behavioral, performance, and life-cycle requirements. Assuming that we do not accept trial and error as the best way to choose an architecture for a system—that is, picking an architecture at random, building the system from it, and hoping for the best—this raises the importance of *architecture evaluation*.

2.2   Architectural Styles, Reference Models, and Reference Architectures

There are three other common concepts that we must define; they are as follows:

1. *An architectural style is a description of component types and a pattern of their runtime control and/or data transfer.*   A style can be thought of as a set of constraints on an architecture—constraints on the component types and their patterns of interaction—and these constraints define a set or family of architectures that satisfy them. For example, client-server is a common architectural style. Client and server are two component types, and their coordination is described in terms of the protocol that the server uses to communicate with each of its clients. Use of the term *client-server* implies only that multiple clients exist; the clients themselves are not identified, and there is no discussion of what functionality (other than implementation of the protocols) has been assigned to any of the clients or to the server. Countless architectures are of the client-server style as we have defined it, but these architectures are different from each other. An architectural style is not an architecture, then, but it still conveys a useful image of the system—it imposes useful constraints on the architecture (and, in turn, the system). Styles are discussed in more detail in Chapter 5.

2. *A reference model is a division of functionality together with data flow between the pieces.*   A reference model is a standard decomposition of a known problem into parts that cooperatively solve the problem. Arising from experience, reference models are a characteristic of mature domains and are often obtained by domain analysis or other group activity. Can you name the standard parts of a compiler or a database management system? Can you explain in broad terms how the parts work together to accomplish their collective purpose? If so, it is because you have been taught a reference model of these applications. Reference models are discussed in more detail in Chapters 6 and 17.

3. *A reference architecture is a reference model mapped onto software components (that will cooperatively implement the functionality defined in the reference model) and the data flows between the components.*   Whereas a reference model divides the functionality, a reference architecture is the mapping of that functionality onto a system decomposition. The mapping may be, but by no means necessarily is, one to one. A software component may implement part of a function or several functions.

Reference models, architectural styles, and reference architectures are not architectures; they are useful steps toward an architecture. Each is the outcome of making a set of early design decisions, and each lays the groundwork for future steps. Each prepares for the later development phases by means such as the identification and formation of work teams corresponding to the components identified.

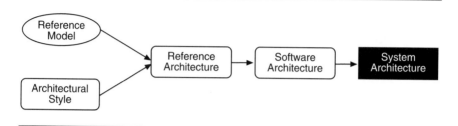

FIGURE 2.2 The relationship between reference models, architectural styles, reference architectures, and implemented software architectures.

Their relationship is shown in Figure 2.2. At each successive phase in this progression more requirements are addressed, and more design and development have taken place.

2.3 Other Viewpoints

Software architecture is a young discipline; hence, there is no single, accepted definition of the term. On the other hand, there is no shortage of definitions, either. Most of the commonly circulated definitions are consistent in their themes—structure, components, and connections among them—but they vary widely in the details and are not interchangeable.

This lack of consensus is troubling at first glance; after all, how can we fruitfully exploit a concept if we cannot even agree on its definition? In practice, however, this lack of an engraved definition will not prevent us from making good use of the concept. To convince yourself of this, try raising your hand at an object-oriented programming workshop and asking as innocently as you can what an *object* is. You will either be given zero answers (and asked to leave the workshop because the participants are tired of debating the question) or be given as many answers as there are people in the room. And yet a full-fledged paradigm shift has occurred around this apparently ill-defined concept.

So it is with architecture: The field is in many ways following practice, not leading it. The study of software architecture has evolved by observation of the design principles that designers follow and actions that they take when working on real systems. It is an attempt to abstract the commonalities inherent in system design, and as such, it must account for a wide range of activities, concepts, methods, approaches, and results. Hence, other definitions of architecture are present in the software-engineering community. Because you are likely to encounter some of them, you should understand their implications and be able to discuss them from an informed position. A few of the most often-heard definitions follow.

- *Architecture is high-level design.*   This is true enough, in the sense that a horse *is* a mammal. But the two are not interchangeable. There are other tasks associated with early design that are not architectural, such as deciding on important data structures that will be encapsulated. The interface to those data structures is decidedly an architectural interface, but their actual choice is not.

- *Architecture is the overall structure of the system.*   This common refrain implies (incorrectly) that systems have but one structure. We know this to be false. If someone takes this position, it is usually entertaining to ask which structure they mean.

- *Architecture is the structure of the components of a program or system, their interrelationships, and principles and guidelines governing their design and evolution over time.*   This is one of a number of process-centered definitions that includes ancillary information such as principles and guidelines. Many people claim that architecture includes a statement of stakeholder needs and a rationale for explaining how those needs are met. We agree that gathering these kinds of information is essential and a matter of good professional practice. However, we do not consider them part of the architecture per se any more than an owner's manual for a car is part of the car. Any system has an architecture that can be discovered and analyzed independently from any discovery of the process by which the architecture was designed, evolved, or intended to satisfy requirements placed on it.

- *Architecture is components and connectors.*   Connectors imply a runtime mechanism for transferring control and data around a system. As such, this definition of architecture concentrates on the runtime architectural structures (such as data- and control-flow structures) and does not map well to the non-runtime structures. A UNIX pipe is a connector, for instance. This is more specific than our more general "relationships" among components, such as emerges from the is-a-submodule-of relation among module components. People who adopt this definition and who think that connectors are only runtime mechanisms would probably not accept the module structure of a system as architectural.

- *Architecture is components, connectors, and constraints.*   We interpret constraints as defining the behaviors of the components, which is consistent with our definition. However, this definition is still lacking the notion of the externally visible properties, which we consider to be crucial in making an architectural description useful.

At the essence of all the discussion about software architecture is a focus on reasoning about the *structural* issues of a system. And although *architecture* is sometimes used to mean a certain architectural style, such as client-server, and is sometimes used to refer to a field of study, such as a book about architecture, it is most often used to describe structural aspects of a particular system. That is what we have attempted to capture in our definition.

2.4   Why Is Software Architecture Important?

People often make analogies to other uses of the word *architecture*, about which they have some intuition. They commonly associate architecture with physical structure (building, streets, hardware) and physical arrangement. A building architect must design a building that provides accessibility, aesthetics, light, maintainability, and so on. A software architect must design a system that provides concurrency, portability, modifiability, usability, security, and the like, and the trade-offs among these needs.

Analogies between buildings and software systems should not be taken literally; they break down fairly quickly. Rather, such analogies help us understand that the viewer's perspective is important and that structure can have different meanings depending upon the motivation for examining it. A precise definition of software architecture is not nearly as important as what investigation of the concept allows us to do.

Fundamentally, there are three reasons why software architecture is important, as follows:

1. *Communication among stakeholders.*   Software architecture represents a common high-level abstraction of a system that most if not all of the system's stakeholders can use as a basis for creating mutual understanding, forming consensus, and communicating with each other.

2. *Early design decisions.*   Software architecture represents the manifestation of the earliest design decisions about a system, and these early bindings carry weight far out of proportion to their individual gravity with respect to the system's remaining development, its deployment, and its maintenance life. It is also the earliest point at which the system to be built can be analyzed.

3. *Transferable abstraction of a system.*   Software architecture constitutes a relatively small, intellectually graspable model for how a system is structured and how its components work together; this model is transferable across systems; in particular, it can be applied to other systems exhibiting similar requirements and can promote large-scale reuse.

We will address each of these points in turn.

ARCHITECTURE IS THE VEHICLE FOR STAKEHOLDER COMMUNICATION

Each stakeholder of a software system—customer, user, project manager, coder, tester, and so on—is concerned with different characteristics of the system that are affected by its architecture. For example, the user is concerned that the system is reliable and available when needed; the customer is concerned that the architecture can be implemented on schedule and to budget; the manager is worried (in addition to cost and schedule) that the architecture will allow teams to work largely independently, interacting in disciplined and controlled ways. The developer is worried about strategies to achieve all of those goals. Architecture provides a common language in which different concerns can be expressed, negotiated, and resolved at a level that is intellectually manageable even for large, complex systems (see following sidebar). Without such a language, it is difficult to understand large systems sufficiently to make the early decisions that influence both quality and usefulness. Architectural analysis, as we will see in Chapters 9 and 10, both depends on this level of communication and enhances it.

"What Happens When I Push This Button?" Architecture as a Vehicle for Stakeholder Communication

The project review droned on and on. The government-sponsored development was behind schedule and over budget and was large enough so that these lapses were attracting Congressional attention. And now the government was making up for past apathy by holding a marathon come-one-come-all review session. The contractor had recently undergone a buyout, which hadn't helped matters. It was the afternoon of the second day, and the agenda called for the software architecture to be presented. The young architect—an apprentice to the chief architect for the system—was bravely explaining how the software architecture for the massive system would enable it to meet its very demanding real-time, distributed, high-reliability requirements. He had a solid presentation and a solid architecture to present. It was sound and sensible. But the audience—about 30 government representatives who had varying roles in the management and oversight of this sticky project—was tired. Some of them were even thinking that perhaps they should have gone into real estate instead of enduring another one of these marathon let's-finally-get-it-right-this-time reviews.

The viewgraph showed, in semiformal box-and-line notation, what the major software components were. The names were all acronyms, suggesting no semantic meaning without explanation, which the young architect gave. The lines showed data flow, message passing, and process synchronization. The components were internally redundant, the architect was explaining. "In the event of a failure," he began, using a laser pointer to denote one of the lines, "a restart mechanism triggers along this path when. . . ."

"What happens when the mode select button is pushed?" interrupted one of the audience members. He was a government attendee representing the user community for this system.

"Beg your pardon?" asked the architect.

"The mode select button," he said. "What happens when you push it?"

"Um, that triggers an event in the device driver, up here," began the architect, laser-pointing. "It then reads the register and interprets the event code. If it's mode select, well, then, it signals the blackboard, which in turns signals the objects that have subscribed to that event. . . ."

"No, I mean what does the system do," interrupted the questioner. "Does it reset the displays? And what happens if this occurs during a system reconfiguration?"

The architect looked a little surprised and flicked off the laser pointer. This was not an architectural question, but since he was an architect and therefore fluent in the requirements, he knew the answer. "If the command line is in setup mode, the displays will reset," he said. "Otherwise an error message will be put on the control console, but the signal will be ignored." He put the laser pointer back on. "Now, the restart mechanism that I was talking about. . . ."

"Well, I was just wondering," said the users' delegate. "Because I see from your chart that the display console is sending signal traffic to the target location module."

"What *should* happen?" asked another member of the audience, addressing the first questioner. "Do you really want the user to get mode data during its reconfiguring?" And for the next 45 minutes, the architect watched as the audience consumed his time slot by debating what the correct behavior of the system was supposed to be in various esoteric states.

The debate was not architectural, but the architecture (and the graphical rendition of it) had sparked debate. It is natural to think of architecture as the basis for communication among some of the stakeholders besides the architects and developers: Managers, for example, use the architecture to create teams and allocate resources among them. But users? The architecture is invisible to users, after all; why should they latch on to it as a tool for system understanding?

The fact is that they do. In this case, the questioner had sat through two days of viewgraphs all about function, operation, user interface, and testing. But it was the first slide on architecture that—even though he was tired and wanted to go home—made him realize he didn't understand something. Attendance at many architecture reviews has convinced me that seeing the system in a new way prods the mind and brings new questions to the surface. For users, architecture often serves as that new way, and the questions that a user poses will be behavioral in nature. In Chapter 9, Section 9.4, we describe an architecture review in which the user representatives were much more interested in what the system was going to do than in how it was going to do it, and naturally so. Up until that point, their only contact with the vendor had been through its marketers. The architect was the first legitimate expert on the system to whom they had access, and they didn't hesitate to seize the moment.

Of course, careful and thorough requirements specifications would ameliorate this, but for a variety of reasons they are not always created or available. In their absence, a specification of the architecture often serves to trigger questions and improve clarity. It is probably more prudent to recognize this than to resist it. In Chapter 10, Section 10.3 we discuss a kind of review that clarifies and prioritizes requirements once architectural decisions have begun to be made. A review of this type that emphasizes synergy between requirements and architecture would have let the young architect in our story off the hook by giving him a place in the overall review session to address that kind of information. And the user representative wouldn't have felt like a fish out of water, asking his question at a clearly inappropriate moment. Of course, he could always go into real estate.

— *PCC*

ARCHITECTURE MANIFESTS THE EARLIEST SET
OF DESIGN DECISIONS

Software architecture represents a system's earliest set of design decisions. These early decisions are the most difficult to get correct and the hardest to change, and they have the most far-reaching effects.

An Architecture Defines Constraints on an Implementation. An implementation exhibits an architecture if it conforms to the structural design decisions described by the architecture. This means the implementation must be divided into the prescribed components, the components must interact with each other in the prescribed fashion, and each component must fulfill its responsibility to the other components as dictated by the architecture.

Resource allocation decisions also constrain implementations. These decisions may be invisible to implementors working on individual components. The constraints permit a separation of concerns that allows management decisions that make best use of personnel and computational capacity. Component builders must be fluent in the specification of their individual components but not in architectural trade-offs. Conversely, the architects need not be experts in all aspects of algorithm design or the intricacies of the programming language, but they are the ones responsible for the architectural trade-offs.

The Architecture Dictates Organizational Structure. Not only does architecture prescribe the structure of the system being developed, but that structure becomes engraved in the structure of the development project. The normal method for dividing up the labor in a large system is to assign different groups different portions of the system to construct. This is called the work-breakdown structure of a system. Because the system architecture includes the highest level decomposition of the system, it is typically used as the basis for the work-breakdown structure. Specifically, the module structure is most often the basis for work assignments. The work-breakdown structure in turn dictates units of planning, scheduling, and budget; interteam communication channels; configuration control and file-system organization; integration and test plans and procedures; and even project minutiae such as how the electronic bulletin boards are organized and how many team picnics there are. Teams communicate with each other in terms of the interface specifications to the major components. The maintenance activity, when launched, will also reflect the software structure, with teams formed to maintain specific structural components.

A side effect of establishing the work-breakdown structure is to effectively freeze the software architecture, at least at the level reflected in the work breakdown. A group that is responsible for one of the subsystems will resist having its responsibilities distributed across other groups. If these responsibilities have been formalized in a contractual relationship, changing responsibilities could become expensive. Tracking progress on a collection of tasks that is being distributed would also become much more difficult.

Thus, once the architecture's module structure has been agreed on, it becomes almost impossible for managerial and business reasons to modify it. This is one argument (among many) for carrying out extensive analysis before freezing the software architecture for a large system.

An Architecture Inhibits or Enables a System's Quality Attributes. Whether a large system will be able to exhibit its desired (or required) quality attributes is substantially determined by the time the architecture is chosen. A small system can achieve its quality attributes through methods such as coding and testing. These techniques become increasingly inadequate as systems grow, however, because quality attributes are increasingly satisfied in a large software system's structure and division of functionality rather than in its algorithms and data structures.

Modifiability, for example, depends extensively on the system's modularization, which reflects the system's encapsulation strategies. Reusability of components depends on how strongly coupled they are with other components in the system. Performance depends on the volume and complexity of intercomponent communication and coordination, especially if the components are physically distributed processes. It should be easy to see how architecture can strongly affect many kinds of quality attributes.

It is important to understand, however, that an architecture alone cannot guarantee the functionality or quality required of a system. Poor downstream design or implementation decisions can always undermine an adequate architectural design. Decisions at all stages of the life cycle—from high-level design to coding and implementation—affect system quality. Therefore, quality is not completely a function of an architectural design. A good architecture is necessary, but not sufficient, to ensure quality.

Predicting System Qualities by Studying Its Architecture.   Is it possible to tell that the appropriate architectural decisions have been made (i.e., if the system will exhibit its required quality attributes) without waiting until the system is developed and deployed? If the answer were No, choosing an architecture would be a hopeless task—random architecture selection would perform as well as any other method. Fortunately, it *is* possible to make quality predictions about a system based solely on an evaluation of its architecture. Architecture evaluation techniques such as the software architecture analysis method of Chapter 9 support top-down insight into the attributes of software product quality that is made possible (and constrained) by software architectures.

An Architecture Makes It Easier to Reason About and Manage Change. The software development community is coming to grips with the fact that roughly 80 percent of a typical software system's cost occurs *after* initial deployment, in the maintenance phase. A corollary of this statistic is that most systems that people work on are in this phase. Many if not most programmers and designers never work on new development—they work under the constraints of the existing body of code. Software systems change over their lifetimes; they do so often and often with difficulty.

Every architecture partitions possible changes into three categories: local, nonlocal, and architectural. A local change can be accomplished by modifying a single component. A nonlocal change requires multiple component modifications but leaves the underlying architecture intact. An architectural change affects the fundamental ways in which the components interact with each other—the style of the architecture—and will probably require changes all over the system. Obviously, local changes are the most desirable, and so an effective architecture is one in which the most likely changes are also the easiest to make.

Deciding when changes are essential, determining which change paths have the least risk, assessing the consequences of proposed changes, and arbitrating sequences and priorities for requested changes all require broad insight into relationships, dependencies, performance, and behaviors of system software components. These are in the job description for an architect. Reasoning at an architectural level can provide the insight necessary to make decisions and plans about proposed changes.

An Architecture Helps in Evolutionary Prototyping. Once an architecture has been defined, it can be analyzed and prototyped as an executable model. This aids the development process in two ways, as follows:

1. Potential performance problems can be identified early in the product's life cycle.

2. The system is executable early in the product's life cycle. The fidelity of the system increases as prototype parts are replaced by complete versions of these parts of the software. These prototype parts can be a lower-fidelity version of the final functionality, or they can be surrogates that consume and produce data at the appropriate rates.

Each of these benefits reduces the potential risk in the project. If the architecture is part of a family of related systems, the cost of creating a framework for prototyping can be distributed over the development of many systems.

ARCHITECTURE AS A TRANSFERABLE, REUSABLE MODEL

The earlier in the life cycle reuse is applied, the greater the benefit that can be achieved. While code reuse provides a benefit, reuse at the architectural level provides tremendous leverage for systems with similar requirements. Not only can code be reused but so can the requirements that led to the architecture in the first place, as well as the experience in building the reused architecture. When architectural decisions can be reused across multiple systems, all of the early-decision consequences we just described are also transferred.

Product Lines Share a Common Architecture.   Product lines are derived from what Parnas referred to as program families [Parnas 76]. It pays to carefully order design decisions so that those most likely to be changed occur latest in the process. In an architecture-based development of a product line, the architecture is in fact the sum of the early design decisions. System architects choose an architecture (or a family of closely related architectures) that will serve all envisioned members of the product line by making design decisions that apply across the family early and by making other decisions that apply only to individual members late. The architecture defines what is fixed for all members of the product line and what is variable.

A familywide design solution may not be optimal for all systems derived from it, but the quality gained and labor savings realized through architectural-level reuse may compensate for the loss of optimality in particular areas. On the other hand, reusing a familywide design reduces the risk that a derived system might have an inappropriate architecture. These same trade-offs are seen in engineering design in many disciplines. For example, people seldom have a house designed from scratch. They either build from a standard design or they make minor modifications to a standard design, and these modifications are seldom structural. In the case of both building and software architecture, using a standard design reduces both risk and development costs, at the risk of nonoptimality.

Similar to other capital investments, the architecture for a product line becomes a developing organization's core asset. The term *domain-specific software architectures* applies to architectures designed to address the known architectural abstractions specific to given problem domains. Such architectures represent a step beyond the simpler reference architectures that we defined earlier in this chapter. Product lines and reference architectures are explained in Chapters 15 and 17.

Systems Can Be Built by Using Large, Externally Developed Components.
Whereas former software paradigms have focused on *programming* as the prime activity, with progress measured in lines of code, architecture-based development often focuses on *composing* or *assembling components* that are likely to have been developed separately, even independently, from each other. This composition is possible because the architecture defines the components that can be incorporated into the system. The architecture constrains possible replacements (or additions) according to how they interact with their environment, how they receive and relinquish control, what data they consume and produce, how they access data, and what protocols they use for communication and resource sharing. We see an example of such a system in Chapter 16.

One key aspect of architecture is its organization of component structure, interfaces, and operating concepts. The most significant principle of this organization is *interchangeability*. In 1793, Eli Whitney's mass production of muskets, based on the principle of interchangeable parts, signaled the dawn of the industrial age. In the days before physical measurements were reliable, this was a daunting notion. Today in software, until abstractions can be reliably delimited, the notion of structural interchangeability is just as daunting and just as significant.

Commercial off-the-shelf components, subsystems, and compatible communications interfaces all depend on the principle of interchangeability. However, there is much about software development through composition that remains unresolved. When the components that are candidates for importation and reuse are distinct subsystems that have been built with conflicting architectural assumptions, unanticipated complications can increase the effort required to integrate their functions. Garlan et al. coined the term *architectural mismatch* to describe this situation [Garlan 95].

To resolve these differences, Garlan identified the need to make explicit the architectural contexts for potentially reusable subsystems. Some design practices, such as information hiding, are particularly important for architectural consistency. Techniques and tools for developing wrappers to bridge mismatches and principles for composition of software are also needed. The most elemental need is for improved documentation practices, the inclusion of detailed preconditions for the use of interfaces, and conventions for describing typical architectural assumptions and mechanisms. These and other mismatch-amelioration mechanisms will be described in Chapter 15.

Less Is More: It Pays to Restrict the Vocabulary of Design Alternatives.
As useful architectural styles and design patterns are collected, it becomes clear that although computer programs can be combined in more or less infinite ways, there is something to be gained by voluntarily restricting ourselves to a relatively small number of choices when it comes to program cooperation and interaction. That is, we wish to minimize the design complexity of the system we are building. Advantages to this approach include enhanced reuse, more regular and simpler designs that are more easily understood and communicated, more capable analysis, shorter selection time, and greater interoperability.

Properties of software design follow from the choice of architectural style. Those styles that are more desirable for a particular problem should improve the implementation of the resulting design solution, perhaps by making it easier to arbitrate conflicting design constraints, by increasing insight into poorly understood design contexts, and/or by helping to surface inconsistencies in requirements specifications. We address styles in detail in Chapter 5.

An Architecture Permits Template-Based Component Development.   An architecture embodies design decisions about how components interact that, while reflected in each component at the code level, can be localized and written just once. Templates can be used to capture in one place the interaction mechanisms at the component level. For example, a template can encode the declarations for a component's public area where results will be left or can encode the protocols that the component uses to engage with the system executive. An example of a set of firm architectural decisions enabling template-based component development can be found in the structural modeling approach to software, as will be discussed in Chapter 14.

Architecture Can Be the Basis for Training.   The structure, plus a high-level description of how the components interact with each other to carry out the required behavior, can serve as the first introduction to the system for new project members. This reinforces our point that one of the important uses of software architecture is to support and encourage communication among the various stakeholders. The architecture is a common reference point.

2.5   Architectural Structures

The contractor, the architect, the interior designer, the landscaper, and the electrician all have a different view of the structure of a building. Although these views are pictured differently, all are inherently related: Together they describe the building's architecture.

Previously we said that software architecture is about software structure, but we also explained that since software systems exhibit many structures, defining the overall structure of a system was an inherently ambiguous concept. So, just as the structure of a building has many meanings depending upon motive and viewpoint, software exhibits many structures, and we cannot communicate meaningfully about software unless it is clear which structure we are describing.

Some of the most common and useful software structures are as follows:

- *Module structure.*   The units are work assignments and have products (such as interface specifications, code, test plans, etc.) associated with them. They are linked by the is-a-submodule-of relation. Module structure is used to allocate a project's labor and other resources during maintenance as well as development.

- *Conceptual, or logical, structure.*   The units are abstractions of the system's functional requirements. These abstractions are related by the shares-data-with relation. A reference model, defined earlier, is an example. This view is useful for understanding the interactions between entities in the problem space and their variation.

- *Process structure, or coordination, structure.*   This view is orthogonal to the module and conceptual views and deals with the dynamic aspects of a running system. The units are processes or threads. Relations represented by the links include synchronizes-with, can't-run-without, can't-run-with, preempts, or any of several other relations dealing with process synchronization and concurrency.

- *Physical structure.*   This view shows the mapping of software onto hardware. It is particularly of interest in distributed or parallel systems. The components are hardware entities (processors), and the links are communication pathways. Relations between the processors are communicates-with. This view allows an engineer to reason about performance, availability, and security.

- *Uses structure*   The units are procedures or modules; they are linked by the assumes-the-correct-presence-of relation. The uses structure is used to engineer systems that can be easily subset or extended such as using an incremental build approach to integration.

- *Calls structure*.   The units are usually (sub)procedures; they are related by the calls or invokes relation. The calls structure is used to trace flow of execution in a program.

- *Data flow*.   Units are programs or modules; the relation is may-send-data-to. The links are labeled with the name of the data transmitted. The data-flow view is most useful for requirements traceability.

- *Control flow*.   Units are programs, modules, or system states; the relation is becomes-active-after. This view is useful for verifying the functional behavior of the system as well as timing properties. If the only mechanism for transferring control is the program call, this is identical to the calls structure.

- *Class structure*.   Units are objects; the relation is inherits-from or is-an-instance-of. This view supports reasoning about collections of similar behavior (i.e., the classes that other classes inherit from) and parameterized differences from the core, which are captured by subclassing.

Table 2.1 summarizes these structures. The table lists the meaning of the nodes and arcs in each structure and tells what each structure might be used for.

Although one often thinks about a system's structure in terms of its functionality, there are system properties in addition to functionality, such as physical distribution, process communication, and synchronization, that must be reasoned about at an architectural level. Each structure provides a method for reasoning about some of the relevant quality attributes. The uses structure, for instance, must be *engineered* (and not merely recorded) to build a system that can easily be extended or contracted. The calls structure is *engineered* to reduce bottlenecks. The module structure is *engineered* to produce modifiable systems, and so forth. Each structure provides the reader with a different view into the system and a different leverage point for design. Some authors use the terms *view* and *structure* synonymously. We will favor the term *structure* but will occasionally use the term *view* when it seems more natural.

Each structure is an abstraction with respect to different criteria. Each abstraction "boils away" details about the software that are independent of the concern reflected by the abstraction. Each structure can be considered to be a software blueprint. Consequently, each structure can use its own notation, can reflect its own choice of architectural style, and can define independently what is meant by components, interrelationships, rationale, principles, and guidelines.

RELATING STRUCTURES TO EACH OTHER

Each of these structures provides a different perspective and design handle on a system, and each is valid and useful in its own right. The conceptual and module

TABLE 2.1   Architectural Structures of a System

Software structure	Units	Relation represented by the links	Useful for
Module	Work assignments	Is a submodule of; shares secret with	Resource allocation and project structuring and planning; information hiding, encapsulation; configuration control
Conceptual	Functions	Shares data with	Understanding the problem space
Process	Programs	Runs concurrently with; may run concurrently with; excludes; precedes; etc.	Scheduling analysis; performance analysis
Physical	Hardware	Communicates with	Performance, availability, security analysis
Uses	Programs	Requires the correct presence of	Engineering subsets; engineering extensions
Calls	Programs	Invokes with parameters	Performance profiling; bottleneck elimination
Data flow	Functional tasks	May send data to	Traceability of functional requirements
Control flow	System states or modes	Transitions to, subject to the events and conditions labeling the link	With timing information, can be basis for automatic simulation and verification of timing and functional behavior
Class	Objects	Is an instance of; shares access methods of	In object-oriented design systems, producing rapid almost-alike implementations from a common template

structures emphasize static properties, and the process and physical structures give us the dynamic or runtime system structure. The conceptual and module structures, although similar, address fundamentally different concerns, as we have described. Some argue that the process and physical structures should be combined. Further, although they frequently do resemble each other, there is no requirement or implication that these structures bear any topological resemblance.

Although the structures give different system perspectives, they are not independent. Elements of one structure will be connected to elements of other structures, and we need to reason about these connections. The connections will be many to many. Furthermore, individual projects tend to consider one structure dominant and cast other structures, when possible, in terms of the dominant structure. Often, but not always, the dominant structure is the module structure. For one reason, it tends to precipitate the project structure. Scenarios, described in Chapter 9, are useful for exercising a given structure as well as its connections to other structures. For example, a software engineer, wanting to make a change to the control view of a system, would need to consult with the process and physical views because control mechanisms typically operate on processes and threads, and physical distribution might involve different control mechanisms than would be used if the processes were colocated on a single machine. If control mechanisms need to be changed, the module view would need to be consulted to determine the extent of the changes.

Not all systems warrant multiple architectural structures. Experience has shown that the larger the system, the more dramatic the difference between these structures; but for small systems, the conceptual and module structures may be so similar that they can be described together. If there is only one process or program, there is clearly no need for the process structure. If there is to be no distribution (that is, if there is just one processor), there is no need for the physical structure. However, in the case of most systems of significant size and complexity, if we were to attempt to combine these structures into one, we would add detail that would cripple the usefulness of the architecture as an artifact. This separation of concerns afforded by multiple structures proves beneficial in managing the complexity of large systems. One of the driving motivations for the use of software architecture is to manage the psychological complexity inherent in dealing with large software systems.

Architecture Déjà Vu

While architecture is undoubtedly a vital part of system development that is enjoying widespread community attention at the moment, it must be pointed out that the field is plowing old ground in several areas. In many ways we are "discovering" fundamental principles that were laid out eloquently and convincingly over a quarter-century ago by Fred Brooks, Edsger Dijkstra, David Parnas, and others.

In programming, the term *architecture* was first used to mean a description of a computer system that applied equally to more than one system. It still carries this meaning today. In 1969, Fred Brooks and Ken Iverson called architecture the "conceptual structure of a computer . . . as seen by the programmer" [Brooks 69]. A few years later, Brooks (crediting G. Blaauw for the term) defined architecture as "the complete and detailed specification of the user interface." [Brooks 75]. A careful distinction was drawn between architecture and implementation. Quoting Blaauw, Brooks writes, "Where architecture tells *what* happens, implementation tells *how* it is made to happen." This distinction survives today, and in the era of object-oriented programming, it thrives.

The term *architecture* is still used today in some communities to refer to the user view of a system, but that's not what we mean by *software* architecture. The structure(s) contained in a software architecture are invisible to the system's end user. However, the conceptual separation between the *what* and the *how* applies. Software architecture is not concerned with how components do what they do, just as the end user is not concerned with how the system does what it does. The notion of architecture as a common description of a class of systems (i.e., an abstraction, where all the instances are said to exhibit the architecture) remains at the heart of the concept that we call software architecture today.

Also in 1968, Edsger Dijkstra was pointing out that it pays to be concerned with how software is partitioned and structured as opposed to simply programming to produce a correct result [Dijkstra 68]. Dijkstra was writing about an operating system and introduced the idea of a layered structure, in which programs were grouped into layers and programs in one layer could communicate only with programs in adjacent ayers. Dijkstra pointed out the elegant conceptual integrity exhibited by such an organization, resulting in increased ease of development and maintenance.

David Parnas advanced this line of observation with his fundamental contributions to software engineering in the early 1970s. Parnas's work, more than that of anyone else, is to be found in many of the fundamental tenets and principles behind software architecture, including the following:

- A design principle for how to break a system into components so as to increase maintainability and (as we shall see in Chapter 5) reusability. If architecture has a fundamental principle, it is this one, which Parnas called information hiding [Parnas 72].

- The principle of using a component via its interface only, the conceptual basis of all object-based design [Parnas 72].

- An observation on the various structures to be found in software systems, with an admonition not to confuse them with each other—a lesson often forgotten by today's "architecturists" [Parnas 74].

- Introduction of the uses structure, a principle for controlling the connections between components in order to increase the extensibility of a system, as well as the ability to field subsets quickly and easily [Parnas 79].

- The principle for detection and handling errors (now called exceptions) in component-based systems that is the underlying approach of most modern programming languages [Parnas 72] [Parnas 76].

- Viewing every program as a member of a *family* of programs, with principles for taking advantage of the commonalities among the members and ordering the design decisions so that the ones that need to be easiest to revise are made last. The coarse structuring of the program—part of its architecture—comprises the set of early, familywide design decisions [Parnas 76].

- Recognition that the structure of a system influences the qualities (such as reliability) of that system [Parnas 76].

Now it is true, and Parnas would agree, that not all of the ideas in his papers were invented by him from whole cloth. About information hiding, for example, he has said that he was writing down what good programmers had been doing for a long time (especially operating-systems programmers writing device drivers). However, taken as a body, Parnas's work is a coherent statement of the theme of software architecture: *Structure matters*. His insights form the backbone of software architecture as a study area, and no book on the subject would be complete without acknowledging his fundamental contributions.

Recently a colleague of mine and I had a fine architectural discussion about what exactly constitutes the *interface* to a software component; clearly it's much more than just the names of the programs you can call and the parameters they take. My colleague worked out that it was really the set of assumptions that you could safely make about the component, and that, moreover, these assumptions varied according to the context of the component's use. I agreed, and pulled out Parnas's paper [Parnas 71] in which he said precisely the same thing. My friend looked a little crestfallen for a moment, and then said, "Now I know how Scott felt when he reached the South Pole and found Amundsen's flag already planted. He probably said, 'Oh, damn. And now I've got to eat my dogs.'"

Parnas's flag is planted deeply, and often, in our field. In the next chapter, we will present a case study of an architecture created by Parnas to put his ideas to practical use in a demanding real-world application. Even though it ran its course long ago, I am aware to this day of no other single project that so clearly laid out and faithfully followed architectural principles such as engineering and maintaining separate structures to achieve quality goals, the strict application of information hiding to achieve reusable components and a reusable architecture, and the painstakingly complete specification of that architecture, its components, and their connections.

While Parnas and others laid the foundations, the field has taken its own turns in the interim. Experience with basic ideas leads to refinement of those ideas, to embellishments rooted in practicalities, and to entirely new concepts. Thus, while Parnas wrote about *program families* a couple of decades ago, we'll see in Chapter 16 that organizational, process, and managerial concerns predominate in the successful development of *product lines*, their conceptual descendant. While Dijkstra wrote about separation of concerns about a quarter-century ago, *objects* (the conceptual descendant) have only fairly recently come into their own as a standard, widely accepted design approach. And while Brooks and Blaauw wrote about architecture even longer ago, we've already seen that architectures cannot be understood except in light of the business issues that spawned them, and we'll see ways to analyze architectures without waiting for the system to be built.

Today, architecture as a field of study is large and growing larger, primarily because it has left the realm of the deep thinkers and visionaries and made the transition into practice. The early ideas have been refined and applied enough so that it, too, is becoming an accepted state-of-the-practice approach to system building.

— PCC

2.6 Summary

This chapter has defined software architecture in a rigorous way and also introduced the related concepts of reference model, reference architecture, and architectural style. We have explained why architecture is a fundamentally useful concept in software engineering, in terms of the early insights it provides into the system, the communication it enables among stakeholders, and the value it provides as a reusable asset. All of these themes will be elaborated on in subsequent chapters.

The definition of architecture is one that makes clear that systems comprise many structures, and we have shown several of the most commonly used ones and explained how each serves as an engineering leverage point into the design process.

The next chapter is the first case study of the book, and its purpose is to show the utility of designing and recording different architectural structures in the design of a complex system.

2.7   For Further Reading

The early work of David Parnas laid much of the conceptual foundation for what became the study of software architecture (see the preceding sidebar). A quintessential Parnas reader would include his foundational article on information hiding [Parnas 72] as well as his works on program families [Parnas 76], the structures inherent in software systems [Parnas 74], and use of the uses structure to build subsets and supersets of systems [Parnas 79].

Barry Boehm [Boehm 95] discusses the process issues surrounding software architecture.

For a survey of recent work on software architecture, see Shaw and Garlan [Shaw 96a], as well as a special issue of the IEEE Transactions on Software Engineering [IEEE 95].

Architectural views as used in industrial development projects are the subject of papers by Soni et al. [Soni 95] and Kruchten [Kruchten 95]. They are also described by Ellis et al. [Ellis 96].

Garlan et al. present an interesting discussion of architectural mismatch in [Garlan 95].

Kruchten [Kruchten 95] describes a 4+1 view of software architecture, which includes four architectural views plus scenarios that tie the views together. This view of software architecture is close to our own.

2.8   Discussion Questions

1.   Software architecture is often compared to the architecture of buildings as a conceptual analogy. What are the strong points of that analogy? What is the correspondence in buildings to software architecture structures and views? To styles? What are the weaknesses of the analogy? When does it break down?

2.   What's the difference between a reference architecture and an architectural style? What can you do with one that you can't do with the other in terms of (a) organizational planning and (b) architectural analysis?

3. Do the architectures in your organization recognize the different views (structures and relations) inherent in architecture? If so, which ones? If not, why not?

4. Is there a different definition of software architecture that you are familiar with? If so, think about the ways in which this definition supports our acid test of an architecture: Does it abstract away information from the system and yet provide enough information to be a basis for analysis, decision making, and risk reduction?

3

A-7E
A Case Study in Utilizing
Architectural Structures

An object-oriented program's runtime structure often bears little resemblance to its code structure. The code structure is frozen at compile-time; it consists of classes in fixed inheritance relationships. A program's runtime structure consists of rapidly changing networks of communicating objects. In fact, the two structures are largely independent. Trying to understanding one from the other is like trying to understand the dynamism of living ecosystems from the static taxonomy of plants and animals, and vice versa.
—E. Gamma, R. Helms, R. Johnson, and J. Vlissides [Gamma 95]

In the previous chapter, we stated that architecture describes components of a system and the connections among those components. We also emphasized that every system has many different kinds of components and that different architectural structures are useful, even necessary, to present a complete picture of the architecture of a system. Each structure concentrates on one aspect of an architecture.

This chapter will present a case study of an architecture that was designed by engineering and specifying three specific architectural structures: the *module* structure, the *uses* structure, and the *process* structure. We will see how the three structures complement each other to provide a complete picture of how the system works, and we'll see how certain qualities of the system are affected by each one. Table 3.1 summarizes the three structures that we will discuss.

3.1 Relationship to the Architecture Business Cycle

Figure 3.1 gives the ABC as it pertains to the A-7E avionics system that we describe in this chapter. The system was constructed beginning in 1977 for the naval aviators who flew the A-7E aircraft and was paid for by the U.S. Navy. The

TABLE 3.1 The A-7E's Architectural Structures

Structure	Components	Relation among components	Has influence over
Module	Modules (work assignments)	Is a sub-module of; shares a secret with	Ease of change
Uses	Procedures	Requires the correct presence of	Ability to field subsets and develop incrementally
Process	Processes; thread of procedures	Synchronizes with; shares CPU with; excludes	Schedulability; achieving performance goals through parallelism

developing organization was the software engineering group at the U.S. Naval Research Laboratory. The developers were creating the software to test their belief that the use of software engineering principles (in this case, information hiding and cooperating sequential processes) was appropriate for high-performance embedded real-time systems.

The architects included one of the authors of this book and also included one of the leaders in the development of software engineering principles, but the architects had little experience in the avionics domain. They did have access to other avionics systems and to experts in avionics. There was no compiler available for the target platform.

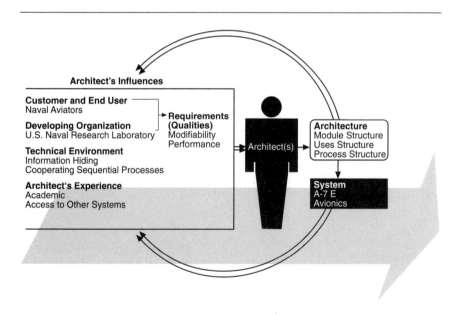

FIGURE 3.1 The ABC as it relates to the A-7E.

We'll start by explaining the application, what the system does, which qualities were important to achieve, and the software's role in performing the system's task.

3.2 Requirements and Qualities

Figure 3.2 shows the A-7E Corsair II. It is a single-seat, carrier-based attack aircraft used by the U.S. Navy throughout the 1960s, 1970s, and 1980s. An earlier version, the A-7C, was among the very first production aircraft in the world to be equipped with an on-board computer to help the pilot with navigation and "weapon delivery" (the military term for attacking a ground target).

The A-7E's on-board computer is a small, special-purpose IBM machine for which no compiler exists; programming is in assembly language only. The computer has special registers connected to analog-to-digital and digital-to-analog converters that let the computer receive and send data to almost two dozen devices in the aircraft's avionics suite.

The A-7E software is responsible, in broad terms, for reading sensors and updating cockpit displays that help the pilot navigate to drop weapons on target. The A-7E software does not actually fly the aircraft as more modern avionics systems do.

The primary sensors that the software reads and manages include the following:

- An air probe that measures barometric pressure and airspeed
- A forward looking radar that can be aimed in azimuth and elevation and returns the straight-line range to the point on the ground at which it is pointed

FIGURE 3.2 An A-7E Corsair II.   Used with permission and under copyright of Squadron/Signal Publications, Inc.

- A Doppler radar that reports ground speed and drift angle (the difference between the direction that the aircraft's nose is pointed and the direction in which it is moving over the ground)

- An inertial measurement set (IMS) that reports accelerations along each of three orthogonal axes—the software must read these accelerations in a timely manner and integrate them over time to derive velocities and must integrate the velocities over time to derive the aircraft's current position in the physical world. The software also must manage the alignment and compensate for the drift of the axes to keep them pointed north, east, and vertical, respectively, so that the measurements accurately correspond to the aircraft's frame of reference.

- An interface to the aircraft carrier's inertial measurement system, through which the aircraft can compute its current position while on board a ship.

- Sensors that report which of the A-7E's six underwing bomb racks have weapons on them and which of over 100 different kinds of weapons in the aircraft's repertoire they are. The software stores large tables of the parameters for each kind of weapon that let it compute how that weapon moves through the atmosphere in a free-fall ballistic trajectory.

- A radar altimeter that measures the distance to the ground

The cockpit display devices managed by the software include some display-only devices and some devices by which the pilot communicate with the software. They include the following:

- A map display that always displays the aircraft's current location by moving a back-lit filmstrip as the aircraft travels—The pilot can choose the map's orientation so that the top corresponds either to the current heading or to true north.

- A head-up display, a device that projects digital and iconographic information on a clear window between the pilot and the windscreen—Since the pilot's head position is assumed fixed and known, the head-up display can be used to overlay information about the real world, such as the position of the target or a line showing the aircraft's direction of travel.

- A keypad and a trio of small alphanumeric display windows—By using the key pad, the pilot can request approximately 100 different kinds of digital information from the computer. A bank of switches on the computer control panel provides a way for the pilot to choose the desired navigation and weapon delivery mode.

- Various lights and dials and an audible signal

The pilot communicates the location of a ground target (or a navigational waypoint) to the software in a number of ways, including the following:

- Keying in its latitude and longitude via the keypad

- Slewing the map using a joystick until its coordinates are under the center crosshairs and then "designating" it by pushing a special button on the control stick
- Aiming the forward-looking radar to the point and designating it
- Slewing a special symbol on the head-up display until it overlays the point of interest on the ground and then designating it

The software then provides navigational information (direction, distance, time to go) and directional cues on the head-up display that get the aircraft to the designated location.

The pilot can choose from over two dozen navigation modes, based on which sensors are most reliable under the conditions of the moment. The software has at least five different direct and indirect ways to calculate the aircraft's current altitude, including a trigonometric scheme using the range and elevation angle of the forward-looking radar as components of a triangle (see Figure 3.3). There are over 20 weapon delivery modes, all demanding in terms of the real-time calculations (repeated 25 times every second) necessary to maintain the A-7E's bombing accuracy.

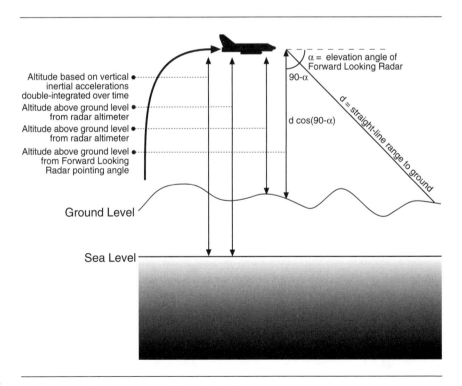

FIGURE 3.3   Calculation of altitute for A-7E.

A-7Es were retired from active duty in the U. S. Navy in the late 1980s, but current-generation fighters feature a head-up display and weapon-delivery and navigation modes that show heavy influence from the Corsair.

3.3   Architectural Approach

The architecture we will present in this chapter is not the architecture for the original software but that of a redesign project launched by Navy software engineers using the A-7E as a demonstration project for their ideas (see sidebar). The qualities that the software system was expected to have included real-time performance and modifiability for expected changes. Three architectural structures play an important role in the A-7E software, and we will discuss each in turn.

About the A-7 Project

"In the mid-1970s, it was clear to computer scientists at the Naval Research Laboratory (NRL) in Washington, D.C., that much of the computer science technology being developed in academe and laboratories was not being used by the developers of software for Navy systems." So began a typical description of the Navy's Software Cost Reduction (SCR) project, or, as it was more popularly known, the A-7 project. Most descriptions went on to say that NRL's response was to choose a high-fidelity challenging Navy program (the software for the A-7E aircraft) and then redesign and reimplement it using that underutilized technology. The point was to create a convincing demonstration of the technology's value in real-world applications.

Between the lines, however, was the fact that those scientists had some very specific computer science technology in mind: primarily, the use of information hiding as the design strategy. This is not surprising, because the impetus behind the A-7 project was the man who first wrote about information hiding as a design technique: David Parnas. Parnas wanted to find out whether his ideas (and others, such as cooperating sequential processes) could be used in a system with inflexible requirements, demanding memory constraints, and tight time budgets. If not, he wanted to find out why not and how to improve his ideas so that they could work. Vague methods demonstrated only on toy problems were clearly not enough. The idea behind the A-7 project was to leave a complete engineering model—documentation, design, code, methodology, principles—that others could emulate, all reported in the open literature.

The project started in 1977 with a couple of people working part time. It soon chose the demonstration application, the software for the A-7E. It was a hard real-time system (meaning it absolutely had to meet its timing requirements), that was embedded (having to interface with all sorts of esoteric hardware devices), was absolutely authentic, and very tightly constrained by the computer's tiny memory capacity: only 32,000 16-bit words. If the new techniques succeeded in duplicating *this* program, they would succeed anywhere.

The first product was a requirements specification for the software. They hadn't intended on producing such a thing, but when Parnas asked the Navy if he could obtain the A-7's requirements document, the response was, "*What requirements document?*" Realizing that they had to have a standard against which to test and judge when they were done, the software engineers at the NRL reluctantly set about documenting the requirements for the software. The team not only produced one but, more important, produced a method for producing one. SCR-style requirements documents are now widely used for real-time embedded software systems.

Then, the small team concentrated on designing the interfaces to all of the modules. This sounds like a long time—which it was—but the few people working on the project were pioneering what would today be called object-based design. In designing to accommodate future changes, they were also building what would today be called a domain model. In creating a standard, reusable design, they were building what would today be called a reference architecture (see Chapter 17). They had to balance their time between inventing new software-engineering approaches, learning the avionics domain, writing papers to get the word out, and last but hardly least, producing the software.

The project implementation phase was staged by deploying a tiny subset of the software to demonstrate the ability to generate executable code and then deploying two successively larger subsets and finally the entire system. The uses structure, one of the three architectural structures highlighted in the case study, allowed them to define these subsets quickly and easily to meet their needs. By the time the second of three subsets was under way, it was clear to the project management that most of what they had set out to learn had been learned and that slogging through to the complete reimplementation was not going to be practical given the small staff size, small budget, and still infantile expertise in the avionics domain. In 1987, the project demonstrated the successful completion of the second subset and was completed. The subset was carefully chosen to include part of every second-level module and to perform a useful and nontrivial navigation function.

They concluded that information hiding is not only compatible with real-time embedded systems, but in many ways it is ideal for it. Careful attention to module interfaces and module interface specifications paid off in essentially eliminating integration as a phase of the project: There were practically no errors of the type usually associated with the integration step. The software was able to meet its timing deadlines but could not compete with years of hand-crafted assembly code in terms of memory efficiency. It is to be hoped that memory efficiency is and will remain less of a concern than it was in 1977.

The architecture we present in this case study is that of the completed design, the one that led to the subset of 1987. There is no reason to believe that it would not have also led, unchanged, to the full reimplementation of the system. In any case, it is a very good example of paying attention to different architectural structures or views in order to achieve particular goals, and we present it in that light.

Why after all this time is the A-7E still interesting? It's because there were two lessons of the A-7E. One is that information hiding is a viable and prudent design discipline. This lesson has been well heeded by the community. The second is that carefully engineering different structures of an architecture yields payoffs in terms of the qualities that can be achieved. This lesson has not been so well heeded, and so we repeat it in the context of the current interest in software architecture in the hope that, through repetition, the lesson will be better absorbed.

— PCC

MODULE STRUCTURE

Unless a program is small enough to be produced by a single programmer, one must give thought to how the work will be divided into work assignments, which are called *modules*, and how those modules will interact with each other. System designers theoretically start out with a clean slate; they can design their systems to maximize or minimize any aspect they choose. Some design strategies attempt to maximize runtime performance. Others try to minimize the time that the design phase takes. The goal of the A-7E designers was to design software from the beginning to be easy to understand and change.

The A-7E module design is based on the decomposition principle known as information hiding. Information hiding works by encapsulating system details that are likely to change independently in different modules. The interface of a module reveals only those aspects considered unlikely to change; the details hidden by the module interface are secrets of the module.

For instance, if a device such as an aircraft altitude sensor is likely to be replaced over the life of an avionics program, the information-hiding principle makes the details of interacting with that device the secret of one module. The interface to the module provides an abstraction of the sensor, consisting perhaps of a single program that returns the most recent value measured by the sensor, because all replacement sensors would probably share this capability. If the sensor is ever replaced, only the internal parts of that module need change; the rest of the software will be unaffected.

Information hiding is enforced by requiring that modules interact with each other only via a defined set of public facilities—their *interfaces*. Each module provides a set of procedures, called *access procedures,* that may be called by any other module in the system. The access procedures provide the only intermodule means for interacting with information encapsulated in a module.

This is, of course, the philosophy underlying object-based design, with a key difference: Whereas objects are created from the physical objects inherent in the application, or conjured up from intuitive insights about the system, information-hiding modules are derived by cataloging the changes to the software that are perceived to be likely over the system's lifetime.

The document produced to record the division of the software into modules is called a *module guide*. It defines the responsibilities of each of the modules by stating the design decisions that will be encapsulated by that module. A module may consist of submodules, or it may be considered to be a single work assignment. If a module contains submodules, a guide to its substructure is provided. The decomposition into submodules and their design is continued until each work assignment is small enough that it could be discarded and begun again if the programmer assigned to do it left the project.

Specific goals of the module decomposition are as follows:

- Each module's structure should be simple enough that it can be understood fully.

- It should be possible to change the implementation of one module without knowledge of the implementation of other modules and without affecting the behavior of other modules.

- The ease of making a change in the design should bear a reasonable relationship to the likelihood of the change being needed; it should be possible to make likely changes without changing any module interfaces; less likely changes may involve interface changes but only for modules that are small and not widely used. Only very unlikely changes should require changes in the interfaces of widely used modules.

- It should be possible to make a major software change as a set of independent changes to individual modules (i.e., except for interface changes, programmers changing the individual modules should not need to communicate). If the interfaces of the modules are not revised, it should be possible to run and test any combination of old and new module versions.

A module guide is needed to avoid duplication and gaps, to achieve separation of concerns, and most of all, to help a maintainer find out which modules are affected by a problem report or change request. It states the criteria used to assign a particular responsibility to a module and arranges the modules in such a way that one can find the information relevant to one's purpose without searching through unrelated documentation.

If one diligently applies information hiding to a large system to achieve the preceding goals, one is certain to end up with a great many modules. A guide that was simply a list of those modules, with no other structure, would help only those who are already familiar with the system. The A-7E module guide follows a tree structure, dividing the system into a small number of modules and treating each such module in the same way until all of the modules are quite small. Each nonleaf node in the tree represents a module that is composed of the modules represented by its descendents.

Applying this principle is not always easy. It is an attempt to lower the expected cost of software by anticipating likely changes. Such estimates are necessarily based on experience, knowledge of the application area, and an understanding of hardware and software technology. Because a designer might not have all of the relevant experience, formal review procedures were used that were

TABLE 3.2   How the A-7E Module Structure Achieves Quality Goals

Goal	How achieved
Ease of change	Information hiding
Understand anticipated changes	Formal review procedure to take advantage of experience of experts in the domain.
Assign work teams so that their interactions were minimized	The modules were structured as a hierarchy and each work team was assigned to a second-level module and all of its descendants.

designed to take advantage of the experience of others—effectively, a kind of domain analysis. Table 3.2 outlines the module structure.

USES STRUCTURE

The second major structure of interest in the A-7E architecture is the uses structure. Whereas modules define loci of change and work assignment, that structure carries no information about runtime execution of the software; you might make an educated guess as to how two procedures in different modules interact with each other in runtime, but this information is in fact not carried in the module structure. The uses structure supplies the authoritative picture of how the software interacts. The concept is based on the uses relation. Procedure A is said to *use* procedure B if a correctly functioning procedure B must be present in order for procedure A to meet its requirements. This relation in practice turns out to be similar to but not quite the same as the calls relation. Procedure A usually calls procedure B because it uses it. However, here are two cases where uses and calls are different:

1. Procedure A is simply required to call procedure B in its specification, but the future computation performed by procedure A does not depend on what procedure B does. Procedure B must be present in order for procedure A to work, but it need not be correct. A calls, but does not use, B.

2. Procedure B performs its function without being called by procedure A, but procedure A uses the results. The results might be an updated data store that B leaves behind. Or B might be an interrupt handler that A assumes exists and functions correctly. A uses, but does not call, B.

The uses relation allows for the rapid identification of functional subsets. If you know that procedure A needs to be in the subset, you also know that every procedure that A uses must also be present. The transitive closure of this relation defines the subset. It therefore pays to engineer this structure, to impose a discipline on it, so that every subset does not need to consist of the entire system. This means specifying an allowed-to-use structure for programmers. After implementation is complete, the actual uses can be cataloged.

The unit of the module structure is, of course, the module. A module may be thought of as defining a group of programs, some public and some private, plus a

TABLE 3.3 How the A-7E Uses Structure Achieves Quality Goals

Goal	How achieved
Incrementally build and test functions of system	Create "is-allowed-to-use" structure for programmers that limits the procedures each can use
Design for portability	Make uses structure define a layered style
Produce usage guidance of manageable size	Where appropriate, define uses to be a relationship among modules

set of private data structures. The relation among modules is is-a-submodule-of or shares-a-secret-with. The unit of the uses (or allowed-to-use) structure is more finely grained: It is the procedure. By dictating what procedures are allowed to use which other procedures (and, by implication, what procedures are *not* allowed to be used by which other procedures), the uses structure is defined.

Although the unit of the uses structure is a procedure, in practice all of the procedures of a module may share the same usage restrictions. Hence, the name of a module might appear in the uses structure; if so, it is a shorthand for all of the procedures in that module.

The uses (is-allowed-to-use) structure is conceptually documented with a binary matrix; the rows and columns each list every procedure in the system. If element (m,n) is true, then procedure m uses (is allowed to use) procedure n. In practice, this is too cumbersome, and a shorthand was introduced in which rules for whole modules (as opposed to individual procedures within each module) were adopted. Table 3.3 shows the uses structure.

PROCESS STRUCTURE

The third structure of architectural importance to the A-7E is the process structure. Even though the underlying aircraft computer was a uniprocessor, one of the modules presents a virtual programming interface that feature multiprocessing capabilities. This was to plan for the day if and when the A-7E computer was replaced with an actual multiprocessor. Hence, the software is implemented as a set of cooperating sequential processes that synchronize with each other to cooperatively use shared resources. The set of processes is arranged using off-line (preruntime) scheduling to produce a single executable thread that is then loaded onto the host computer.

A process is a set of programming steps that are repeated in response to a triggering event or a timing constraint. It has its own thread of control. A process can suspend itself by waiting for an event (usually by invoking one of the event-signalling programs on a module's interface).

Processes are written for two purposes in the A-7E. The first is to compute the output values of the avionics software. They are required to run periodically (e.g., to continuously update a symbol position on the head-up display) or in response to some triggering event (e.g., when the pilot presses the weapon-release button). It is natural to implement them as processes. Conceptually, processes are structured as follows:

- `Periodic_process`: do every 40 milliseconds
  - Call other modules' access procedures to gather the values of all relevant inputs
  - Calculate the resulting output value
  - Call the appropriate Device Interface procedure to send the output value to the outside world
- `End periodic_process`
- `demand_process`
  - Await triggering event
  - Calculate the resulting output result
  - Call the appropriate Device Interface procedure to trigger the action in the outside world
- End `demand_process`

Processes also occur, although less frequently, as a hidden tactic to implement certain access procedures. If the value returned by an access procedure is expensive to compute, a programmer might choose to meet the timing requirements by continuously computing the value in the background and simply returning the most recent value immediately when the access procedure is called. For example,

- `Process`: do every 100 milliseconds
  - Gather inputs to compute value
  - Compute value
  - Store in variable `most_recent`
- `End process`
- `Procedure get_value(p1)`
  - `p1 := most_recent`
  - `return`
- `End procedure`

The process structure, then, consists of the set of processes in the software. The relation contained in the structure is synchronizes-with, a relation based on events that one process signals and one or more processes await. This relation is used as the primary input to the scheduling activity, which includes deadlock avoidance. The off-line scheduling techniques used in the A-7E software are beyond the scope of this treatment, but they avoid the overhead of a runtime scheduler, and they would not have been possible without the information contained in the

TABLE 3.4 How the A-7E Process Structure Achieves Quality Goals

Goal	How achieved
Map input to output	Each process implemented as cycle that samples, inputs, computes, and presents output
Maintain real time constraints	Identify process through process structure and then perform off-line scheduling
Provide the results of time-consuming calculations immediately	Perform calculations in background and return most recent value when queried

process structure. The process structure also allows an optimization trick: merging two otherwise-unrelated processes. This makes scheduling easier in many circumstances and also avoids the overhead of context switching when one process suspends and another resumes. This technique is invisible to programmers; it happens automatically during system construction. Table 3.4 outlines this process structure.

3.4 Architecture for the A-7E Avionics System

We now go into detail about the architecture for the. A-7E avionics system. Because the module structure dominates the other structures (recall they were engineered to be compatible with the module structure), we focus much of our attention on this structure. We also discuss how the uses structure reflects the layering of the modules.

A-7E MODULE STRUCTURE

Recall that the responsibility of the modules is documented in a module guide. The module guide does not describe any runtime relationship among the modules: It doesn't talk about how modules interact with each other while the system is executing. Rather, it simply describes a design-time relationship among the work assignments that constitute the design phase of a project.

To describe the A-7E module structure, and to give an example of how a module structure is documented, we provide excerpts from the A-7E software module guide. The module tree is described beginning with the three highest-level modules. These modules are motivated by the observation that in systems like the A-7E, changes tend to come from three areas: a change to the hardware with which the software must interact, a change to the required externally visible behavior of the system, or a change to a decision solely under the jurisdiction of a project's software designer.

Hardware-Hiding Module.   The Hardware-Hiding Module includes the procedures that need to be changed if any part of the hardware is replaced by a new unit with a different hardware/software interface but with the same general capabilities. This module implements *virtual hardware,* or an abstract device that is used by the rest of the software. The primary secrets of this module are the hardware/software interfaces. The secondary secrets of this module are the data structures and algorithms used to implement the virtual hardware.

Behavior-Hiding Module.   The Behavior-Hiding Module includes procedures that need to be changed if there are changes in requirements affecting the required behavior. Those requirements are the primary secret of this module. These procedures determine the values to be sent to the virtual output devices provided by the Hardware-Hiding Module.

Software Decision Module.   The Software Decision Module hides software design decisions that are based on mathematical theorems, physical facts, and programming considerations such as algorithmic efficiency and accuracy. The secrets of this module are not described in the requirements document. This module differs from the other modules in that both the secrets and the interfaces are determined by software designers. Changes in these modules are more likely to be motivated by a desire to improve performance or accuracy than by externally imposed changes.

The module guide goes on to explain how conflicts among these categories (e.g., is a required algorithm part of the behavior or a software decision?) are arbitrated by a complete and unambiguous requirements specification and then provides the second level decomposition. The following sections describe how the Software Decision Module is decomposed:

Application Data Type Module – The Application Data Type Module supplements the data types provided by the Extended Computer Module with data types that are useful for avionics applications and do not require a computer-dependent implementation. Examples of types include distance (useful for altitude), time intervals, and angles (useful for latitude and longitude). These data types are implemented using the basic numeric data types provided by the Extended Computer; variables of those types are used just as if the types were built into the Extended Computer.

The secrets of the Application Data Type Module are the data representation used in the variables and the procedures used to implement operations on those variables. Units of measurements (such as feet, seconds, or radians) are part of the representation and are hidden. Where necessary, the modules provide conversion operators that deliver or accept real values in specified units.

Data Banker Module – Most data are produced by one module and consumed by another. In most cases, the consumers should receive a value that is as up to date as practical. The time at which a datum should be recalculated is determined both by properties of its consumer (e.g., accuracy requirements) and by properties of its producer (e.g., cost of calculation, rate of change of value). The Data Banker Module acts as a "middleman" and determines when new values for these data are computed.

The Data Banker Module obtains values from producer procedures; consumer procedures obtain data from Data Banker access procedures. The producer and consumers of a particular datum can be written without knowing when a stored value is updated. In most cases, neither the producer nor the consumer need be modified if the updating policy changes.

The data banker provides values for all data that report on the internal state of a module or on the state of the aircraft. The Data Banker also signals events involving changes in the values that it supplies. The Data Banker is used as long as consumer and producer are separate modules, even when they are both submodules of a larger module. The Data Banker is not used if consumers require specific members of the sequence of values computed by the producer or if a produced value is solely a function of the values of input parameters given to the producing procedure, such as $\sin(x)$. The Data Banker Module is an example of the use of the blackboard architectural style (see Chapter 5).

The choice among updating policies should be based on the consumers' accuracy requirements, how often consumers require the value, the maximum wait that consumers can accept, how rapidly the value changes, and the cost of producing a new value. This information is part of the specification given to the implementor of the Data Banker Module.

Filter Behavior Module – The Filter Behavior Module contains digital models of physical filters. They can be used by other procedures to filter potentially noisy data. The primary secrets of this module are the models used for the estimation of values based on sample values and error estimates. The secondary secrets are the computer algorithms and data structures used to implement those models.

Physical Models Module – The software requires estimates of quantities that cannot be measured directly but can be computed from observables using mathematical models. An example is the time that a ballistic weapon will take to strike the ground. The primary secrets of the Physical Models Module are the models; the secondary secrets are the computer implementations of those models.

Software Utility Module – The Software Utility Module contains those utility routines that would otherwise have to be written by more than one other programmer. The routines include mathematical functions, resource monitors, and procedures that signal when all modules have completed their power-up initialization. The secrets of the module are the data structures and algorithms used to implement the procedures.

System Generation Module – The primary secrets of the System Generation Module are decisions that are postponed until system generation time. These include the values of system-generation parameters and the choice among alternative implementations of a module. The secondary secrets of the System Generation Module are the method used to generate a machine-executable form of the code and the representation of the postponed decisions. The procedures in this module do not run on the on-board computer; they run on the computer used to generate the code for the on-board system.

In the previous chapter, we remarked that architectures serve as the blueprint for the developing project as well as the software. In the case of the A-7E architecture, this second-level module structure became enshrined in many ways: Design documentation, on-line configuration-controlled files, test plans, programming teams, review procedures, and project schedule and milestones all used this second-level module structure as their unit of reference.

The module guide describes a third (and in some cases a fourth) level decomposition, but that has been omitted here. Figure 3.4 shows the overall module structure of the A-7E architecture down to the third level of decomposition. Notice that many of the Device Interface modules have the same name as Function Driver modules. The difference is that the Device Interface modules are programmed with knowledge of how the software interfaces with the devices; the Function Driver modules are programmed with the knowledge of what values are required to be computed and sent to those devices. This suggests another architectural relationship that we will explore shortly: how the software in these modules cooperate with each other to accomplish work.

But the module view is not yet complete. Recall from Chapter 2 that our definition of architecture included the behavioral specification for each of the components. As we shall see in the case studies on the World Wide Web (Chapter 7) and distributed object technology (Chapter 8), carefully designed language-independent interfaces are crucial for maintaining portability and achieving interoperability. Here, each module must have an interface specified for it. Whereas architecture representation is one of the themes of this book, explored in detail in Chapter 12, the A-7E provides a glimpse of how an architecture might be represented in practice (as do each of the case studies in this book). We have already seen the module guide. The module interface specifications will complete the module view of the architecture.

DESIGN AND SPECIFICATION OF MODULE INTERFACES

The specification of an information-hiding module's interface should be precise and nonredundant. It should serve as a quick reference document and divulge only the information necessary for the user of the document to perform his or her task.

The organization chosen to achieve these properties consists of the following sections:

- *Introduction.* This section introduces, in informal prose, the features provided by the module. It may define basic concepts that are used in the rest of the specification.

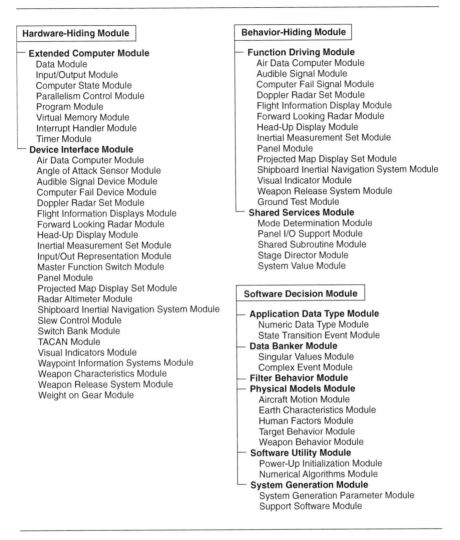

Hardware-Hiding Module

— **Extended Computer Module**
  Data Module
  Input/Output Module
  Computer State Module
  Parallelism Control Module
  Program Module
  Virtual Memory Module
  Interrupt Handler Module
  Timer Module
— **Device Interface Module**
  Air Data Computer Module
  Angle of Attack Sensor Module
  Audible Signal Device Module
  Computer Fail Device Module
  Doppler Radar Set Module
  Flight Information Displays Module
  Forward Looking Radar Module
  Head-Up Display Module
  Inertial Measurement Set Module
  Input/Out Representation Module
  Master Function Switch Module
  Panel Module
  Projected Map Display Set Module
  Radar Altimeter Module
  Shipboard Inertial Navigation System Module
  Slew Control Module
  Switch Bank Module
  TACAN Module
  Visual Indicators Module
  Waypoint Information Systems Module
  Weapon Characteristics Module
  Weapon Release System Module
  Weight on Gear Module

Behavior-Hiding Module

— **Function Driving Module**
  Air Data Computer Module
  Audible Signal Module
  Computer Fail Signal Module
  Doppler Radar Set Module
  Flight Information Display Module
  Forward Looking Radar Module
  Head-Up Display Module
  Inertial Measurement Set Module
  Panel Module
  Projected Map Display Set Module
  Shipboard Inertial Navigation System Module
  Visual Indicator Module
  Weapon Release System Module
  Ground Test Module
— **Shared Services Module**
  Mode Determination Module
  Panel I/O Support Module
  Shared Subroutine Module
  Stage Director Module
  System Value Module

Software Decision Module

— **Application Data Type Module**
  Numeric Data Type Module
  State Transition Event Module
— **Data Banker Module**
  Singular Values Module
  Complex Event Module
— **Filter Behavior Module**
— **Physical Models Module**
  Aircraft Motion Module
  Earth Characteristics Module
  Human Factors Module
  Target Behavior Module
  Weapon Behavior Module
— **Software Utility Module**
  Power-Up Initialization Module
  Numerical Algorithms Module
— **System Generation Module**
  System Generation Parameter Module
  Support Software Module

FIGURE 3.4   The module view of the A-7E software architecture.

- *Interface overview.*   The interface overview section gives a summary description of the facilities provided by the module in a tabular format. This allows quick reference to the major features of the module interface and pointers to more detailed definitions later in the body of the specification. Readers familiar with the module interface can use these tables to refresh their memories about particular facts without having to reread the longer explanations in later sections. Novice readers or those with more detailed questions can use the terms given in the tables to locate specific details quickly.

The interface overview may contain either or both of the following subsections:

– *Access procedure table.*   Where a module provides services used by other modules (e.g. calculating a value such as $\sin(x)$), those services are provided by access procedures, which are defined on the module interface. All of the interactions between modules except synchronization take place through the module's access procedures. An access procedure table lists all access procedures provided by the module, as well as the number, data type, and semantics of the parameters and names the undesired events associated with each procedure. The semantics of access procedures are defined in one of two ways. For procedures that simply deliver values via output parameters (such as a Data Banker procedure that returns a stored value), a dictionary entry defines the meaning of the returned parameter. For procedures that allow users to have an effect on the future operation of the module or the aircraft (such as commands that change the value shown on a display device), an entry in an Effects section specifies the effects (semantics) of invoking the access procedure. The effects are specified in terms of changes or results that are completely observable by using software or a human observer. It is basic to the information-hiding methodology that no information about the implementation or other hidden aspects of a module be divulged in this section. Effects may be given by specifying changes in the values that will subsequently be returned by access procedures or in terms of events that will occur at a later time.

– *Events signaled.*   In a real-time multiprocess system, it is essential that processes be able to detect and report the occurrence of events to each other. This facility represents the highest-level synchronization mechanism. Events may correspond to hardware interrupts, which are in turn reported by the module responsible for encapsulating that hardware, or they may correspond to state changes in the software (e.g., a module may signal event when it has completed its self-initialization phase and is ready to be used). This section is a table that contains a list of all of the events reported by the module. Events are reported via access procedures that do not return until the specified conditions hold. To await an event, a client simply calls the appropriate access procedure.

There are four varieties of event-reporting procedures as shown in Table 3.5. The string *condition* is an entry in the module specification's dictionary. Event meanings are thus defined by the associated dictionary entries.

▪ *Local types dictionary.*   For every procedure parameter, a type is specified in the access procedure table. This section of the specification defines the data types that are used in communicating with the module. Every data type in the A-7E design is implemented by some (not necessarily the same) module. For a module to provide a data type on its interface means that users are told how to declare variables of that type. Once a data type is defined, access

TABLE 3.5   Event-Reporting Procedures

Name of procedure	Meaning
@T*condition*	This procedure will return when (i.e., suspend the caller until) *condition* next changes from false to true.
@F*condition*	This procedure will return when *condition* next changes from true to false.
=T*condition*	This procedure will return when *condition* is true, as soon as the applicable process synchronization rules permit.
=F*condition*	This procedure will return when *condition* is false, as soon as the applicable process synchronization rules permit.

procedures that take parameters of that data type may be specified. All such data types are described in this section except those that are defined in another module interface specification, in which case a reference to that specification is to be given. Some data types are *enumerated types*; their values comprise a set of symbolic names specified by a list of strings or a syntax that defines the list of strings eligible to be passed to the procedure.

- *Dictionary.*   This section of the specification defines terms used in the interface overview to name an output parameter of a procedure or used in the name of a signaled event. The dictionary definition of such a term, then, defines the value returned by the access procedure via the output parameter or defines the meaning of a signaled event. The definition is given only in terms that can be tested by the software or a human user.

- *Undesired event dictionary.*   An undesired event occurs when an assumption about an undesired event is violated, usually when an access procedure is called with an incorrect parameter or in a state in which it cannot be executed successfully. This section defines the conditions that correspond to each undesired event reported by the module. Undesired events correspond to *exceptions* in the Ada programming language. Associating an undesired event with an access procedure imparts an obligation on the procedure implementor to write code to detect, report, and handle any occurrence of the undesired event. Undesired events usually correspond to calling a program with a parameter whose value is illegal or invoking a program when its module is in an inappropriate state (such as trying to retrieve a sensor value from a sensor that has been turned off).

- *System generation parameters.*   This section describes those externally visible characteristics of the module that can be changed by assigning values to parameters at system generation time. Each parameter is named, its data type is given, and its meaning is described. These parameters may be used as symbolic constants by users of the module.

- *Interface design issues.*   This prose section describes any alternative designs that were considered and records the reason for their rejection.

The section serves as a history of design decisions so that issues are not considered repeatedly. It serves as a design rationale providing guidance to maintenance programmers revising the module.

Experience indicates that this section may be one of the most important in an interface specification over the life of the project. Module interfaces are often redesigned, and recording design decisions prevents having to begin at the beginning each time. Many issues and concerns would otherwise have been lost to memory. It is a natural tendency to avoid recording rejected design alternatives or the rationale behind an adopted design, and like so many other professional disciplines, this one usually requires active management to continually remind designers to record their thoughts. Our experience indicates that it is well worth the time and that it doesn't take long for the designers themselves to become converts to the idea. After one takes a bad design path for the second or third time, one usually gets the idea that writing down why this was a bad path is a good idea.

- *Implementation notes.*   During the design of the module interface, certain facts or ideas may come to the designer's attention, ideas that would be necessary or useful to future implementors, and these are noted in this section. On the A-7E project, the people who implemented (programmed) a module were usually different from the people who designed it. The implementation notes gave the programmers a foothold with which to begin their task, and saved them countless hours of research and investigation into alternative implementations.

- *Assumptions lists.*   The information in the assumptions lists is redundant. It is implied by the description of the facilities specified in the rest of the specification. The purpose of the assumption lists is to serve as an explicit medium for review by nonprogrammers. This section has two prose subsections.

  – *Basic assumptions.*   These assumptions contain information that users of the module may assume will never change. In the case of hardware-hiding modules, it consists of information that will remain true about the interface even if the hidden hardware is replaced or modified. In the case of behavior-hiding modules, it consists of information that will remain true even if the hidden requirements are changed. In the case of software decision-hiding modules, it consists of information that will remain true even if the hidden software decisions are changed.

  – *Assumptions about undesired events.*   This section lists assumptions describing incorrect usage of the module at runtime. Violation of each assumption is associated with a runtime undesired event. The development version of the system will be designed to report the undesired event whenever a violation occurs. In the production version of the system, the undesired event that is checking and handling code will be removed for performance enhancement, and violations of the assumptions in this section will result in unpredictable behavior.

TABLE 3.6   Four Audiences for an Interface Specification

	Type of reader			
Section	**User**	**Implementor**	**Reviewer**	**Changer**
Introduction	Yes	Yes	Yes	Yes
Interface Overview	Yes	Yes	Yes	Yes
Local Types	Yes	Yes	Yes	Yes
Dictionary	Yes	Yes	Yes	Yes
Undesired Event Dictionary	Yes	Yes	Yes	Yes
Sysgen Parameter Dictionary	Yes	Yes	Yes	Yes
Design Issues	No	No	No	Yes
Implementation Notes	No	Yes	No	Yes
Assumptions Lists	No	No	Yes	Yes
Efficiency Guide	Yes	Yes	No	Yes
Accuracy Guide	Yes	Yes	No	Yes

- *Accuracy, timing, and efficiency guides.*   These sections contain information about the quantitative costs associated with using the procedures on the module's interface. For systems in which the resource or accuracy constraints are tight, users of a module must have information with which to budget time, space, and/or numerical error. Unlike other sections of the interface specification, these sections may change when the implementation of a procedure changes. If the efficiency of an interface procedure is increased or decreased, the efficiency of the procedure that calls it is correspondingly altered. It is important to note, however, that the correctness of the using procedure is not affected.

Table 3.6 shows the different audiences that tend to use the abstract interface specifications and what sections are important for each.

The transition from abstract interfaces to executable procedures requires more information than is present in the interface specifications; programming conventions are needed. Since the conventions are language dependent, separate documents describe these conventions so as to keep the interface specifications free of language idiosyncrasies.

USES STRUCTURE

Recall that the uses structure is documented in an allowed-to-use specification. This specification for the A-7E architecture is a seven-page table; Table 3.7 is a short excerpt. The two-character preface refers to the second-level modules. The names to the right of the period refer to submodule names that we have mostly omitted from this chapter. Notice the following pattern that emerges:

- No procedure in the Extended Computer module is allowed to use a procedure in any other module, but all other modules are allowed to use (portions of) it.

TABLE 3.7   Excerpt from A-7E Allowed-to-Use Specification

Using procedures: A procedure in . . .	. . . is allowed to use any procedure in . . .
EC: Extended Computer Module	None
DI: Device Interface Module	EC.DATA, EC.PGM, EC.IO, EC.PAR, AT.NUM, AT.STE, SU
ADC: Air Data Computer	PM.ECM
IMS: Inertial Measurement Set	PM.ACM
FD: Function Driver Module	EC.DATA, EC.PAR, EC.PGM, AT.NUM, AT.STE, SU, DB.SS.MODE, DB.SS.PNL.INPUT, DB.SS.SYSVAL, DB.DI
ADC: Air Data Computer Functions	DB.DI.ADC, DI.ADC, FB
IMS: IMS Functions	DB.DI.IMS, DI.IMS
PNL: Panel Functions	EC.IO, DB.SS.PNL.CONFIG, SS.PNL. FORMAT, DI.ADC, DI.IMS, DI.PMDS, DI.PNL
SS: Shared Services Module	EC.DATA, EC.PGM, EC.PAR, AT.NUM, AT.STE, SU,
PNL: Panel I/O Support	DB.SS.MODE, DB.DI.PNL, DB.DI.SWB, SS.PNL.CONFIG, DI.PNL
AT: Application Data Type Module	EC.DATA, EC.PGM
NUM: Numeric Data Types	None additional
STE: State Transition Events	EC.PAR

- Procedures in the Application Data Types module are only allowed to use procedures in the Extended Computer and nothing else.
- Procedures in the Device Interface Module (at least the part shown) are only allowed to use Extended Computer, Application Data Types, and Physical Models procedures.
- Function Drivers and Shared Services procedures can use Data Banker, Extended Computer, Application Data Types, and Device Interface procedures.
- No procedure can use any procedure in the Function Driver module.
- Only a Function Driver procedure can use a Shared Services procedure.

What emerges is a picture of a system partitioned into *layers*. The Extended Computer is the bottom-most layer, with the Application Data Types module built right on top of it. The two of them form a virtual machine. A procedure at a particular level is allowed to use a procedure at the same or any lower level. At the high end of the layering come the Function Drivers and Shared Services modules, which have the freedom to use a wide variety of system facilities to do their jobs. In the middle layers lie the Physical Models, Filter Behavior, and Data Banker modules. The Software Utilities reside in parallel with this structure and are allowed to use anything (except the Function Drivers) necessary to accomplish their individual tasks.

Layered architectures are a well-known architectural style; they will occur in many of the case studies in the book. The A-7E example illustrates three important lessons, as follows:

1. The layering is not clean. That is, all of the procedures in all of the modules are not partitioned into the nice groupings suggested by Figure 3.5. For example, it turns out that a handful of Device Interface procedures need to call a Data Banker procedure or two to get some idea of the system state to know how to present their data. This was a design trade-off, planning for the day when a more sophisticated device would provide the capability in hardware. The designers chose to make the current design less clean in order to make a likely change easier. There are other cases, leading to about two dozen exceptions (out of several hundred procedures) to the nice layered structure shown in the figure.

2. The layering is a generalization of the uses structure, not a substitute for it. It does not show what subsets are possible, which is the point of the uses structure. A *particular* function driver module will use a *particular* set of shared services, Data Banker, Physical Models, Device Interfaces, Application Data Types, and Extended Computer Services. The used shared services

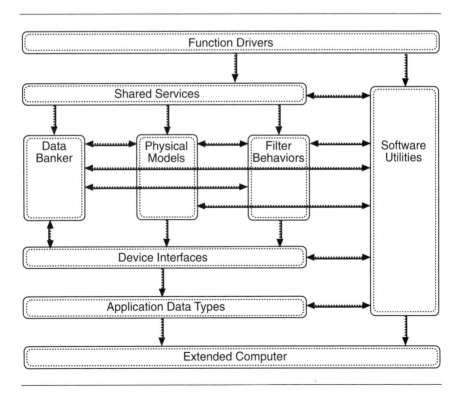

FIGURE 3.5   The layered architecture that emerges from the A-7E uses structure.

will in turn use their own set of lower-level procedures, and so forth. The complete set of procedures derived in this manner constitute a subset.

3. Layering emerges from a structural description of the architecture that is orthogonal to the module structure we saw before. Module grouping information is not visible in this diagram; conversely, no information about layers or uses is available from the module relations. A layered architecture is a statement about the runtime uses relation of its components.

The allowed-to-use structure also provides an image of how the procedures of modules interact with one another at runtime to accomplish tasks. Each Function Driver procedure controls the output value associated with one output device, such as the position of a displayed symbol. In general, a Function Driver procedure retrieves data (via Data Banker procedures) from data producers, applies rules for computing the correct value of its assigned output, and sends that value to the device by calling the appropriate Device Interface procedure. Data may come from one of the following:

- Device Interface procedures about the state of the world with which the software interfaces
- Physical Models procedures that compute predictive measures about the outside world (such as where a bomb will strike the earth if released now, given the aircraft's current position and velocity)
- Shared Services procedures about the current mode, the trustworthiness of current sensor readings, or what panel operations the pilot has requested.

Once the allowed-to-use structure is designed, implementors know what interfaces they need to be familiar with in order to do their work. After implementation is complete, the actual uses structure can be documented so that subsets can be fielded. The ability to deploy a subset of a system may sound esoteric but arises often in practice. When budgets are cut (or overrun) and schedules are slipped, delivering a subset is often the best way to put a positive face on a bad situation. It is probably the case that more subsets would be delivered (instead of nothing at all) if the architectural structure necessary to achieve them—the uses structure—had been carefully designed.

Further, staged delivery of subsets of increasing power and resemblance to the final product is a powerful development technique (discussed in Chapter 13) and it is made possible by the uses structure.

PROCESS STRUCTURE

The process structure emerged after the other structures had been designed. Function Driver procedures were implemented as processes. Other processes existed to compute time-consuming calculations in background so that a value would always be available.

Two kinds of information were captured in the process structure. The first documented what procedures were included in the body of each process. This gave a picture of the threads that ran through the system and also told the implementors which procedures must be coded to be reentrant (that is, able to carry two or more threads of control simultaneously) by using protected data stores or mutual exclusion. It also gave designers early insight into which procedures were going to be invoked most often, suggesting areas where optimization would pay off.

The second kind of information in the process structure documented which processes (or sequential segments of process threads) could not execute simultaneously with each other. The actual regions of mutual exclusion were not finalized until the processes were completely coded, but the early excludes relation among processes let the scheduling team understand some of the quantitative requirements on the off-line scheduler and start planning on areas where automation would be most helpful.

3.5 Summary

This chapter has described the architecture of a highly capable avionics system in terms of three related but quite different structures. A module structure describes design-time relations among its components, which are work assignments for teams. A uses structure describes runtime usage relations among its components, which are procedures in modules. From the uses structure, a picture of a layered architecture emerges. The process structure describes the parallelism of the system and is the basis for assignment for the physical hardware. It is critical to design each structure correctly because each is the key to a different quality attribute: ease of change, ease of extracting a subset, and increased parallelism and performance. It is also critical to document each structure completely because the information about each is duplicated in no other place.

Even though the structures are orthogonal, they are related. Modules contain procedures, which use each other and which are strung together in processes. Other architectural structures could have been specified for this system. One example is a data-flow diagram. It would have looked something like the one in Figure 3.6: All data come from the external world via the Device Interface Modules and work their way through computation and storage modules to the Function Driver Modules that compute output values to send back to the devices. This simplified story also has its exceptions, like those we saw in the uses structure. The A-7E designers never thought data-flow diagrams were useful—what quality attribute do they help achieve that the others do not?—but other designers might feel differently. The point—and the lesson—about architectural structures is that they should enhance understanding and the intellectual control you have over the system and its attributes. If a structure meets these conditions, it is probably one to which you want to pay attention.

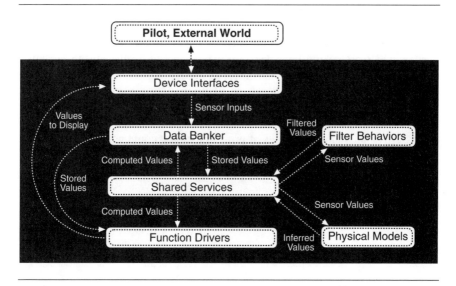

FIGURE 3.6   Coarse-grained data flow diagram for the A-7E software.

We also presented the architecture in terms of the qualities the designers wished to achieve: changeability and understandability. This leads us to the thesis that we explore in the next chapter: Architectures reflect a set of desired qualities.

3.6   For Further Reading

The A7-E avionics project has been documented in [Parnas 85a]. The data that was collected about changes to the system was analyzed and described in [Hager 91] and [Hager 89.]

Much of the text in this chapter about the module structure was taken from the A-7E module guide, which was written by Kathryn Britton and David Parnas [Britton 81].

3.7   Discussion Questions

1. Suppose a version of the A-7E software were to be developed for installation on a flight trainer version of the aircraft. This aircraft would carry no weapons, but it would teach pilots how to navigate using the on-board avionics. What structures of the architecture would have to change, and how?

2. Chapter 13 will discuss using the architecture as a basis for incremental development: starting small and growing the system but having a working subset at all times. Propose the smallest subset of the A-7E software that you can think of that still does something (correctly, in accordance with requirements) that is observable by the pilot. (A good candidate is displaying a value such as current heading on some cockpit display.) Which modules would you need and which could you do without? Now propose three incremental additions to that subset and specify the development plan (i.e., which modules you need) for those.

3. Suppose that monitors were added to ensure that correct values were being stored in the Data Banker and computed by the Function Drivers. If the monitors detected a disparity between the stored or computed values and what they computed as the correct values, they would signal an error. Show how each of the A-7E's architectural structures would change to accommodate this design. If you add modules, state the information-hiding criteria for placing them in the module hierarchy.

PART TWO

CREATING AND ANALYZING AN ARCHITECTURE

Part One of this book introduced the architecture business cycle (ABC) and laid the basic groundwork for the study of software architecture. In particular, it set out the influences that are at work when an architect begins the task of building a system and pointed out that requirements for particular quality attributes such as performance or modifiability often originate from the organization's business goals for that system.

Part Two will focus on the segment of the ABC between the architect and the architecture. One of the tenets of Chapter 2 was that architecture serves as the first opportunity for designing quality attributes into the system. If that is the case, it follows that an architecture can be analyzed or reviewed with respect to those quality attributes. That is, if we can produce an architecture to meet our quality goals for the system, we can evaluate an architecture to see how well we did.

Chapter 4 discusses the quality attributes most commonly sought in today's software systems and points out the architectural achievement of each. Do you require high performance? If so, you need to pay careful attention to intercomponent communication at runtime. Do you need modifiability? If so, your modular structure must realize the appropriate encapsulations. Do you want reusability? If so, the components had better be loosely coupled. And so forth. All of the quality attributes at least begin to be realized at the architectural stage of development.

Chapter 5 continues the theme by showing how concrete architectural decisions—in particular, the use of architectural styles—can lead to the satisfaction of quality attributes. Chapter 6 broadens the perspective to discuss more general engineering principles that can be brought to bear on architectures. *Unit operations* such as replication, separation, and abstraction reflect the kinds of decisions that architects make when refining the architectural structures during development. Unit operations are illustrated using user-interface reference models as an example, showing the evolution of that domain over time in terms of the *standard* architectures that dominated. These reference models evolved in ways explainable by unit operations.

Chapter 9 presents a method for analyzing architectures for quality attributes such as modifiability, interoperability, and portability, thus fulfilling the premise of Part Two: If you can design for quality architecturally, you can analyze for it architecturally. Chapter 10 expands on the topic, presenting the analysis method in the context of an overall review process and focusing on process-oriented issues for architecture reviews as well as organizational goals, investment, and payoff.

Three case studies illustrate the themes of Part Two. Again, as with all case studies, they each illustrate an architectural solution to a specific problem and also reinforce specific topics. Chapter 7 presents the World Wide Web as an architecture responding to specific organizational goals, with enough flexibility to allow it to take off and become the global phenomenon that none of us could live without. Chapter 8 presents the common object request broker architecture (CORBA) as the architectural solution to a business strategy. Yes, CORBA is all about interoperability of separately developed components, but even more than that, it is an organization's response to competitive pressures in the marketplace. Once again, the architecture serves the organization, not just a system. Finally, Chapter 11 shows how extraordinary performance and availability requirements led to an architecture for a large air traffic control system and how the analysis methods of Chapters 9 and 10 were used to evaluate it.

Part Two, then, takes us from the architect to the architecture.

4

Quality Attributes

Every good quality is noxious if unmixed.
— Ralph Waldo Emerson

As we have seen in the ABC, business considerations determine qualities that must be accommodated in a system's architecture. These qualities are over and above that of functionality, which is the basic statement of the system's capabilities, services, and behavior. Although functionality and other qualities are closely related (see following sidebar), functionality often takes not only the front seat in the development scheme but the only seat. Systems are frequently redesigned not because they are functionally deficient—the replacements are often functionally identical—but because they are difficult to maintain, port, or scale or are too slow or have been compromised by network hackers. It is the mapping of a system's functionality onto software structures that determines the architecture's support for qualities. It should be kept in mind that this support is always a compromise: No quality can be maximized in a system without sacrificing some other quality or qualities. (Just ask Ralph Waldo.)

In Chapter 2, we said that architecture was the first stage in system creation in which quality requirements could begin to be addressed. What exactly are quality attributes? Given a set of requirements for a system's quality attributes (which includes functionality, or satisfying the required behavior patterns for the system), how can architecture help to achieve them? This chapter will explore the answers to these questions. After that, the following two chapters will present specific architectural techniques and principles for dealing with quality attributes.

We begin by first looking closely at the concept of quality attributes. What does it mean to say that a system is integrable or portable or secure? In subsequent chapters we look at means for achieving these attributes by examining design ideas in software architecture, object-oriented programming, and more traditional information hiding, as they apply to the concept of quality at the architectural level.

4.1   Architectures and Quality Attributes

There are two broad categories of quality attributes against which a system can be measured (and, in particular, can be measured at the architectural level):

1. *Observable via execution.*   How well does the system, during execution, satisfy its behavioral requirements? Does it provide the required results? Does it provide them in a timely enough manner? Are the results correct or within specified accuracy and stability tolerances? Does the system function as desired when connected to other systems?

2. *Not observable via execution.*   How easy is the system to integrate, test, and modify? How expensive was it to develop? What was its time to market?

Nonfunctional Requirements Is a Dysfunctional Term

Throughout this book, we have taken pains to avoid the term *functional requirements* and its (supposed) antonym *nonfunctional requirements*. Functional requirements usually means the behavior of the system, or what work it is supposed to accomplish. Nonfunctional requirements is a terminological bucket into which all other qualities of the system, such as performance or modifiability, are glibly dumped. We avoid these terms because they are unfortunate anachronisms that shed no useful light on the problem of stating what a system is supposed to do.

First of all, they are based on a word—*function*—that is woefully overused but (more importantly) inappropriate when assigned its most common meaning. Recall that in mathematics, a function is a special kind of relation, which in turn is a set of ordered pairs. No two ordered pairs in a function can have the same first element but different second elements. In computing, we use relations to describe the behaviors of programs: The first element is the state of the program and the input it receives, and the second element is the behavior of the program and the output it produces in that state given that input. Under this model, programs whose behavior is nondeterministic—and there are lots of them—are represented by relations that are *not* functions; hence, these programs strictly speaking have no "functional" behavior at all. The term quickly fails us.

But more insidiously, the terms reflect muddy thinking. They presuppose that the requirements for a system can in fact be cleanly divided into the two halves implied by the terms.

When I was a freshman in college, I took a short story writing course. Shortly before the end of the semester, I saw my professor on campus and she asked me how my final story was coming along. "Fine," I said. "I've got it all written. I just have to go back and put in the symbolism." Suddenly my professor looked very sad, and I knew in that moment that I was not destined to be a short story writer. Of course I know now that you can't just go back and put in all the symbolism; it's an integral part of the story. Software qualities are like that. You can't get the functionality right and then go back and put in all the qualities. They all have to be designed in from the start.

Very well, but can't you specify the "raw" behavior seperately from the qualities? In the most general model of requirements (alluded to in the preceding discussion of functions), systems are specified with relations: ((`old state`, `input`), (`new state`, `output`)). The set of all legal pairs constitutes a specification for a system. (Of course, like mathematical functions, we almost never list all of the ordered pairs but instead find notational means to compactly express large sets of them.)

But notice how this model handles all of the things we commonly refer to as runtime qualities. Consider security: The system sees a valid password in a state where it is expecting one, and it transitions to a state in which a privileged set of commands is allowed and outputs a welcome message. Consider performance: The system sees a stimulus and computes the appropriate response within a time bound (the `old_state` and `new_state` both contain clock information). Consider fault tolerance: The system sees a state in which a processor or other resource has disappeared or become unreliable; it transitions to a degraded state and takes remedial action.

The point is that many traditional quality attributes are bound up inescapably with the behavior of the system, and there is no clean way to separate them in the specification, nor is there a good reason for wanting to do so. One might argue that different parts of the specification could be reviewed by experts in different domains (such as security), so that would be a good reason to separate out those parts of the specification. But even if it were possible to cleanly do so, this argues for many separate sections—one per area of reviewer expertise—and not the simple dichotomy that our two disfavored terms suggest.

In summary, nonfunctional requirements implies something that doesn't exist, a kind of requirement that can be specified independently of the system's behavior. Viewing qualities in this way often leads to their omission until the end of the specification task, leaving them tacked on at the end (like the symbolism in a cheap novel) and poorly specified to boot. Recognizing that the dichotomy is a myth empowers the software engineer to specify the runtime quality attributes with as much discipline as the behavioral aspects of the system and should help to bring their consideration forward in the design process.

Doris Betts, wherever you are, I really did learn something from your short story course.

— PCC

Knowing something in the first category about a system does not tell you anything in the second category about the system. For instance, systems that unfailingly meet all of their runtime requirements may or may not have been prohibitively expensive to develop and may or may not be next to impossible to modify. On the other hand, highly modifiable systems may or may not produce correct results. For that matter, qualities within each category may be unrevealing about each other as well: A highly available system (that never crashes) may be utterly unreliable (producing bad results). A system that took two weeks to build may take two years to modify. And so forth.

Although finer distinctions among attributes may be made (e.g., observable via a single run of a system versus observable by watching all possible runs of the system), we will use this coarse-grained dichotomy to guide us through a tour of quality attributes.

Quality must be considered at *all* phases of design, implementation, and deployment, but different qualities manifest themselves differently during these phases. For example, many aspects of the quality of usability are not architectural; making the user interface clear and easy to use is primarily a matter of getting the details correct. Should you provide a radio button or a check box? What screen layout is most intuitive? What typeface is most clear? Although these details matter tremendously to the end user and inflence usability, they are not architectural because they are almost always encapsulated within a single component. This localization affects modifiability but not usability.

Modifiability, on the other hand, *is* largely architectural. Modifiability is determined by how functionality is divided. A system is modifiable if changes do not involve a large number of distinct components. It is certainly possible to make a system difficult to modify by writing obscure code, but primarily, it is division of responsibility that determines a system's modifiability. This was the basis of the A-7E module structure in Chapter 3, and it underlies the architectural analysis method presented in Chapter 9.

Performance, on the other hand, is an example of a quality that has architectural and nonarchitectural dependencies. Performance depends partially on how much communication is necessary among components (architectural), partially on what functionality has been allocated to each component (architectural), partially on the choice of algorithms to implement selected functionality (nonarchitectural), and partially on how these algorithms are coded (nonarchitectural).

The message of this section is twofold, as follows:

1. Architecture is critical to the realization of many of the qualities of interest in a system, and these qualities should be designed in and evaluated at the architectural level.

2. Some qualities are not architecturally sensitive, and attempting to achieve these qualities or analyze for them through architectural means is not fruitful.

In any discussion of quality attributes, it is important to keep in mind that they exist within complex systems, and their satisfaction can *never* be achieved in isolation. The achievement of any quality attribute will have an effect, sometimes positive and sometimes negative, on the achievement of other quality attributes. For example, security and fault tolerance exist in a state of mutual tension: The most secure system has the fewest points of failure, typically a security kernel. The most fault-tolerant system has the most points of failure, typicaliy a set of redundant processes or processors where the failure of any one will not cause the system to fail. As another example of the tension between quality attributes, it can be seen, upon reflection, that almost every other quality attribute negatively affects performance. Take portability, for instance. The main technique for achieving portable software is to isolate system dependencies. This isolation introduces overhead into the system's execution, typically in the form of process or procedure boundaries, which hurt performance.

Let us begin our tour of quality attributes. We will examine the following three classes:

1. First, there are qualities that can be discerned by observing the system execute (performance, security, availability, functionality, usability) and system qualities that are not discernable at runtime (modifiability, portability, reusability, integrability, testability).

2. In addition to qualities directly attributable to the system, there are business qualities (such as time to market) that are affected by the architecture.

3. Finally, there are qualities about the architecture itself that are important.

SYSTEM QUALITY ATTRIBUTES DISCERNABLE AT RUNTIME

The quality attributes that are discernable at runtime are discussed in the following sections.

Performance.   Performance refers to the responsiveness of the system—the time required to respond to stimuli (events) or the number of events processed in some interval of time.

Performance qualities are often expressed by the number of transactions per unit time or by the amount of time it takes a transaction with the system to complete. Since communication usually takes longer than computation, performance is often a function of how much communication and interaction there is between the components of the system—clearly an architectural issue. This is especially true if the components reside on different computing elements, such as in a distributed system. However, it is still true if the components all occupy the same processor. The amount of interaction by subroutine invocation, process synchronization, or other communication mechanisms still tends to be a performance driver, which makes performance largely a function of architecture.

We can understand, model, and analyze performance at the architectural level by looking at the arrival rates and distributions of service requests, processing times, queue sizes (if applicable), and latency (the rate at which requests are serviced). We can simulate a system's performance by building a stochastic queueing model of the system, based upon anticipated workload scenarios.

For most of the history of software engineering, performance has been the driving factor in system architecture, and this has frequently compromised the achievement of all other qualities. As is demonstrated in almost every case study in this book, this has changed; as the price/performance ratio of hardware plummets and the cost of developing software rises, other qualities have emerged as important competitors to performance.

Security.   Security is a measure of the system's ability to resist unauthorized attempts at usage and denial of service while still providing its services to legitimate users. It is categorized in terms of the types of threats that might be made to system; they include the following:

- *Denial of service.*   This form of attack is aimed a preventing a targeted system from providing, receiving, or responding to network services. The attack typically occurs by flooding the target with connection requests or queries.
- *IP source address spoofing.*   This form of attack attempts to gain access to the target by assuming the identify of a host trusted by the target. The attacker will often inhibit traffic from the genuine trusted host, sometimes by means of a denial of serivce attack on it, and then attempt to gain access to the target using the trusted host's IP address.

The prevention, detection of, and response to an attack will often involve the following architectural strategies:

- An authentication server may be placed between outside users and the portion of the system that provides services.
- Network monitors may be installed for inspection and logging of network events.
- The system may be placed behind a communications "firewall" through which all communication to and from the system must be channelled by a proxy.
- The system may be constructed on top of a trusted kernel that provides security services.

These approaches, and others, involve identifying special components, separating these from the rest of the system's functionality, and arranging the coordination and interaction of the other components through them—all architectural solutions.

Availability.   Availability measures the proportion of time the system is up and running. It is measured by the length of time between failures as well as by how quickly the system is able to resume operation in the event of failure. The steady state availability of a system is the proportion of time that the system is functioning correctly and is typically defined as follows:

$$\alpha = \frac{\text{mean time to failure}}{\text{mean time to failure} + \text{mean time to repair}}$$

Closely related is *reliability*, the ability of the system to keep operating over time. Reliability is usually measured with mean time to failure. These are both quality attributes that are tied to the architecture: The case study of a system designed for air traffic control (Chapter 11) clearly illustrates how high-availability requirements influenced the architecture of that system. Architectural techniques include installing redundant componentry to take over in case of failure, careful attention to error reporting and handling (which involves constraining the interaction patterns among the components), and special kinds of components such as time-out monitors. Availability comes from both mean time to failure and mean time to repair; both are addressed through architectural means. Mean time to failure is lengthened primarily by making an architecture fault tolerant. Fault tolerance, in turn, is achieved by the replication of critical processing elements and connections within the architecture. Mean time to failure can also be lengthened by fielding a less error-prone system, which is addressed architecturally by careful separation of concerns, which leads to better integrability and testability. Mean time to (off-line) repair is lowered by designing components that are easy to modify and by designing a component interaction scheme that helps to identify misbehaving culprits.

Functionality. Functionality is the ability of the system to do the work for which it was intended. Performing a task requires that many or most of the system's components work in a coordinated manner to complete the job, just as framers, electricians, plumbers, drywall hangers, painters, and finish carpenters all come together to cooperatively perform the task of getting a house built. Therefore, if the components have not been assigned the correct responsibilities or have not been endowed with the correct facilities for coordinating with other components (so that, for instance, they know when it is time for them to begin their portion of the task), the system will be unable to perform the required functionality.

Functionality is orthogonal to structure, meaning that it is largely nonarchitectural in nature. Any number of possible structures can be conceived to implement any given functionality. In fact, if the achievement of functionality were the only requirement, the system could exist as a single monolithic component with no internal structure at all.

Software architecture constrains the allocation of functionality to structure when *other* quality attributes are important. For example, systems are frequently divided so that several people can cooperatively build them (which among other things is a time-to-market issue, though seldom stated this way). The interest of functionality is how it interacts with, and constrains, the achievement of those other qualities.

Usability. Usability can be broken down into the following areas:

- *Learnability.* How quick and easy is it for a user to learn to use the system's interface?

- *Efficiency.* Does the system respond with appropriate speed to a user's requests?

- *Memorability.* Can the user remember how to do system operations between uses of the system?

- *Error avoidance.* Does the system anticipate and prevent common user errors?

- *Error handling.*   Does the system help the user recover from errors?
- *Satisfaction.*   Does the system make the user's job easy?

Making a system's user interface clear and easy to use is primarily a matter of getting the details of a user's interaction correct: matching the interface to the user's mental model of the system; using familiar metaphors, standards, and interface conventions; providing adequate performance; and allowing a user to feel in control. Details such as whether a radio button or a check box should be used to indicate selection, screen layout, the use of color and shading as an indication of allowable user activity, and the size and choice of type face matter tremendously to the end user and affect usability, but these details are *not* architectural.

However, making sure that the right information is available to the user at the right time and making sure that the user's instructions get to the right destination in the system are architectural because the information must flow to and across the appropriate components via the connectors. Further, localizing these decisions so that they can be easily modified affects modifiability but not usability (except insofar as a development team will bridle at having to continually change an unmodifiable system). *Efficiency* has performance implications, of course, which we have seen are architectural in nature.

SYSTEM QUALITY ATTRIBUTES NOT DISCERNABLE AT RUNTIME

There are other attributes of a software-intensive system that cannot be discerned at runtime. They are discussed in the following subsections.

Modifiability.   Modifiability, in all its forms, may be the quality attribute most closely aligned to the architecture of a system. The ability to make changes quickly and cost effectively follows directly from the architecture: Modifiability is largely a function of the locality of any change. Making a widespread change to the system is more costly than making a change to a single component, all other things being equal.

There are exceptions, of course. A single component, if excessively large and complex, may be more costly to change than five simple ones. It's also easy to imagine a global change that in each place is simple and systematic: changing the value of a constant that appears everywhere, for instance. However, in large systems, making a change is much more costly than just, well, making the change. Development process costs start to dominate, such as maintaining version control, approving the change across many change control boards, coordinating the change time across many large teams, retesting all the units, perhaps assuring backward compatibility, and so forth. We take as a general principle that local is better.

Since the architecture defines the components and the responsibilities of each, it also defines the circumstances under which each component will have to change. An architecture effectively classifies all possible changes into three categories according to whether the change will precipitate a modification of one component only, of more than one component, or of something more drastic such as a change to the underlying architectural style.

Modifications to a system often flow from changes in the business needs of the owning organization. They can be broadly categorized as follows:

- *Extending or changing capabilities.*   Adding new functionality, enhancing existing functionality, or repairing bugs. The ability to acquire new features is called *extensibility*. Adding new capabilities is important to remain competitive against other products in the same market.

- *Deleting unwanted capabilities.*   To streamline or simplify the functionality of an existing application, perhaps to deliver a less-capable (and therefore less expensive) version of a product to a wider customer base.

- *Adapting to new operating environments.*   For example, processor hardware, input/output devices, and logical devices. This kind of modification occurs so often that the quality of being amenable to it has a special name, *portability*, which we will discuss separately. Portability makes a product more flexible in how it can be fielded, appealing to a broader customer base.

- *Restructuring.*   For example, rationalizing system services, modularizing, optimizing, or creating reusable components that may serve to give the organization a head start on future systems.

Modifiability is sometimes called *maintainability.* Some authors draw a fine distinction between the two terms that has to do with the the type of change being installed, but from the point of view of achieving them via architectural means, they are the same and we will use them interchangeably.

Portability.   Portability is the ability of the system to run under different computing environments. These environments can be hardware, software, or a combination of the two. A system is portable to the extent that all of the assumptions about any *particular* computing environment are confined to one component (or at worst, a small number of easily changed components).

The encapsulation of platform-specific considerations in an architecture typically takes the form of a *portability layer*, a set of software services that gives application software an abstract interface to its environment. This interface remains constant (thus insulating the application software from change) even though the implementation of that layer changes as the system is ported from environment to environment. A portability layer results from a straightforward application of the design principle of information hiding.

Recall the uses structure from the A-7E example in Chapter 3. This structure tells what components (procedures in the case of the A-7E) can use which other ones. A portability layer is only visible in this architectural structure and only provides true portability if usage conventions are enforced: Application software must be constrained to use the portability layer and not directly access the environment that it is charged with abstracting.

Reusability.   *Reusability* is usually taken to mean designing a system so that the system's structure or some of its components can be reused again in future applications (see Chapter 16 for a broad illustration of this). Designing for reusability means that the system has been structured so that its components can be chosen from previously built products, in which case it is a synonym for *integrability* (the discussions of the METOC system in Chapter 18 and CORBA in Chapter 8 provide case studies in which this approach has been particularly successful). In either case, reusability can be conceived of as another special case of modifiability.

Reusability is related to software architecture in that architectural components are the units of reuse, and how reusable a component is depends on how tightly coupled it is with other components. One aspect of this coupling is (again) captured in the uses relation of the A-7E case study of Chapter 3. The uses relation is employed to develop functional subsets. Given that one component would be in a subset, all components in the transitive closure of the uses relation would also have to be in that subset. Reusing a component may be thought of as fielding a small subset of a system employing the uses relation in the same way: To reuse a component in a new system, you must either bring its used components along with it, or the new system must provide those on its own. Either way, loose coupling will lead to fewer unnecessary "tag-along" components, increasing the chances for successful transition.

Reusability is actually a special case of modifiability, although it is seldom considered in that light. To see this, consider the following two stories:

> *Story 1.*   A system S has been built to comprise 100 components, S1 through S100. A new system T is to be built that will also have 100 components, T1 through T100. While building T, the developers discover that component T1 will be identical to S1, and so they of course just reuse S1 instead of building and testing a duplicate. They also discover that T2 will be identical to S2, and so they reuse S2. They investigate further and discover that in fact the first *n* components of T are identical to those of S and can be reused.

> *Story 2.*   System S, comprising 100 components, has been fielded and is now undergoing modification. The modification affects only component S100, which is discarded and rewritten; the remaining 99 components are not changed. The new component is called T100. The new, modified system is called T.

To see that these are two versions of the same story, set *n* in story 1 to 99. In story 1, then, 99 components were "moved" from S to T and reused. In story 2, 99 components were reused to create T. The point is that reuse and modifiability are two sides of the same coin: Building systems to be modifiable yields the gains of reusability.

Integrability.   *Integrability* is the ability to make the separately developed components of the system work correctly together. This in turn depends on the external complexity of the components, their interaction mechanisms and protocols, and the degree to which responsibilities have been cleanly partitioned, all architecture-level issues. Integrability also depends upon how well and completely the interfaces to the components have been specified.

Integrating a component depends not only on the interaction mechanisms used (e.g., procedure call versus process spawning) but also on the functionality assigned to the component to be integrated and how that functionality is related to the functionality of this new component's environment. In our discussion of a design for flight simulators (Chapter 14), we will see a system in which ease of integration was one of the driving considerations in the construction of the system. In addition, Chapter 8 discusses CORBA and its many integration mechanisms. In fact, it can be argued that integrability is the main technical motivator behind the development of CORBA.

A special kind of integrability is *interoperability*. Integrability measures the ability of parts of a system to work together; interoperability measures the ability of a group of parts (constituting a system) to work with another system.

Testability.   Software testability refers to the ease with which software can be made to demonstrate its faults through (typically execution-based) testing. In particular, testability refers to the probability that, assuming that the software does have at least one fault, the software will fail on its *next* test execution. Testability is related to the concepts of *observability* and *controlability*. For a system to be properly testable, it must be possible to *control* each component's internal state and inputs and then to *observe* its outputs.

A system's testability relates to several structural or architectural issues: its level of architectural documentation, its separation of concerns, and the degree to which the system uses information hiding. Incremental development also benefits testability in the same way it enhances integrability.

Table 4.1 summarizes the discussion up to this point.

BUSINESS QUALITIES

In addition to the preceding qualities that apply directly to a system, there are a number of *business* quality goals that frequently shape a system's architecture. We (briefly) distinguish two kinds of business goals. The first concerns cost and schedule considerations; they are as follows:

- *Time to market.*   If there is competitive pressure or if there is a short window of opportunity for a system or product, development time becomes important. This in turn leads to pressure to buy or otherwise reuse existing components. Time to market is often reduced by using prebuilt components such as commercial off-the-shelf (COTS) products or components reused from previous projects. The ability to insert a component into a system depends on the decomposition of the system into components, one or more of which are prebuilt

TABLE 4.1   Summary of Quality Attributes Discussed in This Chapter

System quality attribute	Architectural in nature?	Architectural issues
Discerned by observing the system at runtime		
Performance	Yes	Intercomponent communication; dividing functionality so as to exploit parallelism
Security	Yes	Specialized components, such as secure kernels or authentication servers
Availability	Yes	Fault tolerance with redundant components; controlling component interaction
Functionality	No	Interaction with other quality attributes
Usability	Yes	Modifiability helps to achieve; achieving proper information flow; efficiency related to performance
Not discerned by observing the system at runtime		
Modifiability	Yes	Modularized, encapsulating components
Portability	Yes	Portability layer
Reusability	Yes	Loose coupling among components
Integrability	Yes	Compatible interconnection mechanisms; consistent component interfaces; uses relation allows incremental builds
Testability	Yes	Modularized, encapsulating components; uses relation allows incremental builds

- *Cost.*   The development effort will naturally have a budget that must not be exceeded. Different architectures will yield different development costs; for instance, an architecture that relies on technology (or expertise with a technology) that is not resident within the developing organization will be more expensive to realize than one that takes advantage of assets already in-house.

- *Projected lifetime of the system.*   If the system is intended to have a long lifetime, modifiability and portability across different platforms become important. But building in the additional infrastructure (such as a portability layer) to support modifiability and portability will usually compromise time to market. On the other hand, a modifiable, extensible product is more likely to survive longer in the marketplace, extending its lifetime.

The other business goal deals with market and marketing considerations; they are as follows:

- *Targeted market.*   For general-purpose (mass-market) software, the platforms on which a system runs as well as its feature set will determine the size of the potential market. Thus, portability and functionality are key to market share. Other qualities such as performance, reliability, and usability also play a role. For a large but specific market, a product-line approach should be considered, in which a core of the system is common (frequently including provisions for portability) and around which layers of software of increasing specificity are constructed. Such an approach will be discusssed in Chapter 15, which discusses software product lines.

- *Rollout schedule.*   If a product is to be introduced as base functionality with many options, flexibility and customizability are important. Particularly, the system must be constructed with ease of expansion and contraction in mind.

- *Extensive use of legacy systems.*   If the new system must *integrate* with existing systems, care must be taken to define appropriate integration mechanisms. This is a property that is clearly of marketing importance but which has substantial architectural implications. For example, the ability to integrate a legacy system with an HTTP server to make it accessible from the World Wide Web is currently a marketing goal in many corporations. The architectural constraints implied by this integration must be analyzed.

QUALITIES OF THE ARCHITECTURE

In addition to qualities about the system and qualities related to the business environment in which the system is being developed, there are also qualities related directly to the architecture itself that are important to achieve. We discuss three.

Conceptual integrity is the underlying theme or vision that unifies the design of the system, at all levels. The architecture should do similar things in similar ways. Fred Brooks writes emphatically that a system's conceptual integrity is of overriding importance, and that systems without it fail [Brooks 75]:

> I will contend that conceptual integrity is *the* most important consideration in system design. It is better to have a system omit certain anomalous features and improvements, but to reflect one set of design ideas, than to have one that contains many good but independent and uncoordinated ideas.

Brooks was writing primarily about the way that systems appear to their user, but the point is equally valid for the architectural layout that is invisible to the user. What Brooks' idea of conceptual integrity does for the user, architectural integrity does for the other stakeholders, particular the developers and maintainers. In Chapter 13 we will talk about using patterns to simplify and streamline the design of a system, and it is precisely the quality of conceptual integrity that this is intended to produce. Twenty years later, Brooks still hadn't changed his mind and tells us the architectural secret for achieving conceptual integrity [Brooks 95]:

> I am more convinced than ever. Conceptual integrity is central to product quality. Having a system architect is the most important single step toward conceptual integrity. . . . after teaching a software engineering laboratory more than 20 times, I came to insist that student teams as small as four people choose a manager, and a separate architect.

In Chapter 10, you'll see a recommendation for architecture review that requires that the project being reviewed make the architect available. If no one is identified with that role, it is a sure sign of trouble.

Correctness and *completeness* are essential for the architecture to allow for the meeting of all of the system's requirements and runtime resource constraints.

Buildability is the quality of the architecture that allows the system to be completed by the available team in a timely manner and to be open to certain changes as the system development progresses. Buildability refers to the ease of constructing a desired system. It is usually measured in terms of cost and time. Thus, there is a relationship between the buildability quality and various cost models. Buildability is more complex, however, than what is usually covered in cost models. A system is created from certain materials, and these materials are composed using a variety of tools. For example, a user interface may be constructed from items in a user-interface toolbox (called widgets), and these widgets may be manipulated by a user-interface builder. The widgets are the materials and the builder is the tool. So one element of buildability is the match between the materials that are to be used in the system and the tools that are available to manipulate these materials. Another aspect of buildability is the state of knowledge about the problem to be solved. As we will see in the discussion in Chapter 8 about the goals for CORBA, one decision was to use a well-understood interprocess communication model. The rationale behind this decision was to speed time to market and not to force potential suppliers to invest in the understanding and engineering of a new interprocess communication model. Thus, a design that casts a solution in terms of well-understood concepts is more buildable than a design that introduces new concepts.

4.2 Architectural Means for Achieving Qualities

When developers ask, "What architecture shall I choose?" they are seeking the answer to the following questions:

- What structure shall I employ to assign workers, to derive my work breakdown structure, to exploit already-packaged components, and to plan for modification?

- What structure shall I employ so that the system, at runtime, fulfills its behavioral and quality attribute requirements?

It is not obvious that the first question has a single answer, but in practice it does: A system's modular structure is most often used to coordinate the allocation of *project* (as opposed to system) resources, as well as to achieve the nonruntime quality attributes of modifiability, reusability, etc. This was particularly true in the A-7E system of the previous chapter; we will discuss this further in Chapter 13, which discusses architecture-based development. The modular structure of a system is a purely static concept. When the code from each module is compiled and linked, the modular structure vanishes.

The second question refers to structures that survive through execution. Architectural styles such as pipes and filters, blackboards, and client-servers refer to ways in which components that exist at runtime interact with each other. It is less clear that the second question has a single optimal answer, but one of the goals of the architecture research community is to converge on one. As we have already hinted, architectural styles give us preexisting solutions to certain classes of design patterns, and these will be explored in the next chapter.

Which notion of architecture is the right one, the one whose components are modules or the one whose components are runtime entities such as processes? Obviously they both are. It is an axiom of this book that assuming that the two structures are the same is a fundamental design mistake, since they are optimized to meet completely different criteria.

Nonexecution requirements for a system revolve mainly about building the system to accommodate change of various forms. Choosing a software architecture that accommodates change requires having a strong idea at architecture-creation time of the kinds of changes that will bombard the system during its lifetime. The architecture must handle modifications that may include new computing environments, new platform deployments, new operator interfaces, incorporation of new or modified physical environment models, addition of new sensing devices, and (most likely of all) changes that nobody considered. The goal is to produce a system structure such that each anticipated change will only affect a small number of system components or at worst will affect several components but in a manner in which the large change can be staged as a series of small, independently testable changes.

A wise architect will mine these sources for changes that should be accounted for in the design; they are as follows:

- Changes anticipated for this system or experienced by similar systems. The list of anticipated changes is often augmented by tapping the experience of more mature, already deployed systems with similar purpose.

- Changes anticipated by mining the requirements specifications for areas of uncertainty or ambiguity. These may indicate functionality that might not be met with initial deployments but which may be required subsequently.

- Decreases in functionality brought about because of a management decision to field a subset of the system. This is often done when the cost and schedule of the project exceed original estimates by some "pain threshold," and suddenly some of the features that once were absolutely vital to the project's success now begin to look like expendable frills.

We anticipate changes by exploiting knowledge about the current application and related or similar applications. We choose an architecture to accommodate those predicted changes. We choose an architecture to meet behavioral and performance requirements by exploiting familiarity with architectures of similar systems that produced correct and timely results.

The next chapter carries this theme of exploiting previous knowledge further, by examining a set of standard architectural structures for systems: architectural styles.

4.3   Summary

The set of qualities presented in this chapter is by no means complete, but it does represent those qualities that are most often the goal of software and system architects. We have seen that qualities can be divided into those that apply to the executing system, those that apply to a development or maintenance effort, those that apply to the business environment, and those that apply to the architecture itself. For those that have direct ties to architecture, we have seen general ways in which architecture can affect them.

In the next chapter, we'll explore concrete architectural approaches for following the path from qualities to architecture. And in Chapter 9, we'll see why the simple qualities enumerated in this chapter (although useful for communicating broad requirements) are not up to the task of serving as evaluation criteria.

4.4   For Further Reading

On any list of attributes that can be achieved via architectural means, testability is not normally near the top. Binder treats testability from an object-oriented design perspective [Binder 94].

The IEEE maintains standard definitions for quality attributes (the ones in this chapter and others) [IEEE 91].

Witt, Baker, and Merritt [Witt 94] discuss desirable qualities of architectures (and architects) in their book.

4.5   Discussion Questions

1. How many other qualities of software can you name that were not covered in this chapter? For each, when is it observable? How is it measured? How is it analyzed? With which other qualities does it most often interact?

2. Brooks argues that conceptual integrity is a key to successful systems. Do you agree? Can you think of successful systems that have not had this property? If so, what factors made those systems successful anyway? How would you go about measuring a system to see if it meets Brooks' prescription?

5

Moving From Qualities to Architecture

Architectural Styles

with Mary Shaw

> *We must recognize the strong and undeniable influence that our language exerts on our ways of thinking and, in fact, delimits the abstract space in which we can formulate—give form to—our thoughts.*
> — Niklaus Wirth

The previous chapter explained, in general terms, how architectures affect quality attributes. Qualities provide general guidelines and goals for a system but, as we will see many times in the remainder of this book, qualities by themselves are too vague to enable the design of a system.

This chapter discusses the use of recurring architectural *patterns* in achieving architectural aspects of software quality. Patterns occur in all phases of design. In this book, we will identify and discuss two kinds of patterns: system patterns (which are manifested as *architectural styles*, defined in Chapter 2 and discussed here) and design patterns (discussed in Chapter 13). A third kind of pattern, code patterns, will not be treated in depth because it is not by and large architectural in nature, except insofar as this pattern can be shared across architectural components by means of coding templates. Templates will be discussed in Chapter 13 and illustrated in Chapter 11.

What all patterns have in common is that they are predesigned "chunks" that can be tailored to fit a given situation and about which certain characteristics are known. Each pattern represents a package of design decisions that has already been made and can be reused, as a set. What is most different about them is their scale and hence the time of development when each is applied. System patterns tend to be applied by an architect, design patterns usually occur within the confines

Note: Mary Shaw is a professor at the School of Computer Science, Carnegie Mellon University.

of an architectural component, and code patterns live in the implementor's tool-kit. We begin by discussing architectural styles.

5.1   Introducing Architectural Styles

An architectural style in software is in some ways analogous to an architectural style in buildings such as Gothic or Greek Revival or Queen Anne. It consists of a few key features and rules for combining those features so that architectural integrity is preserved. An architectural software style is determined by the following:

- A set of component types (e.g., data repository, a process, a procedure) that perform some function at runtime
- A topological layout of these components indicating their runtime interrelationships
- A set of semantic constraints (for example, a data repository is not allowed to change the values stored in it)
- A set of connectors (e.g., subroutine call, remote procedure call, data streams, sockets) that mediate communication, coordination, or cooperation among components.

Thus, a style is not an architecture any more than the term *Gothic* determines exactly what a building looks like. Rather, a style defines a class of architectures; equivalently, it is an abstraction for a set of architectures that meet it. Styles are usually ambiguous (intentionally so) about the number of components involved. For example, a pipe-and-filter stream may have two filters connected by a pipe or 20 filters connected by 19 pipes. Styles may be ambiguous about the mechanism(s) by which the components interact, although some styles (main-program-and-subroutine, for example) bind this explicitly. Styles are always ambiguous about the function of the system: One of the components may be a database, for example, but the kind of data may vary.

Mary Shaw and David Garlan have cataloged a set of architectural styles that they have observed by examining a collection of existing systems. Their motivation was the observation that architectural abstractions for complex systems exist, but we do not study or catalog them, as is common in other engineering disciplines.

Styles not only occur regularly in system designs, but they recur in slightly different forms. Style catalogs can help us recognize when two styles are similar, as Figure 5.1 illustrates. In this figure styles are categorized into related groups. For example, an event system is a substyle of independent components. Event systems themselves have two substyles: implicit and explicit invocation. Style catalogs also tell us the circumstances in which it is appropriate to apply a style.

In the remainder of this section, we'll take a brief tour of the architectural style zoo, stopping at each style type shown in Figure 5.1. In the next section,

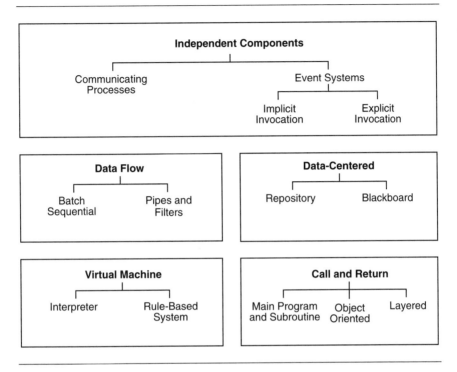

FIGURE 5.1   A small catalog of architectural styles, organized by is-a relations.

we'll take a closer look at how these styles are related to each other and will produce a refinement of the family tree of Figure 5.1.

DATA-CENTERED ARCHITECTURES

Data-centered architectures have the goal of achieving the quality of integrability
of data. The term *data-centered architectures* refers to systems in which the
access and update of a widely accessed data store is an apt description. A sketch
of this style is shown in Figure 5.2. A client runs on an independent thread of
control. The shared data that all of the clients access (and update) may be a passive repository (such as a file) or an active repository (such as a blackboard).
Although the data-centered style shown here has a passive repository (you can
tell this because no control enters it), it can actually occur in a slightly different
guise. At its heart, it is nothing more than a centralized data store that communicates with a number of clients. The means of communication (sometimes called
the coordination model) distinguishes the two subtypes: repository (the one
shown) and blackboard. A blackboard sends notification to subscribers when data
of interest changes, and is thus active. A blackboard differs from Figure 5.2 in
that it would be drawn with control arrows emanating from the shared data.

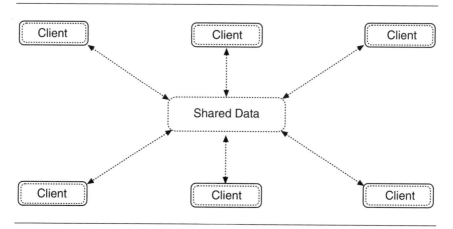

FIGURE 5.2   The data-centered style.

Data-centered styles are becoming increasingly important because they offer a structural solution to integrability. Many systems, especially those built from preexisting components, are achieving data integration through the use of blackboard mechanisms. They have the advantage that the clients are relatively independent of each other, and the data store is independent of the clients. Thus, this style is scalable: New clients can be easily added. It is also modifiable with respect to changing the functionality of any particular client because other clients will not be affected. Coupling among clients will lessen this benefit but may occur to enhance performance.

Note that when the clients are built as independently executing processes, what we have is a client-server style that belongs in the independent-component section of the style catalog. Thus, we see that styles are not rigidly separated from each other.

DATA-FLOW ARCHITECTURES

Data-flow architectures have the goal of achieving the qualities of reuse and modifiability. The data-flow style is characterized by viewing the system as a series of transformations on successive pieces of input data. Data enter the system and then flows through the components one at a time until they are assigned to some final destination (output or a data store). The style has two subtypes, batch sequential and pipe-and-filter. In the batch sequential style, processing steps, or components, are independent programs, and the assumption is that each step runs to completion before the next step starts. Each batch of data is transmitted as a whole between the steps. The typical application for this style is classical data processing. This style is illustrated in Figure 5.3.

The pipe-and-filter style emphasizes the incremental transformation of data by successive components. This is a typical style in the UNIX family of operating systems. Filters are stream transducers. They incrementally transform data (stream

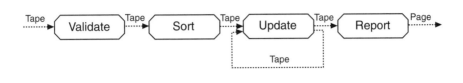

FIGURE 5.3 The batch sequential style.

to stream), use little contextual information, and retain no state information between instantiations. Pipes are stateless and simply exist to move data between filters.

Both pipes and filters are run nondeterministically until no more computations or transmissions are possible. Constraints on the pipe-and-filter style indicate the ways in which pipes and filters can be joined. A pipe has a source end that can only be connected to a filter's output port and a sink end that can only be connected to a filter's input port.

Pipe-and-filter systems, like all other styles, have a number of advantages and disadvantages. Their advantages principally flow from their simplicity—the limited ways in which they can interact with their environment. This simplicity means that a pipe-and-filter system's function is no more and no less than the composition of the functions of its primitives. There are no complex component interactions to manage. The pipe-and-filter style also simplifies system maintenance and enhances reuse for the same reason—filters stand alone, and we can treat them as black boxes. Also, both pipes and filters can be hierarchically composed: Any combination of filters, connected by pipes, can be packaged and appear to the external world as a filter. Finally, because a filter can process its input in isolation from the rest of the system, a pipe-and-filter system is easily made parallel or distributed, providing opportunities for enhancing a system's performance without modifying it.

Pipe-and-filter systems also suffer from some disadvantages. Because of the way that a problem is broken down in this style, a batch mentality is implicitly encouraged. So, interactive applications are difficult to create in this style. Also, filter ordering can be difficult: There is no way for filters to cooperatively interact to solve a problem. Performance in such a system is frequently poor for several reasons, all of which stem from the isolation of functionality that makes pipes and filters so modifiable; these reasons are listed below:

- Filters typically force the lowest common denominator of data representation (such as an ASCII stream). If the input stream needs to be transformed into tokens, every filter pays this parsing/unparsing overhead.

- If a filter cannot produce its output until it has received all of its input, it will require an input buffer of unlimited size. A sort filter is an example of a filter that suffers from this problem. If bounded buffers are used, the system could deadlock.

- Each filter operates as a separate process or procedure call, thus incurring some overhead each time it is invoked.

VIRTUAL MACHINE ARCHITECTURES

Virtual machine architectures have the goal of achieving the quality of portability. Virtual machines are software styles that simulate some functionality that is not native to the hardware and/or software on which it is implemented. This can be useful in a number of ways: It can allow one to simulate (and test) platforms that have not yet been built (such as new hardware), and it can simulate "disaster" modes (as is common in flight simulators and safety-critical systems) that would be too complex, costly, or dangerous to test with the real system.

Common examples of virtual machines are interpreters, rule-based systems, syntactic shells, and command language processors. For example, the Java language is built to run on top of the Java Virtual Machine, which allows the language to be platform independent. Virtual machines have the structure shown in Figure 5.4. The figure shows three kinds of data: the program being interpreted, the program's data (such as the values of variables assigned in the execution of the program), and the internal state of the interpreter (such as the values of registers or the current statement being executed). The interpretation engine selects an instruction from the program being interpreted, updates its internal state, and based on the instruction, potentially updates the program's data.

Executing a program via an interpreter adds flexibility through the ability to interrupt and query the program and introduce modifications at runtime, but there is a performance cost because of the additional computation involved in execution.

CALL-AND-RETURN ARCHITECTURES

Call-and-return architectures have the goal of achieving the qualities of modifiability and scalability. Call-and-return architectures have been the dominant architectural style in large software systems for the past 30 years. However, within this style a number of substyles, each of which has interesting features, have emerged.

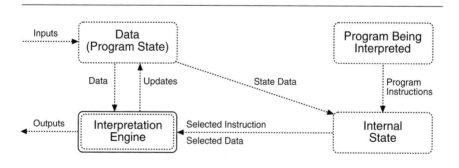

FIGURE 5.4   The virtual machine style.

Main-program-and-subroutine architectures, as shown in Figure 5.5, is the classical programming paradigm. The goal is to decompose a program into smaller pieces to help achieve modifiability. A program is decomposed hierarchically. There is typically a single thread of control and each component in the hierarchy gets this control (optionally along with some data) from its parent and passes it along to its children.

Remote procedure call systems are main-program-and-subroutine systems that are decomposed into parts that live on computers connected via a network. The goal is to increase performance by distributing the computations and taking advantage of multiple processors. In remote procedure call systems, the actual assignment of parts to processors is deferred until runtime, meaning that the assignment is easily changed to accommodate performance tuning. In fact, except that subroutine calls may take longer to accomplish if it is invoking a function on a remote machine, a remote procedure call is indistinguishable from standard main program and subroutine systems.

Object-oriented or *abstract data type systems,* as shown in Figure 5.6, are the modern version of call-and-return architectures. The object-oriented paradigm, like the abstract data type paradigm from which it evolved, emphasizes the bundling of data and the knowledge of how to manipulate and access that data. The goal is to achieve the quality of modifiability. This bundle is an encapsulation that hides its internal secrets from its environment. Access to the object is allowed only through provided operations, typically known as methods, which are constrained forms of procedure calls. This encapsulation promotes reuse and modifiability, principally because it promotes separation of concerns: The user of

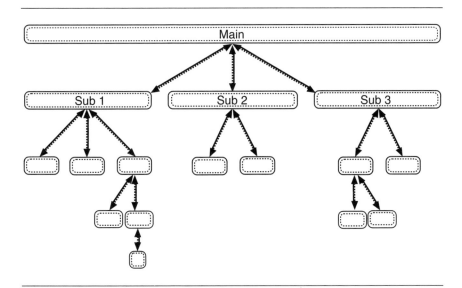

FIGURE 5.5   The main-program-and-subroutine style.

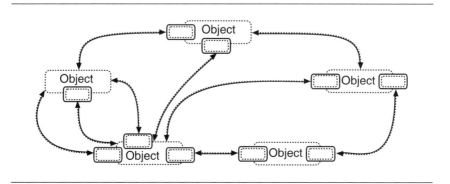

FIGURE 5.6   The object-oriented style.

a service need not know, and should not know, anything about how that service is implemented. The main features that distinguish the object-oriented paradigm from abstract data types are inheritance (the hierarchical sharing of definitions and code) and polymorphism (the ability to determine the semantics of an operation at runtime).

When the object abstractions form components that provide black-box services and other components that request those services, this is a *call-based client-server style* (as opposed to a process-based client-server style, which we will see in the next family).

Layered systems, as shown in Figure 5.7, are ones in which components are assigned to layers to control intercomponent interaction. We first saw layers in Chapter 3. In the pure version of this substyle, each level communicates only with its immediate neighbors. The goal is to achieve the qualities of modifiability and, usually, portability. The lowest[1] layer provides some core functionality, such as hardware, or an operating system kernel. Each successive layer is built on its predecessor, hiding the lower layer and providing some services that the upper layers make use of. The upper layers often provide virtual machines themselves: complete sets of coherent functionality upon which an application, or a more complex virtual machine, can be built. Many of the case studies presented in this book make use of layered hierarchies for portability, modifiability, and ease of system parameterization. In practice, layered systems are frequently not "pure"; functions in one layer may talk to functions in layers other than its immediate neighbors. This is called *layer bridging,* and this practice is used where runtime efficiency is of concern (and the overhead of sending a request through many layers of software cannot be absorbed). But layer bridging compromises the model. If a supposedly portable system is built on a virtual machine—an abstraction of the underlying hardware and software—layer bridging (the direct use of some kernel-level concept, bypassing the portability layer) will make the effort of porting the software greater. On the other hand, if the layering is pure, porting the system

---

[1] Layered architectures are sometimes drawn as concentric circles. In that case, *lowest* becomes *innermost.* There is no conceptual difference.

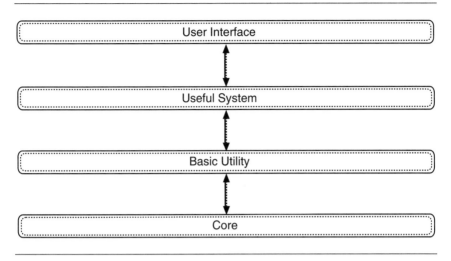

FIGURE 5.7   The layered style.

involves reimplementing only the portability layer, and this can be done once for *all* systems that are built on the virtual machine. For example, a program written in Java requires no porting effort to run it on a large variety of hardware and software platforms, because Java presents a uniform virtual machine abstraction on many platforms. The Java language developers do the porting once so that users of the abstraction need not do so.

INDEPENDENT COMPONENT ARCHITECTURES

Independent component architectures consist of a number of independent processes or objects that communicate through messages. All of these architectures have the goal of achieving modifiability by decoupling various portions of the computations. They send data to each other but typically do not directly control each other. The messages may be passed to named participants or, in the case of event systems using the publish/subscribe paradigm, may be passed among unnamed participants.

Event systems are a substyle in which control is part of the model. Individual components announce data that they wish to share (publish) with their environment—a set of unnamed components. These other components may register an interest in this class of data (subscribe). If they do so, when the data appears, they are invoked and receive the data. Typically, event systems make use of a message manager that manages communication among the components, invoking a component (thus controlling it) when a message arrives for it. In this publish/subscribe paradigm, a message manager may or may not control the components to which it forwards messages. Components register types of information that they are willing to provide and that they wish to receive. They then publish information by sending it to the message manager, which forwards the message, or in some cases an object reference, to all interested participants.

This paradigm is important because it decouples component implementations from knowing each others' names and locations. As mentioned, it may involve decoupling control as well, which means that components can run in parallel, only interacting through an exchange of data when they so choose. This decoupling eases component integration, as has been seen in commercial software engineering tool integration environments and as will be shown in Chapters 13 and 16.

Besides event systems, the other substyle of independent components is the *communicating processes* style. These are the classic multiprocess systems such as we saw in Chapter 3, and will see again in Chapter 11. Of these, client-server is a well-known subtype. The goal is to achieve the quality of scalability. A server exists to serve data to one or more clients, which are typically located across a network. The client originates a call to the server, which works, synchronously or asynchronously, to service the client's request. If the server works synchronously, it returns control to the client at the same time that it returns data. If the server works asynchronously, it returns only data to the client (which has its own thread of control).

HETEROGENEOUS STYLES

Systems are seldom built from a single style, and we say that such systems are heterogeneous. There are three kinds of heterogeneity; they are as follows:

1. *Locationally heterogeneous*, meaning that a drawing of its runtime structures will reveal patterns of different styles in different areas. For example, some branches of a main-program-and-subroutines system might have a shared data repository.

2. *Hierarchically heterogeneous*, meaning that a component of one style, when decomposed, is structured according to the rules of a different style, as Figure 5.8 illustrates.

3. *Simultaneously heterogeneous*, meaning that any of several styles may well be apt descriptions of the system.

This last form of heterogeneity recognizes that styles do not partition software architectures into nonoverlapping, clean categories. You may have noticed this already. The data-centered style at the beginning of this discussion was composed of thread-independent clients, much like an independent component architecture. The layers in a layered system may comprise objects or independent components or even subroutines in a main-program-and-subroutines system. The components in a pipe-and-filter system are usually implemented as processes that operate independently, waiting until input is at their port; again, this is similar to independent component systems whose order of execution is predetermined.

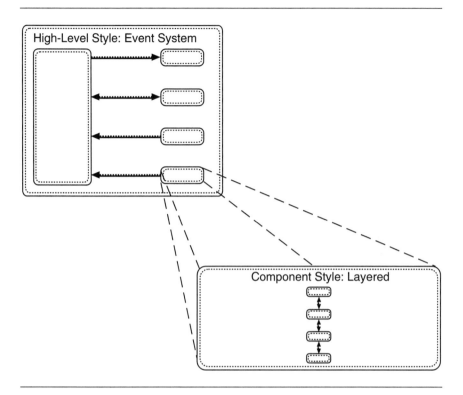

FIGURE 5.8   Hierarchical heterogeneity.

To see an illustration of simultaneous heterogeneity, consider the following A-7E architecture from Chapter 3:

- Its primary control mechanism is call-and-return; its uses structure forms layers with the Extended Computer as its portability layer. Hence, it is a member of the layered style of the call-and-return family.

- Its process structure reveals the classic multiprocess architecture of the communicating processes style in the independent components family.

- Its modular structure forms abstract data types and (except for the lack of inheritance) objects, suggesting an object-oriented style in the call-and-return family.

- Its Data Banker is a blackboard, conforming to the blackboard style of the data-centered family.

- Some input data make a linear trip through the system, in through the Device Interface Module, through the Data Banker, combined with other values in the Function Drivers, and back out through the Device Interface Module again. It is a stretch, but it is possible to describe the A-7E architecture as a data-flow style as well.

In Chapter 11, we'll see another system that consists simultaneously of objects, layers, and communicating processes. In fact, commercial client-server systems such as those that communicate over a CORBA-like infrastructure (see Chapter 8) can often be described as layered object-based process systems, suggesting that this hybrid of three styles may in fact be useful enough as a descriptive vehicle that it deserves its own cage in the style zoo.

These styles are not the full set, or even the only set. They are an early effort at facilitating the architect's job by providing a more sophisticated vocabulary for discussing design alternatives. Other styles will emerge as the field matures.

Should this lack of definitive categorization discourage us? Probably not. Styles exist more as cognitive aids and communication cues than anything else. We can use them as shorthand to convey meaning in a more compact fashion than would otherwise be possible. And just as we know that architectures consist of many structures that do not necessarily resemble each other, it should not surprise us that more than one style may be teased out of (or engineered into) a given system.

In the next section, we take a closer look at styles and the discriminating factors among them. Then we use this information to help us choose specific styles to solve given problems.

5.2   Organizing Architectural Styles

Because an architecture is almost never constructed entirely from one style, an architect needs to understand the interrelationships among styles.

In general, understanding the ramifications of an architecture that is the result of combining styles requires a process of architectural analysis. We will discuss that in Chapter 9. For now, though, we can analyze the set of styles just introduced to see how they are described, what they have in common, and how they might be extended to admit other design possibilities. In this section we begin to organize and classify some of the styles that appear in software descriptions, many of which were introduced in the previous section. We do this for the following reasons:

- By bringing out significant differences that affect the suitability of a style for various tasks, the architect is empowered to make more informed selections.
- By showing which styles are variations of others, the architect can be more confident in choosing appropriate combinations of styles.
- The features used to classify styles will help the designer focus on important design issues by providing a checklist of topics to consider, thereby setting expectations for elements to include in the design.

We first introduce the features that we will use to describe and discriminate styles.

FEATURE CATEGORIES

A system designer's primary impression of an architecture often focuses on the character of the interactions among components. Thus, the major axes of classification are the control and data interactions among components. We can, however, make finer discriminations within these dimensions, such as the following:

- How control is shared, allocated, and transferred among the components
- How data is communicated through the system
- How data and control interact
- The type of reasoning the style permits
- The kinds of components and connectors that are used in the style

Constituent Parts: Components and Connectors.   The allowable kinds of components and connectors are important discriminators among styles. Components and connectors are the primary building blocks of architectures. In this categorization, a component is a unit of software that performs some function at runtime. Examples include programs, objects, processes, and filters. A connector is a mechanism that mediates communication, coordination, or cooperation among components. Implementations of connectors may be distributed over many components; often they do not correspond to discrete elements of the running system. Examples include shared representations, remote procedure calls, message-passing protocols, and data streams.

Selecting the types of constituent parts does not, however, uniquely identify the style, which is why there are other feature categories. Further, some styles rely on finer distinctions within a type of component or connector. Some of these distinctions appear in Table 5.1; a local versus a remote procedure call is an example.

Control Issues.   Control issues describe how control passes among components and how the components work together temporally; they include the following:

- *Topology.*   What geometric form does the control flow for the system take? A pipeline often has a *linear* (nonbranching) or at least an *acyclic* control topology; a main-program-and-subroutines style features a *hierarchical* (tree-shaped) topology; some server systems have *star* (hub-and-spoke) topologies; a style consisting of communicating sequential processes may have an *arbitrary* topology. Within each topology it may be useful to stipulate the direction in which control flows. The topology may be static or dynamic; this is determined by the binding time of the elements as described below.
- *Synchronicity.* How dependent are the components' actions upon each others' control states? In a *lockstep* system, the state of any component implies the state of all others; for instance, a batch sequential system's components are in lockstep with each other because one doesn't begin execution until its

predecessor finishes. Same instruction, multiple data (SIMD) algorithms for massively parallel machines also work in lockstep. In *synchronous* systems, components synchronize regularly and often, but other state relationships are unpredictable. *Asynchronous* components are largely unpredictable in their interaction or synchronize once in a while, and *opportunistic* components such as autonomous agents work completely independently from each other in parallel. Lockstep systems can be *sequential* or *parallel*, depending on how many threads of control run through them. Other forms of synchronicity imply parallelism.

- *Binding time.*   When is the identity of a partner in a transfer-of-control operation established? Some control transfers are predetermined at program *write-* (i.e., source code) time, *compile*-time, or *invocation*-time (i.e., when the operating system initializes the process). Others are bound dynamically while the system is *run*ning.

Data Issues.   Data issues describe how data move around a system; they include the following:

- *Topology.*   Data topology describes the geometric shape of the system's data-flow graph. The alternatives are the same as for control topology

- *Continuity.*   How continuous is the flow of data throughout the system? A *continuous*-flow system has fresh data available at all times; a *sporadic*-flow system has new data generated at discrete times. Data transfer may also be *high volume* (in data-intensive systems) or *low volume* (in compute-intensive systems).

- *Mode.*   Data mode describes how data is made available throughout the system. In an object style, it is *passed* from component to component, whereas in any of the shared data systems it is *shared* by making it available in a place accessible to all the sharers. If the components tend to modify it and reinsert it into the public store, this is a *copy-out-copy-in* mode. In some styles data are *broadcast* or *multicast* to specific recipients.

- *Binding time.*   When is the identity of a partner in a transfer-of-*control* operation established? This is the data analogy of the same control issue.

Control/Data Interaction Issues.   Interaction issues describe the relationship between certain control and data issues.

- *Shape.*   Are the control-flow and data-flow topologies substantially isomorphic?

- *Directionality.*   If the shapes are substantially the same, does control flow in the *same* direction as data or the *opposite* direction? In a data-flow system such as pipe-and-filter, control and data pass together from component to component. However, in a client-server style, control tends to flow into the servers and data flow into the clients.

Type of Reasoning.   Different classes of architectures lend themselves to different types of analysis. A system of components operating asynchronously in parallel yields to vastly different reasoning approaches (e.g., nondeterministic state machine theory) than a system that executes as a fixed sequence of atomic steps (e.g., function composition). Many analysis techniques compose their results from analysis of substructures, but this depends on the ability to combine subanalyses. Thus, different architectural styles are good matches for different analysis techniques. Your choice of architecture may be influenced by the kinds of analysis you require.

Table 5.1 shows a sample set of architectural styles, organized according to these feature categories. We will explore some of these styles in more detail in the next section.

5.3   Refinements of Styles

The classification scheme of Table 5.1 maps out a small part of the space of architectural styles, but it does not capture the richness found in practice, even among this select subset of styles. Each row can be elaborated on to capture more detailed distinctions. In this section we illustrate a refinement of Table 5.1 by partially elaborating on two well-known families of styles that are often used in system development. We do this because the general styles introduced in the previous sections leave many important design decisions unbound. They provide an *approach* to architectural design but are not sufficient in and of themselves to serve as a design. Refinements of those styles are not only possible but necessary before they can lead to an architecture. The refinements we present in this section are more special-purpose tools that can be kept in an architect's conceptual toolkit.

REFINING THE DATA-FLOW STYLE

Data-flow networks describe systems whose components operate on large, continuously available data streams. The components are organized in arbitrary topologies that stream the data with nontransforming connectors. Use of an arbitrary topology makes modification of the system more difficult because interactions among components are unconstrained. Thus, it is natural to wish to place restrictions on the topologies and analyze the results.

Abowd, Allen, and Garlan analyzed what they call the *pipe-and-filter* style by way of formalizing the semantics of architectural styles (as opposed to cataloging their construction, as we have done). They identify three (overlapping) variations of the pipe-and-filter style as follows:

1. Systems without feedback loops or cycles (acyclic)

2. Pipelines (linear)

3. Systems with only fan-out components

TABLE 5.1 A Feature-Based Classification of Architectural Styles

	Constituent parts		Control issues			Data issues				Control/data interaction	
Style	Components	Connectors	Topology [a]	Synchronicity [b]	Binding time [c]	Topology [a]	Continuity [d]	Mode [e]	Binding time	Isomorphic shapes	Flow directions
Data flow: dominated by motion of data through the system, with no "upstream" content control by recipient										*Type of Reasoning: Functional composition*	
Batch sequential	Stand-alone programs	Batch data	Linear	Seq.	r	Linear	Spor. hvol.	Passed, shared	r	Yes	Same
Data-flow network	Transducers	Data stream	Arb.	Asynch.	i, r	Arb.	Cont. lvol. or hvol.	passed	i, r	Yes	Same
Pipes and filters	See Section 5.3.										
Other data-flow substyles	See Section 5.3.										
Call-and-return: dominated by order of computation, usually with single thread of control										*Type of Reasoning: Hierarchy (local reasoning)*	
Main program/subroutines	Procedures, data	Procedure calls	Hier.	Seq.	w, c	Arb.	Spor. lvol.	Passed, shared	w, c, r	No	n/a
Abstract data types	Managers	Static calls	Arb.	Seq.	w, d	Arb.	Spor. lvol.	Passed	w, c, r	Yes	Same
Objects	Managers (objects)	Dynamic calls	Arb.	Seq.	w, c, r	Arb.	Spor. lvol.	Passed	w, c, r	Yes	Same
Call-based client-server	Programs	Calls or RPC	Star	Synch.	w, c, r	Star	Spor. lvol.	Passed	w, c, r	Yes	Opposite
Layered	Various	Various	Hier.	Any	any	Hier.	Spor. lvol., cont.	Any	w, c, i, r	Often	Same or opp.

TABLE 5.1 A Feature-Based Classification of Architectural Styles   *Continued*

Style	Constituent parts		Control issues			Data issues				Control/data interaction	
	Components	Connectors	Topology[a]	Synchronicity[b]	Binding time[c]	Topology[a]	Continuity[d]	Mode[e]	Binding time	Isomorphic shapes	Flow directions
Independent components: dominated by communication patterns among independent, usually concurrent, processes										*Type of Reasoning:* Nondeterminism	
Event systems	Processes	Signals	Arb.	Asynch.	w, c, r	Arb.	Spor. lvol.	Multicast	w,c,r	Yes	Same
Communicating processes	Processes	Message protocols	Arb.	Any but seq.	w, c, r	Arb.	Spor. lvol.	Any	w,c,r	Possibly	If isomorphic, either
Communicating processes substyles	See Section 5.3.										
Data-centered: dominated by a complex central data store, manipulated by independent computations										*Type of Reasoning:* Data integrity	
Repository	Memory, computations	Queries	Star	Asynch. opp.	w	Star	Spor. lvol.	Shared passed	w	Possibly	If isomorphic, opposite
Blackboard	Memory, computations	Direct access	Star	Asynch. opp.	w	Star	Spor. lvol.	Shared mcast	w	No	n/a
Virtual machine: characterized by translation of one instruction set into another										*Type of Reasoning:* Levels of service	
Interpreter	Memory, state machine	Direct data access	Fixed hier.	Seq.	w, c	Hier.	Cont.	Shared	w,c	No	n/a

a. Hier. (hierarchical), arb. (arbitrary), star, linear (one-way), fixed (determined by style).

b. Seq. (sequential, one thread of control), Synch. (synchronous), Asynch. (asynchronous), opp. (opportunistic).

c. w (write-time—that is, in source code), c (compile-time), i (invocation-time), r (runtime).

d. Spor (sporadic), cont. (continuous), hvol. (high-volume), lvol. (low-volume).

e. mcast (multicast)

Their overall pipe-and-filter style corresponds to the data-flow network style of Table 5.1: The components are elements that asynchronously transform input into output with minimal retained state (i.e., transducers). The transducers are connected in various topologies by high-volume data-flow streams.

The pipeline substyle can be seen in Table 5.2 to be a specialization of data-flow network—its data and control topology are restricted from *arbitrary* in the general form to *linear* in the specialized form, but the classifications are otherwise identical. The fan-out and acyclic substyles similarly differ from the general form only by imposing different topological restrictions.

UNIX pipes and filters, a specialization not treated by Abowd and colleagues but widely used elsewhere, can be seen to be a subspecialization of the pipeline style. The hook-ups can only be specified at the time a program—script, in this case—is written or when the command is given to the operating system. Further, its components are those that accept ASCII streams, not generalized data streams.

The classification shows that all of these styles (acyclic, pipelines, fan-out, UNIX pipes and filters) comprise a family that we have called *data-flow network*, in which the members are distinguished mainly by topological restriction. Table 5.2 shows the relationships among the major styles and their family members.

REFINING THE COMMUNICATING PROCESSES STYLE

Andrews analyzed and cataloged a family of styles based on processes communicating with each other via message passing. This family corresponds to the communicating processes style in Table 5.1. Communicating processes are used to achieve the goals of modifiability and scalability, but performance and configuration constraints affect how these goals are achieved. Andrews identifies eight variants that occur in practice and satisfy different goals. The next paragraphs show how each variant is obtained by refining (specializing) the basic communicating processes style.

One-Way Data Flow Through Networks of Filters.   This is a version of the data-flow network substyle implemented with communicating processes. In this version the implementation with messages intrudes on the data-flow abstraction. A piece of data enters the system and makes its way through a series of transformations, each transform accomplished by a separate process. The series need not be linear; Andrews gives an example of a tree of processes forming a sorting network. To analyze this substyle, we note how it differs from both main styles that it resembles. To cast it as a specialization of data-flow networks, we (1) restrict its data and control topologies to one-way flows and (2) relax its data-handling requirements from continuous to sporadic. To cast it as a specialization of communicating processes, we restrict its topologies from arbitrary to one way and its synchronicity to asynchronous. That is, this style lies within the intersection of two major styles: the data-flow network and communicating processes.

TABLE 5.2 Specializations of the Data-Flow Network Style

	Constituent parts		Control issues			Data issues			
Style [a]	Components	Connectors	Topology	Synchronicity [b]	Binding time [c]	Topology	Continuity [d]	Mode	Binding time
Data-flow network	Transducers	Data stream	Arbitrary	Asynch.	i, r	Arbitrary	Cont. lvol. or hvol.	Passed	i, r
▪ Acyclic	Transducers	Data stream	Acyclic	Asynch	i, r	Acyclic	Cont. lvol. or hvol.	Passed	i, r
▪ Fanout	Transducers	Data stream	Hierarchy	Asynch	i, r	Hierarchy	Cont. lvol. or hvol.	Passed	i, r
▪ Pipeline	Transducers	Data stream	Linear	Asynch	i, r	Linear	Cont. lvol. or hvol.	Passed	i, r
– UNIX pipes and filters	Transducers	ASCII stream	Linear	Asynch	i	Linear	Cont. lvol. or hvol.	Passed	i

a. Control/data interaction for all styles is: Isomorphic shapes—yes; Flow directions—same.

b. Asynch. (asynchronous).

c. i (invocation-time), r (runtime).

d. Cont. (continuous), hvol. (high-volume), lvol. (low-volume).

Requests and Replies Between Clients and Servers.   Clients and servers, a popular style, already shown in Table 5.1. It can be seen to be a specialization of the communicating processes style in which the topologies, synchronicity, and mode are restricted from the general form. This is the naive form, which ignores the usual requirement to maintain state for an ongoing sequence of interactions between the client and the server.

Back-and-Forth (Heartbeat) Interaction Between Neighboring Processes.
A heartbeat algorithm causes each node in the process graph to send information out and then gather in new information. An example of applying this algorithm is to discover the topology of a network. On each "beat," each process (representing a processor) communicates with every other process it can, broadcasting its idea of the topology. Between beats, every process assimilates the information just sent to it, combining it with its current idea of the layout. The computation terminates when a completion condition has been met. Andrews proposes two variations of this substyle, depending on whether shared memory is used. We model this form of process interaction by restricting the synchronicity of the communicating processes style to lockstep-parallel (although asynchronous versions are possible) and reflecting the shared-data–distributed-data choice by describing the data and control topologies appropriately.

Probes and Echoes in Graphs.   Probe/echo computations work on (incomplete) graphs. A probe is a message sent by a process to a set of successors; an echo is the reply. Probe/echo algorithms can be used to compute a depth-first search on a graph, discover network topologies, or broadcast using neighbors. The probe/echo substyle can be described as specializing the communicating processes style by restricting the topologies to an incomplete graph, synchronicity to asynchronous, data mode to passed, and flow directions to same.

Broadcasts Between Processes in Complete Graphs.   Broadcast algorithms use a distinguished process to send a message to all other processes. An example is to broadcast the value of a central clock in a soft real-time system. Modeling the broadcast style in our classification simply requires restricting the data topology to star (for that portion of the computation involved in the broadcast) and the data mode to broadcast; the control topology remains arbitrary.

Token Passing Along Edges in a Graph.   Token-passing algorithms use tokens (a special kind of message) to convey temporal rights to the processes receiving the tokens. Token passing is used, for instance, in algorithms to compute the global state of a distributed asynchronous system or to implement distributed mutual exclusion of a shared resource. Token passing is a refinement of the communicating processes style that restricts the synchronicity to asynchronous, data mode to passed, and flow direction to same. The topologies remain arbitrary, and the continuity remains sporadic low volume.

Coordination Between Decentralized Server Processes. In this model, identical servers are replicated to increase the availability of services (for example, in case of the failure or backlog of a single server). The essence of the algorithm is to provide the appearance to clients of a single, centralized server. This requires that the servers coordinate with each other to maintain a consistent state. One server cannot change the "mutual" state without agreement of a sufficient majority of the others. This weighted voting scheme is implemented by passing multiple tokens among the servers. Architecturally, this algorithm is identical to the token-passing substyle discussed previously.

Replicated Workers Sharing a Bag of Tasks. Unlike decentralized servers that maintain multiple copies of data, this style provides multiple copies of computational elements. The replicated-workers style is a primary tool for SIMD machine programmers. Parallel divide-and-conquer is one of its manifestations. One process can be the administrator, generating the first problem and assigning subproblems. Other processes are workers, solving the subproblems (and generating and administering further subproblems as necessary). Subsolutions bubble back up a hierarchical path until the original administrator can assemble the solution to the global problem. To see SIMD algorithms as a substyle of communicating processes, we restrict the topologies to hierarchical, the synchronicity to synchronous, mode to passed or shared (depending on whether shared data is used) and flow direction to same.

Table 5.3 on the next page summarizes these descriptions.

5.4   Using Styles in System Design

Which style should you choose to design a system, then, if more than one will do? The answer (of course) is that it depends on the qualities that most concern you.

If you ask an architect to tell you about the architecture for a system, odds are that the answer will be couched in terms of the architectural solution to the most difficult design problem. If the system had to be ultrareliable and achieving this would be problematic, you would probably first hear about the fault-tolerant redundant warm-restart aspects of the architecture. Perhaps the system had to have high performance as well, but if that were not problematic, you would not hear the solution for that at first. If the architect knew that the system was going to live for a long time, growing and being modified constantly, you would hear about the layered objects and abstract data types used to insulate the system from change. If the system also had to be secure but used an off-the-shelf solution, such as encryption/decryption, you wouldn't hear about the solution for that until later.

Styles are like that. A style can serve as the primary description of a system in an area where discourse and thought are most important to meet uncertainty. Other styles may well apply and be fruitful. But a good rule of thumb is "first

TABLE 5.3 Specializations of the Communicating Processes Style

Style[a]	Control issues			Data issues				Control/data interaction	
	Topology[b]	Synchronicity[c]	Binding time[d]	Topology	Continuity[e]	Mode[f]	Binding time	Isomorphic shapes	Flow directions
Interacting process: dominated by communication patterns among independent, usually concurrent, processes									
Communicating processes	Arb.	Any but seq.	w, c, r	Arb.	Spor. lvol.	Any	w, c, r	Possibly	If isomorphic, either
One-way data flow, networks of filters	Linear	Asynch.	w, c, r	Linear	Spor. lvol.	Passed	w, c	Yes	Same
Client/server request/reply	Star	Synch.	w, c, r	Star	Spor. lvol.	Passed	w, c	Yes	Opposite
Heartbeat	Hier.	Ls./par.	w, c, r	Hier. or star	Spor. lvol	Passed shared ci./co.	w, c	No	Same
Probe/echo	Incomplete graph	Asynch.	w, c, r	Incomplete graph	Spor. lvol.	Passed	w, c	Yes	Same
Broadcast	Arb.	Asynch.	w, c, r	Star	Spor. lvol.	Bdcast.	w, c	No	Same
Token passing	Arb.	Asynch.	w, c, r	Arb.	Spor. lvol.	Passed	w, c	Yes	Same
Decentralized servers	Arb.	Asynch.	w, c, r	Arb.	Spor. lvol.	Passed	w, c	Yes	Same
Replicated workers	Hier.	Synch.	w, c, r	Hier.	Spor. lvol.	Passed shared	w, c	Yes	Yes

a. The Constituent parts for all styles are: Components—processes; Connectors—message protocols.

b. Hier. (hierarchical), arb. (arbitrary), star, linear (one-way).

c. Seq. (sequential, one thread of control), ls./par. (lockstep parallel), synch. (synchronous), asynch. (asynchronous), opp. (opportunistic).

d. w (write-time—that is, in source code), c (compile-time), i (invocation-time), r (runtime).

e. Spor. (sporadic), lvol. (low-volume).

f. Bdcast. (broadcast), Mcast (multicast), Ci./oo. (copy-in/copy-out).

things first." Start with the architectural structure that provides the most leverage on the qualities (including functionality) that you expect to be most troublesome. From there, consider a style appropriate to that structure that addresses the qualities. At that point, other structures and styles can come into play to help address secondary issues.

We expect that the distinctions established in the classification and refinements of Section 5.2 and Section 5.3 provide a framework for offering design guidance of the general form of If your problem has characteristic x, consider architectures with characteristic y. However, organizing this information is a major undertaking for each problem domain. In the interim, we can at least state rules of thumb, as in Table 5.4.

TABLE 5.4   Rules of Thumb for Choosing an Architectural Style

Style	When to use
Data-flow	It makes sense to view your system as one that produces a well-defined easily identified output that is the direct result of sequentially transforming a well-defined easily identified input in a time-independent fashion. Integrability (in this case, resulting from relatively simple interfaces between components) is important.
▪ Batch sequential	▪ There is a single output operation that is the result of reading a single collection of input and the intermediate transformations are sequential.
▪ Data-flow network	▪ The input and output both occur as recurring series, and there is a direct correlation between corresponding members of each series.
– Acyclic	– ...and the transformations involve no feedback loops.
– Fanout	– ...and the transformations involve no feedback loops, and an input leads to more than one output.
– Pipeline, UNIX pipe-and-filter	– The computation involves transformations on continuous streams of data. – The transformations are incremental; one transformation can begin before the previous step has completed.
▪ Closed-loop control	▪ Your system involves controlling continuing action, is embedded in a physical system, and is subject to unpredictable external perturbation so that preset algorithms go awry.
Call-and-return	The order of computation is fixed, and components can make no useful progress while awaiting the results of requests to other components.
▪ Object-oriented/ abstract data type	▪ Overall modifiability is a driving quality requirement. ▪ Integrability (in this case, via careful attention to interfaces) is a driving quality requirement.
– Abstract data types	– There are many system data types whose representation is likely to change.
– Objects	– Information-hiding results in many like modules whose development time and testing time could benefit from exploiting the commonalities through inheritance.

TABLE 5.4   Rules of Thumb for Choosing an Architectural Style   *Continued*

Style	When to use
– Call-and-return-based client-server	– Modifiability with respect to the production of data and how it is consumed is important.
▪ Layered	▪ The tasks in your system can be divided between those specific to the application and those generic to many applications but specific to the underlying computing platform. ▪ Portability across computing platforms is important. ▪ You can use an already-developed computing infrastructure layer (operating system, network management package, etc.).
Independent component	Your system runs on a multiprocessor platform (or may do so in the future). Your system can be structured as a set of loosely coupled components (meaning that one component can continue to make progress somewhat independently of the state of other components). Performance tuning (by reallocating work among processes) is important. Performance tuning (by reallocating processes to processors) is important.
▪ Communicating processes	▪ Message passing is sufficient as an interaction mechanism.
– Lightweight processes	– Access to shared data is critical to meet performance goals.
– Distributed objects	– The reasons for the object-oriented style and the interacting process style all apply.
– One-way data-flow, networks of filters	– The reasons for the data-flow network style and the interacting process style all apply.
– Client-server request/reply	– The tasks can be divided between instigators of requests and executors of those requests or between producers and consumers of data.
– Heartbeat	– The overall state of the system must be assessed from time to time (as in a fault-tolerant system) and the components are working in lockstep with each other. – Availability is a driving requirement.
– Probe/echo	– The topology of the network must be assessed from time to time (as in a fault-tolerant system).
– Broadcast	– All of the components need to be synchronized from time to time. – Availability is an important requirement.
– Token passing	– it makes sense for all of the tasks to communicate with each other in a fully connected graph. – The overall state of the system must be assessed from time to time (such as in a fault-tolerant system), but the components are asynchronous.
– Decentralized servers	– Availability and fault tolerance are driving requirements and the data or services provided by the servers are critical to the system's functionality.

TABLE 5.4   Rules of Thumb for Choosing an Architectural Style   *Continued*

Style	When to use
– Replicated workers	– The computation may be solved by a divide-and-conquer approach using parallel computation.
▪ Event systems	▪ You want to decouple the consumers of events from their signalers. ▪ You want scalability in the form of adding processes that are triggered by events already detected/signaled in the system.
Data-centered	A central issue is the storage, representation, management, and retrieval of a large amount of related long-lived data.
▪ Transactional database/ repository	▪ The order of component execution is determined by a stream of incoming requests to access/update the data, and the data is highly structured. ▪ A commercial database that suits your requirements is available and cost effective.
▪ Blackboard	▪ You want scalability in the form of adding consumers of data without changing the producers. ▪ You want modifiability in the form of changing who produces and consumes which data.
Virtual machine	
▪ Interpreter	▪ You have designed a computation but have no machine to run it on.

5.5   Achieving Quality Goals with Architectural Styles

This section illustrates how different architectural styles lead to different quality attributes by showing how a single system, designed four different ways, differs in its outcome. This example, originally provided by Parnas and modified by Shaw and Garlan, is a case study that shows different architectural alternatives for a Key Word In Context (KWIC) system. One of the main points of this analysis is to show how one system could be designed in a variety of ways. The functionality was the same in each case; what changed was the system's fitness with respect to a portfolio of quality attributes.

A KWIC system takes a set of text lines as input, produces all circular shifts of these lines, and then alphabetizes the results. A KWIC system is primarily used to create an index that is quickly searchable because every key word can be looked up alphabetically even if it does not appear at the beginning of the original index phrase.

The following is an example of the input and output of a KWIC system:

Input: Sequence of lines
   An Introduction to Software Architecture
   Key Word in Context

Output: Circularly shifted, alphabetized lines (ignoring case)
An Introduction to Software Architecture
Architecture an Introduction to Software
Context Key Word in
in Context Key Word
Introduction to Software Architecture an
Key Word in Context
Software Architecture an Introduction to
to Software Architecture an Introduction
Word in Context Key

This case study was originally used by Parnas to make an argument for the use of information-hiding as a design discipline. In Shaw and Garlan's analysis, they discuss four possible architectures for this system: the original "straw-man" architecture, described by Parnas, the improved information-hiding (abstract data type) architecture, an implicit invocation architecture, and a UNIX-style pipe-and-filter architecture.

Parnas's original solutions are shown in Figure 5.9.

Parnas's two solutions—while identical with respect to functionality—differ in their support for the quality attributes of performance, modifiability, reusability, and extendibility. The original shared-memory solution (where shared information is stored in global variables, accessible by all components) has good performance but poor modifiability characteristics. Modifiability is poor because any change to the data format, for example, could potentially affect every component in the system. The abstract data type solution, on the other hand, has better support for modifiability because it hides implementation details (such as data formats) inside abstract data types. An information-hiding approach typically compromises performance somewhat because more interfaces are traversed, and it typically uses more space because information is not shared. It may be difficult to extend the functionality of this solution because there are relatively complex interactions among the abstract data types.

Shaw and Garlan provide two different solutions to this case study: a solution using an implicit invocation architecture and one using a pipe-and-filter solution. These architectures are given in Figure 5.10.

In the implicit invocation architecture, calls to the Circular Shift function are made implicitly, by inserting data into the Lines buffer, as are calls to the Alphabetizer function. In the pipe-and-filter architecture, two filters provide the entire functionality: one to shift the input stream and one to sort the shifted stream. The implicit invocation architecture supports extendibility. If one wanted to add a new function to this architecture, that function would only need to be registered against an event (such as the insertion of a new line into one of the buffers), and the function would be automatically executed whenever the event occurred.

On the other hand, this architecture offers poor control (what is the order of the new function with respect to any functions previously registered with the line insertion?) and poor space utilization (because data is replicated in the two Lines buffers. The pipe-and filter architecture is intuitive and clean and offers the best

Shared-Memory Architecture

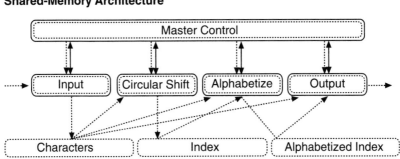

Abstract Data Type Architecture

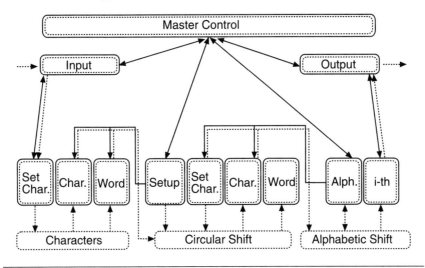

FIGURE 5.9   Parnas's KWIC solutions.

support for reuse of the four alternatives. The Circular Shift and Alphabetizer filters could be picked up and used, unchanged, in another system without affecting
anything in their environments. However, this solution is less efficient than the
others because each filter typically runs as a separate process and may incur some
overhead parsing its input and formatting its output. Also, the pipe-and-filter
solution may not be space efficient.

APPLYING PATTERNS TO ACHIEVE DESIRED ATTRIBUTES

So far we have briefly described each solution to the KWIC problem and provided a laundry list of costs and benefits. Shaw and Garlan, in their analysis,

Implicit Invocation Architecture

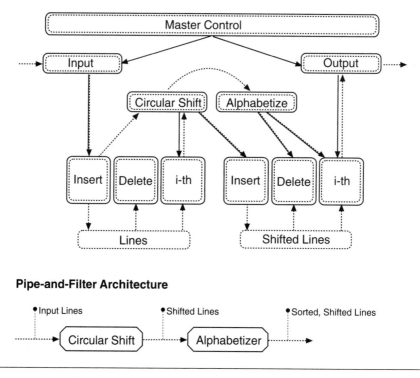

Pipe-and-Filter Architecture

FIGURE 5.10   Shaw and Garlan's KWIC solutions.

present a number of findings with respect to how each of the solutions accommodates a change in the underlying algorithms, a change in the way that data are represented, and a change in the function. They also evaluate each solution with respect to performance and support for reuse. Their results are presented in Table 5.5.

The problem with this table is that it is not repeatable. Or, at the least, it is not repeatable without deep knowledge of the various architectural styles, their costs, their benefits, and an understanding of how each style accommodates the

TABLE 5.5   Rankings of KWIC Architectures with Respect to Quality Attributes

	Shared data	Abstract data type	Implicit Invocation	Pipe-and-filter
Change in algorithm	−	−	+	+
Change in data representation	−	+	−	−
Change in function	−	−	+	+
Performance	+	+	−	−
Reuse	−	+	−	+

problem at hand. This appears to be in conflict with one of the goals of designing with patterns and styles: that a novice should be able to easily apply expert knowledge, as encapsulated and represented by these designs. In practice, however, it is not that simple.

So, how can one go about systematically comparing these (and other) software architectures with respect to their overall satisfaction of a collection of quality attributes? We discuss an alternative technique for analyzing this system in Chapter 9.

We will also discuss the use of patterns in more detail in Chapter 13, where we will concentrate on the use of patterns as a design discipline. There we will look at how the rigorous application of a *small* number of *straightforward* patterns can dramatically simplify a software architecture.

5.6 Summary

This chapter has introduced a set of architectural styles. Styles occur in related groups, and styles in separate groups may actually be closely related. Styles give us a shorthand way of describing a system in ways that make sense, even though the same system may be described with equal fidelity by any of several styles. Styles represent a first-order approach at achieving a system's quality requirements via architectural means, and which style we use to describe a system depends on which qualities we are trying hardest to achieve.

Styles can be described by a set of features, such as the nature of their components and connectors, their static topologies and dynamic control- and data-passing patterns, and the kind of reasoning they admit.

For now, we turn our attention to the primitive design principles that underlie architectural styles (and, as we shall see, design and code patterns). What is it that imparts portability to one design and efficiency to another and integrability to a third? We want to examine these primitives.

We will next turn our attention to these fundamental building blocks, which we call *unit operations*.

5.7 For Further Reading

Shaw and Garlan's catalog of styles may be found in [Shaw 96a]. The classification of styles in Section 5.2 is joint work by Mary Shaw and Paul Clements [Shaw 97]. Their paper contains many more substyles as well as a comprehensive list of references to authors who have written about each of the substyles mentioned in Tables 5.1 through 5.3.

Abowd, Allen, and Garlan [Abowd 95] provide a detailed discussion, and formal analysis, of data-flow styles. Andrews [Andrews 91] provides a detailed discussion of styles of communicating processes.

Parnas [Parnas 72] provided the original KWIC problem which Shaw and Garlan subsequently analyzed [Shaw 96a].

5.8   Discussion Questions

1. Section 5.4 gives rules of thumb for style selection. Pick a few of the styles not mentioned in that section and see if you can write rules of thumb for choosing those styles.

2. A large number of styles are designed to support the quality of modifiability. Give examples and styles of the different types of modification supported by them.

3. Styles, as they are commonly described, are the result of empirical observation, not a taxonomic organization from first principles. As a result, overlap is high: Objects can be cooperating processes that can be layered, and so on. Why is that? Hint: Think about what architectural structures from Chapter 2 are involved in the description of each style.

6

Unit Operations

> *The object of this Handbook is not to enable anyone to erect a works of special character . . . but to illustrate the principles by which plant of any kind may be designed and erected when certain conditions and requirements are known. We cannot make the best use of our abilities unless we are taught to investigate the principles underlying the construction of the appliances with which we have to work.*
> —G. E. Davis, *A Handbook of Chemical Engineering*

Architectural styles are useful if a designer can map one of these styles to the needs of a problem at hand. However, how to create a new style from first principles is not clear. Are there atomic operations of architecture, and if so, what are their effects on quality attributes?

To at least partially answer this question, we present a set of design operations that are commonly used in software architectures and describe how these operations help to achieve qualities. We call these design operations *unit operations,* following the long-time practice in chemical engineering. These software operations are *compression, abstraction,* and *resource sharing, uniform decomposition,* and *replication.*

We will describe each one, give examples of where each is used in large-scale software systems, and discuss them in terms of their effects on the achievement of quality requirements. Once we have described unit operations in general, we explain the history of human-computer interaction models in terms of the unit operations. The goal is to provide better understanding of the atomic design decisions that every architect must make when creating a design and that every architect is implicitly embracing when adopting somebody else's architectural design patterns.

6.1 Introducing Unit Operations

Unit operations are different from architectural styles and design patterns in that they are more primitive. Design patterns and styles *use*, or are derived from, the engineering principles reflected by unit operations. As a consequence, unit operations are more abstract than design patterns, farther from implementation.

We are not presenting a complete set of unit operations, any more than the sets of design patterns or architectural styles appearing in the literature these days can ever be considered complete. However, the set does describe a large number of design decisions made in complex software systems.

SEPARATION

Separation places a distinct piece of functionality into a distinct component that has a well-defined interface to the rest of the world. It is the most primitive and most common tool of a software architect. Separation isolates a portion of a system's functionality. The motivation for determining what portion of a system's functionality to isolate comes from a desire to achieve a set of quality factors. For example, one might separate functionality for performance or ease of creation. Separation permits distribution and hence parallelism. This is important when a large architecture needs to be dissected into smaller pieces for assignment to separate processors or separate development teams.

Separation may also be used to ensure that changes to the external environment do not affect a component, and changes to the component do not affect the environment, as long as the interface is unchanged. Thus, the operation of separation aids both modifiability and portability.

Well-known examples of separation are found in data-flow architectures, compilers, and user-interface management systems. In fact, it is difficult to find a modern software development project that does *not* use separation. However, we seldom use separation per se, but we use its subtypes, such as uniform decomposition or abstraction.

Uniform Decomposition. *Decomposition* is the operation of separating a large system component into two or more smaller ones. *Uniform decomposition* is a restriction of this operation, limiting the composition mechanisms to a small, uniform set. Having uniform composition mechanisms eases integration of components and scaling of the system as a whole. We distinguish two decomposition mechanisms as unit operations as follows:

1. *Part-whole.*   Each of a restricted set of subcomponents represents nonoverlapping portions of the functionality, and every component in the system can be built only from these subcomponents;

2. *Is-a.*   Each of the subcomponents represents a specialization of its parent's functionality.

Replication.   *Replication* is the operation of duplicating a component within an architecture. This technique is used to enhance reliability (fault tolerance) and performance. This unit operation is used in hardware as well as software. When components are replicated, it requires the simultaneous failure of more than one component to make the system as a whole fail. As the amount of replication in a system increases, the available work can be spread among more of the system's components, thus increasing throughput. However the chances that *some* component will fail increase dramatically.

Replication comes in two forms: runtime and static replication. In runtime replication the replicated components perform the same actions at the same times during execution. In static replication the replicated components are written using copies of the same source code but may be performing different functions from each other at any instant depending on their internal state or how they are being used. In Chapter 11, we'll see code templates for fault-tolerance components that back each other up during execution; this is static replication. The space shuttle architecture uses runtime replication, in which multiple versions of the same software decide how to steer the vehicle; differences are resolved through voting.

Runtime replication provides fault tolerance at the cost of performance (the performance that could have been achieved if all of the computing power had been utilized for different things rather than the same thing). Static replication is an approach that compromises between performance and reliability: A backup component can be performing useful but nonessential work until a failure occurs; then it takes over for the failed component.

ABSTRACTION

Abstraction is the operation of creating a virtual machine. A virtual machine is a component whose function is to hide its underlying implementation. Virtual machines are often complex pieces of software to create, but once created they can be adopted and reused by other software components, thus simplifying their creation and maintenance (because they reference a set of abstract functionality).

Virtual machines are found anywhere there is a need to emulate some piece of functionality that is nonnative; an example is to simulate a parallel computation on a single processor. Another common use of virtual machines is in layered systems, as we discussed in the previous chapter. A third use is to provide a common interface to a heterogeneous set of underlying implementations, such as portable user-interface toolkits. In this way, the user-interface portion of the software is written only once, in terms of an abstraction provided by the toolkit. Similarly, abstraction layers are commonly added to single-user systems to allow them to be shared among multiple users.

Separation and abstraction are related but are not the same concept. There are many examples of separation for reasons other than to create a set of abstract services, such as load balancing, parallelizing operations, and dividing work among development teams.

COMPRESSION

Compression is the operation of removing layers or interfaces that separate system functions, and so it is the opposite of separation. These layers may be software (process boundaries, procedure calls) or hardware (separate processors). When one compresses software, one takes distinct functions and places them together. The history of software engineering and computer science has tended away from compression: Abstract data types, the client-server paradigm, distributed and parallel computing, and object-oriented development are all examples of the *addition* of layers (i.e., separation).

Compression serves three main purposes:

1. To improve system performance (by eliminating the overhead of traversing the layers between the functions). For example, Lindstrom discusses the use of layer elimination to meet performance goals in a fault-tolerant, real-time system. Other examples of compression for performance include semantic feedback in user-interface systems and layer straddling in communication protocols.

2. To circumvent layering when it does not provide needed services.

3. To speed system development (by eliminating the requirement that different parts of a system's functionality be placed in separate software components). For example, Microsoft's VisualBasic allows a developer to directly couple individual user-interface objects to application code.

A common technique for automatically achieving compression is the use of macros or in-line procedures. In this technique a user creates code that is packaged into a macro or procedure (and hence separated from the rest of the software), but when the system is compiled, any reference to (or call to) this code is replaced by the actual code. Thus, the compiled system has removed the execution-time overhead of a procedure call at the cost of potentially creating a substantially larger system (if there are 50 calls to an in-line procedure, the code for that procedure will be included 50 times in the resulting compiled version).

RESOURCE SHARING

Resource sharing is an operation that encapsulates either data or services and shares them among multiple independent consumers. Typically there is a resource manager that provides the sole access to the resource. Shared resources, while they are often costly to build initially, enhance the integrability, portability, and modifiability of systems, primarily because they reduce the coupling among components.

Common examples of shared software resources are databases, blackboards, integrated software engineering tool environments, and servers (in a client-server system). In each of these cases, shared resources enhance the integrability of the system. In many cases shared resources are also abstractions. The X-Windowing server, for example, is a shared resource that provides an abstraction of the underlying graphics hardware.

Data repositories such as blackboards and databases are shared resources, and the resource is persistent data to be stored and retrieved. Security kernels also manage shared resources, typically access to privileged system data and functionality. Integrated software engineering environments rely on the notion of a *tool bus* or an explicit shared repository to allow easy integration of tools. Object request brokers permit entire objects and, in fact, entire applications to be encapsulated and remotely and anonymously accessed.

INTERACTIONS AMONG QUALITY ATTRIBUTES
USING UNIT OPERATIONS

We are interested not only in the ways in which these unit operations help or hinder in the achievement of qualities but also in the manner in which quality attributes interact. It is obvious that one cannot maximize all quality attributes. This is the case in any engineering or design discipline. The strongest bridge is not the lightest, quickest to erect, or cheapest. The fastest, best-handling car doesn't carry large amounts of cargo and is not fuel efficient. The best-tasting dessert is never the lowest in calories.

In the realm of software, we are interested in understanding the effect and interactions of unit operations with respect to scalability, integrability, portability, performance (which we separate into sequential performance and concurrent performance, that is, performance given the ability to parallelize operations), fault tolerance, ease of system creation, ease of component creation, overall system modifiability, individual component modifiability, and reusability.

Based on surveys of expert software designers, we can summarize the gross relationships among six unit operations (excluding separation, a supertype of other operations but considering part-whole decomposition and is-a decomposition separately) and the 11 distinct qualities as shown in Table 6.1.

A + in the table indicates a positive relationship between an operation and a quality attribute: that is, the use of this operation aids in the achievement of the quality goal. A − in the table indicates the opposite effect. Finally, a blank cell indicates that, depending on the context of use, the operation might have a positive or negative effect. For example, part-whole decomposition aids in portability if and only if the portions that change from platform to platform have been isolated into a single part. Otherwise, the decomposition actually hinders portability, because the changes to be made are nonlocal; they are spread out among the parts. Similarly, the blank in the portability entry for resource sharing is because portability is enhanced when the shared resource is the only thing that needs to be ported (and hence changes are local) and is reduced when both the shared resource and users of the resource need to be changed (and hence changes are nonlocal). The blank in each of these cases indicates a different scenario of how the unit operation has been applied.

This table is not meant to present a final authority with respect to unit operations and quality attributes. Both qualities and unit operations are abstract and

TABLE 6.1 Summary of Relationships Between Unit Operations and Qualities

	Operation					
	Abstraction	**Compression**	**Part-whole decomposition**	**is-a decomposition**	**Replication**	**Resource sharing**
Scalability					+	
System modifiability	+	−	+	+		
Integrability	+	−	+	+		+
Portability	+	−				
Sequential performance	−	+		−	−	
Concurrent performance		−	+	+	+	−
Fault tolerance	+				+	
Ease of system creation	+	−		+		+
Component modifiability	+	−				−
Ease of component creation	+			+		+
Reusability	+	−	+			

only guide us in our choices among design alternatives. These rankings by themselves tell us little about the context of each question and about how the designers determined the responses. The rationale behind the rankings provides valuable insights into when and how to use a particular operation. In our surveys of expert software designers, we have noted regularly recurring rationales for the use of operations, including constraints on use.

The point here is that these operations have complex interactions, and the effect of a unit operation in terms of a quality attribute is not a simple one. It must be understood in the context of the other design decisions, available materials, cost, time, and the system's operating context. The understanding of this environment is aided by an analysis in terms of unit operations; they aid in focusing discussion and identifying design conflicts.

To realize a complete architecture, quality requirements must, of course, be prioritized so that the order of composition of the unit operations may be determined. This needs to be done because one can't achieve all quality goals at once, and software-transforming operations are not, in general, commutative. The software architect must make hard choices, deciding that greater fault tolerance is more important than greater modifiability or that security is more important than performance.

For example, consider a toy system consisting of a function A. Suppose we wish introduce modifiability by producing an abstraction of A, and we wish to make function A fault tolerant through replication. There are two ways of composing these two operations, as shown in Figure 6.1. The left-hand side does replication first to produce two copies of A and then performs abstraction to produce an interface I. The right-hand side performs the abstraction first to product A and I and then replicates them to achieve fault tolerance.

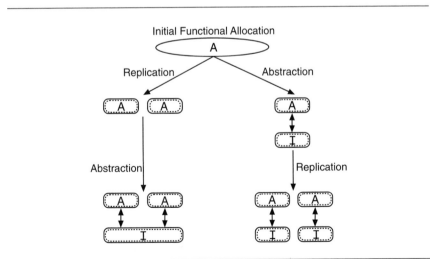

FIGURE 6.1 Non-commutativity of unit operations.

6.2   Applying Unit Operations to User-Interface Software

To understand a software architecture that realizes some set of qualities, we must understand the ramifications of each quality of interest. In particular, we must understand how the functional partitioning is affected by each quality attribute or, put another way, how to achieve a quality by changing the allocation of functionality to structure. As we have already said, this process is currently done intuitively by software developers.

We will now present an example of the ways in which engineering principles, manifested as unit operations applied to architectural decisions, help to meet desired quality goals. The method consists of determining the functions that the architecture must compute and then applying unit operations that transform the structural realization of these functions according to the quality requirements. Unit operations represent a response to each quality attribute in isolation. We see this in many of the case studies presented in this book.

We will provide examples of the use of unit operations in this section. Our examples will be drawn from the domain of human-computer interaction (HCI) and, in particular, from the tools that are used to build user interfaces. There has been an active community creating, using, and modifying both tools and reference models in this field since the early 1980s.

We will not be creating new HCI architectures here because that would prove nothing about the generality of unit operations. Rather, we show how the unit operations have been used over and over in existing, well-known, well-documented HCI architectures and the reference models that underlie them (a fuller discussion of reference models will occur in Chapter 17). It is important to recall at this point that each of the these architectural models, presented here as finished products, is the result of years of research and practical experience by groups of developers and researchers. The unit operations described here are an attempt to codify this knowledge.

A MONOLITHIC ARCHITECTURE

The first step in understanding any class of systems in a given domain is to understand the functions that such a class of systems must compute. Thus, our first step in understanding HCI software architectures is to determine the minimal set of functions that such architectures must support.

There are at least two distinct functions that any system with a user interface must provide: *presentation* (interaction with the user) and *application* (the underlying purpose of the system). Also, there are temporal and hierarchical aspects to HCI—the main task to be accomplished by the user (compose a document, create a spreadsheet, send mail) is broken down into subtasks (create a new file, modify a column, type a paragraph) that are further subdivided until we arrive at the level of physical actions (type a character, click on an icon) that the user performs on the presentation. This decomposition and sequencing can be thought of as a dialogue between the user and the application. Thus *dialogue* is a third type of function that every interactive system must support.

In the monolithic model all of a system's functions are tangled together in a single module. The monolithic model is simply an implementation model. It is widely used because it is obvious (requiring little analysis), and it provides good efficiency because application and interface functions can be directly connected rather than passing through, and incurring the overhead of, intercomponent communication layers. Thus one can think of a purely functional representation of a system as having the structure shown in Figure 6.2. The functions are lumped together in a single structural component.

A program written in a high-level programming language, such as C, with direct calls to a user-interface toolkit, such as the Windows toolkit and Motif, has this structure. An application calls a toolkit function whenever it needs input from the user or wants to present output to the user. The dialogue is implicit; it is embedded in the relationships between these toolkit calls.

THE SEEHEIM MODEL OF HCI SOFTWARE

Now let us look at the monolithic model from the point of view of modifiability and portability because those qualities are frequently demanded of the user-interface portion of the system. The highly influential Seeheim model of HCI software was the result of a workshop of HCI tool developers. These developers attempted to describe a common software architecture for HCI tools that addressed their concerns of modifiability and portability.

Given these goals, the unit operation of abstraction was invoked (although the Seeheim workshop participants certainly did not think of it using that term) because this operation best addressed the achievement of the qualities of modifiability and portability.

As discussed several times, quality requirements are abstract; they are conceptual categories. To make them meaningful for a particular application domain they must be reified as particular tasks. In the HCI domain, we can identify two types of portability concerns: replacing the presentation toolkit (which is quite common) and replacing the application (which is rather more rare).

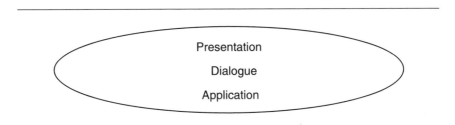

FIGURE 6.2   Allocation of functionality in the monolithic model.

Three of our unit operations can potentially increase the system's portability and increase component modifiability: resource sharing, is-a decomposition, and abstraction. The is-a decomposition operation does not apply because its domain of application is a single component. Resource sharing and abstraction are also ruled out because they have the most deleterious effects on system performance. System performance was a crucial issue in early graphical user interfaces, and poor performance contributed to the demise of many promising early architectures. Also, system designers wanted to mitigate the effects of replacing the presentation toolkit. To achieve this goal, they used the abstraction operation to isolate the presentation function in its own component.

In fact, in most modern HCI architectures the presentation is a shared resource (such as the server in the X-Window system). This is because modern graphics hardware has caught up with the performance demands of graphical user interfaces. As a consequence of the application of separation, the functional partitioning now looks like that shown in Figure 6.3.

In order to insulate against modifications to the dialogue (typically the most heavily modified portion of an interactive system) or to the application, designers once again appealed to the operation of separation: they isolated the dialogue into a separate component, as shown in Figure 6.4

We have now derived the basis of the Seeheim model of software solely from the application of unit operations. We have presented a post facto analysis of the design rationale underlying the Seeheim model, given the resource constraints and quality goals of the time: the desire to remain independent of particular graphics hardware, the desire to be able to easily modify the dialogue, and the performance constraints of the graphics hardware. Deriving design rationale from *reverse engineering* of systems is obviously not definitive; however, published justifications of the Seeheim architecture describe portability and modifiability as benefits of the use of the architecture, and so it is very plausible.

However, we are not quite done with this derivation. The Seeheim model is not exactly as shown in Figure 6.4. There is a fourth element that appeared in the original model, as shown in Figure 6.5.

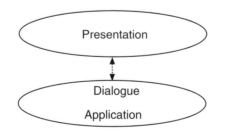

FIGURE 6.3 Applying Part-Whole Decomposition to the monolithic model.

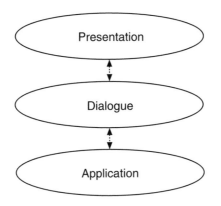

FIGURE 6.4   Two applications of Part-Whole Decomposition.

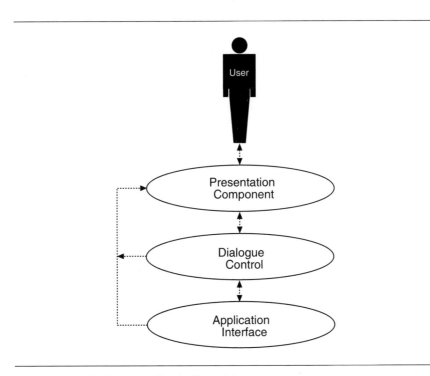

FIGURE 6.5   The Seeheim "Logical" model.

This element, the arrow from application interface to presentation component, was included so that large amounts of data moving from the application interface to the presentation would not have to flow through the dialogue control component. This box is an example of layer bridging, or compression. The unit operation of compression is used to achieve efficiency, at the cost of most other quality factors: modifiability, scalability, and so forth. The designers of the Seeheim model deemed this an acceptable trade-off, given the efficiency demands of user interfaces when providing real-time responses to user input (semantic feedback, for example). The designers attempted to limit the use of this layer bridge to cases in which the dialogue control is not interested in the actual data. Such a restriction is not enforced by the architecture, however.

The Seeheim model is a good example of how designers deal with quality requirements that are in direct conflict with each other. As we shall see, more modern architectures address this problem differently, by the application of a different set of unit operations.

MODEL-VIEW CONTROLLER

The model-view-controller (MVC) paradigm approached the same set of quality concerns as the Seeheim model but in a different fashion. The MVC designers prioritized quality requirements in the same way but applied unit operations differently. This resulted in a different reference model.

To see how MVC addressed modifiability and portability, we will once again begin with the monolithic picture of Figure 6.1 and apply our unit operations in a different order. Let us first consider modifiability. We assume it is likely that one collection of functionality and its dialogue and presentation (say, all of the code associated with a single application object) is going to be modified independently of the rest of the application. This requires the use of the unit operation of part-whole decomposition, which best supports the goal of limiting the effects or scope of modifications. The application of part-whole decomposition results in an architecture such as that shown in Figure 6.6.

The next consideration is that the system must be ported to different input and output devices. To address this consideration we apply separation, this time to the presentation portion of all of the individual components identified above. We want to separate input and output devices not only from the dialogue and application but from each other as well. This yields Figure 6.7, where the presentation has been separated from dialogue and application, and the input and output portions of presentation have been separated from each other.

What we see as a result of applying these operations is the original version of the model (what we call the dialogue and application for a particular object), the view (output), and the controller (input). As with Seeheim, the advantages claimed for the MVC architecture can be understood as the consistent application of unit operations to achieve desired quality attributes.

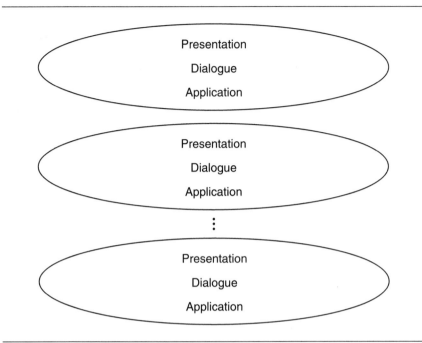

FIGURE 6.6   The application of Part-Whole Decomposition to the entire application.

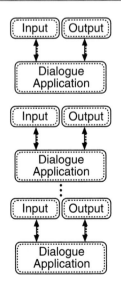

FIGURE 6.7   The application of Separation to the presentation.

COMPARING THE SEEHEIM AND MVC ARCHITECTURES

Note that the two reference models were created from the same base by application of the same techniques. The difference is that Seeheim assumes that the most important scenarios to guard against are porting from toolkit to toolkit and insulating the application, presentation, and dialogue from changes in each other. MVC assumes that modifications are likely to occur between different functional objects and so makes the minimization of the effect of such changes its primary quality goal. These two reference models are graphic evidence of our assertion that qualities are too abstract to be directly useful. Both of the architectures are attempting to minimize the effects of modifications, and both would claim to address modifiability. But each is referring to a different kind of modifiability that affects different architectural components.

MVC and Seeheim represented two fundamentally different approaches to dealing with modifiability. Seeheim's main guard against changes was layering—placing distinct classes of functionality into distinct layers. MVC's guard against changes was part-whole decomposition—placing different pieces of application functionality, along with their input, output, and dialogue, into distinct components. Each of these approaches had its drawbacks, and the next generation of HCI architectures attempted to mitigate these drawbacks.

NEXT-GENERATION DEVELOPMENTS, PART 1: SEEHEIM EVOLVES INTO ARCH/SLINKY

The two architectures we have just discussed underwent some modernization in the late 1980s and early 1990s. Seeheim was elaborated into a model called Arch/Slinky.

The Seeheim model was an important evolutionary step in the engineering of HCI software architectures. Implementations of the Seeheim model have well-known problems, however. For example, given that presentation and dialogue have been separated in the model, there arises the possibility of their interaction. When replacing the presentation toolkit, one should not have to rewrite the dialogue in order to use the idiosyncratic objects and attributes of the new toolkit. Similarly, if one modifies the dialogue, one does not want to have to maintain several related modifications, one per toolkit used. These benchmark tasks motivated an evolution in HCI architectures away from the Seeheim model.

In order to mitigate the interaction of portability and component modifiability (i.e., replacing the toolkit and modifying the dialogue), designers applied the unit operation of abstraction. By applying abstraction, the connection between the presentation and dialogue components is made indirect. A function is inserted between the presentation and dialogue that maps between the two, manifesting a virtual presentation toolkit to the dialogue, thus forcing the dialogue to conform to the abstractions presented by the virtual toolkit.

Finally, designers of the next generation of HCI architecture considered another type of potential modification. If replacing the application (for example, in an interface to a multidatabase) occurs frequently, one would once again appeal to the mechanism of abstraction, inserting a component between the application and the dialogue that maps between the two in the same way that a virtual user-interface toolkit maps between the presentation and dialogue. The application of abstraction creates a virtual application, an analogy with a virtual toolkit. These layers (virtual toolkit and virtual application) add a buffering mechanism to the dialogue from changes in the operating environment.

Thus the reference model motivated by this additional set of benchmark tasks and realized by the unit operation of abstraction evolved into that given in Figure 6.8. Redrawing this figure with Dialogue in the middle gives us Figure 6.9, which was originally called the Arch model. The name Arch was a visual metaphor: The foundations of the Arch are presentation and application; the keystone is dialogue. However, the model depicted in Figure 6.9 was called Arch/Slinky, not just Arch. Here's why.

The "Slinky" portion of the model referred to the ability to expand and contract the allocation of functions to components. (A Slinky is a child's toy—a long loosely coiled spring. One plays with a Slinky by shifting the weight of the spring, which expands one part of the spring while contracting another part.) For example, in a given implementation architecture, the dialogue, virtual application, and application might be placed in distinct structural components or might be implemented in a single structure.

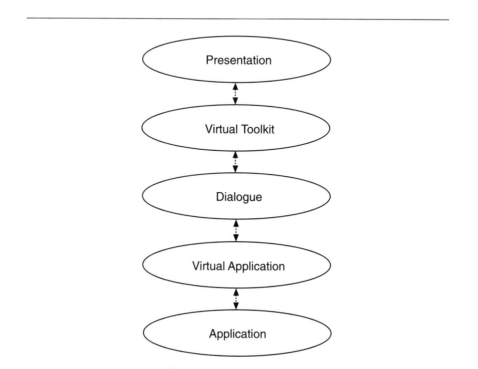

FIGURE 6.8 The functional partitioning of Arch HCI architectures.

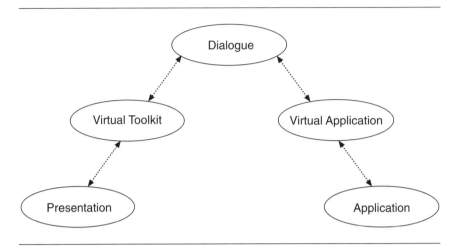

FIGURE 6.9   The Arch/Slinky metamodel.

Furthermore, on occasion an entire Arch is compressed into a single component. For example, most modern toolkits contain a file selection box, a widget
that allows one to navigate around a file system, selecting directories, patterns of
files, and individual files. A file selection box thus contains an application (the file
system and the knowledge of how to navigate around it), a presentation (the buttons, lists, and text input fields that make up the file selection box), and a dialogue
(which controls what occurs when a user selects a directory or file or clicks the
OK button). A sophisticated toolkit might make this file selection box work with
several presentations and several file systems, and so this widget—a single presentation component—would contain an entire miniature Arch structure.

The recognition of the "fluid" or variable nature of allocating functions to
structures led the developers of the Arch model to add the Slinky metaphor to the
metamodel. The Slinky side of the Arch/Slinky metamodel is nothing more than
the opportunistic application of the unit operation of compression to part or all of
the Arch model. Compression increases system throughput and often supports
ease of system creation. The creators of the Arch/Slinky metamodel recognize
that designers often employ compression to speed system creation and system
performance, even at the expense of portability, modifiability, and so forth. This
is, in the hands of experienced designers, a conscious decision, made in the face
of competing requirements. It should be noted that both of these models, Seeheim and Arch/Slinky, were created by a group of expert software designers in
the field of HCI software after substantial contemplation and discussion.

Of course, every unit operation has its costs as well as its benefits. The addition of layers, particularly abstraction layers, incurs a performance penalty. This
penalty is acceptable because graphics hardware has dramatically increased in
performance in the years since the Seeheim model was devised.

We have now shown how the Arch/Slinky model of HCI management systems can be derived entirely from the application of unit operations. Of course, what we have shown in Figure 6.9 is not a software architecture; it is a functional partitioning with an indication of data flow: a reference model. We have not specified the software structure into which this functional partitioning maps. This functional partitioning suggests an architecture that strongly supports the qualities of modifiability and portability. The degree to which the software structure maintains the functional partitioning will affect the eventual success of the architecture with respect to these qualities.

NEXT-GENERATION DEVELOPMENTS, PART 2: MVC EVOLVES INTO PAC

At about the same time that the Seeheim architectural model was evolving into Arch/Slinky, MVC was being elaborated into PAC (presentation, application, control).

The PAC model of HCI software was initially motivated by slightly different quality goals: modifiability and scalability. The concerns of modifiability led to a functional decomposition similar to that shown in Figure 6.2, where the presentation (P), application (A), and dialogue (called control and indicated by a C) were separated, as shown in Figure 6.10. However, the use of separation to isolate presentation from application and dialogue only addresses PAC's modifiability concerns. Given that a complex interactive system is a large piece of software, we would like to support the quality of scalability.

The quality of scalability, applied to a group of components, is supported by the unit operation of part-whole decomposition. Applying this operation, each P-A-C triple can be decomposed into parts. Now the name *control*, rather than *dialogue* is more meaningful, since this subcomponent needs to control its parts as well as mediate the interaction between application and presentation. In this way the structure in Figure 6.10 is completely derived from unit operations.

As PAC was used to build interactive systems, it became apparent that the architectures decomposed in this way did not support portability. This is because a system that is completely decomposed into uniform parts will not be able to localize the effects of porting. For example, each component in the system may have some user-interface–specific code in it. In terms of PAC, each triple may have a presentation subcomponent and each of the subcomponents would have to be individually ported.

When unit operations conflict with each other, either one of the desired quality goals needs to be compromised or the domain of application of a unit operation needs to be limited. The latter strategy was applied in the case of PAC. Given that part-whole decomposition helps ensure scalability of a function, it is applied in a limited fashion, only to the dialogue. This permits the dialogue to be decomposed into manageable, codable chunks, each of which can then be reintegrated to the whole via a regular composition mechanism.

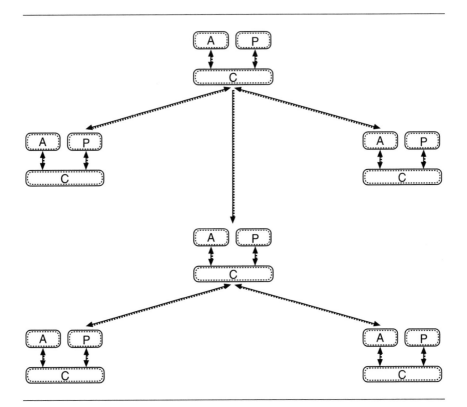

FIGURE 6.10 A typical PAC structure.

To support portability with respect to the underlying application and the presentation toolkit, the Arch/Slinky model described in the previous section is preferred.

UNIFYING PAC AND ARCH/SLINKY: PAC-AMODEUS

Given that part-whole decomposition, as exemplified by PAC, is restricted to apply to only the dialogue component, a PAC model of dialogue can be embedded within the larger Arch/Slinky model of an entire interactive system. This derives the software architecture shown in Figure 6.11, known as the PAC-AMODEUS model. (AMODEUS stands for assimilating models of designers, users, and systems.)

We have now shown how the PAC-AMODEUS model of HCI software was derived. But we have justified this derivation entirely from the application of unit operations. This model, the result of years of research and development, was explicitly designed to promote modifiability, portability, and scalability of the dialogue component. To achieve these conflicting goals, the two threads of HCI software architectures—layered and object-oriented—are combined.

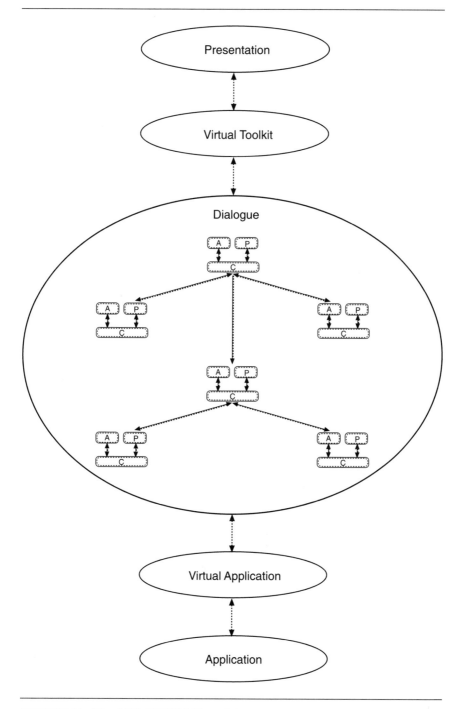

FIGURE 6.11   The PAC-AMODEUS model.

FUTURE DIRECTIONS FOR HCI ARCHITECTURES

The architectures described until this point have been for traditional window, icon, menu, pointer (WIMP) systems. Although most user interfaces built today meet this description, HCI architectures are beginning to be developed for domains that go beyond this characterization: multimodal and multimedia systems, computer-supported cooperative work (CSCW) systems, virtual reality, mobile computing, wearable computer, and so forth. Each of these domains places new pressures on an architecture in terms of the requirements that it must satisfy.

6.3 Ramifications of Addressing Quality Attributes

Engineering principles such as unit operations, which lead to prepackaged design solutions such as patterns and styles, provide ways of dealing with the problem of moving from an abstract set of requirements—some dealing with what the system should do and some dealing with the qualities the system should possess—to a complete architecture.

The problem for the developer in using unit operations is threefold, as follows:

1. Understanding the requirements

2. Mapping the requirements to a structural solution (identified as a design pattern or architectural style that may be derived using unit operations)

3. Identifying and resolving conflicting structural solutions

Most of these conflicts cannot be resolved independently of understanding the problem's context. The conflicts must be analyzed in a context. For this reason, when we elicited the opinions and experience of expert designers with respect to the interaction of qualities and unit operations, many of their responses were qualified.

For example, consider the interaction of is-a decomposition and system modifiability. Does the unit operation of is-a decomposition aid in overall system modifiability? A majority of surveyed experts who gave a negative value to this interaction stated that when changes do not neatly follow the lines of the existing hierarchy, it is necessary to modify the hierarchy. Such a modification can be very difficult because one class is derived from another, and thus many classes may be affected by one change. Respondents who answered positively to this question felt that, provided the changes did not change existing interfaces, the modifications required would be easier, even when not supported by the hierarchy, because of the inherent encapsulation.

The divergence of the experts' opinions on this question is a result of their differing assumptions about the existing system and its environment (principally the proposed change). Those who answered positively assumed that existing interfaces would not have to be changed. It can be concluded that is-a decomposition renders system modification difficult when the modifications are not supported by the class or module hierarchy. Although this is much more difficult than when the changes are supported by the class or module hierarchy, is-a decomposition may make the modifications easier than doing so in a monolithic system due to its encapsulation mechanism.

Thus, although we view unit operations, design patterns, and architectural styles as valuable communication tools and good starting points for the architectural design process, their usage does not replace experience as a requirement for the architect. Rather, they are conceptual tools, ingredients that architects can keep in their bags of tricks. The wisdom precompiled into these design formalisms complements, but is not a substitute for, careful requirements analysis and design walkthroughs and reviews.

We will deal with analyzing designs in Chapters 9 and 10, and design patterns will be addressed in Chapter 13.

6.4   Summary

At a very primitive level, a software architect has a collection of architecture-manipulating techniques that we called unit operations. These operations have been in use for many years, and in this chapter we codified them and discussed their interactions.

Because of the importance of the user interface to most interactive systems and because user-interface reference models provide the oldest, still-evolving collection of reference models, we took a tour of these reference models using the unit operations as a means to understand what motivated the designers.

We saw that the reference models can be understood in terms of the unit operations but not solely in those terms. The same unit operations resulted in both Seeheim and MVC. Unit operations are a portion of understanding design; other techniques such as scenarios, styles, and patterns must be used to achieve desired qualities for a design.

6.5   For Further Reading

Those interested in the history of unit operations can find a brief discussion of how chemical engineers use them in [Shaw 90]. A more detailed treatment can be found in [Furter 80].

Those interested in user-interface reference models can find the original Seeheim model in [Pfaff 85] and a description of MVC in [Krasner 88]. The Arch/Slinky model is documented in [UIMS 92]. PAC is described in [Coutaz 87] and PAC-AMODEUS in [Nigay 91]. Multiuser models are described in [Dewan 95].

6.6   Discussion Questions

1. Consider a large system with which you are familiar. Can you see how unit
    operations were applied to it? In what ways were they used and for what rea-
    sons? If they were not used, has it caused difficulties?

2. Unit operations are extremely coarse grained. Designs are always tempered
    by particular functional requirements and by other quality requirements (as
    Ralph Waldo Emerson—an early software engineer—noted, "Every good
    quality is noxious if unmixed"). Can you think of ways in which the applica-
    tion of unit operations is tempered by the environment in which they are
    applied?

3. Choose an architectural style from Chapter 5 and try to derive it from a
    monolithic model using unit operations. Do the qualities that the unit opera-
    tions impart match those for which the style is known?

4. Choose a blank entry in Table 6.1 and try to decide when the corresponding
    quality is supported by or in conflict with the unit operation.

7

The World Wide Web
A Case Study in Interoperability

*Flexibility was clearly a key goal. Every specification that was needed
to ensure interoperability constrain [sic] the Web's implementation.
Therefore, there should be as few specifications as possible . . . and the
necessary specifications should be made independently. . . . This would let
you replace parts of the design while preserving the basic architecture.*
— Tim Berners-Lee [Berners-Lee 96b]

*In the not-too-distant future, anybody who doesn't have their own
home page on the World Wide Web will probably qualify for
a government subsidy for the home-pageless.*
— Scott Adams, creator of *Dilbert* comic strip

Possibly the most dramatic example of the workings of the architecture business
cycle (ABC) can be found in the way in which the goals, business model, and
architecture of the World Wide Web (WWW) has changed since its introduction
in 1990. No one—not the customers, the users, or the architect (Tim Berners-Lee)—
could have foreseen the explosive growth and evolution of the WWW. In this
chapter, we interpret the WWW from the point of view of the ABC and observe
how the changes in the architecture of the WWW reflect the changing goals and
business needs of the various players. We first look at the origins of the WWW in
terms of the original requirements and the players in the ABC.

7.1   Relationship to the Architecture Business Cycle

The original proposal for the WWW came from Tim Berners-Lee, a researcher
with CERN, the European Laboratory for Particle Physics. Berners-Lee observed
that the several thousand researchers at CERN formed an evolving human "web."
People came and went, developed new research associations, lost old ones,

shared papers, chatted in the hallways, and so on. Berners-Lee wanted to support this informal web with a similar web of electronic information. In 1989, he created and circulated a document entitled "Information Management: A Proposal" throughout CERN. By October of 1990 a reformulated version of the project proposal was approved by management, the name World Wide Web was chosen, and development work began.

Figure 7.1 shows the elements of the ABC as they applied to the initial WWW proposal approved by CERN management. The proposed system was intended to promote interaction among CERN researchers (the end users) within the constraints of a heterogeneous computing environment. The customer was CERN management and the developing organization was a lone CERN researcher. The business case made by Berners-Lee was that the proposed system would increase communication among CERN researchers. This was a very limited proposal with very limited (and speculative) objectives. There was no way of knowing whether such a system would, in fact, increase communication among CERN researchers. On the other hand, the investment required by CERN to generate and test the system was also very limited: one researcher's time for a few months.

The technical environment was familiar to those in the research community. The Internet had been a mainstay of that community since its introduction in the early 1970s. It had weak notions of central control (volunteer committees whose responsibilities were to set protocols for communication among different nodes on the Internet and to charter new newsgroups) and an unregulated, "wild-west" style of human interaction, primarily through specialized newsgroups.

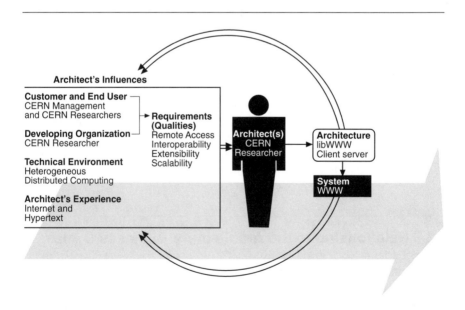

FIGURE 7.1 Initial stages of the ABC at CERN in 1989.

Hypertext systems had an even longer history beginning with the vision of Vannevar Bush in the 1940s. Bush's vision had been explored throughout the 1960s and 1970s and into the 1980s with conferences on hypertext held regularly to bring together researchers. However, Bush's vision had not been achieved in any large-scale way by the 1980s: The uses of hypertext were primarily limited to small-scale documentation systems. That was to change.

CERN management approved Berners-Lee's proposal in October 1990, and by November, he had developed the first WWW program on the NeXT platform. Clearly he had begun working on the implementation before receiving formal management approval. This loose coupling between management approval and researcher activity is quite common in research organizations in which small initial investments are required. By their nature, research organizations tend to generate projects from the bottom up more often than commercial organizations do because research organizations are dependent on the originality and creativity of the researchers and allow them far more freedom than is typical in a commercial organization.

The initial implementation of a WWW system had many features that are still missing from more recent Web browsers: For example, it allowed users to create links from within the browser, and it allowed both authors *and* readers to annotate information. Berners-Lee initially thought that no user would want to write HyperText Markup Language (HTML) or deal with uniform resource locators (URLs). Apparently, he was wrong. Users have been willing to put up with these inconveniences to have the power of publishing on the Web.

7.2 Requirements and Qualities

The World Wide Web, as conceived and initially implemented at CERN, had several desirable qualities. It was portable, able to interoperate with other types of computers running the same software and was scalable and extensible. The business goals of promoting interaction and allowing heterogeneous computing led to the quality goals of remote access, interoperability, extensibility, and scalability, which in turn led to libWWW, the original software library that supported Web-based development and a distributed client-server architecture. The realization of these properties in the original software architecture created an infrastructure that effectively supported the WWW's tremendous growth. libWWW embodies strict separation of concerns and therefore works on virtually any hardware and readily accepts new protocols, new data formats, and new applications. The Web, because it has no centralized control, appears to be able to grow without bound.

We now will deal with these core requirements, and others, in more detail. We will return to the structure of libWWW in Section 7.4. It is worth noting that there is no explicit requirement for ease of use in the original requirements, and it wasn't until the development of point-and-click browsers that the WWW began its tremendous growth. On the other hand, the requirement for portability and the heterogeneous nature of the computing environment led to the introduction of the browser as a separate component, thereby fostering the later development of more sophisticated browsers. As we discussed in Section 6.2, this is an instance of the importance of separating user-interface concerns from the underlying semantic core of the application.

THE ORIGINAL REQUIREMENTS

The initial set of requirements for the WWW, as established in the original project proposals, were as follows:

- *Remote access across networks.*   Any information had to be accessible from any machine on a CERN network.
- *Heterogeneity.*   The system could not be limited to run on any specific hardware or software platform.
- *Noncentralization.*   In the spirit of a human web and of the Internet, there should not be any single source of data or services. This requirement was in anticipation that the Web would grow. The operation of linking to a document, in particular, had to be decentralized.
- *Access to existing data.*   Existing databases had to be accessible.
- *Ability for users to add data.*   Users should be able to "publish" their own data on the Web, using the same interface used to read others' data.
- *Private links.*   Links and nodes had to be capable of being privately annotated.
- *Bells and whistles.*   The only form of data display originally planned was display on a 24×80-character ASCII terminal. Graphics were considered optional.
- *Data analysis.*   One should be able to search across the various databases and look for anomalies, regularities, irregularities, and so on. Berners-Lee gives, as examples, the ability to look for undocumented software or organizations with no people.
- *Live links.*   Given that information changes all the time, there should be some way of updating a user's view of the information. This could be by simply retrieving the information anew every time the link is accessed or (in a more sophisticated fashion) by notifying a user of a link whenever the information has changed.

In addition to these requirements, there were a number of nonrequirements identified. For example, copyright enforcement and data security were explicitly mentioned as requirements that the original project would *not* deal with. The Web, as initially conceived, was to be a public medium. Also, the original proposal explicitly noted that users should not have to use any particular markup format.

Other criteria and features that were common in proposals for hypertext systems at the time but that were missing from the WWW proposal are as follows:

- Controlling the topology of the Web
- Defining navigational techniques and user-interface requirements, including keeping a visual history
- Having different types of links to express differing relationships among nodes

Although many of the original requirements formed the essence of what we think of as the WWW today, several of them either were not realized or only partially realized or their impact was dramatically underestimated. For example, data analysis, live links, and private-link capabilities exist only in a relatively crude fashion to this day. These requirements have gone largely unfulfilled.

Adaptation and selective postponement of requirements is characteristic of unprecedented systems. Requirements are often lists of desirable characteristics. In unprecedented systems, the trade-offs required to realize these requirements are often unknown until a design exists. In the process of making the trade-offs, some requirements become more important and others less so.

The effect of one of the requirements turned out to have been greatly *underestimated*. The bells and whistles of graphics has come to dominate much of today's WWW traffic. Graphics today carry the bulk of the interest and consume the bulk of the Internet traffic generated by the WWW. And yet Berners-Lee and CERN management did not concern themselves with graphics in the initial proposal, and the initial Web browser was line oriented. Similarly, the original proposal eschewed any interest in multimedia research for supporting sound and video.

Some nonrequirements, as the ABC has been traversed, have also become requirements. Security, for example, has proven to be a substantial issue, particularly as the Web has become increasingly dominated by commercial traffic. The security issue is large and complex, given the distributed, decentralized form of the Internet. Security is difficult to ensure when protected access to private data cannot be guaranteed—the Web opens a window onto your computer, and some uninvited guests are sure to crawl through that opening.

However, for the near term at least, the security of commerce on the Web has been dealt with in both a technical and a nontechnical fashion. The technical solution is to use encryption of any private information, such as credit-card numbers. The nontechnical solution is to simply circumvent the Web. In this case, when users want to engage in commercial transactions over the Web, they typically get credit-card authorization through more traditional means (mail, phone, fax) and in return get an account number, which is used in future transactions. Every time this number is used, the user is contacted through e-mail for authorization. In this way, users can avoid ever sending their encrypted credit-card number over the Internet, where it might be stolen and decoded.

REQUIREMENTS COME AND GO

No one could have foreseen the tremendous growth of the World Wide Web, or of the Internet, over the past few years. According to recent statistics, the Web has been doubling in size every three to six months, from about 130 sites in mid-1993 to an estimated 230,000 sites in mid-1996, as shown in Table 7.1. Figure 7.2 shows how the base communication paths for the Internet blanket the United States. Similarly, the number of Internet hosts—at least as counted by registered Internet Protocol (IP) addresses—had grown from 1.3 million in 1993 to 9.5 million by January 1996.

Not only have the Web and the Internet grown, but the Web has grown much faster than the Internet as a whole. This can be seen in the final column of Table 7.1 where we see that the ratio of Internet hosts to Web servers keeps decreasing. This means that an ever-greater proportion of Internet hosts are becoming Web servers. Table 7.2, which reports the breakdown of traffic on the NFSNet backbone by service type, reinforces this point: The percentage of Internet traffic devoted to the Web is steadily increasing. By March of 1995, it was close to dominating the traffic. By today it must surely do so.

In addition to the enormous growth, the nature of the Web has changed, as indicated by the third column of Table 7.1. Although the Web's beginnings were in the research community, it is increasingly dominated by commercial traffic (as indicated by Internet hosts whose names end in *.com*).

The advent of easy, widespread access to the Web had an interesting side effect. Easy access to graphics in a distributed, largely uncontrolled fashion spawned the "cyberporn" industry. This has led to a new requirement: that content be labeled and access to content be controllable. The result of this requirement was the platform for Internet content selection (PICS) specification. PICS is an industrywide set of principles, and specific vendors' implementations of those principles, that allow the labeling of content and flexible selection criteria. In this way, content producers are not limited in what they provide, but content consumers can tailor what they view or what they permit others to view according to their own tastes and criteria. For example, a parent can prevent a child from viewing

TABLE 7.1   Web Growth Statistics

Date	No. of Web sites	% *.com* sites	Hosts per Web server
6/93	130	1.5	13,000
12/93	623	4.6	3,475
6/94	2,738	13.5	1,095
12/94	10,022	18.3	451
6/95	23,500	31.3	270
1/96	100,000	50.0	94
6/96	230,000 (est.)	NA	41

Used with permission of Matthew Gray of the Massachusetts Institute of Technology.

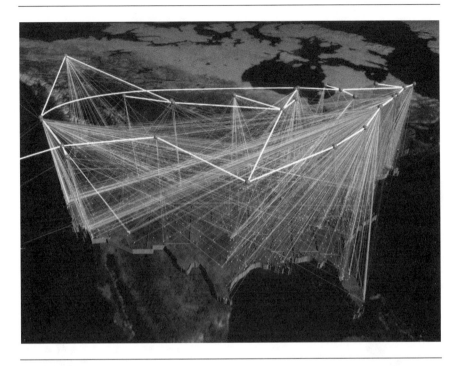

FIGURE 7.2 Internet backbones in the United States.   Copyright 1996 by Donna Cox and Robert Patterson. Produced at the National Center for Supercomputing Applications, University of Illinois at Urbana-Champaign. Used with permission.

movies other than those rated G or PG, and an employer can prevent an employee from accessing non-business-related sites during business hours.

To see how far and how fast the WWW has diverged from its original concept, suppose Berners-Lee had put a requirement for restriction of content to prevent children from accessing pornography into his original proposal. The management of CERN would have tossed his proposal out without discussion. We return to this point about change of customer when we revisit the ABC for the WWW in Section 7.5.

TABLE 7.2   NFSNet Backbone Usage Statistics

Date	% FTP	% TELNET	% netnews	% irc	% Gopher	% e-mail	% Web
6/93	42.9	5.6	9.3	1.1	1.6	6.4	0.5
12/93	40.9	5.3	9.7	1.3	3.0	6.0	2.2
6/94	35.2	4.8	10.9	1.3	3.7	6.4	6.1
12/94	31.7	3.9	10.9	1.4	3.6	5.6	16.0
3/95	24.2	2.9	8.3	1.3	2.5	4.9	23.9

Used with permission of Matthew Gray of the Massachusetts Institute of Technology.

7.3 Architectural Approach

The basic architectural approach used in the WWW was a dependence on clients and servers and on using a library (libWWW) that masks all hardware, operating system, and protocol dependencies. Figure 7.3 shows how the content producers and consumers interact through their respective servers and clients. The producer places content on a server machine and the content is described in HTML. The server communicates with a client using the hypertext transfer protocol (HTTP). The software on both the server and the client is based on libWWW, and so the details of the protocol and the dependencies on the platforms are masked from the software. One of the components on the client is a browser that knows how to display HTML so that the content consumer is presented with an understandable image. Note that this separation of the presentation (from the browser) from the production of the data to be presented (from the server) is an application of the Seeheim model described in Section 6.2. Table 7.3 shows how the WWW achieves its quality goals.

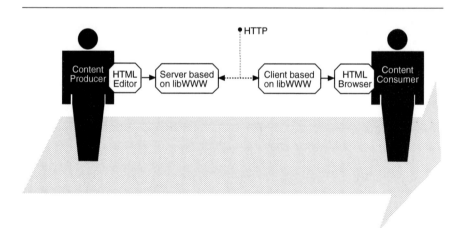

FIGURE 7.3 Content producers and consumers interact through clients and servers.

7.4 Architectural Solution

We now go into more detail about both libWWW and the client-server architecture used as the basis for the WWW. We also briefly discuss a proposal to replace libWWW with a new object-oriented database approach named Jigsaw.

TABLE 7.3   How the WWW Achieves the Quality Goals

Goal	How achieved
Remote access	Build WWW on top of Internet
Interoperability	Use libWWW to mask platform details
Extensibility of software	Isolate protocol and data type extensions in libWWW
Extensibility of data	Each data item is independent except for references it controls.
Scability	Use client-server architecture and keep references to other data local to referring data location.

MEETING THE ORIGINAL REQUIREMENTS: LIBWWW

As stated earlier, libWWW is a library of software used to create applications that run on either the client or the server. This library provides the generic functionality that is shared by most applications: the ability to connect with remote hosts, the ability to understand streams of HTML data, and so forth.

The goals for the libWWW were to create a compact, portable library that could be built upon to create Web-based applications such as clients, servers, databases, and Web spiders. It was organized into five layers, as shown in Figure 7.4.

The generic utilities provide a portability layer on which the rest of the system rests. Layers was one of the architectural styles discussed in Section 5.1. The utilities layer includes basic building blocks for the system such as network management,

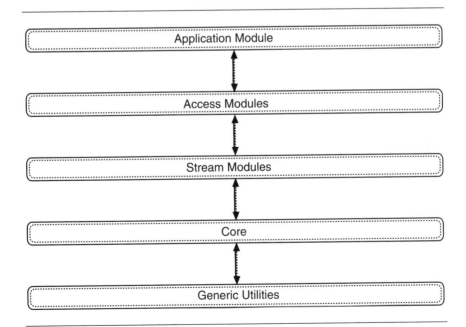

FIGURE 7.4   Layers in libWWW.

data types such as container classes, and string-manipulation utilities. Through the services provided by this layer, all higher levels can be made platform independent, and the task of porting to a new hardware or software platform is almost entirely contained within the task of porting the utilities layer, which needs to be done only once per platform.

The core layer contains the skeletal functionality of a WWW application—network access, data management and parsing, logging, etc. By itself, the core layer does nothing. It provides a standard interface for a WWW application to be built upon. The actual functionality is provided by plug-ins and call-out functions that are registered by an application. *Plug-ins* are modules that are registered by the application at runtime. Plug-ins do the actual work of the core layer—sending and manipulating data. These modules typically support protocols, handle low-level transport, and understand data formats. Plug-ins can be changed dynamically, which means that it is easy to add new functionality or even to change the very nature of the Web application.

Call-out functions provide another means for applications to extend the functionality provided in the core layer. *Call-outs* are arbitrary application-specific functions that can be called before or after requests to protocol modules.

What is the relationship between the generic utilities and the core? The generic utilities provide utility functions in a platform-independent manner, but these utilities could be used to build any networked application. The core layer, on the other hand, provides the abstractions specific to building a WWW application.

The stream layer provides the abstraction of a stream of data. All data transported between the application and the network use this abstraction.

The access layer provides a set of network-protocol-aware modules. The standard set of protocols that libWWW supports are hypertext transfer protocol (HTTP—the underlying protocol of the World Wide Web), Network News Transport Protocol (NNTP—the protocol for Usenet messages), Wide Area Information Server (WAIS—a networked information-retrieval system), file transfer protocol (FTP), TELNET, rlogin, Gopher, local file system, and TN3270. It is a relatively simple matter to add new protocol modules because they are built upon the abstractions of the lower layers.

The uppermost layer consists of the WWW application modules. This layer is not an actual application but rather a set of functionality that is useful for writing applications. The application layer includes modules for common functionality, such as caching, logging, and registering proxy servers (for protocol translation), and gateways (for dealing with security firewalls, for example), history maintenance, and so on.

LESSONS FROM LIBWWW

As a result of building libWWW and the many applications that rest upon this foundation, several lessons have been learned. These lessons have derived in part from the developers' experience in trying to meet the requirements listed in Section

7.2—that Web-based tools be heterogeneous, support remote access across networks, be noncentralized, and so forth. However, the requirement that turned out to be the most challenging to meet was supplying bells and whistles. Or, to put it another way, allowing the growth of features of Web-based applications has driven many decisions in libWWW has led to the following lessons:

- Formalized application program interfaces (APIs) are required: These are the interfaces that present libWWW functionality to the rest of the software architecture, in particular to the programs being built on top of libWWW functionality. For this reason, APIs should be specified in a language-independent fashion (recall the A-7E module interspecifications of Chapter 3) because libWWW is meant to support application development on a wide variety of platforms and languages.

- Functionality and the APIs that present that functionality must be layered. Different applications will need access to different levels of service abstraction. These levels are most naturally provided by a layered style.

- The library must support a dynamic, open-ended set of features. All features of the library must be able to be replaced, and it must be possible to make this replacement at runtime (i.e., without restarting the system).

- Processes built on the software must be thread safe. Web-based applications must support the ability to perform several functions simultaneously, particularly because some operations, such as downloading large files over a slow communication link, may take a considerable amount of real time. To do this, the applications require the use of several simultaneous threads of control. Thus, the functionality exposed by the APIs must be safe to use in a threaded environment.

Currently, libWWW does not support all of these goals as well as it might. For example, the libWWW core makes some assumptions about essential services, so not all features can be dynamically replaced. Furthermore, since libWWW is meant to run on many different platforms, it could not depend on a single-thread model. Thus, it has implemented pseudothreads, which provide some, but not all, of the functionality required. Finally, most current implementations of Web applications do not support dynamic feature configuration; they require a restart before new services are registered.

A SAMPLE CLIENT-SERVER ARCHITECTURE USING LIBWWW

In Figure 7.5 we show the architecture of a typical WWW client-server built using the services of libWWW. We will use this example to make a few points about libWWW. In particular, it should be noted that not all parts of a client-server are built from libWWW. For example, the user-interface functionality is independent of libWWW. Also, the names of the managers do not directly correspond to the names of the layers: Although the access manager, protocol manager,

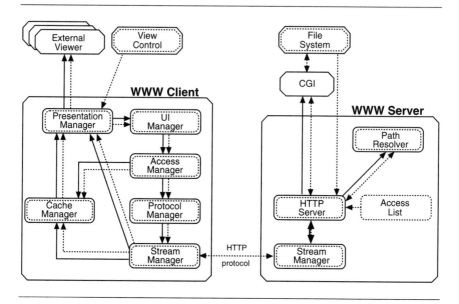

FIGURE 7.5   A World Wide Web client-server pair.

and stream manager are clearly related to the access and stream layers, the cache manager uses the services of the application layer. The stream managers in the client-server manage the low-level communications, thus ensuring, for the other parts of the system, transparent communication across a network.

The user interface (UI) manager handles the look and feel of the client's user interface. However, given that the set of resources that a WWW system can handle is open ended, another component, the presentation manager, can delegate information display to external programs (viewers) to view resources that are known by the system but not directly supported by the UI manager. For example, most Web viewers use an external program to view PostScript files on a bit-mapped display. This delegation is a reasonable compromise between the competing desires of user-interface integration (which provides for a consistent look and feel and hence better usability) and extensibility.

The UI manager captures a user's request for information retrieval in the form of a URL and passes the information to the access manager. The access manager determines if the requested URL exists in cache and also interprets history-based navigation (e.g., "back"). If the file is cached, it is retrieved from the cache manager and passed to the presentation manager for display to either the UI or an external viewer. If the file is not cached, the protocol manager determines the type of request and invokes the appropriate protocol suite to service the request. This protocol is used by the client stream manager for communicating the request to the server. Once the client stream manager receives a response from the server in the form of a document, this information is passed to the presentation manager for appropriate display. The presentation manager consults a static view control configuration file (mimerc, mailcap, etc.) that aids in the mapping of document types to external viewers.

The HTTP server ensures transparent access to the file system—the source of the documents that the Web exists to transfer. The server does this either by handling the access directly (for known resource types) or through a proxy known as common gateway interface (CGI). CGI handles resource types that a native server cannot handle and handles extension of the functionality of the server, as will be discussed next. Currently, the available WWW servers implement a subset of defined HTTP requests. This subset allows for the retrieval of documents, the retrieval of document meta-information, and server-side program execution via the CGI.

When a request is received by the server stream manager, the type of request is determined and the path of the URL is resolved via the path resolver. The HTTP server consults an access list to determine if the requesting client is authorized to access the data pointed to by the URL. The HTTP server might initiate a password authentication session with the client to permit access to secured data. Assuming authentication succeeds, the HTTP server accesses the file system (which is outside the WWW server boundary) and writes the requested information to the output stream. If a program is to be executed, a process is made available (either new or polled) through the CGI and the program is executed, with the output written by the server stream manager back to the WWW client.

In either case, CGI is one of the primary means through which servers provide for extensibility, and ease of extensibility has become one of the most important requirements driving the evolution of Web software. CGI has become such an important aspect of Web-based applications that we now discuss this topic at greater length.

CGI

Most information served by a server is static; it changes only when its author modifies it on its home file system. CGI scripts, on the other hand, allow dynamic, request-specific information to be returned by a server. CGI is used to augment server functionality: for input of information, for searches, for clickable images. The most common use of CGI, however, is to create *virtual documents*— documents that are dynamically synthesized in response to a user request. For example, when a user does an Internet search, the search engine creates a reply to the search request, and a CGI script creates a new HTML document from the reply and returns that to the user.

The use of CGI scripts shows the flexibility of an architecture based on lib-WWW. CGI is shown as external to the server in Figure 7.5. CGI scripts are written in a variety of languages, some of which are compiled (C, C++, Fortran) and some of which are interpreted (Perl, VisualBasic, AppleScript, etc.). These scripts allow a developer to extend a server's functionality arbitrarily and, in particular, to produce information that will be returned, via the server, to the user.

However, because these scripts may contain any functionality that one can write in C, Perl, and so on, they represent an enormous security hole for any system on which they are installed. For example, a script (which runs as a process separate from the server) might be "tricked" into executing an arbitrary command on the host system on behalf of a remote user. The requirement for increased security derived in large part from the use of server-side scripts such as CGI. One means of addressing this requirement will be described in the next section.

Probably the most important additional feature that CGI brought to the WWW architecture was the ability to allow users to "put" information into the Web, in contrast to the "get" operation that servers normally provide. Although the requirement to put information was listed in the original requirements for the World Wide Web project, it still has not been fully achieved. CGI allows only users to put information in application-specific ways, such as adding information to a database by filling out a form.

Although CGI solved many problems inherent in the original design of lib-WWW—principally because it provided much-needed server extensibility to handle arbitrary resources and it allowed users to put data in limited ways—it also had several substantial shortcomings. The security issue was one; another was portability. CGI scripts written in VisualBasic, AppleScript, and C Shell work on Windows-based PCs, Macintoshes, and UNIX-based systems, respectively. These scripts cannot be (easily) moved from one platform to another.

This leads to a discussion of a current proposal for meeting some of the new requirements: Jigsaw. Jigsaw is the result of the realization that the WWW has strayed sufficiently far from its original requirements that its base architecture no longer suffices and that it is time to create a new architecture to support the new requirements of the WWW.

MEETING NEW REQUIREMENTS USING JIGSAW

Jigsaw is an object-oriented server written entirely in Java. Jigsaw was created as a new design from the bottom up that completely bypasses the services provided in libWWW. It was intended to address the quality issues of portability, extensibility, efficiency, security, and ease of creation. The main functional enhancement that Jigsaw was intended to provide was better handling for the put operation, permitting clients to add information directly to Web sites (other than through CGI scripts with their portability and security shortcomings).

Jigsaw supports portability, security, and ease of creation (at least in part) because it is written in Java. Java was designed to run on heterogeneous computing platforms and has been designed from the start to be as secure as possible (since it was designed with the expectation that it would support distributed computing, particularly embedded Web-based applications). Java aids in security in three ways: a lack of pointer arithmetic, automatic garbage collection, and strong type checking. These language features remove the ability to access data outside of the program's address space. Prohibiting uncontrolled data accesses is a major component of ensuring security.

Java helps to ease Web-based program creation (as much as any programming language can) by directly supporting threads. The use of a programming language cannot guarantee any nonfunctional quality, but it can make the achievement of that quality easier, less costly, or more likely, to achieve. The main quality design challenges for Jigsaw, however, were extensibility and efficiency, and these had to be met through architectural means.

Extensibility was provided through the use of resource objects—encapsulated pieces of functionality that know how to handle particular Web resource types. Resource objects were initially designed as a generic replacement for the kind of add-on functionality provided by CGI. Because resource objects are Java objects, they can run in their own thread rather than having to run in a separate processes as CGI scripts do.

A Jigsaw server has a set of rules that indicate what kind of handlers should be used to handle particular resource types. Examples are as follows:

```
/foo/bar/* FileHandler()
/cgi-bin/* CgiHandler()
```

These rules say that any URL with a prefix `/foo/bar` should be handled by a resource object created from the `FileHandler()` class, and any URL with the prefix `/cgi-bin` should be handled by the `CgiHandler()` class.

Linked with the notion of resource objects is the idea of filters. Any request can be filtered before being passed to a resource object. The filters are specified according to the kind of resource that they are protecting. An example is as follows:

```
/protected/* AuthFilter("realm", CgiHandler() )
```

This example says that any URL with a prefix `/protected` must first be sent to `AuthFilter` (with the parameter `"realm"`), and the output of `AuthFilter` is then passed to `CgiHandler()`. In this way, the job of authentication is moved out of the functionality of the server. This example can be seen as evidence of the success of Jigsaw's design goal of extensibility: Jigsaw itself is just a framework with little inherent server functionality. Almost all of its functionality resides in extensions. In fact, Jigsaw can be viewed as an object-oriented database that serves requests by dispatching them to the appropriate object. The main part of the server functionality, then, is concerned with storing, indexing, caching, and dispatching resource objects.

Efficiency was addressed by Jigsaw in several ways. One aspect of efficiency that the designers strived for was to minimize file-system accesses. This is done through the caching of persistent resource objects.

In addition, performance (as compared with efficiency) can be improved by moving Java objects around. In the past, nonserver functionality was divided into applets (programs that execute within a Web browser) and CGI (which executed on the server's platform). However, by using resources that are encapsulated as Java objects, these objects can be made to execute anywhere (because Java is portable, interpreted, and network aware). Because of this, the distinction between clients and servers becomes blurred; any functionality can be executed anywhere. In effect, any Jigsaw process can become a proxy server. When a Jigsaw process becomes a proxy server, performance for the client can be improved through load balancing: moving the execution of the resource object to a local platform if there is sufficient processing power or to a remote platform if there is insufficient processing power locally but adequate bandwidth resources between the local and remote platforms.

7.5   Architecture Business Cycle Today

If we look at the current state of the WWW after several cycles through the ABC, we see a number of phenomena, as follows:

- Several different types of organizations provide the technical environment. These can be divided into service providers and content providers. Service providers are organizations that provide the software that makes the WWW—browsers, servers and search engines. Content providers are organizations that provide data for the WWW. There is heavy competition in all of these areas.

- A separate nonprofit organization, the WWW Consortium, provides basic libWWW/Jigsaw services.

- CERN has no special role in the evolution of the WWW.

Figure 7.6 shows the ABC today for the WWW. The requirements and qualities are the same. The customers for the WWW are the WWW software server and browser providers, the WWW service providers, and the content providers. The end users are intended to be the whole population of the world. The architect's role is provided by the WWW Consortium and the remainder of the ABC remains the same except that the technical environment now includes the WWW, and this adds an upward compatability requirement to the qualities.

We discussed the return cycle of the ABC in Section 1.1. The existence of a system creates new business opportunities both for the developing organization and the customers of that organization. In the case of the WWW, the developing organization, CERN, decided that WWW activity was not its main business: It was a nuclear research organization. The business opportunities that were created by the return loop of the ABC were filled by other organizations. Furthermore, in Section 17.1, we will discuss the role of a reference architecture and a community in defining such architectures; that role today is being filled by the WWW Consortium.

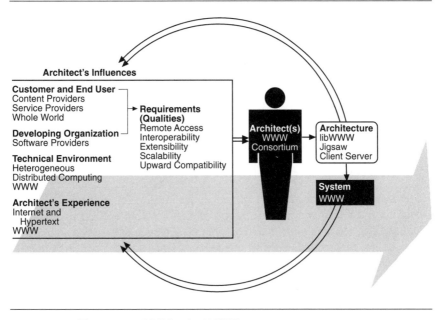

FIGURE 7.6   The current ABC for the WWW.

7.6   Summary

The WWW has been successful because of the manner in which the desired qualities were realized in the architecture. The success of the WWW has meant that the ABC has been traversed multiple times, with each traversal creating new business opportunities and new requirements. For a look at an example of how the background of the architect influenced the architecture, see the sidebar below.

The Importance of the Architect's Background

In 1986, I was asked to design a system that today would be called an intranet. Its requirements were very much those given by Berners-Lee in his proposal to CERN management. The system was to act as a respository for information that was already available within the organization. Such things as trip reports, project information, project reports, and personal schedules were to be encompassed within the system and be available for access both within the organization and, selectively, from outside of the organization.

My first decision was the same as that made by Berners-Lee: No graphics and only textual information would be kept in the system. Given the technology generally available to the customers of the organization, who were expected to access the information from external sites, the restriction to supporting textual terminals was a reasonable one.

My other design decisions were far different from those made by Berners-Lee and when I explain my background, the decisions should be apparent. I had just completed a successful but lengthy development effort on a scientific database management system. This system ran on minicomputers (what today would be called a mainframe) and managed various scientific data gathered from both extensive field studies and laboratory studies. The database management system provided links to a popular statistical analysis system and the scientists who used this system could select one type of data from one database, join it to data selected from another database, and perform some type of statistical analysis.

The key aspect of this system was that the data were centralized. In those days, data and access were both centralized. Users were required to perform their analyses through terminals located in a central room. For a time, I also did development in this central room. The social ambience of computing was far different than it is today. The people in the computer room had social interactions that don't occur today among users of computers.

My exposure to the Internet (not yet called the Internet) in 1986 was limited. I had just discovered newsgroups and had used e-mail in only a limited fashion. Concepts such as ftp and various data-sharing protocols were not familiar to me.

Given this background, it should be clear what kind of system I began designing. In fact, the system was canceled after I worked on it for a very short time, and so I had time to do little but explore the problem. The system outline was clear to me, however. The system would be a classic database system. There would be a central repository of information and users would access the information through one computer. The interesting aspects of the system dealt with the user interface—how to provide for a variety of different types of users wanting and expecting different things from the system.

Contrast my background with that of Berners-Lee. He was a researcher in hypertext and was at home in the Internet and familiar with distributed computing paradigms. Our various solutions to the same general set of requirements very clearly reflected the backgrounds that we brought to the task. He designed a decentralized hypertext system; I designed a centralized database system.

The point to be emphasized is that systems reflect not only the requirements (both in terms of functionality and system qualities) but also, as we asserted in Section 1.1 when we described the ABC, the background and knowledge of the architects.

— LJB

7.7 For Further Reading

The reader interested in discovering more about the hypertext should read Vannevar Bush [Bush 45] and the special issue of the CACM devoted to hypertext [CACM 88].

Information on the history and growth of the WWW can be found primarily on the WWW. We used articles by Berners-Lee [Berners-Lee 1996*a*] and Matthew Gray of MIT.

Information on Jigsaw can be found at *http://www.w3.org/pub/WWW/Jigsaw* and information on Java can be found at *http://java.sun.com/aboutJava/index.html*.

Much of the detail about using libWWW comes from W3C Reference Library, available through the World Wide Web Consortium. This document can be found at *http://www.w3.org/pub/WWW/Library*.

7.8 Discussion Questions

1. We have identified a number of qualities that made the WWW successful: interoperability, portability, remote access, extensibility, and scalability. Which of these do you think contributed most substantially to the Web's success? If any of qualities had been sacrificed, would the Web still have been successful? What trade-offs did these quality goals entail in the architecture of applications based upon libWWW?

2. The WWW did not have performance as one of its early quality goals. This is unusual for a successful system. What, if anything, does this say about the future of computing?

8

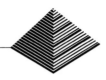

CORBA

A Case Study of an Industry Standard Computing Infrastructure

with Kurt Wallnau

> *The Object Management Architecture is the architecture for a connected world. Heterogeneous, distributed systems, with worldwide connectivity, is here to stay, and OMA provides the tools to build those systems.*
> — Richard Mark Soley
> Vice President and Technical Director
> Object Management Group

This chapter presents object management architecture (OMA) and its better-known communication infrastructure, Common Object Request Broker Architecture (CORBA). Together, they provide a standard software platform in which distributed object-oriented programs can communicate and interact with each other.

Object-oriented technology is not new. Programming languages, such as Simula'67 and its more popular descendant Smalltalk'80, established the core concepts of *object-oriented* software. Programming languages with mass appeal such as C++, ObjectiveC, and most recently Java, have brought these concepts into widespread use. Object technology, as it has come to be known, has made inroads in other areas as well, such as object-oriented database management systems. For some, object orientation has become a philosophy (some might say religion) for software engineering, as evidenced by the use of the term *object-oriented* as a prefix to other well-established terms such as *database management systems*.

When seen in this light, the OMA and CORBA represent just another application of object-oriented concepts to different aspects of computing—in the case of CORBA, to distributed (object-oriented) systems. Thus, an object request broker (ORB) allows objects to publish their interfaces and allows client programs

Note: Kurt Wallnau is a member of the technical staff at the Software Engineering Institute, Carnegie Mellon University.

(and perhaps other objects) to locate them anywhere on the computer network—possibly anywhere in the world—and to request services from these remote objects. Indeed, the initial name for Sun Microsystem's ORB was DOE, for "distributed objects, everywhere."

But CORBA is not an ORB—it is a specification for a *common ORB architecture*. What types of business needs led to the creation of an industry standard architecture for ORBs? How did CORBA address these needs, and how successful is the CORBA design? In what ways has the original need for CORBA changed, and how has CORBA changed in response? These are the questions we consider in this chapter.

8.1 Relationship to the Architecture Business Cycle

The business motivation for development of the OMA comes very clearly from Redmond, Washington, headquarters of Microsoft. Microsoft's success in dominating the personal computing industry throughout the 1980s is well known. Workstation computer manufacturers such as Digital Equipment Corporation, Hewlett-Packard (HP), and Sun Microsystem initially watched the deadly competition among PC manufacturers and among Microsoft, IBM, and Apple with detachment. Toward the end of the 1980s, however, this detachment was gradually replaced by genuine alarm: The price–performance ratio for PCs was improving, and PC processing power was getting close to that of high-end workstations. The hardware distinction between PCs and high-end workstations was disappearing. Workstation manufacturers realized that the competitive fray that they had so far avoided was about to overtake them.

THE FIGHT AGAINST MICROSOFT

Because profit margins for PC hardware are small, hardware is only a small part of the story. Control of the operating system leads to control of the vast market of independent software vendors (ISVs) and their wares. Microsoft's Windows operating system now dominates the PC marketplace. Further, extensions to Windows, such as object linking and embedding (OLE), allow ISVs to develop components—stand-alone applications with a common look and feel—that can be readily integrated into a standard desktop environment. OLE also allows documents (data files) produced by components to be embedded within the documents of other components, essentially supporting the composition of components. The possibility that OLE offers of seamless integration among components such as spreadsheets, word processors, report writers, databases, and so on, was very attractive to end users.

The major computer manufacturers had not, singly, been able to meet these expectations nor had they contributed to the development of the diverse and burgeoning ISV and component marketplace supported by Microsoft Windows. Fortunately for computer manufacturers, however, PCs and OLE were hobbled by the DOS lineage of Microsoft Windows. Although adequate for personal use, Microsoft Windows would not scale, or be sufficiently reliable, for the highly demanding and critical information-management needs of corporate users. The computing manufacturers' best assets were their stable, mature operating systems and the enterprise software built to run in these environments. End users were willing to endure an impoverished, expensive, and unintegrated component marketplace to have the security of stable and mature operating systems.

Microsoft's Windows NT appeared to be the first major threat to this uneasy equilibrium. Unlike Microsoft Windows, Windows NT is an operating system with a solid pedigree. With the PC price–performance ratio not just converging but leveling with that of high-end workstations and "servers," with an advanced operating system to exploit cheap PC hardware, and with OLE and a vast, ready-to-hand component marketplace, it became clear that computer manufacturers needed to unite to provide adequate competition.

OPEN STANDARDS: AN EMBARRASSMENT OF RICHES

The major computer manufacturers had not been idle. One of the major problems facing computer manufacturers in their battle with Microsoft was market and technology fragmentation. Consider, for example, the number of variants of the UNIX operating system: Solaris, SunOS, SystemV, HP/UX, and so forth. Historically, there have simply been too many versions of UNIX (let alone other operating systems such as VMS, MVS, etc.) running on too many different hardware platforms to provide a unified front against Microsoft. To counteract this fragmentation, manufacturers and ISVs with a stake in their non-Microsoft products have spawned numerous industry groups to develop an "open standards" software infrastructure that can remove or accommodate heterogeneity.

Unfortunately, the number of industry groups and the open standards they supported also reflected the diversity of technology and business objectives lurking just beneath the surface. Rivalry between the major vendors (IBM, HP, Digital, Sun) was always apparent. A plethora of organizations and acronyms promoted by one or several of the major vendors assaulted the end user: Open Systems Foundation (OSF), X/Open, distributed computing environment (DCE), POSIX, OpenDoc, Motif, OpenLook, common desktop environment (CDE), common operating system environment (COSE), Berkley/UNIX, and SystemV/ UNIX, were a few of these organizations and systems. This assault increased the appearance of the very fragmentation that these organizations and standards were intended to remedy in the first place. Moreover, the collaborators on these open standards are also competitors in their own right. As a result, standards were often augmented with value-added features as a means of obtaining favorable product differentiation in the marketplace.

But product differentiation runs counter to the needs of ISVs who want and need a uniform computing environment in the face of heterogeneous technology, and the diversity and complexity of choices posed by the open systems standards was a liability.

THE OBJECT MANAGEMENT GROUP

The Object Management Group (OMG) was chartered in 1989—not coincidentally just one year after Microsoft established its Windows NT design team—to "create a component-based software marketplace." Of course, such a marketplace already existed, but it was "owned" by Microsoft. The OMG envisioned a technology whereby applications (components) could execute on different platforms and operating systems, yet still interoperate. This would be an alternative to Microsoft's OLE. But why would OMG succeed where others had failed? What unifying principles could OMG use that could capture the attention of ISVs and unify the disparate complexity of open systems computing?

In a word, the answer is *objects*. In three words, it is object management architecture, OMG's proposed answer to Microsoft hegemony. Figure 8.1 shows the architecture business cycle (ABC) as it pertains to the OMA and CORBA. The customers for OMA and CORBA were hardware and software vendors such as IBM, Digital, and Sun. The end users were the ISVs. The technical environment at the time consisted of OLE (the competition) and object-oriented everything (design, analysis, databases, and so on). The architects were members of a consortium, so they had a variety of backgrounds.

The quality attributes for the OMA and CORBA are discussed in the next section; they include buildability, balanced specificity, implementation transparency, interoperability, evolvability, and extensibility. The architects were the OMG itself, and the final systems were all of the systems to be constructed based on CORBA and the OMA.

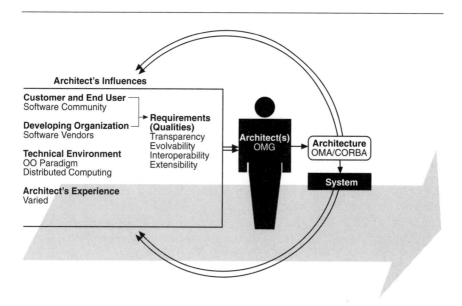

FIGURE 8.1   The ABC as it pertains to OMA and CORBA.

8.2   Requirements and Qualities

This section discusses the goals of the OMG and how these goals were reflected in qualities for the OMA.

NECESSARY CONDITIONS FOR THE SUCCESS OF THE OMG

The idea underlying the OMG is that a component industry that is independent of a particular vendor's infrastructure (i.e., Windows NT and OLE) can be established, provided that

- A component integration infrastructure can be developed that is sufficiently rich in services to support most component integration requirements
- Implementations of these services are readily available on all significant platforms (including Wintel machines, that is, Windows running on Intel processors)
- Clients are portable across vendor implementations of these services and can interoperate with components that use implementations of these services provided by differing vendors.

In addition to these positive success conditions, the OMG also had to avoid numerous pitfalls. These are best illustrated by the failure of the portable common tools environment (PCTE). In Chapter 1, we discussed how systems can influence the environment in which future systems are developed. This influence can be both positive and negative. PCTE is an example of a negative influence.

PCTE was intended to provide standard services for component integration, and yet despite the hundreds of millions of dollars lavished on it, PCTE never succeeded in the marketplace. Although the ultimate cause of the PCTE failure can be argued, the failure does underscore a number of potential pitfalls:

- PCTE was conceived as an integrated (monolithic) system, which meant that the designers had to fully specify all of its technology services and how these services interact (e.g., security, distribution, data, and process management services).
- The complexity of PCTE and the fact that subset implementations of PCTE were not allowed resulted in steep development costs, lengthy time to market, and ultimately few PCTE implementations in the marketplace.
- The PCTE specification required the use of (what was then) immature "research" technologies, for example, distributed object-based data management.
- Producing a formal International Standards Organization (ISO) standard is a lengthy process—PCTE development began in the early 1980s, but it did not become an ISO standard until 1994. By the time it became a standard, its technology assumptions were largely obsolete.

TABLE 8.1 OMA Quality Attribute Requirements

Goal	How achieved
Buildability	Be readily implemented with available technology, across different computing platforms, and work well with existing software development tools and practices
Balanced specificity	Be detailed enough to provide a meaningful standard for component developers and integrators, but general enough to allow vendor-specific features and optimizations
Implementation transparency	Provide compete transparency of implementation details so that client programs can be independent of object implementation details (programming language, object location, operating system, vendor, etc.)
Interoperability	Support interoperation of objects implemented on different vendor implementations of the OMA and allow bridges for interoperability of the OMA to other technologies (including Microsoft technology)
Evolvability	Be responsive to the development of new object and distributed-systems technologies and new market needs (i.e., be open to new services and facilities and accommodate interoperation of many kinds of object technology)
Extensibility	Provide a stable, core set of component-integration and interoperation services needed by most component developers, but be extensible for component integration services needed by market niches.

The business conditions and the lessons from PCTE are reflected in the OMA's desired quality attributes for their specified architecture, as summarized in Table 8.1.

It is interesting to note what is *not* a *required* quality attribute for the OMA. Neither security nor performance is required since the OMA has to balance numerous market factors if it is to become a ubiquitous component-integration standard, as it must to compete with Windows NT/OLE. Each quality attribute implies a set of engineering trade-offs, and each trade-off has consequences that might be anathema to the OMG in certain market segments. For example, rigorous performance requirements might not be acceptable to SmallTalk implementations of the OMA. On the other hand, high-performance implementations of the OMA might be developed by vendors seeking market distinction. Similar vendor differentiations can emerge (and have emerged) to support other quality attributes, such as fault tolerance.

In addition to the challenge of deciding which quality attributes to address and which to leave as vendor enhancements, the OMG also had to develop an architecture that made reasonable trade-offs among the selected quality attributes. For example, buildability is in tension with evolvability; as we will discuss, complete client-side implementation transparency and the generality requirements of OMA specifications (the second clause in balanced specificity) are in tension with each other; and both are in tension with the ORB interoperability requirement. Thus, the OMG needed to ensure that the OMA addressed a wide array of trade-offs— an architecture that is detailed versus general, stable versus flexible, featureful versus implementable, general purpose versus niche optimal, niche optimal versus interoperable, and so on.

8.3   Architectural Approach

The OMG approach to satisfying these quality attributes is through two architectures: the OMA and CORBA. The OMA is the high-level architecture, and its structure reflects quality attributes that relate to extensibility and evolvability. It also reflects the consensus-based design processes inherent in any standards-making efforts and in the OMG design processes in particular. CORBA is an architecture for one component of the OMA, and it reflects the deeper technical requirements that relate to buildability, implementation transparency, and interoperability. Both OMA and CORBA reflect balanced specificity.

The OMA describes what it means to be an object, how objects communicate with each other, and how applications can be made to interoperate through the use of standard object services. Figure 8.2 depicts a high-level view of the OMA. The OMA assumes three different types of objects: objects that provide universally useful services (CORBAServices), objects that provide useful but not universally useful services (CORBAFacilities), and objects that provide application-specific services (application objects). What differentiates these types of objects is the kinds of services they provide; however, they are all objects. In the OMA, all objects communicate via an ORB; CORBA defines a standard architecture (and services) required of OMA-compliant ORBs.

The partitioning scheme outlined in Figure 8.2 is important despite the fact that there are no objective criteria for determining whether an object is a CORBAService, CORBAFacility, or application object. Instead, the partitioning scheme is meant to separate the kinds of services that are needed by most developers (CORBA-Services) from those that are more likely to be niche specific (CORBAFacilities) are those likely to be used by a single application) and from the application itself (application objects). All of these are separated from the services that are necessary to enable object communication—the ORB.

A summary description of CORBAServices (as of October, 1996) is provided in Table 8.2. The CORBAFacilities category is not as mature and is instead

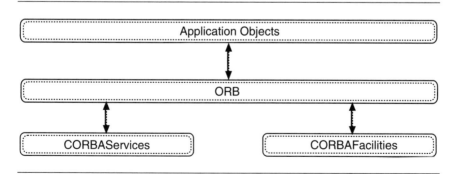

FIGURE 8.2   The object management architecture.

TABLE 8.2 Summary of CORBAServices

Service	Service description
Naming	Provides the ability to bind a name to an object; similar to other forms of directory service
Event	Supports asynchronous message-based communication among objects
Life-cycle	Defines conventions for creating, deleting, copying, and moving objects
Persistent-object	Provides a means for retaining and managing the persistent state of objects
Transaction	Supports multiple transaction models, including mandatory "flat" and optional "nested" transactions
Concurrency-control	Supports concurrent, coordinated access to objects from multiple clients
Relationship	Supports the specification, creation, and maintenance of relationships among objects
Externalization	Defines protocols and conventions for externalizing and internalizing objects across processes and across ORBs

focused on further partitioning of CORBAFacilities into smaller categories organized into "horizontal" facilities such as information, system, task, and user-interface management and "vertical" facilities targeted for particular application domains such as imagery, manufacturing, distributed simulation, accounting, oil and gas exploration, and mapping. Figure 8.3 illustrates how the different classes of objects in the OMA are related to each other. CORBAServices are the most fundamental application building blocks (for using the OMA); CORBAFacilities reuse and

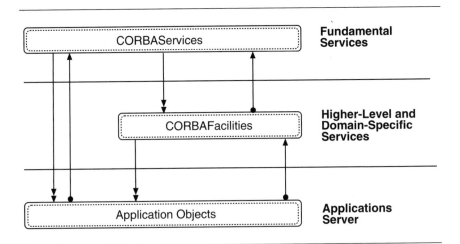

FIGURE 8.3 Contextual relationships among OMG object classes.

extend these building blocks and introduce domain-specific building blocks; application objects reuse and extend both CORBAServices and CORBAFacilities. However, application objects are not a subject for standardization in the OMA.

The partitioning scheme depicted in Figures 8.2 and 8.3 is important for two reasons. First, it provides a different forum for stakeholders who have separate, and sometimes competing, interests. For example, although the OMA is intended to be an infrastructure for component developers, the ORB is really the infrastructure of the infrastructure—it is the communications heart of the OMA. As such, its specification is the most complex part of the OMA, and its implementors are most likely to be the computer manufacturers or ISVs in the CORBA business. In contrast, CORBAFacilities provides a forum for component developers and integrators in specific market niches such as manufacturing (the domain-specific services alluded to in Figure 8.3). CORBAServices are somewhere between these two extremes, and the specification of these services draws accordingly from both manufacturers and ISVs.

A second reason for the OMA partitioning is that it supports several quality attributes. First, the core ORB part is separated from questions concerning the functionality that should be supported by the OMA (such as outlined in Table 8.2). Consequently, ORBs could (and did) appear on the marketplace long before the specification of CORBAServices was complete. Thus, one of the pitfalls of the PCTE—the long time to market—was avoided. Further, the separation of functional services from the ORB set in motion an incremental specification and implementation for the OMA itself. Thus, CORBA (the ORB specification) became an initial stable basis for the OMA, CORBAServices provided commonly needed services, and the CORBAFacilities provided a basis for developing niche-specific services. Finally, the extensible nature of these services—new services can be added more or less independently of each other—supports the ability of the OMA to accommodate new technologies, although as we will see, CORBA also supports this quality attribute.

In addition to the structure and content of the OMA itself, the OMG's process for developing the OMA also contributes to satisfying the OMA quality attributes. The byzantine nature of this development process defies a brief description. The process is also as flexible and evolvable as the OMA itself (i.e., it continues to change). However, the process is one of consensus and compromise, balanced with a clear bias toward already implemented solutions to proposed extensions of the OMA.

Table 8.3 summarizes how the structure of the OMA and the processes of the OMG help to satisfy the quality attributes outlined in Table 8.1. As can be seen, quality attributes are achieved through a combination of technical and nontechnical means. On the technical side, the use of an abstract interface description and the functional partitioning scheme help achieve *balanced* specificity, evolvability, and extensibility. On the nontechnical side, the OMG standardization process helps achieve buildability. Thus, what the OMA depicted in Figure 8.2 lacks in specificity, it makes up for in the harmonization of business considerations (market niches, addressing stakeholder interests, and so on).

TABLE 8.3 How the OMA Supports Its Quality Attribute Requirements

Goal	How achieved
Buildability	OMA standardization process combines a competitive "request-for-proposal" approach for developing specifications with a requirement that selected specifications have commercial quality implementations available within a year of acceptance.
Balanced specificity	Specifications described via an abstract interface definition language (IDL). (See CORBA discussion in Section 8.4 for more details about IDL.)
Evolvability	Specification is partitioned into separately evolvable subcategories. OMA has processes to introduce task forces and special-interest groups.
Extensibility	ORB core and CORBAServices form a stable core.
	CORBAFacilities allow niche-specific extensions.

8.4 Architectural Solution

The ORB provides the fundamental communications services between clients and objects in the OMA. The ORB is responsible for all of the mechanisms required to find the object implementation for a client request, to prepare the object implementation to receive the request, and to communicate the data making up the request. The interface that the client sees is completely independent of the location of the object, the programming language in which the object is implemented, and anything else that is not reflected in the object's interface.

CORBA specifies an architecture for OMA-compliant ORBs. This section focuses on CORBA v2.0, released in July of 1995. However, before getting into the details, it is worthwhile relating the story of CORBA v1.0 and why it was designed as it was. As noted, the OMG issues requests for proposals for specifying OMA technologies. The original CORBA specification was no different, and numerous responses to the OMG's request were submitted. The major computer manufacturers submitted their proposals, but the team led by Sun Microsystems prevailed. Business requirements forced an alternative proposal, submitted by a team led by Digital, to be also incorporated. Certainly it would not satisfy the OMG's objectives to create a schism at this early juncture.

The OMG solution? Combine the Sun and Digital proposals so that no major players would walk away losers. The influence of the original Digital submission can be seen in the CORBA dynamic invocation interface (DII), while the original Sun submission emphasized static invocation via "stubs" and provided the overall structure of what became CORBA. A careful scrutiny of the CORBA specification today will reveal some subtle inconsistencies between the DII and stub-based paradigms. However, this compromise, at the cost of a small degree of impurity, produced harmony in the OMG and resulted in a specification that reflected the interests of most major computer manufacturers.

COMPONENTS OF CORBA

History aside, the overall structure of CORBA is depicted in Figure 8.4, which corresponds (without client and object implementation) to the ORB component of the OMA (see Figure 8.2). Figure 8.4 shows the structure as the OMG presents it. Figure 8.5 shows the structure of a typical CORBA implementation, recast into our notation. In our discussion of CORBA, we will concentrate on how this structure, and the functionality it partitions, achieves the required OMA quality attributes.

First, though, a bit of terminology is in order. Figure 8.4 differentiates client from object implementation. A *client* is a computer program that makes requests of services provided by an object implementation. Of course, an object implementation (or just *object* where this is not confusing) can be a client of other objects. Thus, it is also often useful to distinguish between clients, which can be application programs or objects, and *pure clients*, which are not objects and provide no services that can be accessed via an ORB.

Both clients and object implementations use the same ORB interface (the same for ORBs from any vendor) to do ORB bookkeeping such as binding to an ORB and binding to an object implementation. The individual clients and object implementations could use either a static interface where the interface is described at specification time and does not change for the life of the execution or a dynamic interface where the client dynamically determines the details of the

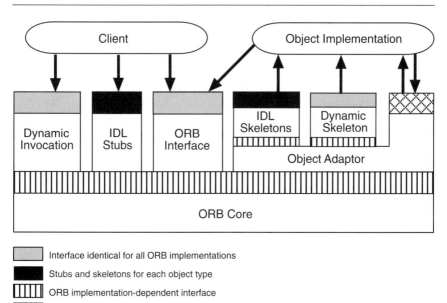

FIGURE 8.4   The structure of CORBA-compliant ORBs as presented by OMG.

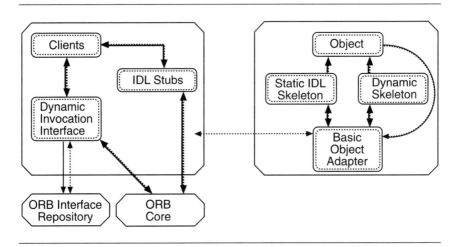

FIGURE 8.5   An example CORBA-compliant implementation.

object implementation's interface. In this discussion, we will focus on the static interface description for simplicity.

Objects in the OMA are described via the OMG's interface description language (IDL). As its name suggests, IDL describes the interface, *not* implementation details, to objects. In fact, this is an important property because clients of objects may assume nothing more about objects than is specified by their interface and perhaps narrative prose concerning the "semantics" of an operation defined in an IDL. A sample IDL is illustrated in Figure 8.6. Although the banking abstraction illustrated is not realistic, it illustrates a number of interesting points. First, C++ programmers will be instinctively familiar with IDL. Replace the IDL keyword `interface` with the C++ keyword `class` and remove the IDL keywords `readonly` and `attribute` (`attribute` is just syntactic sugar anyway), and the example would be legal C++ code.

Why is this important? Recall that one of the OMA quality attributes was that it must be readily implementable with available technology and work well with existing development technology (*buildability*). Selecting a C++-like syntax for IDL made the task of generating C++ code from IDL simpler than it would have been had a more abstract IDL syntax been chosen. Also, the C++ flavor satisfies the principle of least surprise (i.e., don't introduce new concepts where old ones will do). Since C++ programmers constitute the largest object-oriented developer market, meeting them at least halfway was appropriate.

On the other hand, IDL is also considerably more restrictive in interface description capability than is C++. For example, most C++ programmers would overload the account-creation operations defined in `Bank` to be just `open_account` or something similar. Why does IDL not allow overloading? Because overloading is not supported by all programming languages (e.g., C, Fortran). Supporting overloading

```
interface Account {
        readonly attribute string name;
        readonly attribute float balance;
        void deposit (in float amount);
        void withdraw (in float amount);
};

interface CheckingAccount: Account {
        readonly attribute float overdraft_limit;
        void order_new_checks();
};

interface SavingsAccount: Account {
        float annual_interest();
};

interface Bank {
        CheckingAccount open_checking(
                in string name, in float starting_balance);
        SavingsAccount open_savings(
                in string name, in float starting_balance);
};
```

FIGURE 8.6   IDL for a simple bank abstraction.

in IDL would interfere with the objective of making CORBA work with hetero-geneous technologies (i.e., *buildability* and *interoperability*).

Of course, it would still be possible to support overloading in IDL and to then define "name-mangling" approaches for generating nonoverloaded interfaces in languages such as C. However, although this might produce a more elegant and more object-oriented IDL, it would make the IDL translators more complex, make them more costly to develop, and perhaps have a negative effect on both time to market and on the development of IDL processors for non-object-oriented languages. This, in turn, would interfere with OMG's objective of getting OMA implementations rapidly into the marketplace for as diverse a set of platforms and technologies as possible (*buildability*).

Note that IDL is used to specify the interfaces described in Figure 8.4, in particular the ORB interface, dynamic invocation interface, dynamic skeleton interface, and interfaces to the basic object adaptor and interface repository (neither of which is explicit in Figure 8.4). IDL is also used to describe the interfaces of CORBAServices and, when they become sufficiently mature, CORBAFacilities. The use of IDL as a means for describing the OMA helps define interface function-ality while leaving implementation details unspecified; this is useful for ORB developers (*balanced specificity*). This is also useful for application developers, whether they are developing clients or object implementations, since they are insulated from ORB implementation details, and further, clients are insulated from implementation details of object implementations (*implementation transparency*).

IDL completely defines the interfaces of objects in the OMA. The IDL stubs and skeleton components illustrated in Figure 8.4 are generated from IDL interface specifications. Thus, the banking interface illustrated in Figure 8.6 would be "compiled" by an IDL compiler that generates stubs to be used by clients and skeletons to be used by object implementations. The IDL mapping for a programming language defines the rules for performing this code generation. Thus, C++ client programs would access banking services defined in IDL in the same way, regardless of which vendor's IDL compiler was used. Standard IDL mappings are defined for C, C++, and Smalltalk; mappings for other languages such as Ada 95 have also been defined and are under review.

To illustrate the idea of standard mapping, Figure 8.7 shows a small client program written in C++ that makes use of IDL stubs generated from the specification outlined in Figure 8.6.

The main points to note are as follows:

- In theory, this code will be the same regardless of which vendor's ORB (and IDL compiler) and which C++ compiler are used. Thus, ISVs should be able to write applications that are portable across platforms (at least insofar as using the OMA is concerned).

- The C++ code corresponds quite closely stylistically and syntactically to the corresponding IDL interface definition. In contrast, other language mappings are not quite so direct (although compromises in IDL expressivity ensure that mapping to conventional, non-object-oriented languages is still quite feasible).

- There is nothing special about the source of objects in the OMA—they are returned from ordinary object implementations such as a naming service or a bank. Clients need no vendor "magic" for creating these fundamental units of computation and distribution.

Thus, the insulation of clients and objects from ORB-vendor-specific interfaces, the use of IDL to describe standard interfaces to various components of CORBA (interface repository, ORB, dynamic invocation interface, dynamic skeleton

```
main (int argc, char **argv){
        Bank *PNB = ...// look this up from the naming service
        CheckingAccount *my_checking =
                PNB->open_checking("John Doe", (float) 15,000);
        my_checking->order_new_checks();
}
```

FIGURE 8.7 Sample client-side code for bank abstraction.

TABLE 8.4   How CORBA Supports OMA Quality Attribute Requirements

Goal	How achieved
Buildability	IDL compilers are easily implemented with conventional parser-generator technology.
	The IDL language mappings to C and C++ mesh well with existing software-development practices.
Balanced specificity	CORBA interfaces are defined in IDL, effectively deferring implementation decisions to ORB implementors.
Implementation transparency	Clients can rely only on properties of objects that can be expressed in IDL, effectively providing transparency of implementation details.

interface), and the use of standard mappings from IDL to popular programming languages help the OMA satisfy quality attributes concerning buildability, balanced specificity, and implementation transparency. Table 8.4 summarizes the key points from the preceding discussion.

OBJECT ADAPTORS AND THE BASIC OBJECT ADAPTOR

The use of IDL allows clients and object implementors to access ORB services, but this is only part of what is needed. In addition to providing a means for object implementations to access ORB functions, some means must be established for the ORB to access object implementations. Specifically, the ORB must be able to *activate* object implementations in response to requests from clients and, once activated, the ORB must be able to *deliver* those requests.

There are many ways in which ORB vendors may implement the object model—what an object is, how objects are activated, how they are executed—and this is no trivial matter. Consider the following three alternatives:

1. Use a commercial object-oriented database management system to implement objects, and use the database management system as a runtime environment for executing object methods.

2. Use a shared-library approach to implement objects, where the actual methods are resident with client programs.

3. Use a traditional remote procedure call (RPC) model to implement objects, where objects are implemented as server processes.

Given the OMG's desire to allow implementation latitude (*balanced specificity*), CORBA should allow each of these forms of implementation in a way that still maintains implementation transparency. Unfortunately, the means by which objects are located and activated and by which their methods are executed differ radically among the three alternatives listed above. Because the ORB core must make assumptions about how objects are implemented, there is an implementation dependency between the ORB and the type of technology used to implement the CORBA object model. The developers of object implementations (object providers or application developers) have a similar dependency.

So how should the needs of vendors to be able to exploit existing object technologies and support newly emerging object technologies (*evolvability*) be balanced with the need to provide a stable basis for ISVs to develop object implementations that are portable from ORB to ORB across different vendor ORBs (*implementation transparency*)? The CORBA answer to this question is the concept of object adaptor (refer to Figure 8.4) and the requirement that CORBA-compliant ORBs provide an implementation of a particular kind of object adaptor, known as the basic object adaptor. This is an example of what we call a *wrapper* in Section 15.3. Object adaptors provide the following services to object implementations:

- Generation and interpretation of object references
- Mapping of object references to the corresponding object implementations
- Activation and deactivation of object implementations
- Invocation of methods on object implementations
- Registration of object implementations
- Security

The first four items involve the concept of *object reference*, the means by which clients access the services defined (in IDL) for particular objects. Object references are similar to pointers in conventional programming languages, except that they contain more information than pointers. This additional information enables the ORB to perform functions such as locating and activating object implementations. By having a specialized component in the architecture that can generate and interpret object references and by making the form of object reference opaque to all other components in the architecture (including clients), CORBA allows different object-implementation technologies to be "plugged into" an ORB (*extensibility* and *evolvability*).

But object adaptors cover only the ORB-vendor half of the story. The other half of the story—a uniform approach for developing object implementations—is provided by the basic object adaptor. The *basic object adaptor* supports an implementation approach that is quite traditional in modern operating systems and reflects an RPC model. The basic object adaptor equates object implementations with programs that act as object servers. An *object server* (i.e., a program, typically executed as an operating-system process) can be started per method, a separate program per object, or one program for an arbitrary number of objects. The basic object adaptor is easily implemented on all "real" operating systems.

Figure 8.8 illustrates the role of object adaptors and the basic object adaptor in supporting both ORB extensibility to alternative object technology and in supporting (to some extent) uniformity of interfaces for object implementations. The basic object adaptor provides support for object technologies that are implemented using conventional means provided by most operating systems. Thus, it supports a technical approach and development style that is quite similar to RPC,

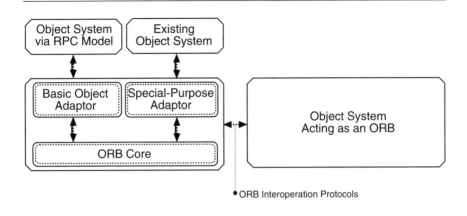

FIGURE 8.8   Object adaptors and integration of alternative object technologies.

is easy to implement using existing and proven technologies, and is standard across all ORBs; this satisfies the buildability quality attribute. Special-purpose adaptors (as illustrated in Figure 8.8) can be developed for other forms of object technology; for example, adaptors for object-oriented database management systems might require database key information in object references, might handle object activation and deactivation differently than the basic object adaptor, etc. The general concept of an object adaptor directly supports the need to allow vendor optimizations and exploitation of new object technologies (*evolvability*).

Figure 8.8 also indicates a third way of introducing new object technologies into CORBA: through interoperation protocols, in this case treating a "foreign" object system as a kind of ORB. The topic of CORBA's interoperation architecture—one aspect of the approach CORBA takes to the question of supporting technology heterogeneity—is considered in the following sections on the CORBA interoperability architecture and interworking architecture. Table 8.5 summarizes the ways in which object adaptors and the basic object adaptor contribute to OMA quality attributes.

CORBA'S INTEROPERABILITY ARCHITECTURE

The ability of clients (pure clients and object implementations that make requests of other objects) to make requests of objects implemented using different vendor ORBs is supported through the CORBA interoperability architecture. It is interesting to note that although interoperability among ORBs is essential to achieving the broadest objectives of the OMA—to provide an open, multivendor infrastructure for component integration to compete with Microsoft's single-vendor solution—the initial CORBA specification did not specify inter-ORB interoperation. It was not until 1995 that the CORBA v2.0 specification dealt directly with the question

TABLE 8.5   How Object Adaptors Support OMA Quality Attribute Requirements

Goal	How achieved
Buildability	The basic object adaptor, in conjunction with the use of IDL stub/skeletons, reflects an RPC approach to the underlying technology and development practices. This approach is mature, implementable on all "real" operating systems, widely used, and well understood.
Balanced specificity	Vendors can develop object adaptors that optimize specific platform capabilities, because the details of which object adaptor is used by an object are transparent to clients of the object. The basic object adaptor itself is not so rigidly specified as to disallow implementation optimizations, for example, optimizations that exploit operating system support for multi-threaded servers.
Implementation transparency	Details of the object adaptor used by an object are transparent to clients of the object.
Evolvability and extensibility	New or alternative object technologies can be integrated with an ORB through the development of special adaptors.

of interoperation. Why the delay? Because inter-ORB interoperation required a degree of vendor cooperation that might have delayed the initial introduction of CORBA. The OMG decided that it was better to get CORBA implementations into the marketplace first and worry about making ORBs interoperable later.

The OMG approach to achieving interoperability was to introduce yet another architecture, the CORBA interoperability architecture. Although what was done in CORBA v2.0 to allow interoperability is not an architecture according to our definition, the OMG calls it an interoperability architecture, and this architecture is based on a number of design goals that augment some of the OMA quality attributes already outlined in Table 8.1. We outline these augmenting quality attributes, taken almost verbatim from the CORBA v2.0 specification, in Table 8.6. Some design goals and quality attributes pertaining to the interoperability architecture (e.g., architecture neutrality, generality, widespread availability) repeat aspects of the OMA requirements and business context already covered in Table 8.1.

TABLE 8.6   CORBA Interoperability Architecture Quality Attributes

Goal	How achieved
Interoperability	Support interoperation of objects implemented on different vendor implementations of the OMA and allow bridges for interoperability of the OMA to other technologies (including Microsoft technology)
Good performance to footprint ratio	Allow high-performance, small-footprint, lightweight interoperability solutions
Backward compatibility	Work with the CORBA-compliant core features of existing ORB implementations
Uniformity	Support all operations implied by the CORBA object model (i.e., no distinction among native and foreign objects in terms of CORBA-defined operations on object references)

The CORBA interoperability architecture uses the concept of bridges that we discuss in Section 15.3. The basic approach is shown in Figure 8.9. Both ORBs in the figure are CORBA compliant, but they do not use the same internal protocols with respect to some concept that they wish to share. The two ORBs communicate to a bridge that provides translation between the internal protocols. Three options are possible, as follows:

1. The bridge is separate as shown in the figure. The bridge is specifically constructed to translate between the protocols of ORB 1 and ORB 2. This leads to a plethora of such bridges and also increases the communication costs, but it has the advantage that neither ORB must be modified to provide interoperate.

2. The bridge is a portion of one of the ORBs, say ORB 1. That is, there is a control as well as a data connection between ORB 1 and the bridge. In this case, it is called a full bridge. ORB 1 is responsible for ensuring that it follows the protocol of ORB 2. This leads to a large number of different protocols that must be supported to ensure interoperability, but it is the most efficient if two vendors wish to cooperate to allow interoperation.

3. The bridge is divided in two between the proxy objects and each half is a portion of one of the ORBs. That is, the bridge is separated, each half is connected to its adjacent ORB using a control and data connection, and the two halves are connected using a data connect. This scheme is called a half-bridge. The two half-bridges communicate using an OMA-defined protocol.

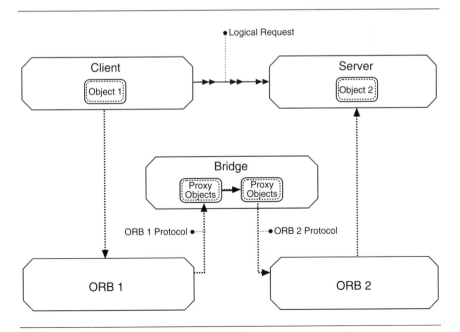

FIGURE 8.9   Use of bridges to achieve CORBA interoperability.

Another way of saying this is that each ORB must support an OMA-defined protocol and is responsible for translating messages received in the OMA-defined protocol into its internal protocol.

8.5 The Web and CORBA

We have seen how the business needs associated with competing with Microsoft and the desire to avoid repeating the experience of PCTE have led to an architecture designed for program extensibility and how the technical aspects of the OMA and CORBA contribute to satisfying the various quality attributes. Evaluating how successful the OMA has been in the marketplace is a different question. Has it been widely adopted, and does it provide an alternative to Microsoft?

One measure, of course, is the number of CORBA-compliant products (i.e., ORBs) that have appeared in the marketplace. Using this measure, the OMA appears to be quite successful, as the following (partial) list of vendors demonstrates: BBN, Digital Equipment, DNS Technologies, ParcPlace, Expersoft, HP, Sun Microsystem, IBM, Iona, and Visigenics. CORBA ORBs are also being developed by university research and development projects, for example, at Stanford, XeroxPARC, and Cornell.

Even more compelling than the number of ORB products is evidence of the use of ORBs in commercial-grade applications (i.e., not just research projects and throw-away prototypes). There is, indeed, indirect evidence of the use of CORBA in "real" application domains. For example, manufacturing, health care, and telecommunications domain task forces have been established by the OMG in response to market demand for CORBA solutions in these different domains. More direct evidence can be found on the home pages of various ORB vendors as a way of advertising their products through testimonials. Iona claims more than a few large-scale uses of their ORB on projects including satellite systems, health care, banking, and trading.

The natural question to ask about the OMA is whether it can somehow exploit the phenomenal growth of Web-based technology, including Java. Alternatively, it is reasonable to ask whether the Web and Java are on the verge of making the OMA obsolete. We take up these questions in turn.

EXPLOITING JAVA AND THE WORLD WIDE WEB

If it is true that mobile and distributed objects are complementary, and that the Web is already a delivery vehicle for mobile objects (via Java), how can the OMA join in? In effect, can the OMA draft in the wake of Java much in the same way that race car drivers and cyclists draft behind their respective front runners? The answer, it turns out, is Yes, and the structure of CORBA has proven resilient enough and flexible to accommodate this. The following paragraphs describe how.

First, we start with the basic notion of a Java "applet," a Java-based computer program that is downloaded from a Web server to a Web browser running at a client location. Applets provide an interface to browsers, which can then make "back" connections to the source of the applet Java code via low-level Transmission Control Protocol/Internet Protocol (TCP/IP) interfaces. What if, instead of using sockets directly, there were some way to access host services at a higher level of abstraction, using CORBA objects instead of sockets? In effect, the Java mobile code would represent a detachable client interface to immobile CORBA objects. The client interface could be a graphical user interface (GUI), or it could perform smart processing on the client machine. In any event, it makes sense to keep some objects remote—maybe they consume too many resources to relocate, or maybe there are administrative or security reasons for not relocating them—while having other objects that are capable of being relocated. It turns out that this scenario is readily implemented using existing browser technology, Java implementations, and CORBA v2.0.

One approach is to generate Java stubs from IDL interface specifications. However, this is insufficient, because stubs typically link in additional ORB code to perform connection management and all the low-level details of interacting with a remote object. One solution is for ORB developers to write their client-side libraries in Java, too, and to download these libraries to the browser at runtime. This is the solution taken by Sun Microsystems' JOE (Java objects everywhere) system. Another nice feature is that if, like JOE, the client-side libraries use the CORBA-defined ORB interoperation protocol, the CORBA-using applet will be able to interact with any CORBA object, from any vendor, anywhere (subject to security restrictions imposed by the browser itself).

Another approach is for the browser to come bundled with an on-board ORB. Thus, given an object reference in the form of a string downloaded to the browser using the conventional HTTP protocol, the on-board ORB could convert the type of the object being referred to and make requests of the remote object. Details about what operations are supported by an object could be acquired by the browser through queries to the remote object's interface repository. Requests could then be made of the object using dynamic invocation. Netscape has announced that the next major release will feature an on-board ORB, so this also seems to be a viable solution to the development of CORBA using applets.

IS CORBA OBSOLETE?

Although Web-based delivery of CORBA objects (or, rather, access to CORBA objects) demonstrates that the OMA was sufficiently flexible to accommodate rapidly emerging changes in distributed computing technology (one of the key OMA quality attributes), CORBA is no longer the only viable distributed-object technology.

For example, Java now supports remote method invocation (RMI), which in effect builds Java-specific ORB functionality into every Java virtual machine. Because Java's RMI is specific to Java, it is more convenient for Java programmers to use than CORBA. For example, interfaces to remote objects can be expressed with Java's own interface definition notation, rather than in IDL, which reflects compromises already described. JavaBeans is a related development, which in many ways mirrors the OMA services built on top of CORBA.

Microsoft has not been idle while its competitors, OMA and CORBA, were being defined and implemented. Microsoft's Distributed Component Object Model (DCOM) supports the distribution of objects. It therefore represents a more direct Microsoft-specific competitor to CORBA for developing distributed Wintel systems. Nor has Microsoft ignored the Java angle. By providing its own Web-browser technology and integration scheme for tying together Java, OLE, browsers, and the like, Microsoft has planted itself on firm footing for competing in the distributed-object technology marketplace.

It is doubtful, however, that the OMA will go quietly into the night. As we have shown in this chapter, the OMA is complex, reflects numerous compromises, and is showing signs of age. However, the qualities that have led to its initial successes—openness, vendor freedom, client-implementation transparency—may serve it well as it struggles for new life in a changing environment.

8.6   Summary

The OMA architecture was developed to serve the business needs of the OMG. These business needs were influenced by the lessons of PCTE, by the competitive pressures of Microsoft, and by the requirement to satisfy the major corporate sponsors of the OMG.

The architecture features a separate infrastructure and an expanding list of services. The quality goals of interoperability and extensibility led to the use of IDL as an integration mechanism. The OMA continues to evolve in response to new competitive pressures, but its basic architectural framework has held up over many years.

8.7   For Further Reading

Much OMG information is available on line. This includes the Object Management Group home page, available at *http://www.omg.org*. The Distributed Software Technology Center in Australia also has a home page with interesting OMG information. It is available at *http://corbanet.dstc.edu.au*.

How CORBA treats security was described by Deng and colleagues [Deng 95], and a comparison of CORBA and OLE was published by Jell and Stal [Jell 95]. Other interesting articles on the OMG and CORBA can be found in *Object Magazine* [Roy 95], [Watson 96]. Hamilton [Hamilton 96] discusses the relationship between Java and CORBA.

8.8 Discussion Questions

1. The discussion of CORBA in this chapter centers around programmatic integration of applications. The discussion of the World Wide Web (WWW) in the previous chapter centered around data integration of applications. What is the major difference between these two approaches? What are the strengths and weaknesses of each? What would be involved in moving CORBA toward a datacentric view or the WWW to a programmatic view?

2. What are the issues involved in using CORBA to obtain real-time performance? To put it another way, what would be involved in maintaining real-time quality of service in a distributed object world (as was required in many of the case studies in this book)?

9

Analyzing Development Qualities at the Architectural Level
The Software Architecture Analysis Method

with Gregory Abowd

> *The Cat only grinned when it saw Alice . . . "Cheshire-Puss," she began, rather*
> *timidly . . . "Would you tell me, please, which way I ought to go from here?"*
> *"That depends a good deal on where you want to go to," said the Cat.*
> *"Oh, I don't much care where—" said Alice.*
> *"Then it doesn't matter which way you go," said the Cat.*
> *"—so long as I get somewhere" said Alice.*
> *"Oh, you're sure to do that," said the Cat, "if you only walk long enough."*
> *— Lewis Carroll, Alice's Adventures in Wonderland*

Alice in Wonderland was, of course, a metaphor for software architecture. (We know this to be true because Carroll's story has been shown to be a metaphor for just about everything.) In this passage, Lewis Carroll was telling us something about analysis of software architectures.

An important role of architecture cited in Section 2.4 was as an early handle for achieving a system's quality attributes. Chapters 4, 5, and 6 discussed how specific quality goals for a system are manifested in architectural decisions. All of the case studies in this book illustrate architectures that satisfy specific quality and behavioral requirements. Since architecture is a key to quality, it follows that analysis of an architecture can (and should) be performed to evaluate it with

Note: Gregory Abowd is a professor at the College of Computing, Georgia Tech University.

respect to how well suited it is for its intended purpose. However, as we infer from Alice's unsatisfying conversation with the Cheshire Cat, analysis is only useful in the presence of clearly articulated goals for the artifact being analyzed. Analyzing an architecture without knowing the exact criteria for "goodness" is like beginning a trip without a destination in mind.

This chapter and the next deal with validation techniques for determining that stakeholder quality goals are met. This chapter introduces the software architecture analysis method (SAAM), a method designed to help articulate those goals and then determine the degree to which an architecture meets them.

An architectural analysis method such as SAAM can be used in two contexts: as a validation step for an architecture being developed or as a step in the acquisition of a software system. SAAM has been used in both contexts, and the results we present here reflect that use.

The best time to evaluate an architecture is early, before problems arise, as part of the standard development process; however, architectural evaluations are often done after the fact by outsiders. As we will see in the next chapter, architectural analysis can be done either in-house (by members of the design team) or by outsiders. Our experience with SAAM has been gained by acting as external consultants, although in some organizations SAAM has been adopted for internal, regular use after we first applied it for them.

9.1 The How and Why of Analyzing Software Architecture

Because of the importance of architectural decisions, it is fitting that they receive close scrutiny. In particular, it is always more cost-effective to evaluate software quality as early as possible in the life cycle. If problems are found early in the software life cycle, they are easier to correct—a change to a requirement, specification, or design is all that is necessary. Software quality cannot be appended late in a project; it must be inherent from the beginning, built in by design. It is in the project's best interest for prospective candidate designs to be evaluated (and rejected, if necessary) during the design phase, before long-term institutionalization occurs. Therefore, an effective technique to assess a candidate architecture—*before* it becomes the project's accepted blueprint—is of great economic value.

Furthermore, when acquiring a large software system that will have a long lifetime within the acquiring organization, it is important that the organization develop an understanding of the underlying architecture of the candidates. This makes possible an assessment of the suitability of the candidates with respect to qualities of importance.

Recall that an architecture cannot guarantee the functionality or quality required of a system. Poor downstream design, implementation, testing, or management decisions can always undermine an acceptable architecture. Decisions at all stages of the life cycle—from high-level design to coding and implementation—will affect quality. Therefore, quality cannot be completely assessed on the basis of an architectural description. An architecture-based assessment provides only one dimension of a system's quality characteristics and is a necessary, but not sufficient, component of evaluating the overall quality of a system. It assesses the ability of the architecture to support the desired qualities. Refinement of the architecture into an implementation that preserves the qualities is necessary for the final product to actually achieve those qualities.

INPUTS TO AND OUTPUTS FROM THE EVALUATION

If the architecture being evaluated is not yet instantiated in a system—as ideally, it should not yet be—what is the basis for the analysis? Obviously a description or specification of the architecture is required. Because, as we have seen, architectures can be described in many levels of detail and from many views, what kind of description or specification is needed for evaluation? The answer is whatever is needed to answer the questions posed by the evaluation technique. If the evaluation will delve into issues of performance or parallelism, a description of the architecture's task and communication structure will probably be required. If modifiability is important, the architecture's decomposition into modules or work assignments will be needed. And so forth. In the beginning of a SAAM analysis, whatever description of the architecture is available is used, and the evaluation proceeds based on this description. If other views or finer-grained depictions of the architecture are needed, SAAM will make their need clear as it progresses.

If two or more candidate architectures are being compared to see which one satisfies its quality requirements more fully, SAAM will produce a relative ranking of the candidates. If a single architecture is being evaluated, SAAM will point out places where that architecture fails to meet its quality requirements and will in some cases show obvious alternative designs that would work better. The results are coarse and broad; this reflects the variance inherent in performing architectural analysis at a very coarse grain.

In no case are absolute numbers on some mythical scale of "architecture excellence" produced. SAAM is predicated on the principle that there is no such scale; an architecture's suitability depends entirely on the context in which it is being developed. The coarse analysis provided by SAAM is justified by its low cost and the ability to apply it very early in the software-development life cycle.

ANALYZING QUALITIES WITH SCENARIOS

People often want to analyze software architectures with respect to quality attributes expressed using words such as maintainability, security, performance, reliability, and so forth. These words provide convenient ways for describing and communicating many common, recurring problems in software. There are even IEEE standards that define many of these quality attributes. However, most software quality attributes are too complex and amorphous to be evaluated on a simple scale, in spite of our persistence in describing them that way. Consider the following two examples:

1. Suppose a system can change the background color of the user interface through a change to a data file, but that same system requires a manual change to dozens of programs to accommodate a new data storage layout. Would you say that this system is or is not modifiable?

2. Suppose the user interface to a system is carefully thought out so that a novice user can use the system with minimal training, but the experienced user finds it so tedious as to be inhibiting. Would you say that this system is usable or not?

The point, of course, is that quality attributes do not exist in isolation but rather have meaning only within a context. A system is modifiable (or not) with respect to certain classes of changes, secure (or not) with respect to specific threats, usable (or not) with respect to specific user classes, efficient (or not) with respect to its utilization of specific resources, and so forth. Statements such as "This system is highly maintainable" turn out to be entirely without operational meaning.

This notion of context-based evaluation of quality attributes has led us to adopt scenarios as the descriptive means of specifying and evaluating quality attributes. A *scenario* is a brief description of a single interaction of a stakeholder with a system. The concept is similar to Jacobson's use cases from the object-oriented community. However, use cases focus on runtime behavior with the stakeholder as the user, whereas SAAM scenarios encompass other interactions with the system as well, such as a maintainer carrying out a modification.

SAAM is a scenario-based method for analyzing architectures; it provides a means to characterize how well an architectural design responds to the demands placed on it by a set of scenarios, where a scenario is a specified sequence of steps involving the use or modification of the system. It is thus easy to imagine a set of scenarios that would test what we normally call modifiability (by proposing specific changes to be made to the system), security (by proposing specific threat actions), performance (by proposing usage profiles that tax resources), and so on.

A scenario actually serves as a representative for an entire class of scenarios. This class consists of all scenarios for which the system under consideration responds in exactly the same way. For example, the scenario "change the background color on all windows to blue" is, under most system designs, essentially equivalent to the scenario "change the window border decorations on all windows." SAAM measures, among other things, how many evaluation scenarios cause changes to the same architectural component; this is called *clustering*. As a consequence, judgment must be exercised as to whether the clustered scenarios represent variations on a similar theme or whether they are substantially different. In the first case, the clustering is a good thing; in the second, it is bad. In other words, if a group of scenarios are similar and they all affect the same component or components in an architecture (i.e., they cluster), that is a good thing because it means that the system's functionality has been modularized in a way that properly reflects the modification tasks. If, on the other hand, a group of similar scenarios affects many different components throughout an architecture, that is bad. We will return to this theme after SAAM has been presented in detail.

As an aid to creating and organizing scenarios, we employ the concept of stakeholders related to the system. Examples of stakeholders include the following:

- The person responsible for executing the software—the end user
- The person responsible for managing the data repositories used by the system—the system administrator
- The person responsible for modifying the runtime functions of the system—the developer
- The person responsible for approving new requirements for the system.

And so on. Stakeholder roles reflect the difference between runtime and developmental qualities, that is, those qualities that are a function of the system's execution (such as performance) and those that reflect operations performed off-line in a development environment (such as modifiability). Scenarios of the former variety would be performed by stakeholders such as end user; scenarios of the latter, by developers or maintainers. One method for discovering the stakeholders of a system is to consider the different business organizations associated with the system—the developers, the acquirers, the marketers, and others.

In summary, SAAM uses scenarios, or concrete descriptions of expected uses of a system, as benchmarks to compare and contrast different candidate architectures. The purpose of SAAM is to provide a way to validate claims about system quality from architectural description, not through vacuous appeal to abstract terms (e.g., our system is scalable). SAAM relies on a description of all candidate architectures that identifies the important components and connections and the overall coordinated behavior of the system. These descriptions are then measured against an agreed set of scenarios to determine the extent to which the candidate architecture supports each scenario or must be modified to support it. Candidate architectures are then compared against each other with attention to how they "perform" for similar scenarios.

9.2   Overview of Software Architecture Analysis Method

In this section, we define the steps of a SAAM evaluation and discuss the interactions among them. Not every SAAM evaluation needs to go through all of these steps. In fact, projects can benefit from performing almost any subset, as some of the case studies will show.

DEVELOP SCENARIOS

Scenarios should illustrate the kinds of activities that the system must support and the kinds of changes that it is anticipated will be made to the system. In developing these scenarios, it is important to capture all important uses of a system, users of a system, and qualities that a system is to satisfy. Thus, scenarios will represent tasks relevant to different stakeholders such as end user, customer, marketing specialist, system administrator, maintainer, and developer. Scenario elicitation requires a certain degree of skill and experience; the SAAM evaluation described in Section 9.4 concentrates on the process of scenario creation.

DESCRIBE CANDIDATE ARCHITECTURE

The candidate architecture or architectures should be described in an architectural notation that is well understood by the parties involved in the analysis. These architectural descriptions must indicate the system's computation and data components as well as all relevant connections. SAAM evaluations have tended to use very simplistic architectural primitives. A typical representation will distinguish between data connections (passing information between components) and control connections (one component enabling another component to perform its function). This simple lexicon provides a reasonable static representation of the architecture. Accompanying this static representation of the architecture is a description of how the system behaves over time, or a more dynamic representation of the architecture. This can take the form of a natural-language specification of the overall behavior or some other more formal and structured specification.

CLASSIFY SCENARIOS

There is an important distinction between scenario types that we introduce at this point. Recall that a scenario is a brief description of some anticipated or desired use of a system. The system may directly support that scenario, meaning that anticipated use requires no modification to the system for the scenario to be performed. This would usually be determined by demonstrating how the existing architecture would behave in performing the scenario (rather like a walk-through simulation of the system conducted in terms of the architectural constructs). If a scenario is not directly supported, there must be some change to the system that we could represent architecturally. This change could be a change to how one or more components perform an assigned activity, the addition of a component to perform some activity, the addition of a connection between existing components, or a combination of these factors.

We refer to the first class of scenarios as *direct* scenarios and the second class as *indirect* scenarios. A scenario is direct or indirect only with respect to a particular architecture. One candidate architecture may execute a scenario directly, and another may require modification before it can be executed. When using SAAM in an acquisition, whether scenarios are direct or indirect is often of great interest and often unknown to the customer before the analysis begins. Obviously, an architecture for which the scenarios of interest are directly supported is more capable than one that requires modification to support those same scenarios, and it will score higher under SAAM.

Having said this, it must be confessed that the distinction between direct and indirect is not a completely reliable indicator of the complexity of a change. Systems might support a scenario directly, but poorly (see sidebar on the next page). Further, a system can be modified in any of several ways: changing source code, changing a data (resource) file that the system reads at start-up, changing some parameters and recompiling, and so on. These degrees of modification must be captured when evaluating a system's response to a scenario.

PERFORM SCENARIO EVALUATIONS

For each indirect scenario, the changes to the architecture that are necessary for it to support the scenario must be listed, and the cost of performing the change must be estimated. A modification to the architecture means that either a new component or connection is introduced or an existing component or connection requires a change in its specification. By the end of this stage, there should be a summary table that lists all scenarios (direct and indirect). For each indirect scenario, the effect or set of changes that the scenario has on the architecture should be described. A weighting of the difficulty must also accompany this stage. Usually, this weighting is coarse grained, based on the understanding of the architecture. A tabular summary is especially useful when comparing alternative architectural candidates because it provides an easy way to determine which architecture better supports a collection of scenarios.

Notice that a monolithic system with little or no substructure will score quite well under this step: Every indirect scenario will require changing only a single component. The next step provides a counterbalance to this result by revealing components that are the focus of too many kinds of changes.

REVEAL SCENARIO INTERACTION

When two or more indirect scenarios require changes to a single component of a system, they are said to *interact* in that component. Scenario interaction is important to highlight because it exposes the allocation of functionality to the product's design. The interaction of semantically unrelated scenarios explicitly shows which system modules are computing semantically unrelated functions. Areas of high scenario interaction reveal potentially poor separation of concerns in a system component. Thus, areas of scenario interaction indicate where the designer should focus subsequent attention. The amount of scenario interaction is related to metrics such as structural complexity, coupling, and cohesion. High interaction among scenarios that are fundamentally different corresponds to low cohesion

"Their Solution Just Won't Work"

The steps of SAAM might suggest that the stakeholders' role is to limited to helping craft the statement of goals for the architecture and then helping articulate the scenarios. However, their presence at the presentation and evaluation of the architecture has been vital on more than one occasion. Only the stakeholders have the depth of knowledge necessary to tell when the architecture—or its presenter—is glossing over an important issue. For example, in the evaluation of the financial management system described in Section 9.4, the SAAM-ites were not expert in the application area of financial management systems. Hence, several exchanges took place during the evaluation such as the following:

SAAM-ite (to vendor). "OK, let's move to the next scenario. Does your system provide that capability?"

Vendor (smiling kindly). "Oh, yes, it sure does. All the user has to do is enter the account number, bring up the accounts receivable table, and transfer the results to the sponsor alert file."

SAAM-ite (nodding, checking "direct" for that scenario, and thinking that this evaluation is going to be easier than he thought). "OK, great. Now the next scenario . . . ."

System user 1 (indignantly). "Wait a minute! You mean there's no way to automatically transfer that data? You're telling me I have to type it all in to *each* alert file?"

Vendor (looking a little nervous). "Um, well . . . ."

System user 1 (sensing vulnerability). "Do you know how many sponsors a major university like this has?"

Vendor (tugging at his collar). "A lot?"

System user 1 (now it's her turn to smile kindly). "Yes. A lot."

System user 2. "And what if I don't know the account number to enter? That was the whole reason you'd initiate this transaction in the first place, right? Because otherwise, you'd just open a payout update voucher."

System user 1 (to the SAAM-ites). "Their solution just won't work."

SAAM-ite (trying to remember what a sponsor alert file is, wondering if he's ever heard of a payout update voucher, and discretely erasing his previous check mark). "OK, well, this sure sounds like an indirect scenario. Now what would you have to change . . . ?"

The point is that expert stakeholders are required to sniff out a problem that outsiders might not catch.

— PCC

and suggests high structural complexity. High interaction among fundamentally similar scenarios signals high cohesion. Therefore, scenario interaction is likely to be strongly correlated with the number of defects in the final product.

OVERALL EVALUATION

If architectures are being compared, a weight should be assigned to each scenario and the scenario interactions in terms of their relative importance, and the weighting should be used to determine an overall ranking of the candidate architectures. The purpose of assigning weights is to resolve the situation in which the first candidate architecture scores well on one half the scenarios, and the second candidate architecture scores better on the other half. Assigning weights is a subjective process involving all of the stakeholders in the system. Rather than offering a single architectural metric, SAAM produces a collection of small metrics, a set of per-scenario analyses. It is left to the users of SAAM to determine which scenarios are most important to them so that they can resolve cases in which the candidates outscore one another on different scenarios. The process of performing a SAAM analysis has also been used to gain a more complete understanding of the competing architectures; this understanding, rather than just a scenario-based table, is useful for performing comparative analysis. The case study of Section 9.4 emphasizes this utility.

Crafting the scenarios and representing the architecture are interdependent steps. Deciding the appropriate granularity for an architecture will depend on the kinds of scenarios you wish to evaluate (although not all scenarios are appropriate, such as a scenario dealing with the number of lines of source code). Determining a reasonable set of scenarios also depends on the kinds of activities you expect the system to be able to perform, and that is also reflected in the architecture.

Figure 9.1 illustrates the steps in a SAAM evaluation, and Figure 9.2 shows the dependencies among SAAM analysis activities.

| Stage 1 | Stage 2 | Stage 3 | Stage 4 | Stage 5 | Stage 6 |
| Scenario development | Architecture description | Classification of scenarios | Individual evaluation of indirect scenarios | Assessment of scenario interaction | Overall evaluation |

FIGURE 9.1   Activities in a SAAM analysis.

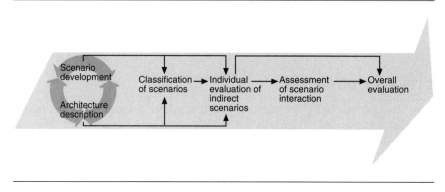

FIGURE 9.2   Dependencies among SAAM analysis activities.

9.3   A Small Example of SAAM Application

In this section, we apply SAAM to the case study first presented in Section 5.5, the keyword in context (KWIC) system. One problem with the analysis presented there was that, even after the presentation of the four structural solutions to the problem, it was unclear how to evaluate and compare these solutions. The original authors of the studies made evaluations of the architectures, but their results were largely intuitive. Our purpose is to illuminate the essential features of SAAM using a small easily understood example that will shed light on how competing architectures can be compared in a repeatable manner. We will concentrate on two of the four structural solutions: the shared memory architecture and the abstract data type (ADT) architecture.

SAMPLE SCENARIOS

The KWIC example has two stakeholders that we will consider: the *end user,* who wishes to produce the KWIC index, and the *developer,* who produces or modifies the code that produces the KWIC index.

Two of the scenarios we use (1 and 2), which have been discussed by various authors, involve the end user. The other two scenarios we will use (3 and 4) involve the developer but are not apparent to the end user. The scenarios are as follows:

1. Make the KWIC program operate in an incremental rather than in a batch fashion. This version of the program would work by accepting one sentence at a time and producing an alphabetical list of all permutations of all sentences that had been given as input to date.
2. Make the KWIC program eliminate entries beginning with "noise" words (articles, prepositions, pronouns, conjunctions, etc.).

3. Change the internal representation of the sentences (e.g., compressed or uncompressed).

4. Change the internal representation of intermediate data structures (e.g., either store the shifted sentences directly or store an index to the shifted words).

CLASSIFYING THE SCENARIOS

We have already represented the architectures in Section 5.5, and so the next step in the method is to classify the scenarios as direct or indirect with respect to each architecture. In this case, each of the scenarios that we have chosen for evaluation of the KWIC architectures is indirect. None can be directly executed by either candidate architecture, so all of the evaluation is dependent upon some modification to the architecture.

EVALUATING THE CANDIDATE ARCHITECTURES

The next step in the method is to evaluate the architectures against the scenarios. The evaluation begins by considering each of the scenarios in turn. Figures 9.3 and 9.4 show the two architectures annotated with the scenarios (the numbers in the various computational components).

Scenario 1.   The first scenario is to operate not in a batch mode but in an incremental mode. That is, operate on one sentence at a time rather than inputting all of the sentences and operating on the total input.

For the shared-memory solution, this requires a modification of the Input routine so that it yields control after each sentence. Master Control must be modified because the sequencing among the subordinate routines is going to be repetitive rather than calling each routine only once. The Alphabetizer will need to be modified because an incremental algorithm, such as insertion sort, must be used rather than one that sorts all of the sentences at once. Presumably, the Circular

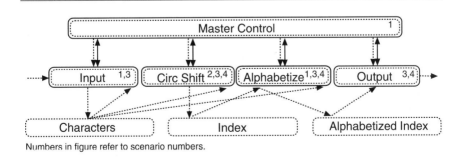

Numbers in figure refer to scenario numbers.

FIGURE 9.3   KWIC—shared memory solution.

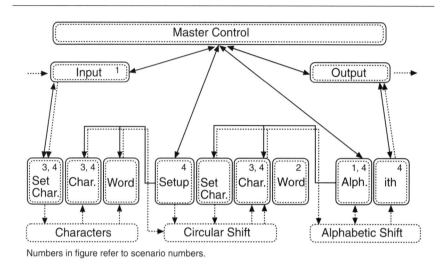

Numbers in figure refer to scenario numbers.

FIGURE 9.4 KWIC—ADT solution.

Shift routine operates on one sentence at a time and the output function outputs whatever is available whenever it is called.

Remember from Section 2.1 that architecture includes behavioral specifications of the components. We don't really have those in this example and so are reduced to making reasonable assumptions in order to proceed. In an actual application of SAAM, the reviewers would either have access to those specifications should the need arise or at least access to an authoritative source of information about the components.

For the ADT solution, shown in Figure 9.4, the Input function must be changed so that only one line at a time is provided as input each time it is called. The Characters abstraction is assumed to be implemented to relinquish control when it has stored its input. Since it receives input one sentence at a time, this need not be changed. The Circular Shift abstraction is also assumed to be implemented to request and shift all available sentences when it is invoked. Thus, this routine also does not need to be modified. The Alphabetic Shift abstraction must be modified as in the shared-memory example. For this scenario, because both candidate architectures have been affected equally, we rate the two architectures as a tie.

Scenario 2. The second scenario is the elimination of noise words. This change is most easily performed by modifying the Circular Shift function in both architectures to eliminate those shifted sentences beginning with noise words. Because the shifter function is localized in both architectures and because noise-word elimination does not affect the internal representation of the sentences, the difficulty of making this modification is equivalent for the two architectures.

Scenario 3.   The third scenario is the modification of the internal representation of an input sentence (e.g., moving from an uncompressed representation to a compressed representation). In the shared-memory architecture, all functions directly access the common representation for the data, and so all of the functions are affected by this scenario, except for the Master Control. In the ADT architecture, the internal representation of the input is an implementation secret that is hidden by the Characters abstraction. Thus, only this abstraction needs to be changed to satisfy this scenario in the ADT architecture. The ADT architecture scores better here.

Scenario 4.   In this scenario—changing the representation of the intermediate data structures—we observe that the shifting and alphabetizing functions maintain indices to the input sentences and only one copy of the input sentence exists.

   For the shared-memory example, this requires a modification of the Circular Shift, the Alphabetizer, and the Output routines. For the ADT solution, it requires a modification of the Circular Shift and the Alphabetic Shift ADTs. Thus the ADT solution affects fewer components and is superior for this example. Figures 9.3 and 9.4 have both been annotated to reflect the influence of each scenario.

Scenario Interaction Analysis.   Examining the candidate architectures to determine which one has more scenario interaction (components with more than one scenario annotation), we see that the ADT is superior in this regard. Although both architectures show scenario interaction in four components, in the shared-memory solution, the contention is among three of the scenarios in two components (Circular Shift and Alphabetize), whereas no component in the ADT solution has contention from more than two tasks.

SUMMARY OF EVALUATION

Table 9.1 summarizes the results of the SAAM evaluation. A 0 indicates that neither architecture is superior with respect to this scenario. In a real evaluation, the evaluation would conclude by weighting the scenarios to represent the organization's priorities. For example, if the addition of functions were the primary concern (as represented by scenario 2), the two architectures would be ranked closely because they do not differ with respect to this task.

   If, on the other hand, a change in the internal representation of sentences (as represented by scenario 3) were of primary concern to the organization, the ADT solution would be superior.

TABLE 9.1   Summary of SAAM Evaluation

Architecture	Scenario 1	Scenario 2	Scenario 3	Scenario 4	Contention
Shared memory	0	0	−	−	−
Abstract data types	0	0	+	+	+

9.4   SAAM Applied to a Financial Management System

This section applies SAAM to an actual financial management system. SAAM can be applied to help choose between the product architectures of competing commercial vendors. The example presented here highlights the scenario selection process, discussing in detail how the reviewers and stakeholders collaborated to produce the set of scenarios against which the products were to be judged. It also illustrates how an architecture review leads to a deeper qualitative understanding of a system design by providing insights into the broad principles that led to the design.

CHOOSING SCENARIOS AND ACHIEVING DEEP UNDERSTANDING

In SAAM, scenarios play a pivotal role. The entire evaluation process revolves around characterizing an architecture in terms of how well it supports (directly by operation or indirectly by facilitating the necessary accommodation) those scenarios that represent the stakeholders' overriding concerns.

The goals for the choice of scenarios are that there be a sufficient number to reflect the views of all of the stakeholders, that they reflect the important quality requirements, that they reflect a variety of different types of possible activities with the system, and that there be a manageable number.

How are scenarios chosen? We have seen that choosing is an interactive process between the evaluators and the stakeholders of the evaluation process. In this section, we describe a process for producing scenarios that was quite successful in a recent application of SAAM. The process was structured and led to a manageable set of scenarios in a reasonable amount of time, and the scenarios were effective at uncovering issues of architectural importance in a competitive situation.

BACKGROUND

The application for this SAAM exercise was a large financial accounting and management system for a major university. The acquisition process had narrowed the field down to two competing vendors. Feeling that the systems being offered were roughly equal in capability, the customer was looking for another evaluation criterion with which to help make the choice. SAAM was offered as a way to illuminate the likely robustness of each system over a long life cycle of evolution, during which its functionality would be continually enhanced.

A characteristic of this situation was that it was clear that neither competing system fulfilled all of the requirements in terms of functional capability. Neither system would simply be delivered off the shelf; a complex implementation phase was part of both proposals. Before SAAM, during the demonstrations and vendor presentations, the customer's representatives asked detailed questions about how to accomplish a precisely detailed set of operations and functions. The answers were often vague, so the users could not always confirm that a system would perform an operation as required.

In SAAM terms, the users had already presented the vendors with operational scenarios that the users *hoped* were direct scenarios. In many cases, they were unable to ascertain whether they were direct. This was the situation when the architectural evaluation process began.

SCENARIO SELECTION PROCESS

The scenario selection process proceeded as follows. First, a four-hour meeting was scheduled. Present were nine representatives of the procuring agency, users and programmers of the university's current financial management system, and users and programmers of systems that shared interfaces with the current system. Many had participated in the procurement and selection process up to its current state and so were familiar with the offerings of the competing vendors.

Two SAAM experts (two of this book's authors) also attended. Before the meeting, we, the SAAM experts (SAAM-ites), read the customer's request for information in which requirements were set forth, as well as the vendors' literature about their systems. This helped us to prepare tentative modification scenarios to keep handy to stimulate discussion. Our function was to ensure that scenarios represented a variety of different types of change and that the concerns of all stakeholders were accounted for in the final set.

An agenda was provided beforehand. A timekeeper, facilitator, and scribe were appointed. The agenda provided time for presentation of the SAAM method, creation and discussion of the initial set of scenarios, and selection of the final scenarios to be used in the evaluation.

After the SAAM method was described, we asked the other attendees if they believed that the process we described would help uncover useful information that would help them make a more informed decision. This allowed the following concerns to be raised:

- Does locality of change necessarily yield lower cost?
- Might there not be contractual mechanisms to achieve low-cost change in spite of the architecture?
- Would SAAM help uncover whether a system actually provided a needed capability?
- How would we know if the vendor representatives were being factual?

And so forth. One of the benefits of this interaction was that the non-SAAM-ites could become comfortable with the SAAM-ites and the type of activity that was under way.

A brainstorming session was conducted in which the attendees posed operational scenarios (usually in the form of operational capabilities that they felt they needed). The scribe wrote down all the suggestions on flip charts. Since the SAAM-ites were unfamiliar with the application except in the most general of terms, they asked clarifying questions as needed and suggested their own scenarios when discussions lagged.

This process produced an unstructured list of almost 50 "protoscenarios." These were recorded on flip charts as phrases such as the following:

- Degraded operation
- New DB platform
- Flex-time
- Sponsored research capability
- WWW client access
- Bottom-up by-person percent budgeting
- Double number of users

The goal of the meeting then became one of choosing the dozen or so "best" candidates for scenarios. This winnowing process took several steps but could have stopped as soon as the desired number had been reached.

First, we asked the participants to reject protoscenarios that represented capabilities deemed of minor importance by the university. Representatives were chosen from the remaining protoscenarios based on this question: "Is the answer likely to be revealing about the architecture?" If the answer was Yes, the group considered whether it was likely to reveal something about the architecture over and above some other candidate from the same cluster. If not, the candidate was deleted or merged with another candidate. If it was, the candidate remained in the running. Of course, whether a scenario is "revealing" about the architecture is a function of the architecture, which the SAAM-ites had not yet seen. This judgment was based on the intuition of the SAAM-ites and the group.

In most clusters, the group was able to articulate a general statement of the concern that was represented by several individual protoscenarios, thus merging many into a few.

At the end of this process, eleven candidates remained, with at least one from each cluster. This was comfortably close to our goal of a dozen. One was added by acclamation because the group was keenly interested in whether either system could provide the capability it described. In SAAM terms, the group wanted to know if the scenario was direct or not.

The next day, the SAAM-ites turned the protoscenarios into actual scenarios. Close inspection revealed that two were special cases of two others, and these were merged, leaving ten. They were e-mailed to all of the meeting attendees for comment, which resulted in minor wording changes to three of the scenarios. The resulting scenarios were mailed to the vendors so that they could prepare their presentations. Table 9.2 lists the scenarios.

TABLE 9.2   Scenarios for the Financial Management System Analysis

Type of Scenario	Characteristics
1. Bottom-up by-person percentage budget, actuals, and forecasting	A user wants to construct a budget, collect actual effort, and perform forecasting by assigning percentages of people to projects (where people may be assigned to several projects in this way) and then constructing project budgets, department budgets, etc., based on these percentages and reporting actual dollars based on percentage of effort.
2. Multiple fiscal year budgets	A user wants to examine budgetary and actual data under different fiscal years without reentering project data.
3. Ability to add major new functionality, tightly integrated with existing functionality	What are the options for integrating major new functionality? For example, how might a Grants Administration function be added to the as-delivered FMP system so that users can use and combine new data with preexisting data with no more effort than combining preexisting data?
4. Exception mail, items in red on screen	The user wants to define exception conditions corresponding to the data, have the system notify a defined list of recipients by e-mail of the existence of an exception condition, and have the system display the offending conditions in red on data screens.
5. Degraded operation mode	A user wants to continue to operate the system (perform useful work) in the presence of one of the following kinds of failures: database server, application server, or partial network failure.
6. Web clients	A user wants to access and modify data via a World Wide Web client.
7. Data transmitted in encrypted form	A user wants to encrypt data (not just passwords) being sent over a network.
8. Non-Web remote access	A user wants to access and modify data from a home computer of some sort and of different type or configuration than the user's office computer.
9. Integration with a variety of e-mail systems	A user wants to attach screen information to an e-mail message and transmit it under a variety of e-mail systems.
10. Upgrade to any system component	What is the cost (in time) and frequency of adapting to upgrades of individual system components such as X11, CPUs, operating systems, and GUI packages?

OBSERVATIONS ON THE SCENARIO SELECTION PROCESS

The relatively short duration of the meeting, its structured agenda, and the high stakeholder interest usually allow the use of the vague protoscenarios as the basic means for communication and winnowing. In this case, although the terms were vague, the discussion about each one was crisp. Ambiguity was surprisingly rare, and everyone could always remember who had proposed a question in the first place if clarification was needed, which the proposer was consistently able to supply.

It is common in scenario generation for the participants to try to resurrect requirements that did not make the original cutoff. It is important to avoid rehashing disputes about what requirements will be satisfied by an initial release of a system.

Granularity of the scenarios matters; proper granularity is a function of the architectures presented and also how those architectures are described. For example, in this exercise, two of the scenarios turned out to be of the wrong granularity. Scenario 4 referred to identifying error conditions in red. The intent of the scenario was to require that error conditions be visually highlighted in some way; the choice of red was arbitrary. One vendor could support the general scenario directly (by using inverse video) but could not support color. If the intent had been realized, it would have been a direct scenario for that vendor. Scenario 3 dealt with the addition of major new functionality. This scenario was too broadly worded to elicit many details about the architectures. On the other hand, it did elicit a discussion about the philosophy of incorporating major changes that was illuminating about both vendors' architectures.

SUMMARY OF SCENARIO SELECTION PROCESS

In summary, to produce the scenarios, the following steps are involved:

- Method presentation
- Participant buy-in and expression of concerns and issues
- Brainstorming session to produce unstructured list of protoscenarios
- Refinement and selection
  - Marking each candidate as likely or unlikely; discarding unlikely ones
  - Clustering remaining candidates into five or six groups by subject area
  - Ranking each member of each cluster by criticality
  - Ranking each member of each cluster by its likelihood to reveal important aspects of the competing architectures
  - Merging or deleting candidates that would probably reveal no additional information about the appropriateness of the architecture
- Wordsmithing of the winning candidates; distribution to participants for review and to vendors to enable them to prepare for evaluation

RESULTS OF FINANCIAL MANAGEMENT SYSTEM EVALUATION

The last step of SAAM is to provide the overall evaluation of the candidate architecture. As indicated previously, this evaluation can be presented in the form of a table showing how each architecture fared on each scenario. Often, however, the customer for the evaluation will desire a more qualitative outcome or comparison of the architectures. Scenarios, after all, often serve as single representatives of larger classes of similar issues.

The following is an excerpt from the final report for the financial management system evaluation; the names of the vendors have been deleted, and identifying details have been changed to protect their identities. First, the results of the scenarios are presented. Following that, however, a broader understanding emerged of the ways in which the philosophies underlying the two architectures differed. These philosophies are described and their implications discussed in general terms.

In this case, the customer for the evaluation found the broad generic comparison at least as helpful as the scenario evaluations and considered that the report would have been incomplete without it. The sidebar below is an excerpt from the final report.

Financial Management Systems Final Report Excerpt

Based on the performance of each system under the ten scenarios, we produced Table A.

In Table A, a + means that the system supports the scenario directly as part of its as-delivered capability. A 0 means that the system would have to be regenerated (e.g., changing resource files and recompiling) in order to achieve the desired capability; this is a much easier change than modifying source code, but is a change nonetheless. A – indicates that the scenario cannot be performed by the delivered system, but requires an implementation change to be supported.

Scenarios in which both vendors scored + are a clear tie—both systems already provide the indicated capability.

Scenarios in which both vendors scored a – (per-person budgeting, new functionality, component upgrades) indicate areas in which both systems would have to be modified significantly to achieve the desired effect. It was our feeling that both vendors' systems were reasonably modifiable with respect to the security authorization scenario. The other two scenarios were similar in that both added unanticipated functionality. Vendor 2 provides extensive support for customers writing their own applications, but the steps

TABLE A

Scenarios	Vendor 1	Vendor 2
Per-person budgeting	–	–
Multiple fiscal years	+	+
New functionality	–	–
Exception mail, highlight screen	0 [a]	0
Degraded operation mode	+	+
Web clients	+	0
Encrypted data	–	+
Non-Web remote access	+	+
Component upgrades	–	–

a. Vendor 1 receives a 0 for this scenario if the requirement is to highlight the error condition in a visually distinguished form, such as reverse video, but a - if the requirement is to highlight the condition on the screen in another color.

would be similar under both systems: identify new tables, identify new applications (or applications that could be enhanced to accommodate the new functionality), and design new forms and screens.

Scenarios in which one vendor scored higher than another (where + is higher than 0 which is higher than −) highlight an area in which that vendor's system is superior.

Our summary evaluation is that the Vendor 1 architecture is more flexible than Vendor 2's with respect to changes to the presentation portion of a system or with respect to the types of database engines that can be used within the system. Vendor 2 applications are more vertically integrated than are Vendor 1 applications and Vendor 1 applications are more horizontally integrated than are Vendor 2 applications.

What Is Meant by "Integrated" and "Flexible"?
Under the Vendor 1 architecture, the database engine(s) may come from a variety of vendors: it could be an Oracle database, an Ingres database, or a Sybase database. Under the Vendor 2 architecture, however, the database engine can only come from a single source. Thus, Vendor 1 is more flexible than Vendor 2 is with respect to the underlying database engine.

On the other hand, Vendor 2's presentation and applications layers are written to take advantage of features that are known to be implemented in the database engine that it uses. For example, the Vendor 2 database engine can delete all occurrences of an employee when the employee leaves the university. Thus, a human resources application that is invoked when an employee leaves the university can be much simpler (easier to write and understand, and producing less network traffic) than one that cannot assume the availability of that feature from the underlying database engine. This is what is meant by *vertically integrated applications*. Since Vendor 1 allows a variety of different types of data base engines, applications written for Vendor 1 must assume the "least common denominator" in terms of database capability, although this is mitigated somewhat by the abstract interface to the database that Vendor 1 provides. . . .

A final type of integration, *horizontal integration of applications*, is not apparent from the initial presentations became apparent during the discussions with the two vendors. Vendor 1 applications are more horizontally integrated. For example, the ability to send e-mail is given to the workflow manager in a Vendor 1 system; if another application wishes to have e-mail sent, it must notify the workflow manager. Any Vendor 2 application could, in principle, send e-mail. The consequence of this is that a Vendor 2 application is easier to create (since it need not worry about conforming to as many constraints) but that Vendor 1 applications are easier to modify. Using our e-mail example, again, suppose the university wished to e-mail a new type of information to an individual. In a Vendor 2 system, each application that sends that type of e-mail would need to be modified. In Vendor 1's system, only the workflow manager would need to be modified (assuming it knew about the information to be sent).

A last distinction became apparent when the two vendors discussed their philosophies for adding new functionality. Vendor 1 would tend to first try to identify existing components that could be "stretched" to accommodate the new functionality; for example, administering grants might be considered a type of customer management because both customers and sponsors produce income. Vendor 2 would tend to write a new component to accommodate the functionality; for them, grants administration would be a new product. These philosophies could have business implications. Vendor 1 tends to fold improvements made for a specific customer back into their product line and, thus, they would be available to all of their customers; Vendor 2 tends to create new and separate user-specific products that might not have the general-purpose capabilities necessary to make them useful to other customers.

Implications of Integration and Flexibility
In general, systems that are integrated in one dimension or another are easier to modify in that dimension and more difficult to modify in the other dimension. We elaborate this notion in Tables B and C.

TABLE B

Feature	Positives	Negatives
Flexibility in database engine	Allows for use of different types of database engines	Does not allow vertically integrated applications
Vertical integration of applications	Simpler to implement application Better performance	Does not allow easy replacement of underlying database engine Some modifications may require changing all applications
Flexibility in presentation	Easier integration of new presentation mechanisms	Increased network traffic Additional CPU requirements to transform representations Difficult to get uniform look and feel for applications
Horizontal integration of applications	Easier to modify since functionality is localized	More difficult to initially implement applications

TABLE C

	System	
	Vendor 1	Vendor 2
Flexibility in database engine	yes	no
Vertical integration of applications	no	yes
Flexibility in presentation	yes	no
Horizontal integration of applications	yes	no

Thus, if downstream modifications to existing applications are assumed to be the highest risks, Vendor 1 will be a better system than Vendor 2 because it has flexibility in the database engine, does not have vertically integrated applications, has flexibility in presentation,[1] and has horizontally integrated applications. On the other hand, if addition of large amounts of new functionality after initial delivery is assumed to be the highest risk, or if performance is perceived to be a crucial issue, Vendor 2 will be a better system than Vendor 1 since its applications are vertically, but not horizontally, integrated.

[1] Flexibility in presentation refers to the ability to adopt totally new presentation paradigms, such as display via a World Wide Web browser. It does not refer to the ability to define layout and appearance of screens and forms, which both systems adequately provide.

9.5   SAAM Applied to a Revision-Control System

In this example, we describe the application of SAAM to a commercially available revision-control system, based on RCS, which we will call WRCS. WRCS enables project developers to create archives, compare files, check files in and out, create releases, back up to old versions of files, and so on. *Project* in this context means any group of related files that, when linked together appropriately, form a finished product. For example, these files might be source code for a computer program, text for a book, or digitized audio and video for the creation of a video clip.

SYSTEM CONTEXT AND PURPOSE

WRCS keeps track of changes made to files as they evolve over time. It allows multiple users to work on the same project within their own private work areas. It also allows each developer to modify and test the system in isolation, without disturbing other developers' work and without corrupting the primary copy of the system. Managerial functions, such as report production, are also provided. WRCS's functionality has been integrated with several program-development environments and can be accessed through these tools or through WRCS's graphical user interface.

SCENARIO AND ARCHITECTURE ELICITATION

In this section we present the steps of SAAM taken to arrive at an architectural evaluation of WRCS. For an evaluation to take place, SAAM requires an architectural representation of the product with a well-specified semantic interpretation (principally what it means to be a component or a connector). Creating an architectural description proved to be one of the most difficult tasks in evaluating WRCS. At the start of this evaluation there was no architectural description of the product, so we began by eliciting this information.

This information had to be analyzed and grouped in a way that would aid the construction of an architectural diagram. Our sources of information were limited. These consisted of interviews with members of the development team, the product's documentation, and the product itself. We had no access to the source code or the product's specifications because software architecture is not supposed to concern itself with code. In essence, our task was reverse engineering: to create a design document out of a finished product.

We developed the product's architectural description iteratively. At each stage, we studied the product's existing description, the product itself (namely, its executables and libraries), and its documentation and then devised new questions. The answers to the questions in each stage helped us clarify and refine the current description. Each new stage allowed us to gain more insight into the product and to generate new questions for the next stage. Since we did not have any representation from which to begin, we chose to begin with a gross listing of the modules along with their basic relationships. From this start we iterated, adding structure as we went. The process of eliciting scenarios helped to clarify the architecture. It took three iterations to obtain a representation that was satisfactory for architectural evaluation. This representation is shown in Figure 9.5.[1]

During the process of describing the architecture, we continually developed scenarios that represented the core values of the stakeholders in the system. For WRCS these stakeholders were users, developers, maintainers, and system administrators. Scenario enumeration is simply a form of requirements elicitation and analysis. These scenarios were developed in discussion with all the stakeholders in the system as a way to characterize all current and projected uses of the system. The scenarios formed the basis for all further architectural evaluation. The scenarios were a subset of the scenarios elicited from the WRCS domain expert.

In total we studied 15 tasks, 6 of which we present here. A complete evaluation of a complex system would involve dozens of scenarios. The following scenarios relate to the user:

Compare binary file representations.   Compare binary files generated by other products. For example, FrameMaker files are stored in a binary representation. But when we are comparing two versions of a FrameMaker file, we want to see our editing changes in a human-readable form, and not the changes to the binary codes stored in the files.

Configure the product's toolbar.   Change the icons and actions associated with a button in the toolbar.

The scenarios that concern the maintainer are as follows:

Port to another operating system.

Make minor modifications to the user interface.   Add a menu item or change the look and feel of a dialog box.

---

[1] Figure 9.5 and all other figures in this section showing architectural descriptions are modified from the originals. The exact details of these architectures are proprietary and do not affect the conclusions.

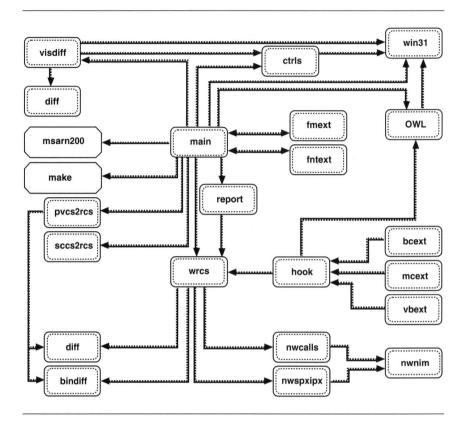

FIGURE 9.5   Architectural representation of WRCS.

The scenarios of the administrator are listed below:

Change access permissions for a project.

Integrate with a new development environment.   Attach, for example, to Symantec C++.

Performing Scenario Evaluations

After categorizing each scenario as direct or indirect, we proceeded to consider the impact of each of the indirect scenarios on the architecture individually.

Per-Scenario Analysis.   At this stage, we want to estimate the difficulty of the change (say, in terms of person-hours required). The change might simply require the modification of an ASCII resource file and a restart of the product, in which case the architectural implications of this indirect scenario are minimal. One might need to change an internal table and recompile, in which case the implications of the scenario are moderate. Or one might need to dramatically recode a component, in which case the implications are considerable.

We indicate the nature of the scenarios and the WRCS modules they affect in Table 9.3.

Revealing Scenario Interactions.   Different indirect scenarios may necessitate changes to the same components or connections. Determining scenario interaction is a process of identifying those indirect scenarios that affect a common set of components. This determination is important because it highlights components that will be affected by multiple modifications. Scenario interaction measures the extent to which the architecture supports an appropriate separation of concerns. For each scenario, the components or connections affected by that scenario must be determined. SAAM favors the architecture with the fewest such scenario contentions *as long as the scenario contentions represent fundamentally different scenarios.*

Table 9.4 shows the number of changes required in each module of the system. In this table, we account for *all* the relevant scenarios elicited in the WRCS analysis, not just the six presented in the preceding section.

TABLE 9.3   Scenario Evaluations for WRCS

Scenario	Description	Direct/ Indirect	Changes Required
1	Compare new binary file representations	Indirect	This requires modifications to **diff** (to make the comparison) and **visdiff** (to display the results of the comparison).
2	Configure the product's toolbar	Direct	
3	Port to another operating system	Indirect	All components that call win31 must be modified (specifically, **main**, **visdiff**, and **ctrls**). If the target operating system does not support OWL, either OWL or all components that call OWL (specifically, **main** and **hook**) must be ported. If the new operating system is not supported by Novell's software, **wrcs** must be modified to work with new networking software.
4	Make minor modifications to the user interface	Indirect	This will require changes to one or more of those components that call the win31 API, specifically, **main**, **visdiff**, and **ctrls**.
5	Change access permissions for a project	Direct	
6	Integrate with a new development environment	Indirect	This requires changes to **hook** as well as the addition of a module along the lines of **bcext**, **mcext**, and **cbext**, which connect the new development environment to **hook**.

TABLE 9.4 Scenario Interactions
by Module for WRCS

Module	Number of Changes
main	4
wrcs	7
diff	1
bindiff	1
pvcs2rcs	1
sccs2rcs	1
nwcalls	1
nwspxipx	1
nwnlm	1
hook	4
report	1
visdiff	3
ctrls	2

SCENARIO EVALUATION MAY LEAD TO A FINER-GRAINED PRESENTATION

Consider the implications of the scenario interaction present in module **wrcs**. This component was tagged by seven different scenarios. What does it mean to have multiple indirect scenarios that affect a single module? There are three possible cases, which follow:

1. The scenarios are all of the same class. That is, they could be variants of the same basic scenario. For this case, the fact that the scenarios are of the same class and cluster together in the same module can be taken to be a good sign. It means the system's functionality is sensibly allocated. Put another way, it means the architecture exhibits high *cohesion* with respect to this class of scenarios.

2. The scenarios are of different classes and module **wrcs** can be further subdivided, but it was not shown subdivided in the original architectural representation. Recall that we said that there is no a priori correct granularity for architectural description but that the scenarios dictate the appropriate level. For example, it might be that module **wrcs** is really composed of three functions, each of which deals neatly with a couple of the scenarios. In this case, the process of scenario-based architectural analysis has helped to refine the detail with which the software architecture of module **wrcs** is presented to represent its true allocation of functionality.

3. The interacting scenarios are of different classes and module **wrcs** cannot be further subdivided. This case reveals a potential problem area within the architecture. If scenarios from different classes are affecting the same module, the architecture is probably not appropriately separating concerns, is probably too complex, and indicates a trouble spot in development and maintenance.

Thus, scenario interaction is not by itself an indicator of architectural quality but leads to questions that either resolve the issue (case 1 or 2) or identify a problem (case 3).

VISUALIZING SCENARIO INTERACTION

The main purposes of software architecture and architectural analysis are to serve as a communication tool within a software team and as a means of documenting the design and design rationale. Therefore we must present the results of an architectural analysis so that they are clearly transmitted and properly emphasize problem areas.

One visualization technique we use to highlight scenario interactions is a fish-eye view. A fish-eye view of a graph shows an area of interest quite large and with detail and shows other areas successively smaller and in less detail. For example, in Figure 9.6, the WRCS architecture is presented with size of the module representation proportional to the number of interacting scenarios that affect

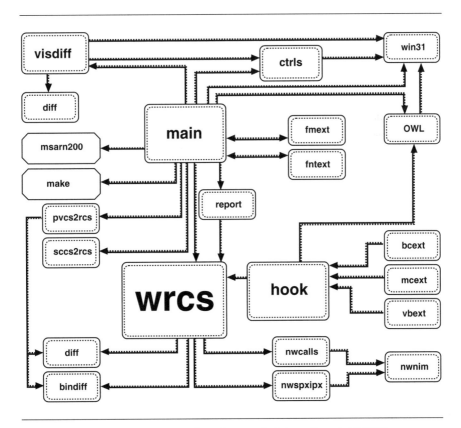

FIGURE 9.6   Fish-eye representation of scenario interactions in WRCS.

it. This figure shows where the scenario interactions lie and the relative scale of the interactions. You can clearly see that the component with most scenario interaction is **wrcs**. Modules **main**, **visdiff**, and **hook** also suffer from high scenario interaction, and **ctrls** has a small amount of scenario interaction.

This information immediately calls attention to the most architecturally problematic features of the system, as it currently exists, and guides designers and developers in their allocation of time and effort. It has proven to be a highly effective device for communication among team members in the WRCS case study. In particular, the representation serves to focus architectural restructuring activities.

Overall Evaluation. Once the scenarios are determined and mapped onto the structural description and all scenario interactions are determined, the implications of the scenarios are made manifest. That is, the changes required by the indirect scenarios have been determined, along with their extent and their interaction with other scenarios. All that remains to be done is to rank these scenarios in priority order to arrive at an overall evaluation of the architecture.

9.6 Observations on SAAM

SAAM is a method that illuminates the management of change and support of different system stakeholders. It relies a great deal on the experience and understanding of the people doing the analysis and, as such, is not a simple "cookbook" approach. A SAAM evaluation will be only as good as the information available to the evaluators. SAAM relies on scenarios that are the explicit articulation of the stakeholders' primary requirements that can be satisfied by the architecture.

This chapter concludes with some observations based on our experience applying SAAM.

THE ROLE OF DIRECT SCENARIOS

Since SAAM focuses on change management, the indirect scenarios appear to take a predominant role in the evaluation step. What about direct scenarios?

First of all, direct scenarios serve as the first-order culling mechanism between competing architectures. An architecture that is thoroughly modifiable to support all the envisioned uses is still less desirable than the architecture that supports those uses directly, and SAAM's scoring will reflect that. Second, direct scenarios turn out to be a good mechanism for eliciting and understanding the dynamics of an architecture or how the parts interact at runtime. Third, the direct scenarios can serve as starting points for analysis of runtime qualities. In SAAM, the cost of carrying out every indirect scenario is estimated. So it can be with direct scenarios. The cost of carrying out a direct scenario is measured in terms of resource utilization, where resources may include time or network traffic (for measuring performance), user effort (for measuring usability), failures consumed out of an allowable maximum (for measuring reliability), and so on. SAAM does not provide any new techniques for assessing these aspects but instead provides a starting point for bringing standard estimation methods to bear.

RESULTS OF SAAM

The results of a SAAM analysis are both technical and social. Technically, the direct output of a SAAM analysis is useful, but also useful is the increased understanding of the architecture that may lead to deeper insights than were previously available. Further, SAAM produces as a by product an explicit statement of the priority-ordered requirements for the architecture. Socially, a SAAM analysis acts as a catalyzing activity on an organization.

SAAM allows insight into system capabilities that could not easily be achieved from inspections of code and design documents. In a simple, straightforward, and cost-effective way, it exposes limitations of a system or design. Not only does it allow an evaluation of differing architectures, but it does this in the context of specific scenarios rather than more general qualities.

The process of defining an architecture necessary for a SAAM analysis is itself useful. All of the participants end up with a better understanding of the architecture under examination, and the organization ends up with an architectural description that has future utility. Furthermore, from a consultant's perspective, conversations with the "owners" of the architecture give insight into philosophies and mind sets that help generate deeper insights into the trade-offs that are implicit in an architecture.

Within an organization, SAAM can act as a communication vehicle. This vehicle enables managers to understand how their business goals are being translated into reality and helps the developers understand what business goals were important to management and how their design either helped or hindered the achievement of those goals. The process of undertaking a SAAM evaluation forces the various stakeholders to communicate, and the scenarios serve as an ideal means for bridging the various views of the system.

STAKEHOLDER PARTICIPATION

Not only are stakeholders crucial in the casting of scenarios, it is also vital to have them present at the presentations of the architectures (see the sidebar on page 196). They can tell the evaluators if a scenario that is technically supported by the system is done in too cumbersome a way to really be considered a direct scenario. Or they may have insights into the cost or complexity of making a change that will be required to support an indirect scenario. Finally, their presence tends to keep the presenters honest and on their toes because end users of a system are much harder to fool than consulting analysts. Not all evaluations are adversarial, of course, but when two competing commercial vendors are presenting their architectures, candor is not always the watchword.

SAAM AND TRADITIONAL ARCHITECTURAL METRICS

Architectural evaluation has an interesting relationship with the more traditional design notions of coupling and cohesion. Good architectures exhibit low coupling and high cohesion in terms of some decomposition of functionality. What does this mean in terms of a SAAM analysis? *Low coupling* means that a single scenario doesn't affect large numbers of components. *High cohesion* means that components are not host to scenario interactions. The implication of this correspondence is that architectural analysis is a means of determining coupling and cohesion in a highly directed manner.

Architectural metrics such as structural complexity, as well as metrics for coupling and cohesion, have been criticized as being crude instruments of measure. SAAM improves on these metrics by allowing one to measure coupling and cohesion with respect to a particular scenario or set of scenarios. In this way the instruments of measure become sharper and hence more meaningful.

For example, in the standard interpretation of coupling, if two components are coupled, they are coupled irrespective of whether they communicate once (say, for initialization) or repeatedly. Similarly, structural complexity measures (based on data inflows and outflows from components) do not consider predicted changes to a given part of the architecture. They simply record a part of the architecture with a high structural complexity as being "bad." The use of scenarios, on the other hand, teases apart these types of cases.

DETERMINING THE PROPER ARCHITECTURAL DESCRIPTION

What is the relationship between scenarios about an architecture and the description used to explain the architecture? As we have already said, one of the benefits of software architecture is the ability to view software abstractly. But the presence of hierarchical structures in software leads to the question of which level of architectural representation is appropriate for presentation during a review. How do the designers of the architecture know what is appropriate? The simple answer is that whatever the scenarios dictate is appropriate. The review will begin using the representation that the designers have prepared, but the scenarios may lead to questions that will be resolved by showing finer-grained representations of the architectural design. High scenario interaction in a component is especially prone to lead to this; interaction may be satisfactorily explained by showing the decomposition of the problematic component and allocating its scenarios to its children. This is exactly what happened when we iterated through our three versions of the representation of the WRCS system.

DETERMINING THE PROPER SET OF SCENARIOS

Given the great emphasis that SAAM places on scenarios, an interesting question is, When have I generated a sufficient number of scenarios to adequately test the architecture? Or, put another way, When should I stop generating new scenarios? There are two possible answers. The simple (and distressingly common) answer is, When you run out of resources.

The more complex, and more meaningful answer involves reflecting on the analysis technique. You can stop generating scenarios when the addition of a new scenario is no longer expected to reveal information about the design, in the judgment of the evaluators. In this way scenario generation is much like software testing: You cannot prove that you have a sufficient number of test cases, but you can determine a point at which the addition of new test cases is providing negligible improvement to the software.

SAAM IN AN OVERALL EVALUATION PROCESS

As suggested earlier, SAAM can serve as a jumping-off point for analysis of system qualities that SAAM itself does not address well. The artifacts produced for a SAAM analysis—the direct scenarios that define the runtime architectural requirements and the representation of the architecture—can be used to perform an architecture-level estimation of performance, reliability, availability, and the like. For example, system reliability can be estimated using standard Markov modeling techniques that project the reliability of the system by reasoning about the reliability of its communicating architectural components, which the SAAM analysis causes to be identified.

In the next chapter, we discuss the results of several gatherings of industrial architecture experts to see what the best industrial practice is for architecture analysis. The concepts of SAAM play a major role in that practice, which augments the basic analysis method with organizational and process concerns.

SAAM as a method can be applied either within a normal development process by developers—as recommended in the next chapter—or by an external team of auditors in the form of a review. Several of the case studies in this chapter fall into the latter category. In Chapter 11, we will describe a high-profile software audit of an air traffic control system in which a SAAM-like evaluation was done by a team of outside consultants.

9.7 Summary

SAAM is a low-cost, coarse-grained method for evaluating an architecture against a set of specific scenarios. In this chapter we have presented the steps of SAAM and given examples from its use.

9.8   For Further Reading

Other architectural analysis methods exist that concentrate on different aspects of the system. For example, Barry Boehm's COCOMO II cost model predicts development time and cost based on architectural information; information about COCOMO II may be found at the World Wide Web site for the Center for Software Engineering at the University of Southern California, */http://sunset.usc.edu.*

Schedulability analyzers such as those based on rate monotonic analysis [Klein 93] can tell whether a set of processes (which are, after all, a variety of architectural component) can be scheduled, given timing parameters for the processes. The process of performance engineering in general is described by Connie Smith [Smith 90, Smith 93].

Ivar Jacobson has described use cases, which are a cousin of scenarios [Jacobson 92].

9.9   Discussion Questions

1.   The distinction between direct and indirect scenarios is a coarse way to measure architectural support for a feature. As we have seen, a direct scenario may be so cumbersome as to be effectively indirect. On the other hand, an indirect scenario may be trivially supported by changing a parameter and recompiling. Propose a finer-grained way to categorize scenarios that takes these considerations into account.

2.   Produce a set of scenarios for an architecture in your organization.

3.   Attendees at an architecture review naturally bring their own agendas to the table, and these agendas often show up in the scenarios they propose. Consider this actual scenario from a recent architecture evaluation using SAAM: Produce a system for the least cost and shortest time possible. What quality attribute of the architecture were they trying to measure? What else were they trying to address? How would you handle this scenario if you were running the evaluation?

10

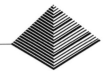

Architecture Reviews

with Gregory Abowd, Linda Northrop, Amy Moormann Zaremski

> *To be good is noble; but to show others how to be good*
> *is nobler and less trouble.*
> — Mark Twain, from
> *Following the Equator*

The use of the software architecture analysis method (SAAM) to analyze architectures (see Chapter 9) is one portion of a systematic review process for architectures. In this chapter we discuss wrapping SAAM (as one technique) into an architecture review and recommend activities to support a review. This chapter, then, is concerned with the process of performing a review: what is reviewed, who the reviewers are, when the review occurs, what the costs and the benefits of such a review are, and so on.

Several portions of the architecture business cycle (ABC) are discussed in this chapter. Most obviously, reviews provide a verification that the path taken from required quality and behavioral attributes to architecture was a sound one. Less obvious is the feedback effect on the organization doing the development. We will discuss, at several points, the maturity of the architecture review process within an organization and the impact of architecture reviews on organizational culture. Since the ABC is organized around artifacts and products instead of processes, this type of feedback does not show up, but it is quite real. Organizations and organizational cultures are changed when activities are institutionalized. The type of review we describe here will have an impact on both organizations and their cultures.

All reviews have certain similarities. The correct people must be identified, information must be provided in advance, and so forth. We will not distinguish in

Note: Gregory Abowd is a professor at the College of Computing, Georgia Tech University.

Linda Northrop is a program manager at the Software Engineering Institute, Carnegie Mellon University.

Amy Moormann Zaremski is a member of the technical staff at Xerox Corporation, Rochester, New York.

our discussion between things that are common to all reviews and things that are specific to architecture reviews. To do so would digress from our point in this chapter.

One natural question whenever anyone proposes a review procedure is, Why bother? Section 10.1 begins this chapter with a discussion of the costs and benefits of an architecture review. Section 10.2 lays out a suite of available review techniques for architecture. Section 10.3 fills in the steps for utilizing the technique of choice in a review.

10.1 Costs and Benefits

There are a number of motivations for performing an architecture review, but there is an associated cost in terms of time and committed resources. An organization must decide whether the benefits are worth the cost.

COSTS

There are three different costs of holding regular architecture reviews; they are as follows:

1. *Staff time.* Three different organizations have provided cost data for architecture reviews.

   a. AT&T, having performed approximately 300 full-scale architecture reviews on projects requiring a minimum of 700 staff days, reported that the average cost of an architecture review was, based upon estimates from individual project managers, 70 staff days.

   b. Rational Software has performed around 30 reviews and charges an average cost of $50,000 for projects of at least 500,000 lines of code in size.

   c. The SAAM reviews done as described in the previous chapter cost approximately 14 to 20 staff days.

2. *Organization overhead for architecture review unit.* Some organizations have established corporate units that are responsible for defining and conducting architecture reviews, a policy we recommend. One of the main reasons for this centralization is that each company is interested in maximizing the amount of corporate reuse at the architectural level. These companies report that the individual start-up costs for such an organization were nontrivial. The management overhead and the additional communication costs for other corporate units are a portion of these costs, as well as staffing of the unit, any relocation costs, and training costs.

3. *Consumption of senior designers for architecture review teams.* Architecture review teams should normally not include members of the development

project—that is, individuals who participated in building the system being examined. Instead, individuals should be selected from within the company to serve on architecture review teams based on their past performance and demonstrated skills with large-scale system organization and design. The question of the membership of the review team brings up two cost-related concerns. First, there is the worry of reduced organization-wide development productivity because superior designers are removed from active involvement. This cost can be mitigated by making membership on the architecture review board nonpermanent. The second concern stems from this temporary engagement on the architecture review team. Each new evaluator needs to be trained in the review techniques and must gain experience in review before becoming a productive member of the review team. There is a cost associated with this learning curve for architecture evaluators.

BENEFITS

We enumerate five different benefits that flow from holding architecture inspections in the following subsections.

Financial Benefits.   At AT&T, each project manager reported perceived savings from an architecture review. On average, over the past eight years, projects receiving a full architecture review have reported a 10 percent reduction in project costs. Given the cost estimate of 70 staff days, the reported 10 percent cost reduction illustrates that on projects of 700 staff days or longer, the review pays for itself.

Other organizations have not publicized such strongly quantified data, but several consultants have reported that over 80 percent of their business was repeat business. Their customers recognized sufficient value in architecture review to be willing to pay for additional reviews.

There are also many anecdotes of estimated cost savings for the customers of reviews, as follows:

- A large company avoided a multimillion-dollar purchase when the architecture of the global information system they were procuring was, upon review, found to be incapable of providing the desired system attributes necessary to support a product line.

- Early analysis of an electronic funds transfer system showed a $50 billion transfer capability per night, which was only half of the desired capacity.

- An architecture review of a retail merchandise system revealed early that there would be peak order performance problems that no amount of hardware could fix; a major business failure was prevented.

- In the architecture review of a revision control system, a number of severe limitations in achieving system portability and modifiability were uncovered. A major redesign of the system was recommended.

There are also anecdotes in which architecture reviews did not occur but should have; they include the following:

- A rewrite of a customer accounting system was estimated to take two years. After seven years, the system had been reimplemented three times. Performance goals have never been met, despite the fact that the latest version uses 60 times the CPU power of the original prototype version.

- In a large engineering relational database system, performance problems were largely attributable to design decisions that made integration testing impossible. The project was canceled after $20 million had been spent.

The problem with all such anecdotes and with evaluating the value of any review process is that there is no method for knowing the results of the path not chosen. Since problems were discovered as a result of the review and had not been discovered prior to the review, it is reasonable to assume that the problem would have persisted for some time. Consequently, the discovery and remedy of the problem would have been much more costly.

Forced Preparation for the Review.   If one gives the reviewees an indication of the focus of the architecture review and the requirement for a representation of the architecture before the review is held, the reviewees are required to document the system's architecture. Many systems do not have an architecture that is understandable to all of the developers. The existing description is either too brief or (more commonly) too long, perhaps thousands of pages. Furthermore, there are often misunderstandings among developers about some of the assumptions for their components. The process of preparing for the review will reveal many of these problems.

Furthermore, the architecture review focuses on a few specific areas with specific questions to be answered. Answering these questions usually involves giving an explanation of the design choices and their rationales. Having a documented design rationale is important later in the life cycle so that the implications of modifications can be assessed. Capturing design rationales after the fact is one of the more difficult tasks in software development. By capturing the design rationale as presented in the architecture review (even by such low-cost methods as videotaping), invaluable information is available for later use.

Early Detection of Problems with the Existing Architecture.   The earlier in the life cycle that problems are detected, the cheaper it is to fix them. The problems that can be found by an architectural level inspection include unreasonable (or expensive to meet) requirements, performance problems, and problems associated with potential downstream modifications. For example, an architecture review that exercises scenarios of typical system activity can manifest rough performance specifications. Exercising system modification scenarios can reveal portability and extensibility problems that will be especially critical if the architecture is to support a product line rather than just a single product. Architecture review, therefore, provides early insight into product capabilities and limitations.

Validation of Requirements.   Discussion and examination of how well an architecture meets requirements also opens requirements up for discussion. What results is a much clearer understanding of the requirements and, usually, prioritization of the requirements. Requirements creation, when performed in isolation from early design, usually results in specification of conflicting system properties. High performance, security, fault tolerance, and low cost are all easy to demand but difficult to achieve and are often impossible to achieve simultaneously. Architecture reviews uncover the conflicts and trade-offs and provide a forum for negotiated resolution.

Improvement in Architectures.   The organizations that practice architecture review as a standard part of their development process report an improvement in the quality of the architectures that are reviewed. As development organizations learn to anticipate the kinds of questions that will be asked, the kinds of issues that will be raised, and the kinds of documentation that will be required for reviews, they naturally position themselves to maximize their performance on the reviews. Architecture reviews result not only in better architectures after the fact, but before the fact. Over time, an organization develops a culture that promotes good architectural design.

Benefits Summary.   Architecture reviews tend to increase quality, control cost, and decrease budget risk. Architecture is the framework for all technical decisions and, as such, has a tremendous impact on the cost and quality of the product. An architecture review does not guarantee high quality or low cost, but it points out areas of risk in a design. Other factors such as testing or quality of documentation and coding will contribute to the eventual cost and quality of the system.

Benefits other than the immediate ones of helping to facilitate the construction of the system also accrue. As we discussed in Section 2.4, architectures reflect existing organizational structures. If, for example, portions of a system are being developed by subcontractors, recognizing commonalities across the portions of the system being developed by the different subcontractors is difficult. An architecture review that has maintenance as one of its focus areas will detect commonalities regardless of organizational considerations.

10.2   Review Techniques

A variety of techniques exist to perform an architecture review. Each of the different techniques has a different cost and can be used to elicit different information. There are two basic categories of these techniques: those that generate qualitative questions to ask of an architecture and those that suggest quantitative measurements to be made on an architecture. *Questioning techniques* can be applied to evaluate an architecture for any given quality. In fact, it is consideration of the quality that drives the development of questions (in the form of checklists or scenarios, as described below). Questioning techniques, however, do not directly provide a means for answering those questions. *Measuring techniques*, on the other hand, are used to answer specific questions. In that sense, they address specific software qualities (for example, performance or scalability) but are not as broadly applicable as are questioning techniques.

We begin by describing three questioning techniques: scenarios, questionnaires, and checklists. These techniques differ from each other in applicability, but they are all used to elicit discussion about the architecture and to increase understanding of the architecture's fitness with respect to its requirements. The techniques are as follows:

1. *Scenario-based techniques.*   These are techniques such as SAAM that describe a specific interaction between a stakeholder and a system.

2. *Questionnaire-based techniques.*   A questionnaire is a list of general and relatively open questions that apply to all architectures. Some questions might apply to the way the architecture was generated and documented (by asking if there is a designated project architect or if a standard description language was used). Other questions focus on the details of the architecture description itself (by asking if all user-interface aspects of the system are separated from functional aspects). The review team is looking for a favorable response and will probe a single question to a level of detail that is necessary to satisfy its concern. The utility of a questionnaire is related to the ease with which the domain of interest can be characterized and circumscribed.

3. C*hecklist-based techniques.*   A checklist is a detailed set of questions that is developed after much experience evaluating a common (usually domain-specific) set of systems. Checklists tend to be much more focused on particular qualities of the system. For example, performance questions in a real-time information system will ask whether the system is writing the same data multiple times to disk or whether consideration has been given to handling both peak and average loads.

There is a natural relationship between these three questioning techniques. Scenarios are intended to be system-specific questions. Experience reviewing a family of related systems can result in generalizing a set of commonly used scenarios, turning them into either domain-specific entries in a checklist or more general items in a questionnaire. Checklists and questionnaires reflect more mature review practices. Scenarios can reflect less mature review practices. Another difference is that scenarios, because they are system specific, are developed as part of the review process for an individual project. Checklists and questionnaires are assumed to exist before a project begins.

As an example of the difference between scenarios and checklists, consider the following checklist item adapted from a checklist used by a large corporation: Is there error recovery code in a process to clean up after it detects an error? The scenario form of this question is, What happens when a divide by zero occurs?

The scenario is specific with respect to the type of error, and it is up to the reviewers to determine that cleanup is required. The checklist specifies that cleanup is required and asks the reviewers (and system architect) to verify that this function has been assigned a place in the design.

This difference reflects organizational maturity in holding architecture reviews. Scenarios are developed by the reviewers of an individual project, whereas the checklist grows out of the scenarios produced by several reviews. An organizational unit that conducts architecture reviews can turn oft-repeated scenarios into a checklist.

We now turn to measuring techniques. These techniques result in quantitative results. Rather than provide ways to generate the questions that will be asked about an architecture, they provide answers to questions a review team might already have about particular qualities of an architecture.

METRICS

Metrics are quantitative interpretations placed on particular observable measurements on the architecture, such as fan in and fan out of components. The most well-researched measuring techniques provide answers on overall complexity, which can suggest places of likely change. With measuring techniques, the review needs to focus not only on the results of the measurement-metric but also on the assumptions under which the technique was used. For example, a calculation of performance characteristics makes assumptions about patterns of resource utilization. How valid are these assumptions? Coupling and cohesion metrics make assumptions about the types of functionalities embodied in the components being examined. How valid are these assumptions?

SIMULATIONS, PROTOTYPES, EXPERIMENTS

Building a prototype or a simulation of the system may help to create and to clarify the architecture. A prototype whose components consist of functionless stubs is a model of the architecture. Performance models are an example of a simulation. Creation of a detailed simulation or prototype just for review purposes is typically expensive. On the other hand, these artifacts often exist as a portion of the normal development process. In this case, using these artifacts during a review or to answer questions that come up during the review becomes a normal and natural procedure.

An existing simulation or prototype may be an answer to an issue raised by a questioning technique. For example, if the review team asks, what evidence supports this assertion, one valid answer would be the results of a simulation.

We can further distinguish the various architecture review techniques we have discussed across a number of different dimensions. Table 10.1 shows a summary of the classification of these review techniques. The dimensions are described in the subsections that follow.

TABLE 10.1   Properties of the Review Techniques

Review technique		Generality	Level of detail	Phase	What is reviewed
Questioning techniques	Questionnaire	General	Coarse	Early	Artifact, process
	Checklist	Domain-specific	Varies	Middle	Artifact, process
	Scenarios	System-specific	Medium	Middle	Artifact
Measuring techniques	Metrics	General or domain-specific	Fine	Middle	Artifact
	Prototype, Simulation, Experiment	Domain-specific	Varies	Early	Artifact

Generality.   Two entries are possible: general purpose and domain-specific. General-purpose techniques focus on general-purpose issues and can be applied to any architecture. Domain-specific techniques focus on issues particular to a given domain. As already discussed, questionnaires are a general-purpose approach, whereas checklists are domain specific. Scenarios are system specific because they are defined for a particular review. Metrics are mostly general purpose, although some may be domain-specific metrics, as in the telecommunications domain. Prototypes, simulations, and experimentation are primarily domain specific, although there are some general-purpose simulation generation tools.

Level of Detail.   Three entries are possible: coarse, medium, and fine. Level of detail indicates how much information on the architecture is required to perform the review. Values here represent a continuum and usually determine when in the development cycle the review technique can be applied. Coarse-grained approaches can be applied early in the design process because they do not require much detailed information such as component specification or connection protocols. Fine-grained approaches generally need more detail and hence must be applied later, when more decisions have been bound.

Phase.   Three entries are possible: early, middle, and postdeployment. The entry in the table lists the earliest that a particular approach can be employed. In general, the approach should be applied as early as possible.

Early-phase review occurs after early, high-priority, coarse architectural decisions have been made, such as the establishment of a reference model for the system. At this point, we can evaluate the preliminary decisions and detect poor preliminary choices. An actual architecture does not yet exist, only the preliminary decisions.

Middle-phase review occurs after some (perhaps all) elaboration of the architectural design. Elaboration is an iterative process; the review can occur at any point here. At this point, there should be an actual architectural design in varying stages of completeness (depending on how much has been elaborated). At this stage we can identify problems with the architectural design.

Postdeployment-phase review occurs after the system has been completely designed, implemented, and deployed. At this stage, both the architecture and the system exist, so we can answer additional questions about whether the architecture matches the implementation. If the product has been in existence for a while, we can also check for architectural *drift*—movement away from the original design.

What Is Reviewed?   There are two different kinds of questions that could be answered in a review. The first has to do with the architecture as an *artifact* or product. Here the focus is on evaluating the architecture itself. Issues include the assignment of functionality, the nature of intercomponent connections, and the achievement of quality goals. This is the most common subject of a review. Another kind of review looks at the *process* of creating and using the architecture in the development. Issues here include how responsibility for the architecture was allocated, how the architecture is made known to the project personnel, how conformance is ensured, and how the architecture will be maintained.

Questionnaires and checklists can evaluate both the artifact and the process, depending on what kind of question is asked. Examples of questions that address the process at the early phase include: Do you have an architect? How will you go from here to develop the architecture? Examples of questions that address the process at a later stage include: Do people understand the architecture? and What happens if we split the development team? Examples of questions at the postdeployment stage include: Is the architecture adhered to when you change the system? Does the implementation match the architecture?

Scenarios and prototypes by their nature are geared toward evaluating only the artifact. It is possible to come up with scenarios that focus on the process, but that is not really their intent. Metrics can address either product or process.

WHICH TECHNIQUE SHOULD I USE?

Given these different techniques, the question then becomes, Which one should I use for my project? The answer depends on several different factors: the development process, the maturity of architecture review within an organization, and the particular qualities being examined during the review.

If, during the development process, simulations, prototypes, or experiments have been developed, they should be used to provide information during an architecture review that is within their scope. That is, a prototype may have been developed to test particular performance characteristics. The use of this prototype to answer questions concerned with modifiability is probably inappropriate. Specifically, simulations and prototypes are recommended to answer performance questions.

Questionnaires and checklists are evolved over time, and so if an organization is just beginning to perform architecture reviews and does not have questionnaires and checklists in place, scenarios are the technique of choice. Development of a collection of scenarios is an activity performed during a review so that after performing a collection of reviews, an organization can build a database of scenarios and turn them into questionnaires and checklists. Even if an organization has questionnaires and checklists already in place, scenarios should be used to deal with issues not covered in the questionnaires or checklists; they can also be used to grow the questionnaires and checklists for future reviews.

10.3   The Review Practice

We have summarized the costs and benefits for architecture review and categorized different review techniques. Next, we describe how to prepare, execute, and report the results of an architecture review.

PRECONDITIONS

Preconditions are the set of necessary assets and conditions that must be in place before a successful review can proceed. We identify five preconditions: an understanding of the review context, involvement of the right people, creation of a review team, organizational expectations and support, and review preparation, including an appropriate representation of the architecture being examined.

Context.   Reviews can be planned or unplanned. In a planned review, the review is considered a normal part of the project's development cycle. The review is scheduled well in advance, built into the project's work plans and budget, and follow-up is expected. In an unplanned review, the review is unexpected—usually the result of a project in serious trouble taking extreme measures to try to salvage previous effort. These two kinds of review are fundamentally different. They have different goals and different agendas, are subject to different expectations, and produce different results.

The planned review is ideally considered an asset to the project. At worst, it is a distraction to the work of getting on with the project. The review can be perceived not as a challenge to the technical authority of the project's members but as a validation of the project's initial direction. Planned reviews are proactive and build teams.

An unplanned review, however, is more of an ordeal for project members. It consumes project resources and schedule from a project already struggling with both factors. It tends to be more adversarial than constructive. It is used only when management perceives that a project has a substantial possibility of failure and needs to make a midcourse correction. Unplanned reviews are reactive.

Because we are describing *best* practices in this chapter, we will not deal with unplanned reviews. Architecture reviews should be an integral part of the development process, planned and scheduled in advance, with follow-up activities accounted for.

The second contextual question is the timing of the review. Sometimes it is useful to hold an early, lightweight *architecture discovery review* at a point during development after requirements have been set but before architectural decisions have become firm. This is the ideal time to challenge requirements on the basis of their feasibility or cost of implementation. Such a discovery review would be held in addition to (not in lieu of) the type of full architecture review that examines a set of architectural decisions against a presumably unbending set of behavioral and quality requirements.

These two reviews are aimed at different kinds of decisions and can analyze for different kinds of qualities. The discovery review should be timed so that some architectural decisions have been made (otherwise there can be nothing to discuss) but the decisions have not been strongly bound and can be changed without great expense. Discovery reviews are less costly, but because most architectural decisions have not been determined at the time of this review, the benefits are less.

It is important that the scope of the review be kept under control. To focus the review, a small number of explicit goals should be enumerated. The number of goals upon which to focus should be kept to a minimum, around three to five. An inability to define a small number of high-priority goals for the review is an indication that the expectations for the review (and perhaps the system) may be unrealistic. These goals define the purpose of the review and should be made an explicit portion of the review contract discussed subsequently.

Finally, review sponsors should make sure that the benefits of the review are likely to exceed the cost, as discussed in the previous section. The type of review we are describing here is suitable for medium and large-scale projects but may not be cost effective for small projects.

Project Representatives.   The project should be represented by the system architect, the designers for each major component, and the system stakeholders. It is imperative to secure the time of the architect or at least someone who can speak authoritatively about the system's architecture and design. This person (or these people) should be primarily able to communicate the facts of the architecture quickly and clearly as well as the motivation behind the architectural decisions.

For very large systems, the designers for each major component need to be involved to ensure that the architect's notion of the system design is in fact reflected and manifested in the more detailed levels of the design. These designers will also be able to speak to the behavioral and quality attributes of the components.

As we discussed in the previous chapter on SAAM, the stakeholders need to be identified and represented at the review. It is essential to identify the customer(s) for the review report and to elicit their values and expectations.

Review Team.   The second group of people whose participation is essential is the review team. As we have already indicated, software architecture review teams ideally are separate entities within a corporation. The review team must be assembled in a way so that the following occurs:

- The team is perceived as impartial, objective, and respected. The team must be seen as being composed of people who are appropriate to carry out the review so that the project personnel will not regard the review as a waste of time and so that the team's conclusions will carry weight.
- Team members must dedicate their work time to the review. It is not possible for a review team member to continue normal responsibilities during the review. Late-night planning sessions and off-the-record breakfast meetings with project personnel are the norm.
- The team includes people highly fluent in architecture and architectural issues and is led by someone with solid experience in designing and evaluating projects at the architectural level.
- The team includes at least one system domain expert—someone who has built systems *in the area being reviewed.*
- The team includes a librarian responsible for organizing and making available the documentation about the project.
- The team has the services of support staff to assist in handling logistics and preparing the report.
- The team is located as close as possible to the source of the artifacts it will be examining. Locality will simplify logistics and enhance communication with project personnel.
- The team includes an "apprentice" reviewer to propagate architecture review capability and provide reviewer turnover to avoid burnout.

Organizational Expectations. Critical to review success is a clear, mutual understanding of the expectations of the organization sponsoring the review as well as support for the review in terms of organizational resources.

Senior managers need to set expectations for the review for both the review team and the project personnel. A mechanism for this is a contract that determines the following:

- Who will be told what upon completion of the review.
- What will be the review criteria (and, by implication, what will not).
- What and who will be made available to the review team.
- What follow-up is expected on the part of the review team and the project.
- What the expected maximum time is for the review to take.

The process of negotiating the contract may be as important as the contract itself. The eye-to-eye communication necessary to forge a contract may be the largest factor in setting realistic expectations.

It must be understood by the managers contracting for the review that analysis at the architectural level is not a definitive analysis. All that can be determined at the architectural level is that it is feasible that the resulting system will have the desired qualities. There are no guarantees: A poor implementation of a good design is likely to perform poorly. Thus, an important part of expectation setting is making sure that all review stakeholders understand the nature of the results.

Review Preparation. An agenda is needed for focus. The agenda should be detailed but flexible. Often, information elicited during a review will launch an area of investigation not previously considered. The goals for the review and the review criteria must be clearly spelled out. For example, rather than saying that the system should be integrable, a criterion should state a more specific goal, such as that the system should integrate with system X with no more than 10 staff-days of effort.

Any questionnaires or checklists that are going to be used during the review should be presented to the development group prior to the review. In fact, if these are organization-wide artifacts, they should be presented to the development group when the project is initiated. If system-specific scenarios are going to be used, they will be crafted as part of the review process itself, in response to input from the various stakeholders.

The following material should flow from the project to the review team:

- Materials that describe the architecture and discuss the rationale behind architectural decisions. Expectations should be set beforehand about the level of detail of the material; 50 pages would be preferable to 500 or 1. This assumes that the architecture and the requirements are in a concrete enough form to have been unambiguously documented. If this is not the case, elicitation of this information will be the first order of business in the review itself.

- In organizations in which this review process is part of the culture, it is far less likely that the architecture and requirements will not have been adequately documented by the time the review begins. In organizations without standard representations for requirements and architectures, the review team may distribute templates for desired documents to illustrate to project personnel the kind of information required and the approved forms for conveying it.

- A ranking of the three to five top quality and behavioral requirements of the system. Such a ranking of requirements serves the project by preventing the architecture from being muddied by the lobbying from representatives of a large number of conflicting quality attributes. If more desired quality attributes are expressed, they should be ranked as *essential* or *desirable*. Essential attributes *must* be addressed by the architecture. Desirable attributes may be sacrificed due to their impact on deadlines, budgets, or software complexity.

Industrial reviewers tell us that no standard architecture representations (beyond box-and-line diagrams) have been used in formal architecture reviews. However, this is not an impediment. Reviews are primarily vehicles for focused discussion where there are usually no right answers, only compelling ones. Any representation of the architecture that helps facilitate the exchange of information will do.

REVIEW ACTIVITIES

During the review, the review team should highlight critical issues that are raised in support of or (more important) against the architecture. Each issue raised during the review is documented. For example, these issues could be written on index cards and pinned to a board or stored in a widely accessible location, such as a corporate database. At convenient points during the review, the participants' comments on critical issues are organized by theme. The review team then rates the themes as *project threatening*, *major*, or *minor*. Thus, at the conclusion of the review, there is a prioritized list of issues that can be reported to higher management and used to determine follow-up activities.

Every architecture review should consider the cost consequences of the proposed design. There are a variety of cost models that can be used to estimate cost and most are organization dependent. The goal is not to come to a precise determination of projected cost during an architecture review but to see whether there are any features in the architecture that are suspected to be sources of undue risk and, potentially, unbounded cost.

The review team should understand the essential functions of the system and should look to see how each function is unambiguously defined in the architecture representation or succinctly described by the architect. A response to the question, How is X done? that takes the form, I'm not sure or X could be done either here or there, indicates a potential problem that should be recorded as an issue. Other functionality-related issues that are important to examine include the following:

- Making sure there are written requirements in all key areas
- Checking that the functionality of the architecture is complete with respect to the behavioral requirements
- Checking that system acceptance criteria exist

To evaluate the achievement of performance goals, usually in terms of resource utilization, several pieces of information are required. The exact set depends upon the nature of the system and the performance goal being reviewed but typically will include the following:

- Workload information, which consists of the number of concurrent users, request arrival rates, and performance goals
- A specification of execution paths and programs, components to be executed, timing information about and probability of execution of each component, the number of repetitions of each software component, and the protocol for contention resolution used by the software component
- Environmental information (when binding decisions have been made), consisting of system characteristics such as configuration and device service rates, overhead information for operating-system services, and scheduling policies

Resource utilization can be derived from the three types of information given above; it consists of CPU usage (or number of instructions executed per unit time), input–output activity, number of database calls, amount of communication and other device usage, amount of service routine usage, and memory usage. This resource usage is then compared to the resource budget for the system to determine (as a rough estimate) whether a performance issue exists.

Evaluating for modifiability is best addressed via questioning techniques. The scenarios, checklists, or questionnaires can reveal how vulnerable the architecture is to specific modifications. Finally, there should be a check for the following nine early-warning signs of architecture problems:

1. The architecture is forced to match the current organization.

2. Top-level architecture components number more than 25.

3. One requirement drives the rest of the design.

4. The architecture depends upon alternatives in the operating system.

5. Proprietary components are being used when standard components would do.

6. The component definition comes from the hardware division.

7. There is redundancy not needed for reliability (e.g., two databases, two start-up routines, two error-locking procedures).

8. The design is exception driven; that is, the emphasis is on the extensibility and not core commonalities.

9. The development unit is unable to identify an architect for the system.

Each serious issue raised during the review needs to be examined from the points of view of modifying the architecture and of modifying the requirement(s) that caused the issue to be raised. For example, if there is a performance issue, the issue can be resolved either by increasing the performance of the system in some manner or by relaxing the performance requirements. Sometimes requirements are set without careful examination of the system context, and the specific requirement that is driving an issue should be revisited. There also may be a tendency to "gold plate" a system by requiring functionality and performance levels that are not really needed. Sometimes this is justified by a business case, but other times this should be resisted. An architecture review is an early opportunity to ferret out nonessential or conflicting requirements.

The final review activity is to create and present a report in which all of the issues, along with supporting data surfaced during the review, are described. The report should be circulated in draft form to all of the review participants to catch and correct any misconceptions and biases and to correlate elements before it is finalized.

REVIEW OUTPUT

The categorized and ranked issues recorded during the review activities are formally documented, along with the data supporting the issue identification. A formal report is delivered to the party or parties sponsoring the review, and to the review participants, as specified in the contract. The report can also contain architectural descriptions and results of individual analyses if they are particularly illuminating or are produced as a result of the review and not located elsewhere in the system documentation.

The set of scenarios that was used to exercise the architecture during the analysis becomes part of the system configuration and can be used to analyze an improved system or a related system, as well as to form the basis of eventual test cases. As already indicated, scenarios developed for common systems will, over time, be used to formulate more generalized questionnaires and checklists.

Predictions about the eventual system that emerged during the review should be kept. If performance was one of the key architecture review criteria, it is likely that, as a result of the review, some rough worst-case–best-case performance predictions are available. If system modification was a key criterion, preliminary predictions of the kinds of modifications the system can support will surface. It is likely that the set of potentially reusable design structures that could be shared by multiple similar systems will be among these predictions.

Information about the review process itself should also be collected. The aggregated output from multiple reviews may lead to courses, training, and improvements to system development and the architecture review processes. Costs and benefits of the review should be collected. Estimates of the benefits are best collected from the manager of the development. The information about the review should be retained by the reviewing organization and used to improve future reviews and to provide cost–benefit summaries to the managers of the reviewing organization.

10.4   Summary

In summary, the main guidelines for architecture reviews are as follows:

- Have a formal review with external reviewers as a planned part of the project's development life cycle.
- Time the review to best advantage. Consider an early architecture discovery review.
- Choose an appropriate review technique.
- Create a review contract.
- Limit the number of qualities to be reviewed.
- Make sure the review team includes an architecture expert, a domain expert, a librarian, and support staff.
- Insist on a system architect.
- Collect scenarios and grow them into checklists.

Having a separate organizational entity that performs architecture reviews is desirable, but it may be helpful to gain experience with the costs and benefits of architecture reviews prior to creating such an entity. Using external consultants who have experience with such reviews is one mechanism for gaining experience and training internal staff to subsequently take the lead in establishing an internal architecture review organization.

10.5 For Further Reading

The material in the chapter was derived from the report "Recommended Best Industrial Practice for Software Architectural Evaluation" [Abowd 96] that in turn was derived from a series of workshops organized by the authors and others at the Software Engineering Institute and attended by representatives of eight industrial and consulting organizations.

Architecture reviews based on checklists or questionnaires are a form of *active design review* as described by Parnas and Weiss [Parnas 85b]. An active design review is one in which the participants are asked to take an active part in the review by using the documentation to answer specific questions that are prepared in advance as opposed to an opportunistic or unstructured review in which the participants are merely asked to report any anomalies they might discover.

Fred Brooks [Brooks 95] writes about conceptual integrity flowing from a chief architect.

Some of AT&T's rich experience with performing architecture reviews is also documented [AT&T 93].

10.6 Discussion Questions

1. How are architectures currently reviewed in your enterprise? What are the good points of that practice? What are ways in which it could be improved?

2. AT&T's data suggest that an architecture review saves a typical project about 10 percent. This is an organization that builds systems in a fairly mature domain, using checklists and questionnaires that the architects have access to beforehand. Why would a review save anything (after all, every project knows what is going to be asked of it)? Discuss this apparent paradox.

3. How much do you think institutionalized architecture reviews would save in your organization? Why?

4. Try to write a checklist for an architecture review for a system in your organization's domain. Write one for artifact review and one for process review.

11

Air Traffic Control
A Case Study in Designing
for High Availability

> *The FAA has faced this problem [of complexity] throughout its decade-old attempt to replace the nation's increasingly obsolete air traffic control system. The replacement, called Advanced Automation System (AAS), combines all the challenges of computing in the 1990s. A program that is more than a million lines in size is distributed across hundreds of computers and embedded into new and sophisticated hardware, all of which must respond around the clock to unpredictable real-time events. Even a small glitch potentially threatens public safety.... Now running five years late and more than $1 billion over budget, the bug-infested program is being scoured by software experts at Carnegie Mellon and the Massachusetts Institute of Technology to determine whether it can be salvaged or must be canceled outright.*
> — W. Wayt Gibbs [Gibbs 94]

Air traffic control (ATC) is among the most demanding of all software applications. It is *hard real time*, meaning that timing deadlines must be met absolutely; ATC is *safety critical*, meaning that human lives may be lost if the system does not perform correctly; it is *highly distributed*, requiring dozens of controllers to work cooperatively to guide aircraft through the airways system. In the United States, whose skies are filled with more commercial, private, and military aircraft than is any other part of the world, ATC is an area of intense public scrutiny. Aside from the obvious safety issues, building and maintaining a safe, reliable airways system requires enormous expenditures of public money. ATC is a multibillion-dollar undertaking.

This chapter is a case study on one part of a planned next-generation ATC system for the United States. We will see how its architecture was the key to achieving its demanding and wide-ranging requirements. Although this system was never put into operation because of budgetary constraints, it was implemented and demonstrated that the system could meet its quality goals.

We will also see how an intensive audit of the system was performed to assess its ability to meet these and other requirements. The architecture was evaluated using a variety of techniques including an analysis using software archite-cure analysis method (SAAM)-like scenarios, as presented in Chapter 9 and analysis of artifacts produced by methods described in Chapter 10.

In the United States, air traffic is controlled by the Federal Aviation Agency (FAA), a government agency responsible for aviation safety in general. The FAA is the customer for the system we will describe. As a flight progresses from its departure to its arrival airport, it deals with several different ATC entities that guide it safely through each portion of the airways (and ground facilities) it is currently using. *Ground control* coordinates the movement of aircraft on the ground at an airport. *Towers* control aircraft flying within an airport's *terminal control area*, a cylindrical section of airspace centered at an airport. Finally, *en route centers* divide the skies over the country into 22 large sections of responsibility.

So, consider an airline flight from Key West, Florida, to Washington, D.C.'s Dulles Airport. The crew of the flight will communicate with Key West ground control to taxi from the gate to the end of the runway, Key West tower during takeoff and climb-out, and then Miami Center (the en route center whose airspace covers Key West) once it leaves the Key West terminal control area. From there the flight will be handed off to Jacksonville Center, Atlanta Center, and so forth, until it enters the airspace controlled by Washington Center. From Washington Center, it will be handed off to the Dulles tower, which will guide its approach and landing. When it leaves the runway, the flight will communicate with Dulles ground control for its taxi to the gate. This is an oversimplified view of ATC in the United States but suffices for our case study. Figure 11.1 shows the hand-off process, and Figure 11.2 shows the 22 en route centers.

The system we will study is called the Initial Sector Suite System (ISSS). ISSS was intended to be an upgraded hardware and software system for the 22 en route centers in the United States. It was part of a much larger government pro-curement that would have, in stages, installed similar upgraded systems in the towers and ground control facilities, as well as the transoceanic ATC facilities. The fact that ISSS was to be procured as only one of a strongly related set of sys-tems had a profound effect on its architecture. In particular, there was great incentive to adopt common designs and components where possible because the ISSS developer also intended bidding on the other systems. After all, these differ-ent systems (en route center, tower, ground control) share many components: interfaces to radio systems, interfaces to flight plan databases, interfaces to each other, interpreting radar data, requirements for reliability and performance, and so on. Thus, the ISSS design was influenced broadly by the requirements for all of the upgraded systems, not just the ISSS-specific requirements.

The complete set of upgrade systems was to be called the Advanced Auto-mation System (AAS). Ultimately, the program was canceled in favor of a less ambitious, less costly, more staged upgrade plan. The ISSS program survived the cancellation of AAS but not for long. It too was eventually scrapped in favor of a

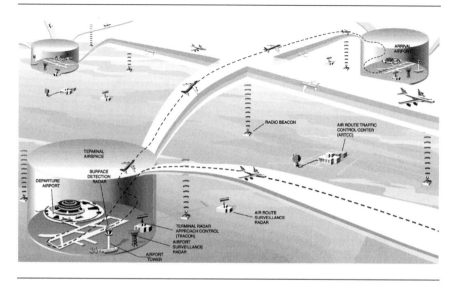

FIGURE 11.1   Flying from point A to point B in the U.S. air traffic control system.
Courtesy of Ian Worpole/*Scientific American*, 1994.

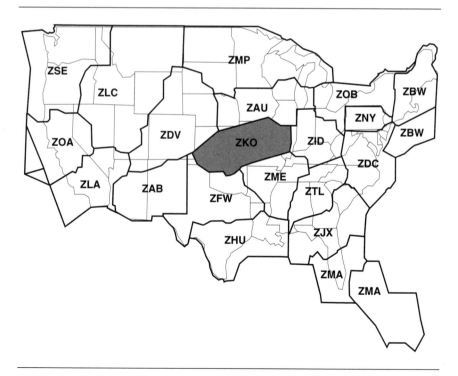

FIGURE 11.2   En route centers in the United States.

scaled-back program that concentrated on replacing the decades-old display consoles that were regularly breaking down in centers across the nation and filling those new consoles with software that was simpler (and did less) than ISSS. Nevertheless, ISSS is still an illuminating case study because when the program was canceled the design and most of the code were actually already completed. Furthermore, the architecture of the system (as well as most other aspects) was studied by an independent audit team and found to be well suited to its requirements. Finally, the system that was deployed instead of ISSS borrowed heavily from the ISSS architecture. Hence, we will present the ISSS architecture as an actual solution to an extremely difficult problem. ISSS is also an interesting case study for us because its audit included an early and important application of SAAM.

11.1   Relationship to the Architecture Business Cycle

Figure 11.3 shows how the air traffic control system relates to the architecture business cycle (ABC). The end users are federal air traffic controllers; the customer is the Federal Aviation Administration. The developing organization is a

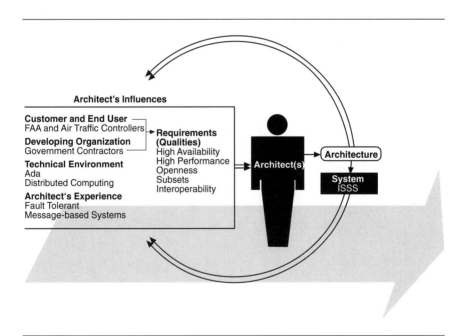

FIGURE 11.3   The ABC applied to the ATC system.

large corporation that supplies many other important software-intensive systems to the U.S. government. Factors in the technical environment include the mandated use of Ada as the language of implementation for large government software systems and the emergence of distributed computing as a routine way to build systems and approach fault tolerance.

11.2   Requirements and Qualities

Given that air traffic control is highly visible, with huge amounts of commercial, government and civilian interest, and given that it involves the potential loss of human life if it fails, its two most important quality requirements are as follows:

1. Ultrahigh availability, meaning that the system is absolutely prohibited from being inoperative for longer than very short periods of time
2. High performance, meaning that the system has to be able to process large numbers of aircraft without "losing" any of them. Networks have to be able to carry the communication loads, and the software has to be able to perform its computations quickly and predictably.

In addition, the following requirements, although not as critical to the safety of the aircraft and its passengers, are major drivers in the shape of the architecture and the principles that form the shape:

- Openness, meaning that the system has to be able to incorporate commercially developed software components, including ATC functions and basic computing services such as graphics display packages
- The ability to field subsets of the system, necessary in case the billion-dollar project falls victim to reductions in budget (and hence functionality)—as indeed happened
- The ability to make modifications to the functionality and handle upgrades in hardware and software (new processors, new I/O devices and drivers, new versions of the Ada compiler)
- The ability to operate with and interface to a bewildering set of external systems, both hardware and software, some decades old and others not yet implemented

Finally, the requirements of this system are unusual in that they must satisfy a great many stakeholders, particularly the controllers who are the system's end users. While this doesn't sound unusual, the difference is that controllers have the ability to reject the system if it is not to their liking, even if it meets all its operational requirements. The implications of this situation were profound for the process of determining requirements and designing the system and slowed it down substantially. Table 11.1 shows how the quality goals were met by the ATC system.

TABLE 11.1 How the ATC System Achieves Its Quality Goals

Goal	How achieved
High availability	Hardware redundancy (both processor and network) and, software redundancy (layered fault detection and recovery)
High performance	Distributed multiprocessors, front-end schedulability analysis, and network modeling
Openness	Interface wrapping and layering
Modifiability	Templates and table-driven adaptation data
Ability to field subsets	Appropriate separation of concerns
Interoperability	Client-server division of functionality and message-based communications

11.3 Architectural Approach

The ISSS architecture has a number of characteristics that distinguish it as an inherently complex and largely unprecedented system. The inherent complexity is mainly a function of demanding requirements, including the following:

- *Distributed multiprocessor.*   Distributed multiprocessor systems are increasingly common because of the decreasing cost of computing power and the increasing effectiveness of communication protocols. Given that they were used, however, a front-end effort in analyzing the schedulability of the system and the network loads was necessary.

- *Message based.*   Message-based systems are typical of command and control types of applications and serve as a unifying paradigm under which each unit can determine its processing requirements based on the set of messages it is allowed to receive.

- *Client-server.*   Client-server architectures are meant to promote modularity and cohesion and make coupling explicit and limited.

- *Built-in redundancy.*   Redundant hardware is used to provide backup processing and communications capacity. Software redundancy is used to provide backup processing for hardware failures and backup processing for software faults.

- *Table-driven start-up configuration.*   Table-driven "adaptation data" provide the capability to configure the ISSS for different sites without changing the code.

- *Templates.*   Patterns of software that are repeated throughout the system are used to promote reuse and extract the similar aspects of processing units to minimize necessary creativity and to improve maintainability. It also allows easy extensibility of the system.

11.4   Architectural Solution

Before we dive into the considerable details of the architectural solution, some background is in order. The term *sector suite* refers to a suite of controllers (each sitting at a control console like the one in Figure 11.4) that together control all of the aircraft in a particular sector of the en route center's airspace. Our oversimplified view of ATC is now enhanced by the fact that aircraft are not only handed off from center to center but also from sector to sector within each center. Sectors are defined in ways unique to each center. A center's sectors may be defined to balance the load among the center's controllers; for instance, less-traveled sectors may be larger than densely flown areas.

The ISSS design calls for flexibility about how many control stations are assigned to each sector; anywhere from one to four are allowed, and the number can be changed administratively while the system is in operation. Each sector is required to have at least two controllers assigned to it. The first is the radar controller, who monitors the radar surveillance data, communicates with the aircraft, and is responsible for maintaining safe separations. This controller is responsible for managing the tactical situation in the sector. The second controller is the data controller, who retrieves information (such as flight plans) about each aircraft that is either in the sector or soon will be. The data controller provides the radar

FIGURE 11.4   Controllers at a sector suite.   Courtesy of William J. Hughes Technical Center; FAA public domain photo.

controller with the information needed about the aircraft's intentions to safely and efficiently guide it through the sector.

How big is the ISSS system? Here are some numbers to convey a sense of scale:

- ISSS is designed to support up to 210 consoles per en route center. Each console contains its own workstation-class processor; the CPU is an IBM RS/6000 series processor.
- ISSS requirements call for a center to control from 400 to 2440 separate aircraft tracks simultaneously.
- There may be 16 to 40 radars to support a single facility.
- A center may have from 60 to 90 control positions (each with one or several consoles devoted to it).
- The code to implement ISSS contains about 1 million lines of Ada.

In summary, the ISSS system must do the following:

- Acquire radar target reports that are stored in an existing ATC computer system called the Host Computer System.
- Convert the radar reports for display and broadcast them to all of the consoles. Each console chooses the reports that it needs to display; any console is capable of displaying any area.
- Handle conflict alerts (potential aircraft collisions) or other data transmitted by the host computer.
- Interface to the Host for input and retrieval of flight plans.
- Provide extensive monitoring and control information, such as network management, to allow site administrators to reconfigure the installation in realtime.
- Provide a recording capability for later playback.
- Provide graphical user-interface facilities, such as windowing, on the consoles. Special safety-related provisions are necessary, such as window transparency to keep potentially crucial data from being obscured.
- Provide reduced backup capability in the event of failure of the Host, the primary communications network, or the primary radar sensors.
- Be constantly available. The actual availability requirement for ISSS is targeted at 0.99999, meaning that the system should be unavailable for less than 5 minutes a year. (However, if the system is able to recover from a failure and resume operating within 10 seconds, that failure is not counted as unavailable time.)

ISSS SYSTEM ARCHITECTURE

ISSS is a distributed system, consisting of a number of components connected by local area networks. Figure 11.5 is intended to provide an overview of the major facets of the system architecture. It does not show any of the ISSS support systems

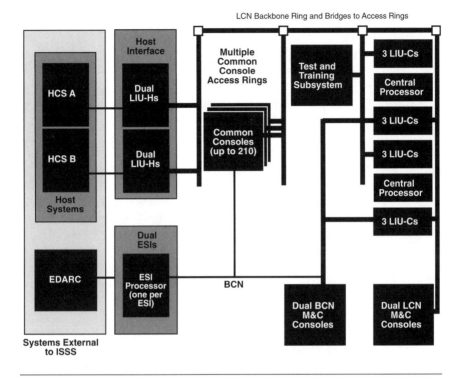

FIGURE 11.5   ISSS architecture.

or their interfaces to the ISSS equipment. It also does not show any structure of the ISSS software. The major components of the ISSS system architecture and their roles are as follows:

- The Host Computer System is the current heart of the en route automation system. At each en route center there are two host computers, one primary and the other ready to take the primary role should there be some problem with the first computer. The Host provides processing of both surveillance data and flight-plan data. Surveillance data is displayed on the en route display consoles used by controllers. Flight data is printed as necessary on flight-strip printers, and some flight data elements are displayed on the data tags associated with the radar surveillance information.

- Common consoles are the air traffic controller's workstations. They provide displays of aircraft position information and associated data tags in a plan-view format (the radar display), displays of flight-plan data in the form of electronic flight strips, and a variety of other information displays. They also allow controller entries to modify the flight data and to control the information being displayed and its format. Common consoles are grouped in sector suites of from one to four consoles, with each sector suite serving the controller team for one airspace control sector.

- The common consoles are connected to the Host computers by means of the Local Communications Network (LCN), the primary network of ISSS. Each Host is interfaced to the LCN via dual LCN interface units that act as a fault-tolerant redundant pair.

- The LCN is composed of four parallel token ring networks for redundancy and to balance overall loading. One network supports the broadcast of surveillance data to all processors; one processor is used for point-to-point communications between pairs of processors; one provides a channel for display data to be sent from the common consoles to recording units for layer playback; and one is a spare. Bridges provide connections between the networks of the access rings and those of the backbone. The bridges also provide the ability to substitute the spare ring for a failed ring and to make other alternative routings.

- The Enhanced Direct Access Radar Channel (EDARC) provides a backup display of aircraft position and limited flight data block information to the en route display consoles. EDARC is used in the event of a loss of the display data provided by the Host. EDARC provides essentially raw unprocessed radar data.

- The Backup Communications Network (BCN) is an Ethernet network using TCP/IP protocols. It is used for other system functions besides the EDARC interface and is also used as a backup network in some LCN failure conditions.

- Both the LCN and BCN have associated *Monitor and Control* (M&C) consoles. These give system maintenance personnel an overview of the state of the system and allow them to control its operation. M&C consoles are ordinary consoles that contain special software to support M&C functions and also to provide the top-level or global availability management functions.

- The Test and Training subsystem provides the capability to test new hardware and software and to train users without interfering with the ATC mission.

- The central processors are mainframe-class processors that provide the data recording and playback functions for the system in an early version of ISSS.

Each common console is connected to both the LCN and the BCN. Because of the large number of common consoles that may be present at a facility (up to 210), multiple LCN access rings are used to support all the consoles. This, then, is the system architecture for ISSS, in which the software resides.

ISSS SOFTWARE ARCHITECTURE

Just as architecture affects behavior, performance, fault tolerance, and maintainability, so an architecture is shaped by stringent requirements in any of these areas. In the case of ISSS, by far the most important driving requirement is the extraordinarily high requirement for system availability: less than 5 minutes per year of down-time. This requirement, more than any other, motivated architectural decisions for ISSS.

ISSS has two categories of software. Operational software facilitates air traffic control. Support software exists to help generate, develop, install, and initialize operational software. The two categories are roughly the same size, as measured by lines of source code. Our case study will focus on the operational software, to which the hard real-time and availability requirements applied. Support software will become important when addressing maintainability.

We will describe the ISSS software architecture by first describing its components, then describing the connections among them, and finally describing the way in which the components and connections form layers.

ISSS Components.   As always, when one examines an architectural structure of components and the relationship among them, it is important to be clear about what kind of components they are. ISSS, like most systems, can be described using different kinds of components. The kinds of components most often referred to in this architecture are as follows:

- Computer software configuration items (CSCIs)
- Applications
- Ada-level entities such as programs
- Threads

Put another way, these components form the basis of useful structures of the architecture, as discussed in Section 2.5.

CSCIs – The largest components of the ISSS operational software are CSCIs, defined in the government software development standard whose use was mandated by the customer. CSCIs correspond largely to work assignments; a large team is devoted to designing, building, and testing a CSCI. There is usually some coherent theme associated with each CSCI, some rationale for grouping together all of the small software elements that it contains (such as packages, processes, etc.). There are five CSCIs in ISSS; they are as follows:

1. Display Management, comprising approximately 350,000 lines of source code and responsible for producing and maintaining displays on the common consoles.

2. Common System Services, comprising approximately 345,000 lines of source code and responsible for providing utilities generally useful in air traffic control software—recall that the developer was planning to build other systems under the larger AAS program.

3. Recording, Analysis, and Playback, comprising approximately 31,000 lines of source code and responsible for capturing ATC sessions for later analysis.

4. National Airspace System Modification entailing a modification of the software that resides on the Host (outside the scope of this chapter).

5. The IBM AIX operating system, providing the underlying operating system environment for the operational software.

These CSCIs are components in that they form units of deliverable documentation and software, they appear in schedule milestones, and they are each responsible for a logically related segment of ISSS functionality.

Applications – CSCIs are composed of applications. An application corresponds roughly to a process, in the sense of Dijkstra's cooperating sequential processes, and is at the core of the approach the ISSS designers adopted for fault tolerance. An application is implemented as an Ada "main" unit (a process schedulable by the operating system).

ISSS is constructed to operate on a plurality of processors. Processors are logically combined to form a *processor group*. The purpose of a processor group is to host separate copies of one or more applications. This concept is critical to support fault tolerance and (therefore) availability. One executing copy is primary, and the others are secondary; hence, the different copies of applications are referred to as *primary address space* (PAS) or *standby address space* (SAS). The collection of one primary address space and its attendant standby address spaces are called an *operational unit*. A given operational unit resides entirely within the processors of a single processor group, which can consist of up to four processors. Those parts of the ISSS that are not constructed in this fault-tolerant manner (i.e., of coexisting primary and standby versions) simply run independently on different processors; these are called *functional groups*. Functional groups are present on each processor as needed, with each copy a separate instance of the program, maintaining its own state.

In summary, an application may be either an operating unit or a functional group. The two differ by whether the application's functionality is backed up by one or more secondary copies that keep up with the state and data of the primary copy and wait to take over in case the primary copy fails. Operational units have this fault-tolerant design; functional groups do not. An application is implemented as an operational unit if its availability requirements dictate it; otherwise it is implemented as a functional group.

Applications interact with each other in a client-server fashion; the client of the transaction sends the server a *service request message*, and the server replies with an acknowledgment. (As in all client-server schemes, a particular participant—or application, in this case—can be the client in one transaction and the server in another.) Within an operational unit, the PAS sends state change notification to each of its SASs, which look for time-outs or other signs that they should take over and become primary if the PAS or its processor fails. Figure 11.6 summarizes how the primary and secondary address spaces of an application coordinate with each other to provide backup capability and give their relationship to processor groups.

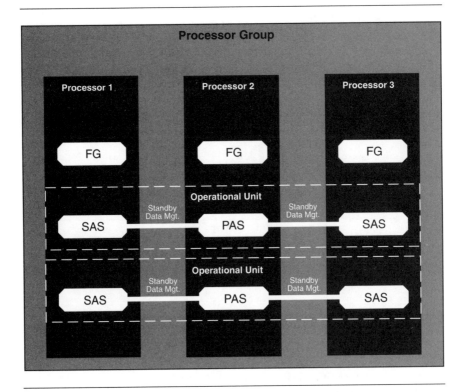

FIGURE 11.6 Functional groups, operational units, processor groups, and address spaces.

When a functional group receives a message, it need only respond and update its own state as appropriate. Typically, the PAS of an operational unit receives and responds to messages on behalf of the entire operational unit. It then must update both its own state and the state of its SASs, which involves sending additional messages to the SASs. Figure 11.7 shows how the applications operate in a client-server relationship.

In the event of a PAS failure, a switchover occurs as follows:

1. A SAS is promoted to the new PAS.

2. The new PAS reconstitutes with the clients of that operational unit (a fixed list for each operational unit) by sending them a message that means, essentially: The operational unit that was serving you has had a failure. Were you waiting for anything from us at the time? It then proceeds to service any requests received in response.

3. A new SAS is started to replace the previous PAS.

4. The newly started SAS announces itself to the new PAS, which starts sending it message as appropriate to keep it up to date.

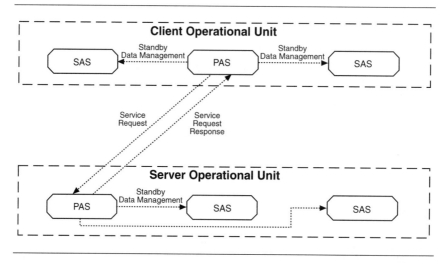

FIGURE 11.7 Applications as clients and servers.

If failure is detected within an SAS, a new SAS is started on some other processor. It coordinates with its PAS and starts receiving state data.

Programming language entities – An Ada (main) *program* is created from one or more source files; it typically comprises of number of *subprograms*, some of which are gathered into separately compilable *packages*. The ISSS is composed of a number of such programs, many of which operate in a client-server manner.

An Ada program may contain one or more *tasks*, which are Ada entities capable of executing concurrently with each other. The ISSS relies on Ada tasks for concurrent execution of individual threads of control in individual programs. Because Ada tasks are managed by the Ada runtime system, the ISSS also employs a mapping of Ada tasks onto UNIX (AIX) processes, which means that all individual threads of control (whether separate Ada programs or tasks within a single Ada program) are independent AIX processes operating concurrently.

Applications (i.e., operational units and functional groups) are decomposed into Ada packages, some of which include only type definitions and some of which are reused across applications. *Packaging* is a design activity intended to embody abstraction and information hiding, and it is carried out by an operational unit's chief designer.

Threads – Another kind of component is a thread. A *thread*, in this context, consists of software that, when taken as a unit and executing as one or more cooperating sequential processes, fulfills a logically related piece of functionality. Threads form the basis for test plans and in fact formed the basis for defining major deliverable versions of the ISSS software.

ISSS CONNECTIONS

The complement to architectural components is the connections among them. In the case of ISSS, the connection type most used to convey system information was the message-passing structure among applications. Sequential messages were used to define threads.

Interapplication communication is by message passing. We have already seen messages passed between clients and servers and between primary and secondary address spaces in an operational unit. There are almost no Ada rendezvous or other synchronization operations used because developers could not be sure about the timing performance of those mechanisms (for meeting hard real-time deadlines).

Figure 11.8 depicts the programs that provide the main operational ATC application functions of the ISSS and the major data flows among them.

TEMPLATES FOR STRUCTURING APPLICATIONS

Recall that the primary-secondary address space scheme described earlier relies on redundancy to achieve fault tolerance: Copies of the software are stored on different processors. While the primary copy is executing, it sends state information

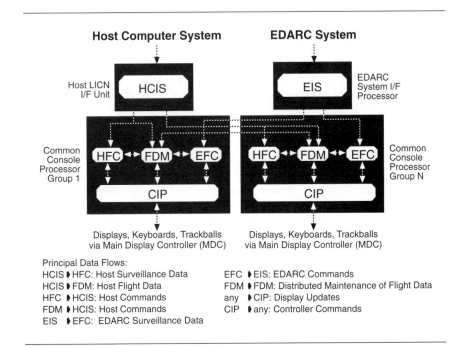

FIGURE 11.8   Data flows among application programs.

from time to time to all of the secondary copies so that they can take up execution when called on. The implementation plan for these copies called for both to come from true copies of the *same source code*. Even though the primary and secondary copies are never doing the same thing at the same time (the primary is performing its duty and sending state updates to its backups, and the secondaries are waiting to leap into action and accepting state updates), both programs come from identical copies of the same source code. To accomplish this, the contractor developed a standard code template for each application; the pattern is illustrated in Figure 11.9.

The structure is a continuous loop that services incoming events. If the event is one that causes the application to take a normal (non-fault-tolerant-related) action, it carries out the appropriate action, followed by an update of its backup counterparts' data so that the counterpart can take over if necessary. Most applications process between 50 and 100 normal events. Other events involve the transfer (transmission and reception) of state and data updates. The last set of events involves both the announcement that this unit has become the primary address space and requests from clients for services that the former primary address space (now failed) failed to complete.

This template has architectural implications: It makes it simple to add new applications to the system with a minimum of concern for the actual mechanics of the fault-tolerant mechanisms that were designed into the approach. Coders and maintainers of applications don't need to know about message handling mechanisms except at an abstract level, and they do not need to ensure that their applications are fault tolerant—that has been handled at a higher (architectural) level of design.

ISSS AS A LAYERED ARCHITECTURE

To support the operation of the ATC application programs on the ISSS processors system, support software is needed. Part of the necessary support is provided by a commercial UNIX operating system, AIX. However, UNIX does not provide all the services necessary to support a fault-tolerant distributed system such as ISSS. Therefore additional system services software was added to provide these functions. Figure 11.10 shows the overall software environment in a typical ISSS processor.

The lowest two rows of components above AIX represent extensions to AIX that run within the AIX kernel's address space. Due to performance requirements and for compatibility with the AIX operating system, these extensions are generally small programs written in the C language. Since they run within the kernels address space, faults in these programs can potentially damage AIX itself; hence, these must be relatively small trusted programs.

The Atomic Broadcast Manager plays a key role in the communication among the Local Availability Manager (LGSM) modules within a sector suite to manage the availability of functions within the suite. The Station Manager provides datagram services on the LCN and serves as the local representative of the

```
terminate:= false
initialize application/application protocols

ask for current state (image request)
Loop
   Get_event
   Case Event_Type is

   -- "normal" (non-fault-tolerant-related) requests to perform actions;
   -- only happens if this unit is the current primary address space
   when X=> Process X
           Send state data updates to other address spaces
   when Y=>Process Y
           Send state data updates to other address spaces
 ..
   when Terminate_Directive => clean up resources; terminate := true

   when State_Data_Update => apply to state data
   -- will only happen if this unit is a secondary address space, receiving
   -- the update from the primary after it has completed a "normal" action

   -- sending, receiving state data
   when Image_Request =>  send current state data to new address space
   when State_Data_Image => Initialize state data

   when Switch_Directive => notify service packages of change in rank

   -- these are requests that come in after a PAS/SAS switchover; they
   -- report services that they had requested from the old (failed) PAS
   -- which this unit (now the PAS) must complete. A,B, etc. are the names
   -- of the clients.
   when Recon_from_A=>reconstitute A
   when Recon_from_B=>reconstitute B
   ...
   when others=>log error
   end case
exit when terminate
end loop
```

FIGURE 11.9   Code structure template for fault-tolerant ISSS applications.

LCN network management services. The Network Interface Sublayer provides a similar function for the point-to-point messages, sharing its network information with the Station Manager.

   The next two rows represent operating system extensions that execute outside the AIX kernel's address space and therefore cannot directly damage AIX if they should contain faults. These programs are generally written in Ada.

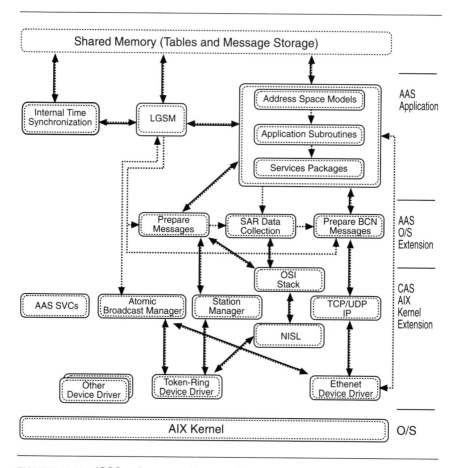

FIGURE 11.10 ISSS software architecture layers.

Prepare Messages handles LCN messages for application programs. Prepare BCN Messages performs a similar function for messages to be sent on the BCN. One function these programs need to perform is to determine which of the multiple redundant copies of an application program within a sector suite is the primary copy and thus is to receive messages. LGSM provides the control information needed to make this determination.

The top layer is where the applications reside. The Local Availability Manager and the Internal Time Synchronization programs are application-level system services. The Local Availability Manager is responsible for managing the initiation, termination, and availability of the application programs. It communicates with each address space on its own processor to control its operation and check its status. It communicates with the Local Availability Manager on the other processors within its sector suite to manage the availability of the sector-suite functions, including switching from a primary to a backup copy of an application program when appropriate. The Local Availability Manager communicates with the global availability management application that resides on the M&C consoles to report status and to accept control commands. The Internal Time Synchronization program synchronizes the processor's clock with that of the other ISSS processors, which is crucial to the operation of the availability management functions.

The Coordination task provides the connection between the address space availability management and the system availability management by communicating with the Local Availability Manager program on its processor. The Initialization task performs certain address space initialization functions when the address space is initiated. This includes reading adaptation data and inserting it into the address space's data structures. The Device tasks are optional and are only present for applications that directly communicate with a device driver. The Function tasks are the tasks that provide the application-specific functions.

FAULT TOLERANCE

The high availability requirements for ISSS elevated fault tolerance to an important role in the design of the system. For one thing, a cold restart of the system in the event of a failure is out of the question. Immediate (or at least rapid) switchover to a component on standby seemed the best approach. As design progressed and this idea became clearer, a new architectural structure emerged: the fault-tolerant hierarchy (Figure 11.11). This structure describes how faults are detected and isolated and how the system recovers. Whereas the PAS/SAS scheme traps and recovers from errors that are confined within a single application, the fault-tolerant hierarchy is designed to trap and recover from errors that are the result of cross-application interaction.

The ISSS system fault-tolerant hierarchy provides various levels of fault detection and recovery. Each level asynchronously

- Detects errors in self, peers, lower levels
- Handles exceptions from lower levels
- Diagnoses, recovers, reports or raises exceptions

Each level is meant to produce another increment in system availability above that produced by the lower levels. The levels are as follows:

- Physical (network, processor, and I/O devices)
- Operating system
- Runtime environment
- Application
- Local availability
- Group availability
- Global availability
- System monitor and control

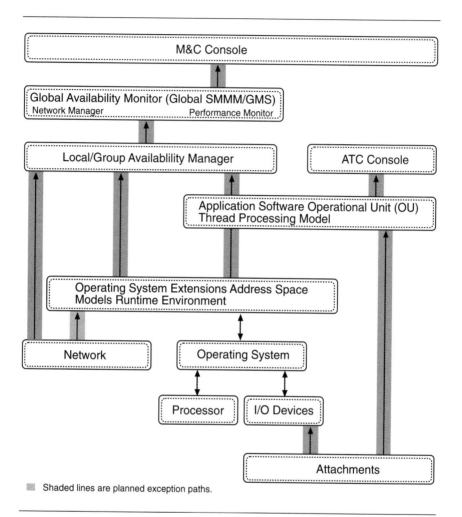

FIGURE 11.11   ISSS software components for fault tolerance.

Fault detection and isolation are performed at each level in the hierarchy. The fault detection is performed by built-in tests, event time-outs, network circuit tests, group membership protocol, and as a last resort, human reaction to alarms and indicators.

Fault recovery is performed at each level in the software hierarchy and can be automatic or manual. For the local, group, and global availability managers, the recovery methods are table driven. There are four types of recovery from failure in a PAS. The type of recovery used depends on the current operational status and is determined by the LGSM using decision tables, as follows:

- In a switchover, the SAS takes over almost immediately from its PAS.
- A warm restart uses checkpoint data (written to nonvolatile memory).
- A cold restart uses default data and loses state history.
- A cutover is used to transition to new (or old) logic or adaptation data.

Redundancy is provided by network hardware (LCN, BCN, and associated bridges), processor hardware (up to four processors per processor group, redundant recording), and software (multiple address spaces per operational unit).

This concludes our presentation of the ISSS architecture. The remainder of the chapter discusses the approach taken when the customer, troubled by cost and schedule overruns, asked if the architecture was up to the task required of it.

11.5   Assessing the Architecture for Maintainability

In our terminology, maintenance refers to the process of finding and correcting bugs and modifying the system to satisfy new requirements. These new requirements may include adding new functionality, changing the performance or availability requirements, altering the behavior (e.g., the user interface), inserting new hardware, making the system interoperable with new systems in its environment, or incorporating third-party (including commercial) software.

As we have seen, there is no scalar measurement of product maintainability; it is not possible to simply say whether or to what degree a system is maintainable in the absence of specific changes. Often, at the time of development or deployment, a system's precise maintenance history cannot be predicted, and so a set of specific changes (that would allow us to give a precise measure of maintainability) is not available. In this situation, there are two approaches that can be taken. The first is to assess whether generally accepted software engineering practices were followed that, in the past, have resulted in systems that were easily modified. We call this *general maintainability*. The second is to assess the estimated impact of changing the system with respect to a set of whatever specific planned changes are known. For instance, in the case of ISSS, we might wish to evaluate whether the system was maintainable with respect to the specific change of deleting electronic flight strips[1] from the requirements or with respect to replacing the RS/6000 processors with a chip of similar capability. We call this *specific maintainability*.

---

[1] A strip of paper, printed by the system, containing flight-plan data about an aircraft currently in or about to arrive in a sector. Before ISSS, these flight strips were annotated by hand in pencil. As a cost-saving measure, the customer was considering deleting the requirement for ISSS to deal with flight strips. For one thing, no printers would need to be acquired or maintained.

Both methods are important in assessing maintainability. This section will describe a SAAM-like maintainability assessment that was performed for ISSS by a software audit team.

In attempting to assess general maintainability, the software audit focused upon the principles and abstractions used to create the major units of design and code in the system. architecturally, this includes the CSCIs and their subcomponents. At the design level, this includes the rationale for packaging and the use of abstraction, encapsulation, and separation of concerns. The audit also focused upon the quality of the implementation, relying on quantitative analysis of the Ada code by an outside contractor and inspection of the code by the team itself. These steps are outside the scope of this chapter.

To assess specific maintainability, the team asked the developer to conduct a series of hands-on exercises in which the team proposed a set of requirements modifications and observed the artifacts (documents, code units) that each modification affected. Some were changes that the developer had already made or considered making to ISSS; others were new. The exercises included the following:

- Making major modifications to the Monitor and Control position's human-computer interface
- Importing third-party-developed air traffic applications into the ISSS system
- Deleting the requirement to support electronic flights strips in ISSS
- Increasing the system's maximum capacity of flight tracks by 50 percent
- Adding new ATC views to the system

During all of these exercises, the audit recorded the process that was followed to make each change and viewed and cataloged the documentation that was or would have been produced, accessed, or modified as a result of the change. Because much of the system had already been coded at the time of the review, it was possible to catalog the code units that were or would have been modified in some of the exercises.

These exercises were, of course, SAAM scenarios. Because the assessment was focused on maintainability, they were all intentionally indirect scenarios—scenarios whose satisfaction required changing the architecture.

RESULTS

The results of the exercising scenario are discussed in the following subsections.

Importing Third-Party Software.   The ability to import third-party software was a quality important to the ISSS customer. The fact that ISSS uses a commercial operating system, commercial network hardware and software, commercial processors, and the Ada language and runtime support environment are de facto evidence of the architecture's ability to import third-party software. Further, development history showed how the system easily handled version upgrades of all of these items during development. Finally, the developer had built a working prototype whose display driver was the commercial X-Windows system. However, the customer was also interested in how amenable the architecture was to importing third-party ATC applications. The developer was able to point to an ATC system built for Taiwan based on the ISSS architecture. In this system, a Taiwanese component had been integrated into the ISSS architecture. This integration required rehosting it onto the RS/6000 and writing a wrapper that made this application resemble an operational unit. We will discuss wrappers more in Chapter 17.

Modifiability. Modifiability with respect to requirements changes is also important, and the ISSS architecture passed this test quite well. None of the scenario exercises showed any architectural impact except for the one that deleted the requirement for electronic flight strips. Here, the change to the architecture was primarily the wholesale deletion of components, a straightforward change. This exercise showed that the ISSS design is amenable to extracting functionally useful subsets. Given the subsequent cancellation of ISSS in favor of a similar but simpler system, this exercise proved to be prescient. Further, the project's error-correction history was available and showed that of over 5600 trouble reports, only 10 had architectural ramifications (meaning that a component was added, deleted, or its interface was substantially changed).

The extensive use made of adaptation data in ISSS has broad implications for maintenance. *Adaptation data* refers to data that the ISSS system reads during initialization that tells it how to configure itself. There is site-specific adaptation data used to tailor the ISSS system across the 22 en route centers in which it was planned to be deployed and so-called preset adaptation data, which exists to tailor the software to changes that arise during development and deployment but which will not represent site-specific differences. Adaptation data represent an elegant and crucial shortcut to modifying the system in the face of site-specific requirements, user- or center-specific preferences, configuration changes, requirements changes, and other aspects of the software that might be expected to vary over time and across deployment sites. In effect, the software has been designed to read its operating parameters and behavioral specifications from input data; it is therefore completely general with respect to the set of behaviors able to be represented in that data. For example, one of the change exercises followed a requirements change to split the data in one ATC window view into two separate windows. The exercise revealed that this change required that only a few lines of code be modified and was primarily handled by changing the adaptation data.

The negative side is that adaptation data present a complicated mechanism to maintainers. For example, although it is trivial (from an operational point of view) to add new commands or command syntax to the system, the implementation of this flexibility is in fact a complicated interpretive language all its own. Also, complicated interactions may occur between various pieces of adaptation data, which could affect correctness, and there are no automated or semiautomated mechanisms in place to guard against the effects of such inconsistencies. Finally, adaptation data significantly increases the state space within which the operational software must correctly perform, which has broad implications for system testing.

One kind of modification appeared problematic. There is a fairly complicated procedure for adding a new operational unit to the system. The process includes the following:

- Beginning with the template shown in Figure 11.9 for the operational unit, consisting of a skeletal control structure that is common across all operational units

- Identifying the necessary input data and where they reside

- Identifying which operational units require output data from the new operational unit

- Fitting this operational unit's communication patterns into a systemwide acyclic graph in such a way that the graph remains acyclic so that deadlocks will not occur

- Designing messages to achieve the required data flows

- Identifying internal state data that must be used for checkpointing and the state data that must be included in the update communication from PAS to SAS

- Partitioning the state data into messages that fit well on the networks

- Defining the necessary message types

- Planning for switchover in case of failure: planning updates to ensure complete state capture

- Ensuring consistent data in case of switchover

- Ensuring that individual processing steps are completed in less time than a system "heartbeat"

- Planning data-sharing and data-locking protocols with other operational units

This complicated protocol can be navigated straightforwardly by experienced team members, but without adequate documentation it represents a gauntlet of confusion to a newly baptized maintainer.

Use of COTS Software.   The customer for ISSS applied considerable pressure to have the developer use as much commercial off-the-shelf (COTS) software as possible. There is general agreement that using COTS software is usually good practice; however, such usage may be in fundamental conflict with the extraordinarily high availability requirements to which ISSS is being held. To certify the availability of the system, it is necessary to be able to certify the availability and reliability of its components. In the case of ISSS, the developers had access to proprietary reliability and fault-injection data about the IBM AIX operating system, a situation they do not enjoy with respect to arbitrary off-the-shelf products (and indeed, a situation that most developers do not enjoy with respect to their chosen operating system). It is not possible to test a system completely to verify that it will be unavailable no more than seconds per year; therefore, meeting availability requirements must be done by analyzing the availability of components. Such fine-grained reliability information is not available for COTS software in general.

Thus, requiring or encouraging the use of COTS software may be in conflict with maintaining the ultrahigh reliability requirements of the system. There is a choice to be made between requiring COTS software and maintaining the reliability standards with assurance. Any availability figures claimed for ISSS are the result of making certain availability assumptions about the COTS that it employs.

Performance.   The version of ISSS that the team audited had in fact met most of its performance requirements, indicating the de facto ability of the architecture and design to satisfy the performance constraints. However, the change exercise to increase by 50 percent the maximum number of flight tracks monitored by the system revealed that the networks and network interface units would be highly stressed and might not be able to support the new load. However, the fact that the architecture relegated hardware dependencies to specific levels in the layered design meant that performance upgrades to the hardware should be straightforward. Thus, the ability of the architecture to absorb change pays dividends in achieving increased performance.

11.6 Summary

The Initial Sector Suite System illustrates how architectural solutions can be the key to achieving the demanding needs of an application. Because of its projected long life, high cost, large size, important function, and high visibility, ISSS was subject to extraordinary change pressures over and above its demanding operational requirements. Human-computer interfaces, new hardware, new commercial components, operating system and network upgrades, and capacity increases were not just likely but were foregone conclusions. The architecture, by using standard fault-tolerant mechanisms (and code templates) including hardware and software redundancy and layered fault detection, and by using distributed computing with message passing, was able to satisfy its complex, wide-ranging operational requirements.

The second half of the chapter presented the results of a SAAM-like evaluation of the ISSS architecture. (SAAM scenario analysis was but one part of the audit.) The architecture, by manifesting strict encapsulation and separation of concerns (particularly in its software layering) and by the widespread use of adaptation data was able to easily satisfy the audit's change scenarios.

11.7 For Further Reading

The saga of the FAA's attempts to upgrade its air traffic control software has been written about extensively; for example, by Gibbs [Gibbs 94]. The effort to audit the ISSS system for salvageability was reported by Brown [Brown 95a,b]. In these papers, maintainability is treated as a dual quality related not only to properties of the system but also to the capabilities of the organization slated to perform the maintenance. This important aspect of maintainability—the necessary fit between the maintenance that a system needs and the maintenance that an organization is prepared to provide for it—is not usually discussed.

11.8 Discussion Questions

1. High reliability was a main impetus behind the architecture presented in this chapter. How were other quality attributes, such as performance, affected by this requirement? How might the architecture change if this requirement is removed?

2. How many architectural styles can you recognize in the architecture for ISSS?

PART THREE

MOVING FROM ARCHITECTURES TO SYSTEMS

Part Three continues our tour around the architecture business cycle. Whereas Part Two took us from the architect to the architecture, Part Three focuses on the segment between the architecture and the system or systems that are built from it.

One of the tenets of Chapter 2 was that architecture serves as a common vehicle for stakeholder communication. What role does formal representation play toward that end? Chapter 12 discusses architecture description languages, which are formal languages for specifying the architecture of a system. Several such languages exist in universities and research departments; a few exist in the commercial world. We will take an in-depth look at one of the latter and show how its use can add to the early analysis capabilities we illustrated in Chapters 9 and 10.

Once an architecture has been specified (or at least the first iteration of it), how does it help expedite the process of building a sytem that conforms to it? Chapter 13 discusses architecture-based development, how it differs from conventional development, and how techniques such as architecture-based team composition and component templates can help to shorten the production schedule and increase reliability and predictability.

Chapter 14 is the case study of Part Three. Structural modeling is an architectural style that has been used to build several flight simulation systems for the U.S. Air Force. Structural modeling features a small number of component types; each component in a type has an identical substructure, an identical data interchange protocol, identical interactions with the process scheduler, identical error-reporting conventions, and a limited and easily identifiable correspondence with

265

the part of the aircraft being simulated. The result of this overall consistency and conformity is a system in which all the components "look" alike even though their functionality may differ. This results in an architecture that is not only highly scalable and integrable, but one whose components can be implemented essentially by filling in the blanks of standard coding templates. Structural modeling is a style of architecture that allows the advantages of architecture-based development to be epitomized.

Part Three, then, brings us to the system-building stage of the architecture business cycle.

12

Architecture Description Languages

with Jeromy Carrière

> *A good notation should embody characteristics familiar to any user of mathematical notation: Ease of expressing constructs arising in problems, suggestivity, ability to subordinate detail, economy, amenability to formal proofs.*
> — Ken Iverson, creator of the APL programming language [Iverson 87]

We have seen how architecture can be used as the vehicle to achieve quality attributes important to a business enterprise. Up to this point, the treatment of the topics has been independent of any technology (or technique, for that matter) for describing or representing an architecture. In the A-7E case study of Chapter 3 we showed that architecture-based design and development did not require a high-level programming language. In our treatment of architecture-level evaluation in Chapters 9 and 10, the evaluation techniques were largely carried out by hand, except for the creation of simulators—which are usually hand-crafted.

To date, architectures have largely been represented by box-and-line drawings in which the nature of the components, their properties, the semantics of the connections, and the behavior of the system as a whole are poorly (if at all) defined. Even though such figures often give an intuitive picture of the system's construction, they usually fail to answer such questions as the following:

- What are the components? Are they modules that exist only at design-time but are compiled together before runtime? Are they tasks or processes threaded together from different modules, assembled at compile-time, that

Note: Jeromy Carrière is a member of the technical staff at the Software Engineering Institute, Carnegie Mellon University.

form runtime units? Or are they something as nebulous as "functional areas," as in data-flow diagrams, or something else entirely?

- What do the components do? How do they behave? What other components do they rely on?

- What do the connections mean? Do they mean "sends data to," "sends control to," "calls," "is a part of," some combination of these, or something else? What are the mechanisms used to fulfill these relations?

Architecture description languages (ADLs) result from a linguistic approach to the formal representation of architectures, and as such they address the shortcomings of informal representations. Further, as will be shown, sophisticated ADLs allow for early analysis and feasibility testing of architectural design decisions.

The case studies in this book have a carefully defined notation that, among other things, draws clear distinctions among the kinds of components shown in the diagrams, but this notation is not an ADL. Thus, it is possible to get by with informal descriptions of architectures as long as one is careful. In Section 2.4, we identified three reasons why architecture is important:

1. Mutual communication

2. Embodiment of early design decisions suitable for analysis

3. Transferable abstraction of a system

All of these purposes would be better served if there were a standard notation—an *architecture description language*—for representing architectures.

Such a language would enhance communication because both the author and the reader of the architectural description would share a common understanding, saving time spent asking clarifying questions about the drawings. A language would support the analysis of early design decisions and would enable tools to be built to assist in the development process. A language would provide a mechanism to construct the artifact that is to be transferred to subsequent systems; for example, it might be possible to generate executable code for (at least part of) a system based on its formal architectural description. Finally, a formal architecture representation is more likely to be maintained and followed than an informal one, can more readily be consulted and treated as authoritative, and can more easily be transferred to other projects as a core asset.

Do such languages exist? Yes; perhaps there are more than you think. ADLs are emerging as a technological solution for representing and analyzing architectures. Nearly all are still in the research stage, and so it is premature to choose any of them as the most promising, most powerful, most useful, or most likely to succeed. Because of the immaturity of ADLs, this chapter will focus on the requirements that an ADL must satisfy and how you might evaluate an ADL if you are choosing among alternatives. Commercial-quality ADLs are emerging, however, and we discuss one of them at the end of this chapter.

12.1   Architecture Description Languages Today

There is a surprisingly large variety of ADLs emerging from industrial and academic research groups. A few ADLs are commercial products, such as the one we describe in Section 12.5; a dozen or so are emerging from university environments. Most trace their lineage to government research sponsorship. And many languages that were not intended to be ADLs, it turns out, are suitable for representing and analyzing an architecture. ADLs lie at the conceptual intersection among requirements, programming, and modeling languages, and yet they are distinct from all three.

In principle, ADLs differ from requirements languages because the latter describe problem spaces, whereas the former are rooted in the solution space. In practice, requirements are often divided into behavioral chunks for ease of presentation, and languages for representing those behaviors are sometimes well suited to representing architectural components, even though that was not the original goal of the language.

In principle, ADLs differ from programming languages because the latter bind all architectural abstractions to specific point solutions, whereas ADLs intentionally suppress or vary such binding. In practice, architecture is embodied in and recoverable from code, and many languages provide architecture-level structures of the system. For example, Ada offers the ability to view a system just in terms of its package specifications, which are the interfaces to components. However, Ada offers little or no architectural analytical capabilities, nor does it provide architecture-level insight into how the components are "wired" together. We would not be comfortable claiming that Ada is an ADL, but it does offer an architectural structure.

In principle, ADLs differ from modeling languages because the latter are more concerned with the behaviors of the whole rather than of the parts; ADLs concentrate on representation of components. In practice, many modeling languages allow the representation of cooperating components and can represent architectures reasonably well.

Languages that are today generally considered mainstream ADLs provide abstractions, structures, and analysis capabilities that are clearly architectural in nature. This is in contrast to a programming or requirements language that tends to show other kinds of information. Analysis capabilities include a discrete event simulator that uses behavioral information about each component to generate partially ordered event sets and a rate monotonic analyzer that uses black-box performance information about each component in order to compute schedulability.

Nearly all ADLs have the following in common:

- They feature a graphical syntax; most also have a textual form, and nearly all feature formally defined syntax and semantics.
- They provide features for modeling distributed systems.

- They provide little support for capturing design rationale and/or history, other than through general-purpose annotation mechanisms.

- They handle data flow and control flow as interconnection mechanisms; other kinds of connections are less well supported.

- They feature the ability to represent hierarchical levels of detail and handle multiple instantiations of a template as a quick way to copy substructures during creation.

A glaring commonality is the lack of in-depth experience and real-world application that ADLs currently offer. This is a reflection of our assertion earlier that ADLs were common in the research community but had not yet reached common practice.

ADLs vary widely, however, with respect to their underlying models, their analytical capabilities, and the kinds of systems about which they embody knowledge. For instance,

- ADLs differ markedly in their ability to handle real-time constructs at the architectural level. Roughly half seem to deal with hard real-time constructs such as deadlines; only a small number deal with soft real-time constructs such as task priorities.

- ADLs vary in their ability to support the specification of particular architectural styles. Nearly all ADLs can represent pipe-and-filter architectures, either directly or indirectly. Other styles do not fare as well. Most provide hierarchical structuring of components and can represent objects, but few handle object-oriented class inheritance. Few handle dynamic architectures.

- Nearly all ADLs provide built-in internal consistency and completeness rules for artifacts rendered in those languages, only a few allow the user to define what was meant by consistency, and only a few deal with consistency between different artifacts (e.g., between an architecture and component designs).

- ADLs vary widely in their ability to support analysis, as mentioned above.

- ADLs differ in their ability to handle variability or different instantiations of the same architecture. All support component variability through simple rewrite capability, but few support maintaining different instantiations of the same architecture simultaneously. That is, ADLs do not yet support product line architectures in a helpful way.

After considering the requirements for ADLs, and after seeing how ADLs resemble and differ from each other, what can we conclude about what makes a language an ADL? The following is a minimal set of requirements for a language to be an ADL:

- The ADL must be suitable for communicating an architecture to all interested parties. All of the architecture's structures must be available through the ADL, including a range of dynamic and static structures. Components and connectors and their types must be identified in each of the structures, and the level of granularity of the information must be customizable for the readers of the architecture.

- An ADL must support the tasks of architecture creation, refinement, and validation. It must embody rules about what constitutes a complete or consistent architecture.

- An ADL must provide the ability to represent (even if indirectly) most of the common architectural styles.

- An ADL must have the ability to provide structures of the system that express architectural information but at the same time suppress implementation or nonarchitectural information.

- The ADL must provide a basis for further implementation. It must be possible to add information to the ADL specification to enable the final system specification to be derived from the ADL.

- If the language can express implementation-level information, it must contain capabilities for matching more than one implementation to the architecture-level structures of the system. That is, it must support specification of families of implementations that all satisfy a common architecture.

- An ADL must support either an analytical capability, based on architecture-level information, or a capability for quickly generating prototype implementations.

12.2   Capturing Architectural Information in an ADL

Architecture description languages represent architectural structures that can be divided into types, static and dynamic information.

STATIC INFORMATION

The ability to declare a component and name its type is an essential feature of an ADL language that provides static structures. Each component would then be explicitly declared, for example, as a pipe or a server or a repository. Then, the semantics of being that particular type could be enforced both by the compile time system and the runtime system. Thus, for example, a pipe might be constrained to be connected only to a filter.

Defining the semantics of a component is hard, however. To see the problem, consider a pipe. In Section 5.1 we defined a *pipe* as being stateless and simply existing to move data between filters. A pipe may be stateless from an external perspective, but it almost certainly has to have some internal state. Furthermore, the relationship between pipes and filters is a statement of intent and a statement of the allowable types to which a pipe might be connected, but it is not testable unless it is possible to verify that a component is a filter.

The data that enter a standard pipe are identical to the data that exit. It seems reasonable that a new kind of pipe should be allowed to do some format conversion as long as the data that exit the pipe are *semantically* equivalent to the data that enter the pipe. This is now a slippery slope because testing whether a format conversion adds additional information is an unsolvable problem.

The point of this discussion is not that having an ADL that allows declaration of component types impossible, but that having such an ADL involves difficult issues that are currently in the research realm. If component and connector types could be strongly defined, it would be possible to defer their binding until later in the development cycle. A standard technique in software engineering is to defer decisions to as late as possible in the development cycle. The advantage of deferring decisions is that at a later time in the development cycle more information is available to enable a decision to be made more correctly or more easily. The disadvantage is that, for a certain class of decisions, errors can remain undetected until they become expensive to correct. (We have just summarized 30 years of discussion between the proponents and opponents of strong typing in programming languages.)

In the architectural context, one decision that can be deferred is the binding of function to component types. Consider the properties exhibited by the subroutine call, the ancestor of all connectors: It connects two components of type "procedure"; it transfers data bidirectionally; it imbues the called program with control; it blocks the caller; the caller specifies its partner at design time, whereas the called program does not know the identify of its partner. How many of these and other qualities are explicitly required when a subroutine call is chosen as the connection mechanism between two elements? In all likelihood, very few. But by embedding that choice in the architecture, the actual requirements are lost. Substituting another connector (e.g., when porting to a distributed environment or when interacting with a different kind of component that is not callable) becomes problematic. Further, components that are written to coordinate via a particular mechanism are not nearly so reusable as are components written with their coordination requirements specified but with the choice of mechanism left unbound.

Deferring the choice of connector type, for example, could be accomplished by adding statements such as "bind to module x, furnishing y and z" to a standard programming language. Then, at runtime, based on system environment (distributed or single process) and quality of service (fast connection to module x), a choice could be made that the binding mechanism is a standard procedure call, a remote procedure call, a process initiation, and so forth.

As with the discussion of the declaration of component types, such issues are currently in the realm of research and do not appear in commercially available packages.

DYNAMIC INFORMATION

Understanding how the various components interact at execution time is essential for understanding the behavior of a system. This behavior can be communicated by using execution models such as Petri nets or by utilizing animation techniques.

A dynamic structure frequently requires a simulator to perform analysis, although models exist for many kinds of analysis that do not involve simulation (e.g., Markov models for availability analysis and Rate Monotonic Analysis for real-time scheduling). The information provided for the simulation is dependent on the type of analysis to be done. If a performance analysis is to be done, the resource usage of the components must be estimated. If a reliability analysis is to be done, the reliability of each component must be estimated. These and other kinds of information can be readily captured by an ADL, which then launches the appropriate analysis tool with the required information.

Once resource information is provided, portions of the system (such as the real-time scheduler) can be generated automatically. For scheduler generation to occur, the resource consumption for each component needs to be known and the data dependencies among the components also need to be known. Other portions of the code can also be generated. The CODE (Computation-Oriented Display Environment) system for parallel programs lets an architect specify the data flows among components and then generates all the Ada wrappers that establish the parallel processes and the data transfer among them. The programmer must fill in the body of the templates with the functionality of each component, but all of the coordination infrastructure is produced by the tool.

12.3   How Do ADLs Help System Development?

An ADL that achieves all of the goals we enumerated for it must be a part of an integrated development environment that supports the incremental addition of information. A generic scenario of how an ADL can be used to build a system as follows:

- The system would be initially described through a texual or (more typically) graphical input procedure that is based on architectural styes and component types. Major subsystems are described in terms of the information that they accept and produce. A description of behavior is associated with each component, which might include the kinds of events they produce and respond to, timing information, and resource usage information.

- Information that describes the behavior of the system, perhaps via use cases or scenarios or some more formal trace language, is entered and maintained along with the high level description.

- Those types of analyses that can be performed at this level of detail are performed. Changes to the component types are allowed without the necessity of reentering any information that has already been furnished.

- Resource estimates and descriptions for the ADL simulator or model analyzer are also entered into the ADL system. These allow for further analyses, such as analyses of performance, availability, or security.

- The components are refined, as necessary, for each type of analysis. At any time a component can be viewed along with any information about that component entered thus far and the results of any analyses that affect the component.

- Once the system yields acceptable results for the different analyses, the components are refined into code. The code, or at least code templates, is generated where possible from the descriptions associated with the components.

12.4   Choosing an ADL

The most compelling question to an architect about an ADL is, Which ADL should I choose for my project? Just as choosing the best architecture depends upon stating the goals for it, choosing the best ADL depends upon what the architect wishes to achieve by using it. While we cannot give an answer to the question—ADLs are rapidly emerging and evolving—we can give advice about how you can answer this question for yourself: Evaluate a candidate ADL against a set of applicability criteria. In this section, we provide criteria.

This section gives a list of questions to ask about an ADL to see how it compares to other ADLs in terms of inherent capability, tool support, maturity, and other criteria. ADLs can be evaluated or described by listing the following:

- System-oriented attributes
- Language-oriented attributes
- Process-oriented attributes

SYSTEM-ORIENTED ATTRIBUTES

System-oriented attributes are related to the application system derived from the software architecture that was encoded in the ADL. Although all are attributes of the end system, they reflect the ability of the ADL to produce such a system. System-oriented attributes characterize an ADL by enumerating the types of systems for which they are especially applicable or which they were intended to support. We characterize a system by its predominant architectural style, its broad taxonomic category such as real-time or distributed, and its application domain. Table 12.1 shows questions used to elicit system-oriented attributes with respect to the architectural style(s) supported by an ADL.

LANGUAGE-ORIENTED ATTRIBUTES

There is also a large class of language-oriented attributes. These are attributes of the ADL itself, independent of the system(s) it is being used to develop. These attributes include the kind of information usually found in a language reference manual, if one exists. Table 12.2 illustrates the questions used to elicit the language-oriented attributes of an ADL.

TABLE 12.1   System-Oriented Attributes of an ADL

Questions about the system-oriented attributes of an ADL
How suitable is the ADL for representing a particular type of application system?
How well does the ADL allow description of architectural styles?
What broad classes of systems (e.g., hard real-time, distributed, embedded systems with dynamic architectures) can have their architectures represented with the ADL?

TABLE 12.2   Language-Oriented Attributes of an ADL

Questions on the language-oriented attributes of an ADL
Are the ADL's syntax and semantics formally defined?
Does the ADL define *completeness* for an architecture description? How? To what extent does the ADL allow an incomplete architecture description?
Is self-consistency defined for an architecture description (internal)? Is it defined between two different descriptions or between an architecture description and some other rendering of the system such as a requirements specification or coded implementation (external)?
How much nonarchitecture information can the ADL represent? What type?
How well does the ADL support different structures that highlight different perspectives of the architecture? Which structures are supported? Does the ADL support mapping between structures?
How much detailed knowledge is needed to use the ADL to represent an architecture?
How does the ADL address presentation control?
Does the ADL support the ability to define new types of components, connectors, etc., including composite types?
Does the ADL support domain-specific extensions?
Does the ADL have the ability to define new statements or abstractions?
Does the ADL support multiple instantiation (the ability to create copies of a component that are identical to the original or that vary in specified ways)?
Does the ADL have a subset capability (the ability to partition the architecture description into smaller pieces that can be examined or analyzed in isolation)?
Does the ADL allow for embedded commentary?
How easily modified is the software architecture description?
How well does the ADL support scalability; the representation of large, complex systems?
Does the ADL support arbitrary abstraction levels (hierarchical levels of detail)?
Does the ADL support arbitrary cross-referencing (the ability to have pointers to related information within the architecture description)?
How well does the ADL represent the variations in the application systems that can be derived from an architecture?

PROCESS-ORIENTED ATTRIBUTES

Process-oriented attributes tell how the ADL is used to create, validate, analyze, and refine an architecture description and to build an application system. Included are attributes that measure or describe how or to what extent an ADL allows predictive evaluation of the application with respect to that attribute. They are related to the semantics of the language that support analysis, evaluation, and verification of the architecture. These attributes test whether the ADL contains enough information to allow analysis of an architecture, and whether tools that exploit the capability actually exist.

We are ignoring the distinction between a language and any tools or environmental infrastructure to support it. The likelihood that any organization would adopt a language but eschew all tool support for it, presumably preferring to write its own or proceed manually, is quite small. Process-oriented attributes exist to explicitly describe the reasoning ability provided by the language and the tool support available to exploit that ability. They answer whether the ADL is executable in any sense or just exists to facilitate human-to-human communication.

Table 12.3 presents a set of issues to be aware of when evaluating an ADL's support for the software development process.

TABLE 12.3   Process-Oriented Attributes of an ADL

Questions on the process-oriented attributes of an ADL
Is there a textual editor, a tool (specific to the ADL) for directly manipulating textual descriptions of architectures?
Is there a graphical editor, a tool (specific to the ADL) for directly manipulating graphical descriptions of architectures?
Can a tool (specific to the ADL) import information from other descriptions into the architecture?
Is there a syntax checker (e.g., parser), a semantics checker, a completeness checker, an internal consistency checker, or an external consistency checker?
Is there a browser, interactive support for undirected navigation of the description?
Is there a search tool, interactive support for directed navigation of the description?
Does the ADL support incremental refinement?
Is version control directly supported?
Does the ADL support comparing two architecture representations to see if they represent the same architecture?
What support is provided by the ADL for analyzing architecture-level information to predict or project qualities of the end system (e.g., schedulability, throughput, memory usage, completeness, correctness, security, interoperability, maintainability, reliability, usability, etc.)?
Does the ADL support building a compilable or executable software system from a design?
Does the ADL allow a system description to be composed of or integrated with components' bodies to produce a compilable or executable software system (particularly for diverse platform types and environments such as heterogeneous distributed)?
Is test case generation supported?
Can the ADL generate documentation?
Is there a documented sequence of steps for using the ADL?

12.5   An Example of an ADL

Now that we've told you about ADLs and architecture representation in general, it is time to show an example of how they are used. There are many ADLs in the research labs, and a few have made their way into the marketplace. We will present one of the latter.

The tool that we will present is called ObjecTime,[1] and its design method and ADL are called real-time object-oriented modeling (ROOM). This system appears to be representative of the current generation of ADL tools. It is already widely and successfully used in the telecommunications industry.

ROOM is a graphical modeling ADL designed for the development of systems characterized by such properties as timeliness, dynamic internal structure, reactiveness, concurrency, and distribution. ROOM is based on a set of modeling abstractions centered around active objects or *actors*. Actors are the structural elements of a system modeled using ROOM, providing hierarchical decomposition and inheritance. Actor interfaces are defined by *protocols* that specify sets of direction-dependent messages or *signals* that may be exchanged between actors. Protocols, like actors, may be organized into an inheritance hierarchy. *Ports* are protocol endpoints associated with actors and are connected by *bindings*. The final element of a ROOM model is the definition of actor behavior via *ROOM-charts,* based on Harel's Statechart formalism [Harel 88]. A ROOMchart identifies the possible states of an actor, the *signals* that initiate transitions between states, and the actions performed on transitions.

A fundamental principle of ROOM is that of the *operational model.* Once a ROOM model has been fleshed out sufficiently, it may be executed. The purpose of this execution is to validate requirements and to demonstrate behavior. Thus, ROOM models may act as system prototypes early in the development life cycle. This is one of ObjecTime's selling points: that an executable model is available early in the design cycle and this model can be progressively refined.

When a model is *fully* specified, it may be compiled into an executing system when fleshed out with actor bodies coded in a procedural programming language such as C++. The ObjecTime toolset provides an environment for ROOM modeling, execution, and compilation.

Because of this feature, a design can be analyzed for runtime defects even when little of its detailed functionality has been specified, and there is no conceptual gap to bridge when moving from specification to design to execution.

Figure 12.1 shows a simple example of the ROOM notation, constructed using the ObjecTime tool. The figure shows the following:

- An actor with two subactors, `subactor1` and `subactor2`
- A *relay port*, `protocol1Port1`

---

[1] ObjecTime is a registered trademark of ObjecTime Limited.

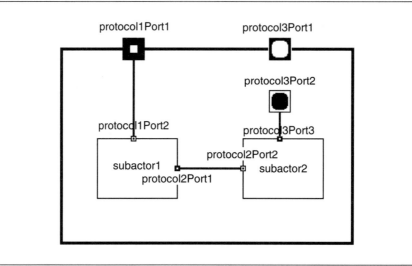

FIGURE 12.1   An example of the ROOM notation.

- An *end port*, `protocol3Port1`
- An *internal port*, `protocol3Port2`

The relay port, `protocol1Port1`, is used to pass messages between `subactor1` and an external actor, through the boundary of the containing actor, while the end port, `protocol3Port1`, is used for communication between this actor and other actors. The internal port, `protocol3Port2`, provides a mechanism for communication between the containing actor and its subactors, specifically `subactor2`. The types (relay port or end port) of the ports on the subactor boundaries are deliberately hidden by the notation because we need not know whether these ports terminate with the subactors or are relay ports to their internal structure. The containing actor need only know that the subactors will fulfill the contracts defined by the protocols.

The protocols to which ports refer define two sets of messages, incoming and outgoing, relative to the actor to which a port is attached. Figure 12.2 gives an example.

To bind two ports, one must be *conjugated* to indicate that it plays the inverse role relative to the definition of the protocol. That is, a conjugated port receives the outgoing messages defined by the protocol and sends the incoming ones. Conjugated ports are depicted with a light outer portion and a dark inner portion.

Figure 12.3 shows a ROOM model for IBM's AIX Common Data Link Interface (CDLI) operating system. In AIX, the CDLI provides the networking infrastructure into which new messaging protocols and device drivers are integrated. Conceptually, the CDLI operates on top of a layer called *networkServices* that provides functionality for registration and lookup of new network device

```
PROTOCOL CLASS Protocol1
      SERVICE BasicCommunication
      IN MESSAGES
            {
            DEFINE InSignal1 ISA Null;
            DEFINE InSignal2 ISA Boolean;
      }/* end of in messages */
      OUT MESSAGES
            {
            DEFINE OutSignal1 ISA Integer;
            DEFINE OutSignal2 ISA String;
            } /* end of out messages */
      ;/* end of Protocol1 */
```

FIGURE 12.2   Example of port attachment.

drivers, network interface drivers, network demuxers, and message protocols. Network device drivers provide the interface to the physical device, network interface drivers provide data-link layer functionality for outgoing packets, and network demuxers route incoming mesages to the appropriate message protocol. All of these components are loaded dynamically by the AIX kernel at runtime.

ObjecTime was used to model and simulate this framework. In Figure 12.3, we see actor references (referring to actor classes) for each of the primary components, networkInterfaceDriver, networkDeviceDriver, network-Demuxer, and MessageProtocol, defined as subcomponents of the networkServices actor. Each is connected to an internal end port (called networkService) of networkServices for access to the operations that it provides. This internal port is also connected to a relay port, called network-ServiceIn, that allows external actors to access networkService functionality. (The same capability could have been provided using an end port on the boundary of the actor, at the expense of one additional port.)

Each of the actors shown is a reference to an "abstract" actor class. These are subclassed to define concrete actors that provide capabilities for particular network devices and message protocols. However, ROOM models are always fully operational, so the system may be simulated by using the abstract actors in place of concrete instances, providing that they implement appropriate functionality. For example, passing a message through without performing any processing would be one appropriate abstract behavior for a networkInterfaceDriver.

Figure 12.4a shows the internal structure of the networkInterface-Driver actor class. The NIDView actor reference is used to provide a mechanism for dynamic interaction between networkInterfaceDriver actors and other actors. Another actor can communicate with a networkInterface-Driver by importing its NIDView and using it as a pass through. The message-Protocol actor, shown in Figure 12.4b, is an example; when a signal is sent by

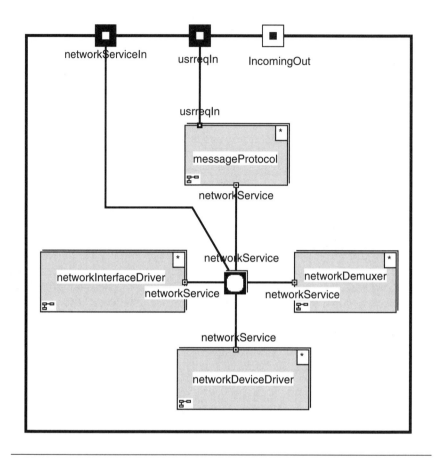

FIGURE 12.3 A ROOM model of the AIX CDCI.

a messageProtocol actor to its OutgoingOut internal port, the NIDView that it has imported passes the message through to its OutgoingOut port and thus to the containing networkInterfaceDriver's OutgoingIn port. We see this pattern replicated within the NetworkInterfaceDriver itself: it has an "imported" actor called NDDView, which it uses to communicate with a networkDeviceDriver actor.

Initialization of the system begins with instantiation of actors. Upon initialization, each of the actor types registers itself with networkService according to the capability that it provides. Figure 12.5 shows the code executed when the behavior of a networkInterfaceDriver makes its initial transition. We see the creation of the NIDView actor (via the incarnate message on line 3) and the registration of the networkInterfaceDriver with networkService

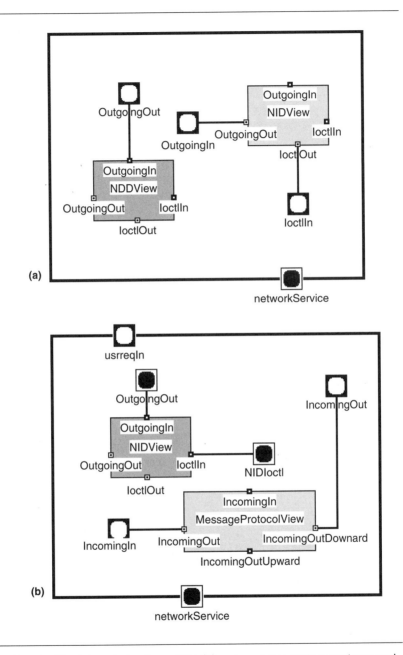

FIGURE 12.4 The internal structure of the (a) `networkInterfaceDriver` and (b) `messageProtocol` actors.

```
 1 NetworkInterfaceDriver::Initialize
 2 | registration |
 3 ViewID := frame incarnate: NIDView.
 4 registration := Registration new.
 5 registration ActorID: ViewID.
 6 registration Identifier: msg data.
 7 SEND networkService
 8   SIGNAL %ifattach
 9   DATA registration
10 ENDSEND
```

FIGURE 12.5   The initialization of the `NetworkInterfaceDriver` actor.

(via the ifattach signal sent on lines 7 to 10). The data provided to the `ifattach` signal are a structure (initialized on lines 4 to 6) containing an identifier that was provided to the `Initialize` signal by the configuration element of the system (not shown) as well as a reference to the `NIDView`. When another actor wishes to communicate with the registered `networkInterfaceDriver`, it can send an `ifunit` signal to `networkService`, specifying the identifier (again provided by an external configuration element); `networkService` returns the `NIDView` reference to the signaling actor.

Once the system has completed initialization, there will a path from `messageProtocols` to `networkInterfaceDrivers` to `network-DeviceDrivers` and another path from `networkDeviceDrivers` to `networkDemuxers` to `messageProtocols`. The former provides outgoing messaging functionality, and the latter provides incoming messaging functionality. A user of the system accesses messaging capabilities via another actor, `SocketInterface` (not shown). The `SocketInterface` actor imports `MessageProtocolView` actors as necessary to provide access to different message protocols. When users wish to initiate messaging, they request a socket of a particular type using the `SocketInterface`; the `SocketInterface` imports a `MessageProtocolView` of the appropriate type, associates this view with a newly allocated socket identifier, and returns this identifier to the user. To send a message, a user provides the `SocketInterface` with the socket identifier, addressing information and the message data. The `Socket-Interface` passes the addressing information and message data to the `messageProtocol` via its view using the `usrreqIn` relay port of `network-Services`. The `messageProtocol` chooses the appropriate `network-InterfaceDriver` (using the ifunit signal as described above) and forwards the request. The `networkInterfaceDriver` finally forwards the request to a `networkDeviceDriver` for transmission to a hardware device. The incoming message path operates similarly.

As we can see from this example, ROOM indeed serves the following purposes of an ADL:

- It facilitates mutual communication via clearly defined semantics for components, connectors, and component behavior.
- It aids in the documentation of the system, through the direct documentation provided by the ROOM models and through secondary products, such as message sequence charts that ObjecTime can automatically generate.
- It provides a continuous refinement paradigm, culminating in code generation facilities, to aid in the seamless construction of an executable system.
- It delivers a formal representation that can be easily consulted and treated as authoritative.

In addition, because ObjecTime models are executable, many kinds of defects can be discovered early in a product's development. In particular timing defects and problems with fault-tolerant mechanisms can be discovered at design time.

12.6 Summary

Communicating an architecture to a stakeholder is a matter of representing it in an unambiguous, understandable form that contains the information appropriate to that stakeholder. Current trends in ADL development are focusing on enhancing the analysis and system-generation capabilities of the languages. Architecture is, after all, only a means to an end, and information that developers can infer about the end system is more valuable than is information about just the architecture. Being able to quickly develop a system or manage qualities of the final product are the real payoffs of ADLs.

ADLs are emerging from research laboratories into the commercial marketplace. When choosing an ADL, it is important to consider system-, language-, and process-related issues, and to make sure you know what you wish to gain by using an ADL.

12.7 For Further Reading

Many ADLs are emerging from academic institutions and research labs, and you can read about most of them in the literature. Among the prominent ones are Rapide [Luckham 95], UniCon and Wright [Shaw 96a], and MetaH [Vestal 93].

There are other languages that, although not created as ADLs, could nevertheless be used to represent the architectures of systems and perform useful preimplementation analyses. Examples include Statechart [Harel 88], its more recent cousin Modechart [Jahanian 94], and the parallel-program development environment CODE [Newton 92].

At least two reports [Clements 96] and [Medvidovic 96] compare and contrast a fair number of architecture description languages.

Details on ROOM and ObjecTime are described by Selic [Selic 94].

12.8 Discussion Questions

1. Ada lets you represent a system by its package specifications, "hiding" the implementations, a very architectural notion. Is Ada, therefore, an architecture description language? Why or why not?

2. Are data flow diagrams an architecture description language? Why or why not?

3. If you could choose one or two kinds of analysis that an architecture description language could perform for you, what would they be?

13

Architecture-Based Development

> *Evolve a modular and horizontal design architecture, mirroring*
> *the product structure in the project structure.*
> — Michael Cusumano and Richard Selby [Cusumano 95]

Up to this point, we have been concerned with the creation, documentation, and analysis of an architecture. We now turn our attention to the process of creating a system from an architecture. That is, after all, the whole point. The most beautiful architecture, if it impedes implementation, is worthless. Here, we will emphasize those aspects of the creation process that specifically relate to architecture. The architecture-specific portions of the creation process are

- Forming the team structure and its relationship to the architecture
- Using the architecture to create a skeletal version of the system
- Using design and coding patterns within an architectural structure
- Checking the conformance of the final system to the architecture
- Using domain-specific languages to exploit multisystem architectural commonality

13.1 Forming the Team Structure

As long ago as 1968, the close relationship between an architecture and the organization that produced it was a subject of comment. Conway makes the point as follows [Conway 68, 29]:

> Take any two nodes x and y of the system. Either they are joined by a branch or they are not. (That is, either they communicate with each other in some way meaningful to the operation of the system or they do not.) If

there is a branch, then the two (not necessarily distinct) design groups X and Y which designed the two nodes must have negotiated and agreed upon an interface specification to permit communication between the two corresponding nodes of the design organization. If, on the other hand, there is no branch between x and y, then the subsystems do not communicate with each other, there was nothing for the two corresponding design groups to negotiate, and therefore there is no branch between X and Y.

Conway was describing how to discern organizational structure (at least in terms of communication paths) from the structure of a system, but the relationship between organizational structure and system structure is bidirectional, and necessarily so.

The impact of an architecture on the development of organizational structure is clear. Once an architecture for the system under construction has been agreed upon, teams are allocated to work on the major components and a work breakdown structure is created that reflects those teams. Each team then creates its own internal work practices (or a systemwide set of practices is adopted). For large systems the teams may belong to different subcontractors. The work practices include items such as bulletin boards and Web pages for communication, naming conventions for files, and the version control system. All of these may be different from group to group, again especially for large systems. Furthermore, quality assurance and testing procedures are set up for each group and each group needs to establish liaisons and coordinate with the other groups.

So, the teams within an organization work on components. Within the team there needs to be high-bandwidth communications: Lots of information in the form of detailed design decisions is being shared constantly. Between teams, low-bandwidth communications are sufficient (and, in fact, crucial. Brooks's thesis [Brooks 95] is that the overhead of interteam communication, if not carefully managed, will swamp a project). This is, of course, assuming that the system has been designed with appropriate separation of concerns. Highly complex systems result when these design criteria are not met. In fact, team structure and control of team interactions often turn out to be the factors affecting a large project's success. If interactions between the teams need to be complex, it means either that the interactions between the components they are creating are needlessly complex or that the requirements for those components were not sufficiently "hardened" before development commenced. In this case, there is a need for high-bandwidth connections *between* teams, not just within teams, requiring substantial negotiations and often rework of components and their interfaces. Teams, like software systems, should strive for loose coupling and high cohesion.

The question remains, Which architectural structure does the team structure mirror? The best bet is the module or logical structure. Information-hiding, the design principle behind the module structure of systems, holds that modules should encapsulate, or hide, changeable details by putting up an interface that abstracts away the changeable aspects and presents a common, unified set of services to its users (in this case, the software in other modules in the system). This implies that each module constitutes its own small domain; we use *domain* here in the sense of domain analysis: an area of specialized knowledge or expertise. For example,

- The module is the presentation layer of a human-computer interaction (HCI) system (see Section 6.2). Then the interface it presents to other modules is one that is independent of the particular user-interface devices (radio buttons, dials, dialogue boxes, etc.) that it uses to present information to the human user, because those might change. The domain here is the repertoire of such devices.

- The module is a process scheduler that hides the number of available processors and the scheduling algorithm. The domain here is process scheduling and the list of appropriate algorithms.

- The module is the Physical Models module of the A-7E architecture (see Chapter 3). It encapsulates the equations used to compute values about the physical environment. The domain is numerical analysis (because the equations must be implemented to maintain sufficient accuracy in a digital computer) and avionics.

Recognizing modules as minidomains immediately suggests that the most effective use of staff is to assign members to teams according to their expertise. Only the module structure permits this. As the sidebar discusses, organizations sometimes add specialized groups that are independent of the architectural structures.

The impact of an organization on an architecture is more subtle but equally strong as the impact of architecture on the organization (of the group that builds the system described by the architecture). Suppose you are a member of a group that builds database applications and you are assigned to work on a team designing an architecture for some application. Your inclination is probably to view the current problem as a database problem, to worry about what database system should be used or whether a home-grown one should be constructed, to assume data retrievals are constructed as queries, and so on. You will therefore press for an architecture that has distinct subsystems for data storage and management, query formulation and implementation, and so on. A person from the telecommunications group, on the other hand, will view the system in telecommunication terms, and for this person the database is a single (possibly uninteresting) subsystem.

We discussed in Chapter 1 how organizational issues and a desire to employ or develop certain sets of skills will have an effect on the architecture. The scenario above is a concrete example of how that effect might be manifested As an organization continues to work in a particular domain, it develops particular artifacts to use as a means of obtaining work, and it also has organizational groups whose purpose is the maintenance of these artifacts. We will see this in Chapters 15 and 16.

Organizational and Architectural Structures

We had no sooner written Section 13.1 about the relationship between organizational structure and architectural structure than someone who has experience in the telecommunications area proposed a counterexample. The organization he described is committed to responding quickly to customer's complaints and requests for changes. In this scheme, every customer-generated request for change is assigned to an individual whose responsibility is to implement the change. Any particular change may require modifications to a variety of architectural components, and so the individuals in the customer-response team make modifications to the whole system and must be outside of any team that has responsibility for any particular group of components. Thus, an organizational structure that is aligned only with architectural structure is not adequate.

At first blush, this counterexample made the authors nervous but on further probing, we discovered that the organization in question actually made each modification twice: once by the customer-service organization to provide quick reaction to the customer and once by the organizational entity that owned the components affected. Any other possibility would result in rapid degradation of any architecture that is not based strictly on separate components to implement each end-user function.

To explore the argument somewhat further, an architecture, as we have emphasized repeatedly, must satisfy many conflicting demands. An architecture that is based on a separate component to implement each end-user function is very good with respect to the modifiability of these functions *as long as the modification is not based on a physical element that affects other functions.* In the maintenance phase, as in the counterexample, this architecture enables modifications to a particular function to be limited to a single component. Of course, such a function-based architecture does not allow reuse of components or sharing of data and is not very efficient with respect to implementation.

The organization under discussion, in fact, had an architecture that attempted to maximize reuse and had organization units that mirrored component structure. Because modifications would (potentially) involve separate organizational units and the activities of these units had to be coordinated (read this as saying that the reaction time of organizations is slow when multiple units are involved), a separate rapid response unit was established at the cost of making each modification twice.

— LJB

13.2   Creating a Skeletal System

In this section we describe the benefits not only of defining a software architecture early in a system's life cycle, but also of using that architecture in the first implementation task: the creation of a *skeletal* system. The analogy here is meant to give the idea that an architecture forms the bare bones of the system. Coding the pieces, the subsystems and components, fleshes out the design, but the basic shape and relationship of the parts is already determined: The knee bone's connected to the shin bone. . . .

The idea is to implement the major behavioral aspects of the architecture. That is, each of the components described in the architecture is implemented to the extent that it demonstrates the behavior of that subsystem, even if that behavior is only a "canned" sequence of actions. Even this low level of functionality provides a skeleton that can be executed.

Classical software engineering practice recommends "stubbing out" sections of code so that portions of the system can be tested independently. The classic practice, however, gives no guidance about which portions should be stubbed. By using the architecture as a guide, a sequence of implementation becomes clear. First, implement the software that deals with the execution and interaction of architectural components. This may require producing a scheduler in a real-time system, implementing the rule engine (with a prototype set of rules) to control rule firing in a rule-based system, implementing process synchronization mechanisms in a multiprocess system, or implementing client-server coordination in a client-server system. At this point, the execution/interaction software is all that exists in true form; everything else is stubbed out. You can now choose which of the stubbed components should be implemented with more fidelity. The choice may be based on lowering risk by addressing the most problematic areas first or it may be based on the levels and type of staffing available.

The skeletal system that first results from this approach serves as an integration harness. One of the benefits of creating a skeletal system first and then populating it with parts is that individual implementation teams can create a complete (but still mostly skeletal) system—one with limited functionality or low fidelity—long before the majority of the system has been coded, debugged, integrated, or tested. The only difference between the skeletal and the final version of the system is that in the final system all the flesh is on the bones—that is, all software slots are filled in with real code. In the skeletal version, empty slots are initially filled only with stub implementations. These stubs adhere to the same interfaces that the final version of the system requires, so they can help to understand and test the interactions among components. These stub components can simulate this interaction in two ways: They can either produce hard-coded canned output or can read the output from a file. The stubs can also generate a synthetic load on the system to approximate the amount of time the actual processing will take in the completed working version. This aids in early understanding of system performance requirements, including performance interactions and bottlenecks.

The skeletal development just discussed may be characterized as building the system broad but shallow: Every component is part of the working prototype, but the functionality has low fidelity. An alternative version of this scheme can be used when a particular aspect of the system is expected to be problematic or when the staffing levels for the entire project are initially low. The idea is to build narrow but deep by fielding a small subset of the system. Initially, the subset can be the smallest one that will actually execute and do recognizable work. In a multiprocess system, this means implementing one task. Then use the uses structure (see Chapter 3) to see what other portions of the software that task requires and implement those. Each implementation is valid, meaning that it exhibits its behavior to the highest fidelity possible. In the A-7E architecture of Chapter 3, an initial subset might be as follows:

- A process in the Function Driver module that causes the aircraft's magnetic heading to be displayed on the head-up display
- Two procedures in the Device Interface Module: one that reads the magnetic heading from the aircraft's compass and one that displays a value in the "heading" field of the head-up display
- Two procedures in the Data Banker module: one that stores the magnetic heading and one that retrieves its current value
- The part of the Extended Computer that allows for the creation and scheduling of a process
- The part of the Abstract Data Types module that provides the abstract type "angle" (which is used to represent a heading)

This simple subset has the advantage that it could be implemented quickly by a few people, but that no shortcuts were taken: It would survive through the deployment of the full system. Subsequent subsets could concentrate on areas of uncertainty or areas suggested by the levels and expertise of available staffing at the time. Thus, having a skeletal version of the entire system from the earliest time in the system's development is important for several reasons, as follows:

- The early creation of a working skeletal version of the system and the ability to iteratively refine that version into successively more comprehensive or higher fidelity versions has a large impact on productivity and team morale—the system exists and "works" early on.
- It allows early concentration on those aspects of the system expected to be most troublesome to implement or about which the most uncertainty exists.
- It lowers integration time and costs and, perhaps most important, makes explicit the costs of integration. These costs are moved to the *front* of the development life cycle where they cannot be ignored. This is in contrast to current development practice, where integration is frequently not budgeted for, underestimated, and not controlled.
- It aids the testing and review process because a testable system always exists. Thus, testing and review can be done incrementally, as each subsystem comes on-line. As an example, performance measures can be taken frequently and performance problems recognized and addressed early. Compared to what frequently occurs—the entire system is built and turned on, and the whole staff holds their breath and crosses their fingers to see if the performance goals are met—this approach yields a big advantage. Further, the stubs can generate synthetic loads, providing a high-fidelity and early look into performance: The system is essentially its own simulation.
- Because more integration planning and development work occur earlier in the product's life cycle, complex dependencies are found earlier. Furthermore, temporal dependencies among development teams are reduced. Each team

can proceed, for a time, by developing its portion of the system in isolation, integrating it only with the current version of the skeletal system. This final point is crucial. In traditional development, project teams proceed in isolation (and hence independently) of each other without a common framework to constrain them and provide feedback.

According to Cusumano and Selby [Cusumano 95], skeletal system development is the strategy that Microsoft uses, although we do not advocate their particular invocation of this strategy. In Microsoft's version of the skeletal system approach, a "complete" skeletal system is created early in a product's life cycle and a "working," but low-fidelity, version of the product is rebuilt at frequent periods—often nightly. This part of their process is fine. It results in a working system for which the features can, at any time, be judged sufficient and the product rolled out. The problem with their process, however, is that the first development team to complete a portion of the system gets to define the interface, and all subsequent subsystems must adhere to that interface. This effectively penalizes the complex portions of the system, because they will require more analysis and hence will be less likely to have their interfaces defined first. This has the effect of making the complex subsystems even more complex. Our recommendation, therefore, is first to negotiate the interfaces in the skeletal subsystem and then use a process that rewards development efficiency.

13.3   Exploiting Patterns in Software Architecture

Being able to analyze and build a system with a regular set of building blocks provides substantial benefits. These include better human comprehension of complex systems, which aids both development and maintenance. Such a regular set of building blocks represents common patterns of usage. Simply put, patterns allow humans to understand complex systems in larger conceptual chunks, thus reducing the cognitive burden. Procedures already perform this function for us, providing complex functions as atomic operations, but patterns can be of larger granularity than individual procedures and hence increase the size of chunk that a human can understand as an atomic unit.

A *pattern* is a small collection of atomic units and a description of their relationships. Patterns are ubiquitous throughout software development and are regularly used subconsciously by experienced programmers. We use them in design-in-the-large, in design-in-the-small, and in coding. In object-oriented design patterns, for example, a pattern is a collection of object classes and the inheritance and uses (method call) relationships among them. We see patterns in other areas as well. For example, in Chapter 14 we will see the repeated use of structural patterns in the design of flight simulators. We also see code patterns: Iterating through a data structure is a common example and has formed the basis for much of the work on template libraries to support component programming.

More and more frequently patterns are being documented and communicated as a way of transferring hard-won experience from experts to novices. This form of documentation is common in other design and engineering disciplines but was, until recently, rare in software engineering.

In this section we will concentrate on design patterns because they are of most importance during the architecture-to-system phase of development that is the subject of this chapter. (Architectural patterns—styles—were treated in Chapter 5 and code patterns, although useful, are not of architectural import.)

Even though patterns can and do operate at different levels of scope, these types of patterns share many features. They all do the following:

- Serve as exemplars to programmers, designers, and architects, which they can quickly adapt for use in their projects.

- Emphasize solutions: discovering patterns (as applied in previous situations) rather than inventing them.

- Represent codified, distilled wisdom: solutions to recurring problems, if those solutions have well-understood properties.

- Allow programmers and designers to program and design using bigger chunks; this also eases those aspects that involve understanding an architecture: architectural reviews, reverse engineering, maintenance, and system restructuring.

- Aid in communication among designers, between designers and programmers, and between a project's technical team members and its nontechnical members.

- Identify and name abstract, common themes in object-oriented design, themes that have known quality properties.

- Form a documented, reusable base of experience which would otherwise be learned only through an informal oral tradition or through trial and error.

- Provide a target for reorganization of software because a designer can attempt to map (parts of) an existing system to a set of patterns. If this mapping can be done, the complexity of the resulting reorganized system will be less than the original version.

DESIGN PATTERNS

Similar to the use of architectural patterns, programmers and designers reuse larger chunks of software, code that spans several modules, objects, or object classes. This is the basis for the study of object-oriented design patterns. An object-oriented design pattern is a small collection of objects or object classes that cooperate to achieve some design goal.

Gamma and colleagues, in the introduction to their book [Gamma 95], note that expert programmers and designers regularly make use of patterns but seldom document or communicate these patterns. Expert designers analyze a problem, particularly in terms of its quality requirements and, whenever possible, adopt a proven solution to satisfy those requirements. Nonexperts do not have access to this wealth of experience and so program a solution to their problem in some novel (and typically less than optimal) way. To address this shortcoming, a substantial amount of effort is going into the task of documenting object-oriented design patterns, and even metapatterns. These patterns are being documented because of the reasons enumerated above.

For example, consider the pattern given in Figure 13.1, the Abstract Factory (adapted from [Gamma 95]). This pattern is used for portability: to create instances of some appropriate resource at runtime without having to worry about how that resource is bound. In this case two different user-interface toolkits are presented to a programmer as a single abstraction—`WindowKit`—which contains methods that the programmer can use. The methods are bound to different instantiations, however, depending on what toolkit the implementation platform actually uses.

This decision, and this binding, is dealt with outside the responsibility of the programmer who uses `WindowKit`. The point here is that design patterns represent architectural solutions to *recurring* problems, in this case the problem of separating application code concerns from user-interface concerns. By solving the problem once and canonizing the design, users of the design patterns are aided considerably.

Clearly we would like to design as much of a system as possible with patterns. This should shorten design and development time and result in fewer cases of costly system restructuring that result from poorly understood designs. But how can this goal of maximizing the use of patterns be achieved in practice? The

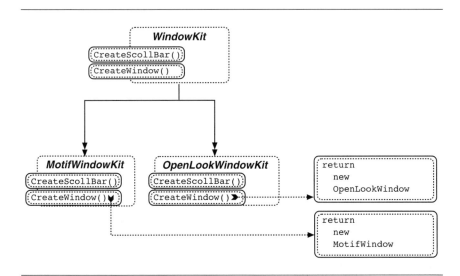

FIGURE 13.1   Abstract factory design pattern.

first step is to understand system requirements well enough to be able to map them onto the kinds of canonical solutions that patterns provide.

Patterns aid in the achievement of qualities principally by being well-understood, time-honored solutions to recurring problems. In addition to being well understood, these solutions are widely used across *different* application domains. For example, consider the strategy design pattern (from [Gamma 95]) shown in Figure 13.2.

The strategy pattern is meant to be used when a single task might be implemented in a variety of ways, depending on the nature of the input. In this case, a text editor needs to handle different kinds of composition strategies, and the choice must be made at runtime. It might choose one kind of strategy for line breaking in formatted text to produce text that is both left and right justified (TeXCompositor), a different kind of strategy for breaking regular tables of information (ArrayCompositor), and a simple, efficient compositor for breaking lines when the right-hand margin does not need to be justified (SimpleCompositor). In each case, the client using the Composition class's Repair method is not bound to a single strategy. The client can choose which Compose method will be applied.

But design patterns are useful only if they are general. The strategy pattern is. It has known uses in a variety of fields, including compiler code optimization (different register allocation strategies and instruction set scheduling policies must be adopted for different architectures), Borland's ObjectWindows (validation

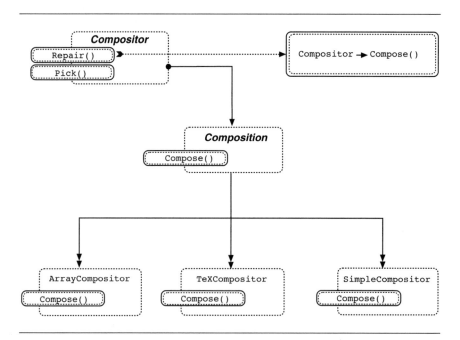

FIGURE 13.2 The strategy design pattern.

of information entered by a user is done through assigning strategies to dialogue boxes), and so forth.

Such a design pattern has some obvious implications for software architecture, once we concern ourselves with an architecture's fitness with respect to qualities. For example, the strategy pattern is clearly useful for modifiability in general (because it cleanly separates modification concerns) and portability in particular, as the compiler code optimization example shows. On the other hand, because the knowledge of which strategy to use is kept in the client rather than in the strategy itself, the use of this pattern couples (perhaps unnecessarily) the client of the strategy with the strategy's realization. This may have negative implications for modifiability.

Consider a final example, that of the decorator (or wrapper) pattern. The decorator pattern is used in cases where an object's capabilities need to be extended, but where subclassing is not an appropriate mechanism for doing this. Consider the example shown in Figure 13.3. In this example a text entry field (a common component of any user-interface toolkit) is the base component. The application being built requires a text entry field that is larger than the available screen space, and the standard solution is to scroll the text field within a larger virtual window. Furthermore, the text field might require a border, either for decoration or to provide "handles" for moving and resizing.

One way to meet these requirements would be to provide a `ScrolledText` class, a `BorderedText` class, a `ScrolledBorderedText` class, and so on. However, this solution, taken to its extreme, results in an enormous number of classes, many of which may seldom or never be used. For example, we would need to provide a horizontally scrolled text field class, a vertically scrolled text field class, a bordered horizontally scrolled text field class, and so on.

The alternative solution taken by the decorator pattern is to augment the abilities of an object (rather than a class) at runtime. Thus, when a request for services is made of the decorated object, the request is first examined by the decorating objects and then, where appropriate, is handed to the original object. In this way, the original object does not know that it has been decorated, and so its functionality does not need to be altered. In this way, an object can have functionality added (or withdrawn) at runtime. This ease of modification comes at a cost, of course; the cost is the additional performance overhead that accrues with the addition of each enclosing class.

Thus, each design pattern exists to solve a well known, well-analyzed *class* of problems. It does so in a way that transfers expert experience to a programmer

FIGURE 13.3   The decorator design pattern.

who might not have this wealth of examples to draw from. Alternative designs have already been considered and discarded in design patterns, saving the programmer the trouble of finding out the hard way. The fact that design patterns are general suggests that there is a "right way" to solve some related class of problems. The meaning of *right* typically is with reference to some set of quality attributes. The strategy pattern was motivated primarily by modifiability and portability rather than, say, efficiency or security.

Design patterns aid in the voyage from quality requirements to a system by providing prepackaged *pockets* of focused design expertise that even a relatively inexperienced programmer can use. The novice does this by matching functional and quality requirements to the database of patterns.

This can still be a large job, however. The set of patterns is already large and is growing rapidly. For example, Table 13.1 shows the set of design patterns given in just a single source [Gamma 95]. And there is a problem: The result of numerous design decisions, each of which properly address some small set of quality requirements, may not compose well. That is, the resulting architecture may not have the composition of the quality strengths that the parts possess. Take usability, for example. The usability of an interface is determined mainly by how well the various portions of the interface work together and use the same conventions. Having a system in which each interface is usable is not the same as having a usable system. This applies to many other qualities as well.

The answer to the problem of compositionality as it applies to the satisfaction of quality attributes is found in architectural styles, which address more global questions of satisfying quality requirements by focusing on systemwide organizational properties: data flows, control flows, loci of computation, and coordination.

PATTERN-BASED SIMPLICITY

The purpose of this section is not to present a full study of design patterns; they fill whole books. We have presented a couple of patterns by way of illustration and talked in general terms about the advantages of design reuse. The real purpose of

TABLE 13.1   A Set of Design Patterns

	Purpose		
Scope	**Creational**	**Structural**	**Behavioral**
Class	Factory method	Adapter (class)	Interpreter Template method
Object	Abstract factory Builder Prototype Singleton	Adapter (object) Bridge Composite Decorator Facade Flyweight Proxy	Chain of responsibility Command Iterator Mediator Memento Observer State Strategy Visitor

this section is to show how exploiting patterns can lead to development-time benefits, in a word, to templates.

Design and architectural patterns both resolve the component interconnection mechanisms, and it turns out that a great deal of the implementation energy on large projects is spent implementing those interconnections: headers for processes, declaration blocks for objects, data communication and consistency protocols for data-sharing components, access synchronization mechanisms to guard shared resources, and so forth. By imposing a consistency on these and other interactions, the implementations can be speeded up by using coding templates in which the commonality forms the framework and the variation is manifested by the blanks.

Chapter 14 will present a case study that is largely about patterns. A structural model is a style that imposes broad consistency on the constituent components: Their data-sharing protocols, interaction with the scheduler, and substructures are all regular and tightly constrained. Hence, implementing a structural model system is largely a matter of filling in templates. The air traffic control system presented in Chapter 11 also illustrates templates. Components in that system were required to implement a complicated protocol to achieve fault tolerance and a warm-restart capability. The template allowed all of the components to be coded identically where possible and differently where necessary. This simplifies things in the following ways:

- Reliability is enhanced because once the template is correct, that templatized portion of every using component is correct.

- Coding time is reduced because the template is copied verbatim into each component.

- Testing is simplified because each component has a standard structure that all-paths-testing can exploit.

- Flexibility is enhanced because the conforming components are largely interchangeable. In addition, a systematic change to an aspect captured by the template can be carried out in one place.

13.4   Ensuring Conformance to an Architecture

Once the requirements for a system have been analyzed, its patterns developed, its skeletal system created and fleshed out, and its testing and integration done, it will become a product. As the ABC states, and as we all know from experience, at that moment the requirements will change. The system will enter a maintenance phase that will last the rest of its useful life.

Is the architecture still meaningful in this phase? Of course. The system still has an architecture, although it may well be different from the architecture that it started out with. The issue, then, is how to keep the description of the architecture and the actual architecture in conformance with each other. It is sadly true that this important piece of documentation is seldom given the maintenance attention that it deserves: Architectures drift away from the documents that describe them, and nothing kills a document so quickly as being unreliable. Hence, documentation that is not valid will not be used, and who wants to spend time updating a document that isn't used anyway? This vicious spiral continues until the code is the only authoritative source of what the system does and what its architecture is. It doesn't take a very large system for this situation to become untenable.

Therefore, it is crucial to keep the architectural documentation up to date. And the good news is the spiral this leads to: Documentation that is valid tends to be kept up to date. The first change is the hardest one to make, but it is also the most important. So, to borrow a phrase, just do it. You will be rewarded.

Well, suppose that you keep all of *your* documentation up to date, naturally, but you've just inherited a system from those less enlightened than yourself. It is your job to modify it in some way, and the documentation that came with it is still in its (dusty) shrink-wrap cover, dated sometime around the invention of dirt. What are your options?

One option is to attempt to reverse engineer the system to determine its conformance to the published architecture and to act on areas of variation, by changing either the system or the architectural representation.

Reverse engineering is a complex topic, far beyond the scope of this book. However, we will briefly review the available technologies and assess their implications for determining architecture conformance. The discipline of reverse engineering has two main areas, one based on technical approaches to deriving information about a system from its existing artifacts and one based on human knowledge and human powers of inference.

Cognitive strategies in reverse engineering center on the question of how humans understand software. Typically, human investigators use the following:

- Top-down strategies, starting at the highest level of system abstraction and recursively filling in understanding of the subparts and sub-subparts
- Bottom-up strategies, understanding the lowest-level components and how these work together to accomplish the system's goals
- Model-based strategies in which the investigator already has a mental model of how the system works and tries to deepen the understanding of selected areas
- Opportunistic strategies, some combination of the above approaches, as dictated by the investigator's current level of understanding and needs.

Technical approaches center on extracting information from any and all of the existing system artifacts, including source code, comments, user documentation, executable modules, system descriptions, and so forth. These approaches include using the following:

- Existing compiler technology to extract software relationships, such as cross-reference information
- Data-flow analysis to determine the static data relationships among components
- Profiling to determine the execution behavior of the system

- Natural language analysis techniques to discern relationships in the code via its documentation

- Architectural-level pattern matching to distill relevant information about structural relationships from the source code

We call the result of these techniques *discovery* information. Each of these techniques will provide a partial and possibly erroneous picture of the system. Even techniques within the same area do not provide consistent discovery information, as a study of call-graph extraction tools has shown. None of the tools surveyed extracted the same information, and none of the discovered architectures was a proper superset of the others. Given this state of the practice, one cannot rely entirely on tool support as an extraction mechanism.

In addition to the challenges inherent in these techniques, two obstacles must be overcome before reverse engineering, either automated or manual, will be a practical tool to support gauging architectural conformance. The first obstacle is related to the enormous volume of information produced. To deal with the flood of information that reverse engineering produces one needs to either filter the information, based on some specification of the current needs, or visualize the information and allow a user to navigate through it. The second obstacle is the integration of expert- and tool-derived information.

Finally, even if this discovery information is accurately culled from a legacy system, there remains the problem of what to do with it. Or, put another way, how can one use discovery information to improve the system being examined? There are the following two options:

1. It can be used to measure the conformance of the architecture "as planned" to the architecture "as executed." This is a use of reverse engineering that we recommend. As an extension to this principle, the discovery information can be used as a basis to enforce design rules and to flag violations. There might be a rule, for example, that there are no direct calls to window system functions; all such functions must be routed through a portable user-interface layer. The discovery information could then detect and flag violations to this rule.

2. It can be used to make engineering changes to the system. The discovery information provides a snapshot of the current state of the software architecture. Such information can be used to find areas of high complexity, areas that violate design principles, or subsystems with similar functions and structures. Each of these can be targets for reengineering efforts.

13.5 Building Domain-Specific Languages

As we have seen, every architecture defines three classes of change to a system: those that only change the internal workings of one or more components, those that affect an interface among the components, and those that affect the architecture.

Also as we have seen, a successful architecture for a system that evolves over its lifetime—and what system doesn't?—is one that puts the likeliest changes into the easiest bucket. When such a change arises, all of the design decisions represented by the architecture, including what the components are and how they interact and cooperate with each other, are carried over from version to version of the system.

Another way to think about this is that the architecture embodies the commonalities across all the versions of the system that will exist, whether before (during prototyping) or after (during product variation) initial deployment. The variation across the versions is captured in the implementations of the components. If we are lucky (because it is very hard to know all the changes that a system will have to endure), the component interfaces will also embody the commonality rather than the variation.

In many cases, it is possible to know the specific variations that the system will be asked to accommodate, and this leads to an even more powerful possibility. If the variations can be codified in a systematic fashion, it is possible to design a simple language to express them. And from a simple language, it is usually a short step to an application generator to implement them.

Application generators are programs that take specifications of other programs as input and produce those programs as output. Strictly speaking, a compiler is an application generator, but there are more straightforward examples. A parser generator such as YACC is a typical example. YACC accepts a specification for a parser as input and produces the parser as output. The specification is in the form of a modified BNF (Backus-Naur form) grammar for the language that the parser accepts. All the parsers that YACC generates are the same, except for the language that they accept. The language constitutes the variability. The architecture of the parser, the data structures it uses, and the algorithms it employs all are part of the commonality; hence, the input language to YACC has no way (or need) to express anything about those aspects.

Other application generators exist across many domains. There are generators to produce cyclic executives (schedulers) in real-time systems, data structure packages, and whole database management systems. There are even application-generator generators emerging from the research field. Application generators have obvious productivity advantages; generating code is faster, cheaper, and more reliable than writing it by hand.

Lucent Technologies' FAST process exemplifies this approach to domain-specific language generation. FAST has been used to build dozens of small application generators for software that helps Lucent manage, maintain, and reprogram their very large telephone switching systems. The steps of FAST are as follows:

- Conduct a series of meetings in which application experts work out the commonalities and variations in the family of systems that is being considered. The commonalities are expressed as *basic assumptions* that are written down and circulated for review. These meetings may, depending on the size of the systems, continue for several weeks.

- Agree on a codification of the variations—that is, design a language to express the variations.
- Design an architecture that encompasses the commonalities identified in the meetings. This includes identifying the components that will hide the variations within their implementations, behind their interfaces.
- Build the application generator.

Of course, this process entails significant overhead, and it is not appropriate for every situation. It would not be practical, for example, for a one-of-a-kind system, for a very small and simple system, or for a system whose lifetime is expected to be quite short. An economic analysis, even if quick and dirty, should be sketched to see whether the benefit will be worth the effort.

13.6   Summary

Architecture-based development has many similarities to normal development such as moving to detailed design from the architecture, a requirement for configuration management, and testing. This is to be expected because some concept of architecture is required for all development (whether the architecture is explicit or implicit). In this chapter we have focused on those aspects of the development process that are not fully realized, such as the relationship between organizations and the architecture of the systems developed by them, or that are specific to having an architecture.

In particular, using the architecture to build a skeletal system that can be executed, using design patterns as a method of fleshing out an architecture with known solutions to common problems, attempting to discern an architecture from an existing system, and building an application using a domain-specific language are all aspects of architectural development that differ from normal development.

13.7   For Further Reading

Christopher Alexander's seminal and innovative work on design patterns for architecture (the house-building kind) served as the basis for the work on software design patterns. His books [Alexander 77] and [Alexander 78] are essential reading to gain an intuitive understanding of what design patterns are all about. (They are also useful if you're planning to build a house someday.)

The most often-cited book on software design patterns is the so-called "gang of four" book [Gamma 95]. Buschmann and colleagues [Buschmann 96] have documented a set of architectural styles as design patterns, thus bridging these two important conceptual areas.

Fred Brooks's *The Mythical Man Month* [Brooks 95] is required reading for any software engineer, and his revised version discusses the virtues and advantages of architecture-based iterative development, especially as practiced by Microsoft.

The FAST process, in which small domain-specific languages are crafted to help quickly produce variants of a family of systems, is described at length in [Lai 97].

For an empirical study that shows the strengths and weaknesses of a common kind of extraction tool, called graph extractors, see [Murphy 96].

13.8　Discussion Questions

1. Architectures beget the teams that build the components that compose the architectures. The architectural structure that is usually reflected in the teams is the modular or logical structure. Why do you think that is the case? What would be the advantages and disadvantages of basing teams around components of some of the other common architectural structures, such as the process structure?

2. How are design patterns, considered as a group, different from architectural styles, considered as a group?

14

Flight Simulation
A Case Study in Architecture for Integrability

> *The striking conclusion that one draws . . . is that the information processing capacity of [flight simulation computation] has been increasing approximately exponentially for nearly thirty years. There is at this time no clear indication that the trend is changing.*
> — Laurence Fogarty [Fogarty 67]

Modern flight simulators are among the most sophisticated software systems in existence. They are highly distributed, have rigorous timing requirements, and must be amenable to frequent updates to maintain high fidelity with the vehicles and environment they are simulating. The creation and maintenance of these large systems present a substantial software development challenge: for performance, for integrability, and for modifiability. Scalability, a particular form of modifiability, is needed to grow these systems so that they can simulate more and more of the real world and further improve the fidelity of the simulation.

This chapter will discuss some of the challenges of flight simulation and introduce a new architectural style created to address them. The style is called a *structural model*, and it emphasizes the following:

- Simplicity and similarity of the system's substructures
- Decoupling of data and control passing strategies from computation
- Minimization of types of components
- A small number of systemwide coordination strategies
- Transparency of design

These principles result in an architectural style that, as we will see, features a high degree of component integrability as well as the other quality attributes necessary for flight simulation.

14.1   Relationship to the Architecture Business Cycle

The segment of the archtecture business cycle (ABC) that connects desired qualities to architecture is the subject of this case study. Figure 14.1 shows the ABC
for structural-model-based flight simulators. Flight simulators are acquired by the
U.S. Air Force. The end users of the systems are pilots and crews for the particular aircraft being simulated. The flight simulators are used for pilot training in the
operation of the aircraft, for crew training in the operation of the various weapons
systems on board, and for mission training for particular missions for the aircraft.
Some of these simulators are intended for stand-alone use, but more and more
they are intended to train multiple crews simultaneously for cooperative missions.

   The flight simulators are constructed by a contractor selected as a result of a
competitive bidding process. Sometimes the contractor is a prime contractor, and
portions of the flight simulator are constructed by specialized subcontractors. The
flight simulator systems are large (some as large as 1.5 million lines of code),
have long lifetimes (the aircraft being simulated often have lifetimes of 40 years
or longer), and have stringent real-time and fidelity requirements (the simulated
aircraft must behave exactly as the real aircraft in various situations).

   The beginning of the structural model design dates from 1987 when the U.S.
Air Force began to investigate the application of object-oriented design techniques.

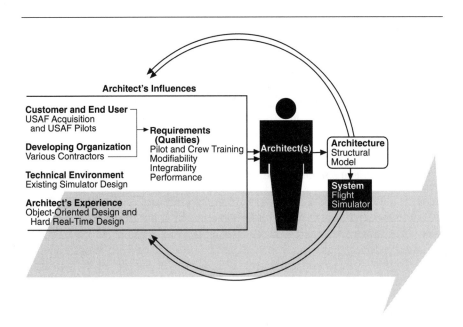

FIGURE 14.1   Initial stages of the ABC for the flight simulator.

Electronic flight simulators have been in existence since the 1960s and so exploration into new design techniques was motivated by the existing designs and the problems associated with them. The problems observed in existing flight simulators included construction problems (the integration phase of development was increasing exponentially with the size and complexity of the systems) and life cycle problems (the cost of some modifications was exceeding the cost of the original system). Structural models have been used in the development of the B-2 Weapons System Trainer, the C-17 Aircrew Training System, and the Special Operations Forces family of trainers, among others.

14.2   Requirements and Qualities

Flight simulation has always been an application that needed to be distributed in order to be computable at all. Although examples of single-processor flight simulators exist, they are typically of low fidelity, often games. True flight simulation has extremely high-fidelity demands: The virtual environment that the simulator creates must be as lifelike as possible in order to train the aircrew as effectively as possible.

Even in simulators created 30 years ago, distribution was used [Perry 66]:

> Linear computing operations, such as summation, integration and sign changing, are performed by d.c. operational amplifiers, consisting of high gain drift correct amplifiers with appropriate resistive or capacitive feedback networks. There are 150 such operational amplifiers. . . . The nonlinear part of the computing equipment consists of servo-multipliers, electronic time-division multipliers, and diode function generators. In addition, forty-eight high gain amplifiers are available for special computing circuits which may be built up for each simulation. . . . The individual computing amplifiers, potentiometers, multipliers, etc. are connected together to form the overall computation network by means of a central patching panel, having over 2300 terminations.

Although the effects produced by such a simulator are primitive by today's standards, many of the principles behind the system's architecture have not changed. A single computer typically cannot provide the raw computation power to serve a flight simulator, or if it could, it would be horrendously expensive. This situation is not likely to change: As computer power increases, so do our demands and so does the complexity of the air vehicles being simulated. Thus, a number of computers were hooked together through a patch panel 30 years ago in order to create a flight simulator; today, they would typically be connected through a fiber-optic network.

Flight simulation is characterized by the following six properties:

1. *Real-time performance constraints.*   Flight simulators must execute at fixed frame rates that are high enough to ensure fidelity. For instance, the simulated aircraft must respond to control inputs as quickly as the real aircraft would.

Different senses require different frame rates. Within a frequency class—say, 30 Hz or 60 Hz—all simulations must be able to execute to completion within the base time frame—one-thirtieth or one-sixtieth of a second.

All portions of a simulator run at an integral factor of the base rate. If the base rate is 60 Hz, slower portions of the simulation may run at 30 Hz, 20 Hz, 15 Hz, or 12 Hz, and so on. They may not run at a nonintegral factor of the base rate, such as 25 Hz. One reason for this restriction is that the sensory inputs provided by a flight simulator for the crew being trained must be strictly coordinated. It would not do to have the pilot execute a turn but not begin to see the change visually or feel the change for even a small period of time (say, one-tenth of a second). Even for delays so small that they are not consciously detectable, a lack of coordination may be a problem. Such delays may result in a phenomenon known as *simulator sickness*, a purely physiological reaction to imperfectly coordinated sensory inputs.

2. *Continuous development and modification.*   Simulators exist for only one purpose: to train users when the equivalent training on the actual vehicle would be much more expensive or dangerous. In order to provide a realistic training experience, a flight simulator must be faithful to the actual air vehicle. However, air vehicles, whether civilian or military, are continually being modified and updated. The simulator software is, therefore, almost constantly modified and updated in order to maintain verisimilitude. Furthermore, the training for which the simulators are used is continually extended to encompass new types of problems (malfunctions) that might occur to the aircraft.

3. *Large size and high complexity.*   Flight simulators typically comprise from tens of thousands of lines of code for the simplest training simulation to over a million lines of code for complex, multiperson trainers. Furthermore, the complexity of flight simulators, mapped over a 30-year period, has shown exponential growth.

4. *Developed in geographically distributed areas.*   Military flight simulators are typically developed in a distributed fashion for two reasons, one technical and one political. The technical reason is that different portions of the development require different expertise, and so it is common practice for the general contractor to subcontract portions of the work to specialists. The political reason is that high-technology jobs such as simulator development are political plums, and so many politicians fight to have a piece of the work in their jurisdiction. In either case, the integrability of the simulator—already problematic because of the size and complexity of the code—is made more difficult because the paths of communication are long.

5. *Very expensive debugging, testing, and modification.*   The complexity of flight simulation software, its real-time nature, and its tendency to be modified regularly all contribute to making the costs of testing, integrating, and modifying the software usually exceed the cost of development.

6. *Unclear mapping between software structure and aircraft structure.*   Flight simulators have traditionally been built with runtime efficiency as their primary quality goal. This is not surprising given their performance and fidelity requirements and given that simulators were initially built on platforms with extremely limited, by today's standards, memory and processing power.

Traditional design of flight simulator software was based on following control loops through a cycle. These, in turn, were motivated by the tasks that caused the loop to be activated. For example, suppose the pilot turns the aircraft left. The pilot moves the rudder and aileron controls and this in turn moves the control surfaces, which affects the aerodynamics and causes the aircraft to turn. In the simulator, there is a model that reflects the relationship between the controls, the surfaces, the aerodynamics, and the orientation of the aircraft. In the original flight simulator architecture, this model was contained in a module that might be called Turn. There might be a similar module for level flight, another for takeoff and landing, and so forth. The basic decomposition strategy is based on examining the tasks that the pilot and crew perform, modeling the components that actually perform the task, and keeping all calculations as local as possible.

This strategy maximizes performance since any task is modeled in a single module (or a small collection of modules) and thus the data movement necessary to perform the calculations is minimized. The problem with this architecture is that the same physical component is represented in multiple models and hence in multiple modules. The extensive interactions among modules causes problems with both modifiability and integration. If the module controlling turning is being integrated with the module controlling level flight and a problem is discovered in the data being provided to the turning module, that same data are probably being accessed by the level flight module, and so there were many coupling effects to be considered during integration and maintenance.

The growth in complexity (and its associated growth in cost) caused the U.S. Air Force organization that is responsible for the acquisition of flight simulators to begin to emphasize the software qualities of integrability and modifiability. This new emphasis was in addition to the requirement for high-fidelity performance.

By *integrability* we mean the ability to reconcile different portions of the system during the integration phase of initial development. One of the consequences of the growth in complexity was the growth of the cost of integration. With a new system under development that was projected to be 50 percent larger than the largest prior system (1.7 million lines of code), the integration phase alone would break the project's budgets for time and cost.

14.3   Architectural Approach

To manage the numerous challenges that flight simulation posed for its software designers, a new culture of software design for flight simulation needed to be created. This design framework, called *structural modeling,* will be discussed for the remainder of this chapter. In brief, the design framework consists of an object-oriented design to model the subsystems and components of the air vehicle and

TABLE 14.1 How the Structural Modeling Paradigm Achieves Its Quality Goals

Goal	How achieved
Performance	Small number of systemwide coordination strategies and periodic scheduling strategy
Integrability	Separation of computation from coordination and indirect data relationships
Modifiability	Transparency of design, simplicity and similarity of substructures, and indirect data relationships

real-time scheduling to control the execution order of the simulation's subsystems so that fidelity could be guaranteed. To expand slightly on what we said in the introduction, the main tenets of structural modeling are as follows:

- Simplicity and similarity of the architecture's substructures so that the architecture is easy to understand and, hence, modify.

- Small number of systemwide coordination strategies, which simplifies the complex performance and scheduling issues in making a high-fidelity real-time system.

- Indirect data relationships so that passing data between subsystems is done through intermediary components. In this way subsystems do not need to directly know of each others' existence or the details of where data come from and go to. This greatly simplifies the integrability and modifiability of the architecture.

- Separation of computation from decisions about how data and control are passed.

- Transparency of design (making the objects in the flight simulator directly analogous to physical parts of the air vehicle being modeled). This makes the flight simulator easier to design, modify, and maintain over time.

The driving design goals and the techniques that allowed these goals to be met are summarized in Table 14.1.

14.4 Architectural Solution

Logically, flight training simulators have three interactive roles. The first role is that of training the pilot and crew. They sit inside a motion platform, surrounded by instruments intended to replicate exactly the aircraft being simulated, and look at visuals that provide a representation of what would be seen outside of an actual aircraft. We are not going to describe the specifics of either the motion platform or the visual display generator. These are driven by special-purpose processors and are outside the scope of the architecture we describe here. The purpose of a flight simulator is to instruct the pilot and crew in how to operate a particular aircraft, how to perform maneuvers such as mid-air refueling, and how to respond to situations such as an attack on the aircraft. The fidelity of the simulation is an important element in the training. For example, the feel of the controls when particular maneuvers are performed must be captured correctly in the simulation. Otherwise, the pilot and crew are being trained incorrectly and the training may actually be counterproductive. Figure 14.2 shows a collection of modern flight simulators.

The second role associated with a flight simulator is that of the environment. Typically, the environment is a computer model rather than individuals operating in the environment, although with multiaircraft training exercises the environment can include individuals other than the pilot and crew we have been discussing. The environment includes the atmosphere, threats, weapons, and other aircraft. For example, if the purpose of the training is to practice refueling, the (simulated) refueling aircraft introduces turbulence into the (modeled) atmosphere.

The third role associated with a flight training simulator is that of instructor for the simulation. Usually, a training session has a very specific purpose, and specific circumstances will occur during the training. During the training exercise, the instructor is responsible for monitoring the performance of the pilot and crew and for initiating training situations. Sometimes these situations are scripted

FIGURE 14.2 Modern flight simulators. Courtesy of the Boeing Company.

in advance, and other times the instructor introduces them. Typical situations include malfunctions of equipment (e.g., landing gear that does not deploy correctly during landing), attacks on the aircraft from foes, and weather conditions such as turbulence caused by thunderstorms. The instructor has a separate console that is used both to monitor the activities of the crew and to inject malfunctions into the aircraft and control the environment.

Figure 14.3 shows a reference model for a flight simulator. Typically, the instructor is hosted on a different hardware platform from the air vehicle model. The environment model may be hosted either on a separate hardware platform or on the instructor station.

The division between the instructor station and the other two portions is clear from a real-time execution perspective. The instructor station is typically scheduled on an event basis—those events that emanate from the instructor's interactions—and the air vehicle model is scheduled by using a periodic scheduling procedure. The environment model can be scheduled using either regime, depending on the complexity and richness of the environment being modeled. This requirement to coordinate and match two different scheduling paradigms will be revisited when we discuss the details of the structural model.

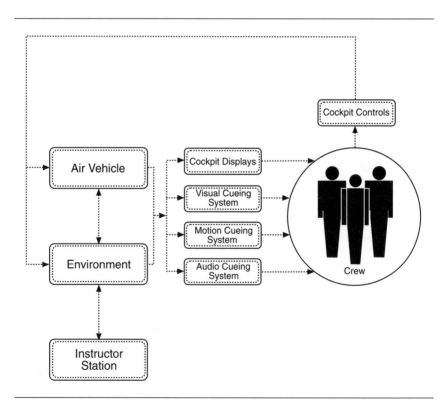

FIGURE 14.3 Reference model for a flight simulator.

The division between the instructor station and the other two portions is not as clean. For example, if an aircraft launches a weapon, it is logically a portion of the air vehicle until it leaves the air vehicle, at which point it becomes a portion of the environment. On firing, however, the aerodynamics of the weapon will be influenced initally by the proximity of the aircraft. Thus, any modeling of it must remain, at least initially, tightly coupled to the air vehicle. If the weapon is always considered a portion of the environment, the modeling of the weapon involves tight coordination between the air vehicle and the environment. If it is modeled as a portion of the air vehicle and then handed off to the environment when fired, control of the weapon needs to be handed from one scheduling regime to another. Even if the environment is scheduled using a periodic scheduling regime, it is likely to operate on a different granularity from that of the environment model.

The simulated behavior of the air vehicle is not calculated from first physical principles. Such simulations are used during the engineering process and are called *engineering simulations*, but they cannot yet be done within the constraints that real-time processing impose. Consequently, the simulations are performed using models supplemented with empirical data. For example, the thrust of an engine might be measured using the whole engine, but the impact of an individual rotor is not measured. Thus, if a rotor is replaced, keeping the simulation correct can be difficult.

For the rest of this section we focus primarily on the architecture of the air vehicle model. But before we can do that, we need a basic understanding of the ways in which time is treated in this domain.

TREATMENT OF TIME IN A FLIGHT SIMULATOR

Time and how it is managed is a critical consideration in the development of a flight simulator. Time is important because a flight simulator is supposed to reflect the real world, and it does this by creating time-based behaviors as they would occur in the real world. Thus, when the pilot in a simulator pushes on the flight control, the simulator must provide the same response in the same time as the actual aircraft would. "In the same time" means both within an upper bound of duration after the event and also within a lower bound of duration. Reacting too quickly is as bad for the quality of the simulation as reacting too slowly.

There are two fundamentally different ways of managing time in a flight simulator: periodic and event-based.

Periodic Time Management.   A periodic time-management scheme has a fixed (simulated) time quantum that is the basis of scheduling the system processes. It typically uses a nonpreemptive cyclic scheduling discipline. The scheduler proceeds by iterating through the following loop:

- Set initial simulated time.
- Iterate next two steps until the session is complete.

- Invoke each of the processes for a fixed (real) quantum. Each of the invoked processes calculates its internal state based on the current simulated time and reports its internal state based on the next period of simulated time. Each invoked process guarantees to complete its computation within its real-time quantum.
- Increment simulated time by quantum.

A simulation based on the periodic management of time will be able to keep the simulated time and the real time in synchronization as long as each individual process is able to advance its state to the next period within the time quantum that it has been allocated.

Typically, this is managed by adjusting the responsibilities of the individual processes so that they are small enough to be computed in the allocated quantum and then using multiple processors, if necessary, to ensure enough computation power to enable all of the processes to receive their quantum of computation.

A periodic simulator scheduling scheme is used when many activities are happening in parallel in simulated time. Thus, for example, when the simulation is based on the simultaneous solution of a collection of differential equations, a solution technique based on finite differences leads to a periodic scheduling strategy.

Event-Based Time Management.   An event-based time-management scheme is similar to interrupt-based scheduling used in many operating systems. The schedule proceeds by iterating through the following loop:

- Add initial simulated event to the event queue.
- While there are events remaining in the event queue:
  - Choose event in event queue with smallest (i.e., soonest) simulated time.
  - Set current simulated time to time of chosen event.
  - Invoke process that processes the chosen event. This process may add events to the event queue.

In this case, simulated time advances by the invoked processes placing events on the event queue and the scheduler choosing the next event to process. There is no guarantee about the relationship of simulated time to real time and no guarantee about the amount of resources consumed by each process that is invoked.

Event-based simulations assume that the management of the event queue is not a major drain on resources. That is, the number of events occurring at a single instant of simulated time is small compared to the effort of managing those events.

Mixed-Time Systems.   Flight simulators must marry periodic time simulation (such as in the air vehicle model) with event-based simulation (such as in the environment model, in some cases) and with other event based activities that are not predictable (such as an interaction with the instructor station or the pilot setting a switch). Many scheduling policies are possible in such a marriage.

A simple policy states that periodic processing occurs immediately after the synchronization interval and is completed before any aperiodic processing. Aperiodic processing then proceeds within a bounded interval, during which as many messages as possible will be retrieved and processed. Those not processed during a given interval must be deferred to subsequent intervals, with the requirement that all messages be processed in the order received from a single source.

Given this understanding of the issues involved in managing time in a flight simulator, we can now present the architectural style that manages this complexity.

THE STRUCTURAL MODEL ARCHITECTURAL STYLE

The structural model is an architectural style as we defined it in section 2.2. That is, it consists of a collection of component configurations and a description of how these configurations coordinate at runtime. In this section, we present the structural model and discuss the considerations that led to its design. The structural model we present here is focused on the air vehicle model. One aspect to keep in mind is that the air vehicle model may itself be spread over several processors. Thus, the elements of the air vehicle structural model must coordinate internally as well as coordinate with the environment model and the instructor portions of the simulation.

A flight simulator can execute in several states including the following:

- *Operate* corresponds to the normal functioning of the simulator as a training tool.

- *Configure* is used when modifications must be made to a current training session. For example, suppose the crew has been training in an environment in which they have been flying in a single-aircraft exercise, and then the instructor wishes to train them for a mid-air refueling exercise. The simulator is then placed into a configure state.

- *Halt* stops the current simulation.

- *Replay* uses a journal to move through the simulation without crew interaction. Replay is used, among other functions, to demonstrate to the crew what they have just done because the crew may get caught up in the operating of the aircraft and not reflect on their actions.

The structural modeling architectural style is divided, at the coarsest level, into two parts: *executive* and *application*.

The *executive* part handles coordination issues: real-time scheduling of subsystems, synchronization between processors, event management from the instructor–operator station, data sharing, and data integrity.

The *application* part handles the actual computation of the flight simulation: modeling the air vehicle. The application's functions are implemented by subsystems and their constituent components. First we will discuss the executive style in detail and then return to a discussion of the application style.

COMPONENT CONFIGURATIONS FOR AIR VEHICLE MODEL EXECUTIVE

Figure 14.4 shows the air vehicle structural model with the executive component configurations given in detail. These are the *timeline synchronizer*, the *periodic sequencer*, the *event handler*, and the *surrogates* for other portions of the simulator.

Timeline Synchronizer. The timeline synchronizer is the base scheduling mechanism for the air vehicle model. It also maintains the simulation's internal notion of time. The other three elements of the executive—the periodic sequencer, the event handler, and the surrogates—all must be allocated processor resources. The timeline synchronizer also maintains the current state of the simulation.

The timeline synchronizer passes both data and control to the other three elements and receives data and control from them. It is also responsible for coordinating time with other portions of the simulator. This can include other processors responsible for a portion of the air vehicle model, which also have their own timeline synchronizers. Finally, the timeline synchronizer implements a scheduling

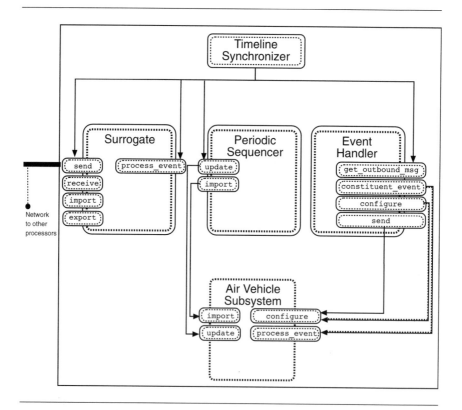

FIGURE 14.4 The structural model style of an air vehicle system processor with focus on the executive.

policy for coordinating both periodic and aperiodic processing. For the sake of continuity, precedence is given to the periodic processing.

Periodic Sequencer.   The periodic sequencer is used to conduct all periodic processing performed by the simulation's subsystems. This involves invoking the subsystems to perform periodic operations according to fixed schedules.

The periodic sequencer provides two operations to the timeline synchronizer. The `import` operation is used to request the periodic sequencer to invoke subsystems to perform their `import` operation. The `update` operation requests that the periodic sequencer invoke the `update` operations of the subsystems.

To conduct its processing, the periodic sequencer requires two capabilities. The first is to organize knowledge of a schedule. By *schedule* we mean the patterns of constituent invocations that represent the orders and rates at which changes are propagated through the simulation algorithms realized by the constituents. The enactment of these patterns essentially represents the passage of time within the air vehicle simulation in its various operating states. The second capability is to actually invoke the subsystems through their periodic operations by means of some dispatching mechanism.

Event Handler.   The event-handler element is used to orchestrate all aperiodic processing performed by subsystems. This involves invoking the subsystems by aperiodic operations appropriate to the current system operating state.

The event handler provides four kinds of operations to the timeline synchronizer: `configure` (used to start a new training mission, for example), `constituent_event` (used when an event is targeted for a particular instance of a component), `get_outbound_msg` (used by the timeline synchronizer to conduct aperiodic processing while in system operating states, such as `operate`, that are predominantly periodic), and `send` (used by subsystem controllers to send events to other subsystem controllers and messages to other systems).

To perform its processing, the event handler requires two capabilities. The first is a capability to determine which subsystem controller receives an event, using knowledge of a mapping between event identifiers and instances. The second is a capability to invoke the subsystems and to extract required parameters from events before invocation.

Surrogate.   Surrogates are responsible for system-to-system communication between the air vehicle model and the environment model or the instructor station. Surrogates are aware of the physical details of the system with which they communicate and are responsible for issues such as representation, communication protocol, and so forth.

For example, the instructor station monitors state data from the air vehicle model and displays the data to the instructor. The surrogate gathers the correct data when it gets control of the processor and sends that data to the instructor station. In the other direction, the instructor may wish to set a particular state for the crew. This is an event that is received by the surrogate and passed to the event processor for dispatching to the appropriate subsystems.

This use of surrogates means that both the periodic scheduler and the event handler can be kept ignorant of the details of the instructor station or the platform on which the environment model is operating. All of the system-specific knowledge is embedded in the surrogate. Any change to these platforms will not propagate further than the surrogate in the air vehicle model system.

COMPONENT CONFIGURATIONS FOR AIR VEHICLE MODEL APPLICATION

Figure 14.5 shows the component configurations that exist in the application subpart of the air vehicle srtuctural model. There are only two of them: the *subsystem controller* and its *components*. The term *component*, as used in the structural model, refers to a specific component type. This terminological ambiguity is restricted to this section, and we hope it will not cause confusion. Subsystem controllers pass data to and from other subsystem controller instances but only to their child components. Components will pass data only to and from their parents and not to any other component. They will also receive control only from their parents and return it only to their parents. These restrictions on data and control passing preclude a component from passing data or control even to a sibling component. The rationale for these restrictions is to assist in integration and modifiability by eliminating any coupling of a component instance with anything other than its parent. Any effect of modification or integration is mediated by the parent subsystem controller.

Subsystem Controller.   Subsystem controllers are used to interconnect a set of functionally related components to do the following:

- Achieve the simulation of a subsystem as a whole
- Mediate control and aperiodic communication between the system and subsystems

They are also responsible for determining how to use the capabilities of their components to satisfy trainer-specific functionality such as malfunctions and the setting of parameters.

A subsystem controller must provide the capability to make logical connections between its components and those of other subsystems. Inbound connections supply inputs produced outside of the subsystem that the subsystem's components need for their simulation algorithms. Outbound connections satisfy similar needs of other subsystems and of surrogates. These connections appear as sets of names by which a subsystem controller internally refers to data considered to be outside of itself. When such a name is read or written, the appropriate connections are assumed to be made. How the connections are actually made is determined later in the detailed design.

Subsystem controllers must both order the `update` operations of their components and interconnect their inputs and outputs. This achieves the desired

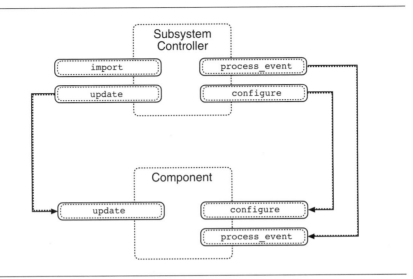

FIGURE 14.5 The application component configurations.

propagation of changes through the components and satisfies the subsystem's outbound connections. The subsystem controller synthesizes, from its components, a simulation algorithm for the subsystem as a whole. In addition to updating components, the controller may be responsible for making intermediate computations as well as data transformations and conversions.

As we mentioned, a flight simulator can be in one of several states. This is translated through the executive to particular executive states. The executive then informs the subsystem controller of its current state. The two states that are relevant here are *operate* and *stabilize*. The operate state instructs the subsystem controller to perform its normal computations relevant to advancing the state of the simulation. The stabilize state informs the subsystem controller to terminate its current computation in a controlled fashion (to prevent the motion platform from harming the crew through uncontrolled motion), as follows:

- Retrieve and locally store the values of inbound connections under the direct control of an executive. Such a capability is provided to address issues of data consistency and time coherence.
- Stabilize the simulation algorithms of its components under the control of executive instances and report whether it considers the subsystem as a whole to be currently stable.

Subsystem controllers *must* be able to do the following:

- Initialize themselves and each of their components to a set of initial conditions in response to an event
- Route requests for malfunctions and the setting of simulation parameters to their components based on knowledge of component capabilities

Finally, subsystem controllers may support the reconfiguration of mission parameters such as armaments, cargo loads, the starting location of a training mission, and so forth. Subsystem controllers realize these capabilities through periodic and aperiodic operations made available to the periodic sequencer and event handler, respectively.

There are two periodic operations provided by system controllers: `update` and `import`.

The `update` operation causes the subsystem controller to perform periodic processing appropriate to the current system operating state, which is provided as an input parameter. In the *operate* state, the `update` operation causes the subsystem controller to retrieve inputs needed by its components by means of inbound connections, execute operations of its components in some logical order so that changes can be propagated through them, and retrieve their outputs for use in satisfying another's inputs or the subsystem's outbound connections. More than just a sequencer, this algorithm provides logical "glue" that cements the components into some coherent, aggregate simulation. This glue may include computations as well as data transformations and conversions.

In the *stabilize* state, the `update` operation is used to request the subsystem controller to perform one iteration of its stabilization algorithm and determine whether locally defined stability criteria are satisfied. The `update` operation provides one output parameter, indicating whether the subsystem controller considers the subsystem to be currently stable. This makes the assumption that such a determination can be made locally, which may not be valid in all circumstances. Subsystem controllers *may* provide the capability to do the following tasks.

The `import` operation is used to request the subsystem controller to complete certain of its inbound connections by reading their values and locally store their values for use in a subsequent `update` operation. There are two aperiodic operations provided by subsystem controllers: `process_event` and `configure`.

The `process_event` operation is used in operating states that are predominantly periodic, such as *operate*, to ask the subsystem controller to respond to an event. A characteristic of this operation is that effects of servicing the event are reflected only in the subsystem's periodic outputs, which are not made available until the next *update* operation. The event is provided by an input parameter to the operation. Several events from the instructor–operator station fall into this category, such as `process_malfunction`, `set_parameter`, and `hold_parameter`.

The `configure` operation is used in system operating states, like *initialize*, in which the processing is predominantly aperiodic. The operation is used to establish a named set of conditions such as some training device configuration or training mission. The information that the subsystem controller needs to establish the condition may be provided as an input parameter on the operation, as a location in a memory on secondary storage, or in a database where the information has been stored for retrieval. To complete the operation, the subsystem controller invokes operations of its components that cause the components to establish the conditions.

Component.   Air vehicle model components can be simulations of real aircraft components, such as a hydraulic pump, an electrical relay, an engine rotor, a fuel tank, and the like. They can support simulator-specific models such as forces and moments, weights and balances, and the equations of motion. They can be used to localize the details of cockpit equipment, such as gauges, switches, and displays. But no matter what specific functionality they are used to simulate, components are all considered to be architecturally equivalent.

In general, components are used to support the simulation of an individual part, or object, within some functional assembly. Each component provides a simulation algorithm that determines the state of the component based on the following:

- Its former state
- Inputs that represent its connections with logically adjacent components
- Some elapsed time interval

A component makes this determination as often as it is requested to do so by its subsystem controller, which provides the required inputs and receives the component's outputs. This capability is called *updating*.

A component can support the capability to produce abnormal outputs, reflecting a malfunction condition. In addition to potentially modeling changes in normal operating conditions that can result in malfunctions over time, such as wear and tear, components can be told to start and stop malfunctioning by their subsystem controller.

A component can also support the capability to set a simulation parameter to a particular value. Simulation parameters are external names for performance parameters and decision criteria used in its simulation algorithm. Each component supports the capability to initialize itself to some known condition. Like the other capabilities of components, parameter setting and initialization must be requested by the subsystem controller.

The capabilities of updating and those of malfunctioning, parameter setting, and initializing differ in the incidence of their use by the subsystem controller. The component is requested to update on a periodic basis, effecting the passage of time within the simulation. Requests for the other capabilities are made only sporadically.

Components support these capabilities through a set of periodic and aperiodic operations made available to the subsystem controller. The `update` operation is the single periodic operation and is used to control the periodic execution of the simulation algorithm. The component receives external inputs and returns its outputs through parameters on the operation. Two aperiodic operations are provided by the components `process_event` and `configure`.

All logical interactions among components are mediated by the subsystem controller, which is encoded with knowledge of how to use the component operations to achieve the simulation requirements allocated to the subsystem as a whole. This includes the following:

- Periodically propagating state changes through the components using their *update* operations

- Making logical connections among components using the input and output parameters on these operations

- Making logical connections among components and the rest of the simulation using the subsystem's inbound and outbound connections

Component malfunctions are assumed to be associated with abnormal operating conditions of the real-world components being modeled. Therefore, the presence and identities of component malfunctions are decided by the component designer and are made known to the subsystem controller designer for use in realizing subsystem malfunction requests. Subsystem malfunctions need not correspond directly to those supported by the components, and certain subsystem malfunctions can be realized as some aggregation of more primitive failures supported by components. It is the subsystem controller's responsibility to realize some mapping between the two.

Likewise, the presence and identities of simulation parameters are decided by the component designer based on the characteristics of the component's simulation algorithm. They are made known to the subsystem controller designer for use in realizing subsystem requests or for other purposes for which they are intended or are suitable to support.

Skeletal System and Pattern-Based Simplicity.   What we have now described is a skeletal system, as defined in Section 13.2. We have a framework for a flight simulator, but none of the details—the functionality—have been filled in. In fact, this framework has also been used for helicopter simulation and even nuclear reactor simulation. The process of realizing a working simulation consists of fleshing out this skeleton with subsystems and components, as dictated by the functional partitioning process, which will be discussed next.

An entire flight simulator, which can easily exceed 1 million lines of code, can be described completely by six component types: components, subsystem controllers, timeline synchronizer, periodic sequencer, event handler, and surrogate. This is an example of pattern-based simplicity, as we discussed in Section 13.3, and it renders the architecture easier to build, understand, integrate, grow, and otherwise modify.

Equally important, with a standard set of fundamental patterns, one can create specification forms, code templates, and exemplars that describe those patterns. This allows for consistent analysis. When these patterns are mandated, an architect can insist that a designer use *only* the provided building blocks. While this may sound draconian, a small number of fundamental building blocks can, in fact, free a designer to concentrate on the functionality, the reason that the system is being built in the first place.

Both of these architectural approaches—skeletal system framework and pattern-based simplicity—have contributed significantly to the success of the structural modeling approach.

REFERENCE ARCHITECTURE

Now that we have described the architectural style with which the air vehicle model is built, we still need to discuss how operational functionality is allocated to instances of that style. That is, we need to define the reference architecture. We do this by defining instances of the subsystem controllers.

The reference architecture is the place where the specifics of the aircraft to be simulated are detailed. The actual partitioning depends on the systems on the aircraft, the complexity of the aircraft, and the types of training for which the simulator is designed. In this section, we sketch a reference architecture.

We begin with a desire to partition the functionality to components based on the underlying physical aircraft. To accomplish this we use an object-oriented decomposition approach. This has a number of virtues, as follows:

- It maintains a close correspondence between the aircraft partitions and the simulator, and this provides us with a set of conceptual models that map closely to the real world. Our understanding of how the parts interact in the aircraft helps us understand how the parts interact in the simulator. It also makes it easier for users and reviewers to understand the simulator. They are familiar with the aircraft (problem domain), and they can easily transfer this understanding to the simulator (solution domain).

- Experience with past flight simulators has taught us that a change in the aircraft is easily identifiable with aircraft partitions. Thus the locus of the change in the simulator corresponds to analogous aircraft partitions. This tends to keep the simulator changes localized and well defined. It also makes it easier to understand how changes in the aircraft affect the simulator, therefore making it easier to assess the cost and time required for changes to be implemented.

- The number and size of the simulator interfaces are reduced. This derives from a strong functional cohesion within partitions, placing the largest interfaces within partitions instead of across them.

- Localization of malfunctions is also achieved. Malfunctions are associated with specific pieces of aircraft equipment. It is easier to analyze the effects of malfunctions when dealing with this physical mapping, and the resulting implementations exhibit good locality. The effects of malfunctions are readily propagated in a natural fashion by the data that the malfunctioning partition produces. Higher-order effects are handled the same as first-order effects.

In breaking down the air vehicle modeling problem into more manageable units, the airframe becomes the focus of attention. Groups exist for the airframe, the forces on the airframe, those things outside the airframe, and those things inside the airframe but ancillary to its operation. This results in the following specific groups:

- *Kinetics group.*   Elements that deal with forces exerted on the airframe
- *Aircraft systems group.*   Those parts concerned with common systems that provide the aircraft with various kinds of power or distribute energy within the airframe

- *Avionics group.* Those things that provide some sort of ancillary support to the aircraft but are not directly involved in the kinetics of the air vehicle model, the vehicle's control, or operation of the basic flight systems

- *Environment group.* Those things associated with the environment in which the air vehicle model operates

GROUP DECOMPOSITION

In this section we motivate the coarsest decomposition of the air vehicle model—the group decomposition. Groups decompose into systems which, in turn, decompose into subsystems. These subsystems provide the instances of the subsystem controllers. Groups and systems are not directly reflected in the architecture and exist to rationalize the functionality assigned to the various instances of subsystem controllers. For now, we begin with groups.

N-Square Charts. One method of presenting information about the interfaces in a system is provided by *n*-square charts. We will make use of this presentation method to illustrate how the partitions we selected relate to each other. Because some of the factors we consider in making partitioning decisions are based on the interfaces between the partitions, *n*-square charts are useful in evaluating the decisions. They are a good method for illustrating the overall view of interfaces and can be used to illustrate the abstractions utilized in various parts of the design.

An example *n*-square chart is shown in Figure 14.6. The boxes on the main diagonal represent the system partitions. Their inputs are found in the column in which the partition lies. The outputs from the partition are shown in the row in which the partition lies. Therefore the full set of inputs to a partition is the union of all the cell contents of the partition's column. Conversely, the full set of outputs is the union of all the cell contents in the row in which the partition resides. The flow of data from one partition to another is to the right, then down, to the left, and then up.

Partition 1	**Inputs** ↓	
Outputs ←	Partition 2	**Outputs** →
	↑ **Inputs**	Partition 3

FIGURE 14.6 The *n*-square chart.

Kinetics Group	Loads	Vehicle State Vector	Vehicle Position
Power	**Aircraft Systems Group**	Power	
Inertial State	Loads	**Avionics Group**	Ownship Emissions
Atmosphere, Terrain, and Weather Data		Environment Emitter Data	**Environment Group**

FIGURE 14.7   Air vehicle model domain *n*-square chart for groups.

Figure 14.7 shows an *n*-square chart depicting the interfaces between the groups we identified above. Interfaces external to the air vehicle model have been omitted to simplify the chart. The external interfaces terminate in interface subsystems. The data elements shown on this chart are aggregate collections of data to simplify the presentation. The interfaces are not named here, nor are they typed. As we investigate partitions, looking at more limited sets of elements, the detail of the information presented increases accordingly. Systems engineers can use this approach to the point where all of the primitive data objects in the interfaces are shown. During detailed design, the interface types and names will be determined and the structure finalized.

Not all of the air vehicle models will have a correspondence to aircraft structure. The aerodynamics models are expressions of the underlying physics of the vehicle's interaction with the environment. There are few direct analogs to aircraft parts. Partitioning this area will mean relying on the mathematical models and physical entities used to describe the vehicle's dynamics. Partitioning correctly based on mathematical models that affect the total aircraft is more difficult to do than partitioning based on the physical structure of the aircraft.

DECOMPOSING GROUPS INTO SYSTEMS

The next step is to refine the groups into systems. A system and a group can be units of integration: The functionality contained within the system is a relatively self-contained solution to a set of simulation problems. These units are a convenient focus for testing and validation. Partitions of groups exist as collections of code modules implemented by one engineer or a small group of engineers. We can identify systems within the groups we have defined above. We will look briefly at the kinetics group systems.

Systems in the Kinetics Group.   These systems consist of elements concerned with the kinetics of the vehicle. Included in this group are elements directly involved in controlling the motion of the vehicle and modeling the interaction of the vehicle and its control surfaces with the environment. The systems identified in this group are as follows:

- Airframe
- Propulsion
- Landing gear
- Flight controls

All of the subsystems in the propulsion system shown in Figure 14.8 deal with the model of the aircraft's engines. Multiple engines are handled by creating multiple sets of state variables and duplicate instances of objects, where appropriate. This system's principal purpose is to calculate engine thrust, moments caused by rotation of engine parts, and the forces and moments caused by mass distribution of fuel.

The aircraft's fuel system is grouped here because the primary interface for the fuel system is to the engines. The fuel system calculates the forces acting on the airframe from movement of the fuel within the tanks as well as the gravitational effect of the fuel mass. At this point the reference architecture for the propulsion subsystem is complete. We have identified the division of functionality, its allocation to subsystems and subsystem controllers, and the connections among subsystems.

To complete the architecture, we would need to do the following:

- Identify the component instances for the propulsion subsystem.
- Similarly decompose the other groups, their systems, and their subsystems.

This, however, concludes the presentation of the architecture in this case study.

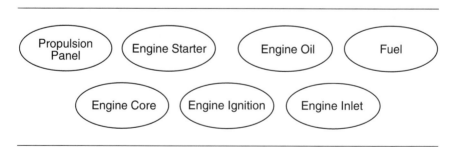

FIGURE 14.8   Propulsion subsystems.

14.5   Achievement of Goals

Structural modeling has been an unqualified success. Chastek and Brownsword describe some of the results achieved through the use of this architectural style [Chastek 96, 28]:

> In a previous data-driven simulator of comparable size (the B-52), 2000–3000 test descriptions (test problems) were identified during factory acceptance testing. With their structural modeling project, 600–700 test descriptions were reported. They found the problems easier to correct; many resulted from misunderstandings with the documentation. . . . Staff typically could isolate a reported problem off-line rather than going to a site. . . . Since the use of structural modeling, defect rates for one project are half that found on previous data-driven simulators.

At the start of this chapter we identified three quality goals of structural modeling: performance, integrability, and modifiability for operational requirements. In this section, we recap how the structural model achieves these quality goals.

PERFORMANCE

A key quality goal of the structural model is real-time performance. This goal is achieved primarily through the operation of the executive and the use of a periodic scheduling strategy. Each subsystem that is invoked by the executive has a time budget, and the hardware for the simulator is sized so that it can accommodate the sum of the time budgets of the subsystems. Sometimes this involves a single processor, other times, multiple processors. Given this scheduling strategy, the achievement of real-time performance comes from requiring the sum of the times allocated to the subsystems involved in the control loops to be within one period of the simulator. Thus, real-time performance is guaranteed by a combination of architectural style (the executive component configurations) and the functional decomposition (how the instances are invoked).

INTEGRABILITY

In Chapters 4 and 5, we discussed how qualities are embedded into an architecture. In this chapter, we see an example in which the architectural style is designed to minimize integration problems. This approach is to minimize the connections between the various component configurations used in the structural model.

In the structural model, both the data connections and the control connections between two subsystems are deliberately minimized. First, within a subsystem, the components can neither pass control nor data directly to any sibling component. Any data or control transfer occurs only through the mediation of the subsystem controller. Thus, integrating another component into a subsystem involves ensuring that the data in the subsystem controller are internally consistent and that the data transferred between the subsystem controller and the component are correct. This is a much simpler process than if the new component communicated with other components because all of them would be involved in the integration. That is, the integration problem has been reduced to a problem that is linear, rather than exponential, in the number of components.

When integrating two subsystems, none of their components interact directly and so the problem is again reduced to ensuring that the two subsystems pass data consistently. It is possible that the addition of a new subsystem will affect several other subsystems, but because the number of subsystems is substantially less than the number of components, this problem is limited in complexity.

In the structural model, therefore, integrability is simplified by deliberately restricting the number of possible connections. The cost for this restriction is that the subsystem controllers often act purely as data conduits for the various components, and this adds complexity. The benefits of this approach, however, far outweigh the cost in practice. Every project that has used structural modeling has reported easy, smooth integration.

MODIFIABILITY

Modifiability is simplified when there are few base component configurations for the designer and maintainer to understand and when functionality is localized so that there are fewer subsystem controllers or components involved in a particular modification. The technique of using n-square charts begins with the premise of reducing connections.

Furthermore, for those subsystems that are physically based, the decomposition follows the physical structure, and modifications also follow the physical structure. Those subsystems that are not physically based, such as the equations of motion, are less likely to be changed. Users of structural modeling reported that side effects encountered during modifications were rare.

14.6   Summary

In this chapter we have described an architecture for flight simulators that was designed to achieve the qualities of performance, integrability, and modifiability. And projects were able to achieve these results with cost savings. For example, on-site installation teams were 50 percent of the size previously required because they could locate and correct faults more easily. The design achieved those qualities by restricting the number of component configurations in the structural model architectural style, by restricting communication among the components, and by decomposing the functionality according to anticipated changes in the underlying aircraft.

The improvements in these simulators have principally accrued from a better understanding of, and adherence to, a well-analyzed and well-documented software architecture.

14.7   For Further Reading

For an historical introduction to the computation and engineering involved in creating flight simulators, see [Fogarty 67], [Marsman 85], and [Perry 66].

The structural modeling paradigm has evolved over the past 10 years. Some of the early writings on this paradigm can be found in [Lee 88], [Rissman 90], and [Abowd 93b]. A more recent description can be found in [Chastek 96].

The reader interested in more details about the functional decomposition used in example flight simulators is referred to [ASCYW 94].

14.8   Discussion Questions

1. The strong relationship between the structure of the system being simulated and the structure of the simulating software is one of the things that makes the structural modeling style so flexible with respect to mirroring the modeled system in the event of change, extension, or contraction. Suppose the application domain were something other than simulation. Would structural modeling still be a reasonable approach? Why or why not? Under what circumstances would it or would it not be?

2. Structural modeling is a combination of several of the architectural styles described in Chapter 5. What are they and how are they used? Does this use conform to the advantages of those styles that we described in Chapter 5?

3. The data and control flow constraints on subsystem controllers and components are very stringent. As a component designer and implementor, do you think you would welcome these constraints or find them too restrictive?

PART FOUR

REUSING ARCHITECTURES

It is a basic premise of the architecture business cycle that architectures affect organizations as much as organizations affect architectures. Part Four explores the feedback portion of the cycle. Today, many organizations recognize that a software architecture is the result of significant investment—at the very least, the time and energy and design expertise of the higher-paid help. It makes sense to wring as much use out of it as possible, far beyond just the single system that necessitated it. These organizations consider their architectures to be capital assets, to be maintained and reused as much as their buildings or their staff. Thus, an architecture serves not only the system it was developed for but also subsequent systems for which it is applicable and appropriate. Knowing this up front and planning for it facilitates the process; an architecture built with reuse across many products in mind will be more likely to be used again and again. Planning for architectural reuse tends to be self-fulfilling and also nudges the organization toward places in the market where it can profitably reuse its architectural assets, thereby completing the cycle.

There are two settings in which architectures can be reused: within the developing organization and within a community across organizations. Chapter 15 deals with the first case. An organization can use an architecture as the basis for a product family, where each member of the family is a system sharing the common architecture (and scores of other reusable assets that flow from the common architecture, such as test cases).

But as suggested, architectures can be used across organizations as well. If your organization has built a compiler recently or a database system or an avionics program or any of a hundred other examples, it's doubtful that its architecture was brand new. More than likely, it was "borrowed" from the appropriate community. Common architectures lead to markets for common components, but for these components to work together, there must be consensus on their interfaces, their behavior, their resource consumption, and so forth. In other words, there must be standards. Chapter 17 explores the world of component-based development from the point of view of open systems and component vendors, including the process for how specifications become open standards.

The two case studies in Part Four underscore each kind of architectural reuse. Chapter 16 tells the story of a company that has used a common architecture to build a wide variety of large command and control systems. As always, we present the architecture as an example in its own right, but this case study also illuminates other important issues that must be addressed when fielding a product line, such as organizational culture, reporting relationships, customer interaction, and training. The company was able to show remarkable reductions in time to market and cost for systems in its family, while at the same time increasing the reliability of the systems as well as the satisfaction of their customers. The company was also able to enter new business areas based on the kinds of systems that could be built from its architecture.

Chapter 18 is an example of rapid system development using commercial off-the-shelf components. This approach depends on the existence of and conformance to open system standards and illustrates how vendors in different markets with no contact with each other were able to make compatible (if not common) architectural assumptions that allowed their products to interact and this system to be built.

Chapter 19 concludes our tour of the architecture business cycle by recapping what we have learned and laying out some future directions for the field.

15

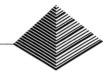

Product Lines
Reusing Architectural Assets within an Organization

with Patricia Oberndorf, Kurt Wallnau, Amy Moormann Zaremski

> *In 1969, McIlroy first recognized the need for an industry of reusable software components, but since then, this has continued to be an elusive goal for the software community. It is therefore fair to ask the question: If the benefits of reusable software components are so overwhelming, why doesn't this practice already pervade the whole of computer science?*
> — Grady Booch [Booch 93]

Up to this point we have been discussing the construction of an individual system. However, for an organization an architecture represents a significant investment of both time and effort of its senior talent. It is natural to want to maximize this investment by reusing an architecture on multiple systems. When an organization is producing multiple similar systems and reusing the same architecture (and components associated with that architecture), it enjoys some substantial benefits including reduced cost of construction and reduced time to market. This is the lure of the *software product line*: a collection of systems sharing a managed set of features constructed from a common set of core software assets. These assets include a base architecture and a set of common, perhaps tailorable, components that populate it. The feedback loops of the architecture business cycle (ABC) that feed back to the organization reflect the impact on an organization of having a product line.

Note: Patricia Oberndorf is a member of the technical staff at the Software Engineering Institute, Carnegie Mellon University.
Kurt Wallnau is a member of the technical staff at the Software Engineering Institute, Carnegie Mellon University.
Amy Moormann Zaremski is a member of the technical staff at the Xerox Corporation, Rochester, N.Y.

331

Product lines epitomize reuse, sometimes in ways that are not immediately evident. Consider the following assets over and above the architecture that can be reused across members of a product line:

- *Components.*   Components are applicable across individual products. Far and above mere code reuse, component reuse includes the (often difficult) initial design work. Design successes are captured and reused; design dead ends are avoided, not repeated. This includes the design of the component's interface, its documentation, its test plans and procedures, and any models (such as performance models) used to predict or measure its behavior. One reusable set of components is the system's user interface, which represents an enormous and vital set of design decisions that can be reused.

- *Personnel.*   Personnel can be transferred among projects as required because of the commonality of the applications. Their expertise is applicable across the entire line.

- *Defect elimination.*   Overall quality increases because errors eliminated in a component on one product raise the quality of the corresponding components in all the other products.

- *Project planning.*   Budgeting and scheduling are more predictable because past experience is a high-fidelity indicator of future performance. Work breakdown structures need not be invented each time. Teams, team size, and team composition are all known quantities.

- *Performance issues.*   Performance models, schedulability analysis, distributed system issues (such as proving absence of deadlock), allocation of processes to processors, fault-tolerance schemes, and network load policies all carry over from product to product.

- *Processes, methods, and tools.*   Configuration control procedures and facilities, documentation plans and approval processes, tool environments, system generation and distribution procedures, coding standards, and a host of other day-to-day engineering support activities can all be carried over from product to product.

- *Exemplar systems.*   Deployed products serve as high-quality demonstration prototypes. Customer satisfaction increases (and risk decreases) because feasibility is not an issue. Deployed products also serve as high-quality engineering prototypes, providing highly detailed performance, security, safety, and reliability models.

The production of a product line is not a simple matter. In the quotation that began this chapter, we see that reuse has been a byword of software engineering for a long time. It is our belief that one reason why reuse has been so long in arriving is that large-scale reuse depends on having a product line approach to software and this, in turn, requires significant organizational restructuring. In the next chapter we see how a particular organization, CelsiusTech, created a product line and the impact it had on both their business and their organization. In this chapter, we discuss the various elements of a product line. These include how products (individual members) of the product line are created, how the product line base architecture and base system are made to evolve, the inclusion of outside components in the base system, and the organizational impact of having a product line.

Achieving a product line is complicated and the approach will vary from organization to organization depending on a wide variety of factors including business area, willingness to invest, desired time to market, existing software base from which the product line is to be constructed, and organizational culture. We will not discuss how an organization that wishes to achieve a product line should attack any of these areas but will instead show how they are manifested in an organization that has achieved a successful product line.

15.1   Creating Products and Evolving a Product Line

An organization that has a product line will have in place an architecture and a collection of components that are associated with the product line. From time to time, the organization will create a new product that is a member of the product line. This product will have features that are in common with the other members of the product line and may have features that are different from any other member.

One problem associated with a product line is managing its evolution. As time passes, the product line—more precisely, the set of core assets from which products are built—must evolve. Product line evolution will be driven by three sources:

1. New versions of existing components within the product line will be released by their vendors, and future products will need to be constructed from the new versions.

2. New externally created components may be added to the product line. Thus, for example, functions that previously were performed via internally developed components may be performed via components acquired externally, or vice versa. Or future products will need to take advantage of new technology, as embodied in externally developed components.

3. New features may be added to the product line to keep it responsive to user needs or competitive pressures.

A second problem is managing the evolution of individual products (i.e., members of the product line) after they have been created. Suppose new functions need to be added to a product. Are these functions within the product line's scope? If they are, the product can simply be built anew from the asset base. But if they are not, a decision must be made. Either the product spins off from the product line, following its own evolutionary path, or the asset base must be updated to expand its scope to include the new functions. Updating the product line may be the wisest choice if the new functionality is likely to be used in future products, but this capability comes at the cost of the time necessary to update the product line assets.

A third problem is what to do with already deployed products when the product line evolves. Even if the organization is in a position to issue a recall and replace old products with ones built from the most up-to-date version of the asset base, should it? Keeping products compatible with the product line takes time and effort. But not doing so may make future upgrades of the product more time consuming because either it will need to be brought into compliance with the then-latest product line components or it will not be able to take advantage of new functions added to the product line.

These and other issues make the relationship between the product line and its members (or more properly the owners of the product line assets and the owners of the individual products) resemble the relationship between a software vendor and its customers. We discuss this in the next section.

15.2   Organizational Implications of a Product Line

A product line affects an organization in its structure, in its relationship with its customers, and its training of staff. These changes arise because the existence of a product line requires an organization to consider the elements of the product line—the architecture, the components, the test cases, and all of the items we enumerated in the beginning of this chapter—as assets to be managed. This leads to an organizational entity to manage these assets and, typically, a separate organizational entity to produce products for customers.

STRUCTURE

How the existence of a product line affects an organization's structure in part depends on the number of simultaneous products an organization is producing and how the organization decides to deal with the problems of keeping the products and the product line in synchronization. Regardless of these factors, however, if an organization has a product line and the product line architecture is going to evolve (as it must), there must be an organizational entity that has responsibility for the architecture and other core assets of the product line. Clearly, the developers of each product cannot be the owners of the asset base since modifications of the core will affect all of the products, not just the one to be modified. Thus, once an artifact has been recognized as an important core asset, an organizational unit must manage it and the other core assets.

Having separate organizational entities, one of which manages the core assets and one of which actually builds the products, means that both organizational managers and the product marketers must understand what it means to have a product line and how that affects both future products and customers. Figure 15.1

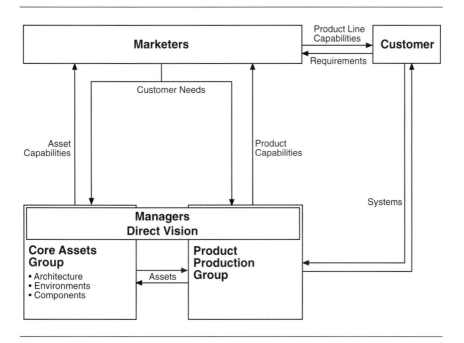

FIGURE 15.1   Relationship of players in a product line organization.

shows some of the relationships that arise because of the existence of both the product line and products. The marketers are responsible for communicating customer needs to both organizations, and the managers are responsible for deciding which needs are satisfied by the core assets group and which by the product production group.

It is not enough to understand the organizational structure; the skills required within the various units also must be understood. The personnel within the core assets group must know how to do abstraction and continually look for generalizations of functions. The personnel within the product production group must understand how to engineer from existing components and must understand the customer problems. Figure 15.2 shows the skill set of both the core assets group and the product production group.

RELATIONSHIP WITH CUSTOMERS

At this point, the relationship between the owner of the core product line assets (especially the architecture and components) and the developers of the products becomes similar to the relationship between a commercial vendor and its customers. The developers of the products become agents for the end customers, lobbying the core asset owners to provide for their individual customers' needs. Formal

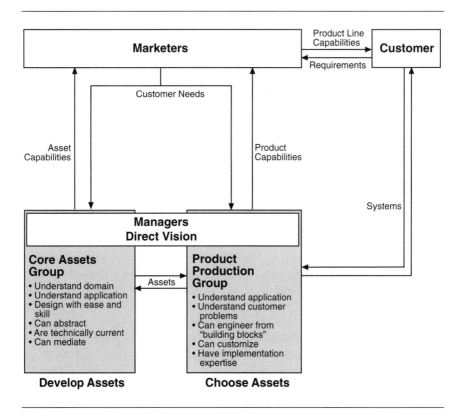

FIGURE 15.2   Product line skill set.

mechanisms are created for feedback to the core architecture owner and cross-cutting groups that must understand the implications of a modification to the core architecture and approve them. Furthermore, modifications to the core architecture become grouped into releases so that the developers or maintainers of the products can manage the integration into their systems.

Finally, product lines spawn different relationships with the end users and customers. The salesperson can offer a better deal to customers who are willing to accept products within the scope of variation of the product line. This means that the salesperson will be more likely to negotiate the customer's requirements based on existing products. Typically, the dialogue might go something like this:

CUSTOMER (*pointing to a thick stack of paper*): "Here are my requirements. Can you meet them?"

SALESPERSON (*fondly remembering the good old days when all that was required was a smile, a nod, and going back to the home organization with a fat contract in hand*): "I'm sure we can. However, I should tell you that if you were able to relax this requirement here, and this one here, and change this one over here just a smidge, we'd be able to satisfy your requirements using a straightforward variant of our product line."

CUSTOMER: "Good for you. What's it to me?"

SALESPERSON: "Because to meet your requirements will cost you $6 million, take two years, and you'll have a system unlike any other. To meet the slightly modified requirements will take two months, cost you $1 million, and you'll be using components that have been used by other customers for over six years now. Which would you like? It's completely up to you."

CUSTOMER (*who's never, ever had a vendor offer a viable choice like this or been made to understand how much the "special" requirements actually cost so their worth could be judged*): "Really? I'll take the modified version. See you in two months."

15.3 Component-Based Systems

For the remainder of this chapter we will concentrate not on the product line itself but on the components that populate a product line's architecture. It is seldom the case these days that every part of a software system must be programmed by the organization that is fielding it. The percentage of systems constructed from preexisting components is much higher than only a few years ago. "Buy, don't build" is the anthem of the software community today. But buying means less control over every aspect of a system's development. How can this loss of control be reconciled with our desire for quality? Part of the answer lies in our assertion that, for large systems, quality lives primarily in the architecture. The other part of the answer is that one must take care to integrate components so that they do not compromise the architecture and the qualities that it helps to manifest.

In Chapter 8, we saw an infrastructure explicitly intended to accommodate the inclusion of preexisting components. In Chapter 18, we will see a system constructed utilizing the Common Object Request Broker Architecture (CORBA) and built almost completely from off-the-shelf components that communicate and cooperate with each other even though they were developed in complete absence of knowledge about each other.

Building systems as component-based product lines promises a dazzling array of benefits, including the following:

- Being able to take faster advantage of new products and new technology
- Significantly reduced time-to-market because off-the-shelf components are ready to use
- Higher employee productivity, with the emphasis not on coding but on reusing and integrating
- Allowing developers to specialize in the application area of the organization

- More reliable components because the components used in your system were developed for a whole class of systems, and other users will probably have found more of the problems than if the component was built specifically for one system.

- More changeable systems because replacement components can be inserted in place of older, less satisfactory ones.

- More extensible systems because new kinds of components can be inserted, allowing the system to perform some function it wasn't able to do before.

If the components conform to communitywide standards, even more benefits are possible as will be discussed in Chapter 17. Of course, not all the promises are easily achieved. Not all components work together—even if they are commercial products that claim to. Think about the difficulty of replacing one database management system with another. Components are often *almost compatible*, where *almost* is a euphemism for *not*. More insidious is the case where components appear to work together—the assembled code compiles and even executes—but the system produces the wrong answer because the components don't work together quite as expected. The errors can be subtle, especially in real-time or parallel systems in which the components might rely on seemingly innocuous assumptions about the timing or relative ordering of each other's operations or, even more likely, may have been developed assuming that no other components are even involved in their operations.

Components that were not developed specifically for *your* system may not meet all of *your* requirements—they may not even work with the other components you pair them with. Worse, you may not know if they are suitable or not until you buy them and try them, because component interfaces are notoriously poor at specifying their quality attributes: How secure is the compiler you're using right now? How reliable is the mail system on your desktop? How accurate is the math library that your applications depend on? And what happens when you discover that the answer to any of these questions is, "Not enough?"

At the 1995 International Conference on Software Engineering, Garlan, Allen, and Ockerbloom coined *architectural mismatch* to describe problems in integrating component-based systems. They stated the problem as a mismatch between the assumptions that are embodied in separately developed components. This mismatch often manifests itself architecturally, such as when two components disagree about which one invokes the other. Architectural mismatch usually shows up at system integration time—the system won't compile, won't link, or won't run.

Architectural mismatch is a special case of *interface mismatch*, where interface is as Parnas [Parnas 71] defined it: the assumptions that components can make about each other. This definition of interface goes beyond what has, unfortunately, become the normal concept of interface in current practice: a component's application program interface (API)—for example, an Ada package specification. An API names the programs and their parameters and says something about their behavior, but this is only a small part of the information needed to correctly use a component. Side effects, consumption of global resources, coordination requirements, and the like are necessary parts of an interface and are included in a complete interface specification. Interface mismatch can manifest itself at integration time, just like an architectural mismatch, but it can also precipitate the insidious run-time errors mentioned before.

Interface assumptions can take two forms. *Provides* assumptions describe the services a component provides to its users or clients. *Requires* assumptions detail those services or resources that a component must have available in order to correctly function. A mismatch between two components occurs when each other's provides and requires assumptions do not match up.

What can you do about an interface mismatch? Besides changing your requirements so that yesterday's bug is today's feature (which is often a viable option), you have the following three choices:

1. Avoid it—make sure it doesn't occur by carefully specifying and inspecting the components for your system

2. Detect those cases you haven't avoided by careful *qualification* of the components

3. Repair those cases you've detected by *adapting* the components

We now discuss interface mismatch from two perspectives. The first is the perspective of the consumer who wishes to integrate outside components into a product line. From this perspective, there is no alternative to repairing interface mismatch. The second perspective is that of a developer for a component intended to be used within the product line. From this perspective, the goal is to avoid interface mismatch.

TECHNIQUES FOR REPAIRING INTERFACE MISMATCH

A first step toward a disciplined approach to interface repair is to categorize the basic techniques and their qualities. An obvious repair method is to change the code of the offending component. However, this is often not possible. Commercial products seldom arrive with their source code. An old component's source code may be lost, or the only person who *understood* the old component's source code may be gone. Even if it is possible, changing a component is often not desirable. If it is used in more than one system—the whole premise of component-based systems—now it must be maintained in multiple versions if the change to make it work in the new system would render it unusable for some of the old systems.

The alternative to changing the code of one or both mismatched components is to insert code that mediates their interaction in a way that fixes the mismatch. There are three classes of repair code: wrappers, bridges, and mediators.

Wrappers.   The term *wrapper* implies a form of encapsulation whereby some component is encased within an alternative abstraction. The term simply means that clients access the wrapped component services only through an alternative interface provided by the wrapper. Wrapping a component can be thought of as yielding an alternative interface to the component. We can interpret interface translation as including the following:

- Translating an element of a component interface into an alternative element
- Hiding an element of a component interface
- Preserving without change an element of a component's interface

As an illustration, assume we have a legacy component that provides programmatic access to graphics rendering services, where the programmatic services are made available as Fortran libraries, and the graphics rendering is done in terms of custom graphics primitives. In our illustrative scenario, we wish to make the component available to clients via CORBA, and we wish to replace the use of custom graphics primitives with X-Windowing System graphics.

CORBA's Interface Description Language (IDL) can be used to specify the new interface that makes the component services available to CORBA clients rather than through linking with Fortran libraries. The repair code for the interface would be the C++ skeleton code automatically generated by an IDL compiler. Also included in the repair code is handwritten code to tie the skeleton into component functionality.

There are various options for wrapping the component's interface to accomplish the switch from custom graphics to X-Windowing System. One is to write a translator library layer whose API corresponds to the API for the custom graphics primitives; the implementation of this library translates custom graphics calls to X-Windowing System calls.

Bridges. A bridge will translate between some requires assumptions of an arbitrary component to some provides assumptions of some other arbitrary component. The key difference between a bridge and a wrapper is that the repair code constituting a bridge is independent of any particular component. Also, the bridge must be explicitly invoked by some external agent—possibly but not necessarily by one of the components that the bridge spans. This last point is intended to convey the idea that bridges are usually transient processes. Moreover, the specific translation is defined at the time of bridge construction (e.g., bridge compile-time). The significance of both of these distinctions will be made clear in the discussion of mediators.

Bridges typically focus on a narrower range of interface translations than the wrappers do. This is because bridges address specific assumptions. The more assumptions a bridge tries to address, the fewer components it will apply to. To illustrate, assume we have two legacy components, one that produces PostScript output for design documents and another that displays Portable Document Format (PDF) documents, and we wish to integrate these components so that the display component can be invoked on design documents.

In this scenario, a straightforward interface repair technique would be a simple bridge that translates PostScript to PDF. The bridge can be written independently of specific features of the two hypothetical components (i.e., the mechanisms used to extract data from one component and feed it to another). The scenario brings to mind the use of UNIX filters, although this is not the only mechanism that can be used in this scenario.

A UNIX shell script can be written to execute the bridge. The script would need to address component-specific interface peculiarities for both integrated components. Thus, the external agent–shell script would not be a wrapper, in our definition, because it would address the interfaces of both endpoints of the integration relation. Alternatively, either component could launch the filter. In this case, the repair mechanism would involve a hybrid wrapper and filter. The wrapper would invoke the repair code necessary to detect the need to launch the bridge and to launch it.

Mediators.   Mediators exhibit properties of both bridges and wrappers. The major distinction between bridges and mediators, however, is that mediators incorporate a *planning* function that in effect results in runtime determination of the translation (recall that bridges establish this translation when the bridge is constructed).

Mediators are also similar to wrappers insofar as the mediator becomes a more explicit component in the overall software architecture. That is, semantically primitive, often transient, bridges can be thought of as incidental repair mechanisms whose role in a design can remain implicit; in contrast, mediators have sufficient semantic complexity and runtime autonomy (persistence) that they may play more of a first-class role in a software architecture.

Mediators are a speculative and less well-explored technique than either bridges or wrappers. To illustrate mediators, we focus on the runtime planning function of mediators because this is the key distinction between mediators and bridges.

One scenario that illustrates mediation is intelligent data fusion. Consider a sensor that generates a high volume of high-fidelity data. At runtime different information consumers may arise that have different operating assumptions about data fidelity; perhaps a low-fidelity consumer requires that some information be "stripped" from the data stream. Alternatively, some other consumer may have similar fidelity requirements but have different throughput characteristics, requiring temporary buffering of data. In each of these cases, a mediator can accommodate the differences between the sensor and its consumers.

Another scenario involves the runtime assembly of sequences of bridges to integrate components whose specific integration requirements arise at runtime. For example one component may produce data in format D^0, while another may consume data in format D^2. It may be that there is no direct bridge from D^0 to D^2, but there are separate bridges from D^0 to D^1 and from D^1 to D^2 that can be chained. The mediator in this scenario would assemble the bridges to complete the D^0 to D^2 translation. UNIX pipes-and-filters are often used in this type of scenario.

TECHNIQUES FOR AVOIDING INTERFACE MISMATCH

In this section, we adopt the approach of a component developer where the component is intended to be used in a variety of different (but currently unknown) contexts. One technique for avoiding interface mismatch is to undertake, from the earliest phases of design, a disciplined approach to specifying as many assumptions about a component's interface as is feasible.

Is it feasible or even possible to specify all of the assumptions that a component makes about its environment or that using components are allowed to make about it? Of course not. Is there any evidence that it is practical to specify an important subset of these assumptions, and that it pays to do so? Yes. The A-7E software design presented in Chapter 3 partitioned the system into a tree of modules. Recall that there were three modules at the highest level, decomposed into about 120 modules at the leaves of the tree. An interface specification was written for each leaf module. The specification included the access procedures (what would now be called methods in an object-based design), the parameters they required and returned, the visible effects of calling the procedure, system generation parameters that allowed compile-time tailoring of the module, and a set of assumptions (on the order of a dozen for each module).

Assumptions stated assertions about the *sufficiency* of the services provided by each module and the *implementability* of each service by identifying resources necessary to the module. Specific subject areas included the use of shared resources, effects of multiple threads of control through a module's facilities, and performance information. These assumptions were meant to remain constant over the lifetime of the system, whose main design goal was modifiability. The assumptions were used by module designers to help ensure that they had thought of all areas of change to be appropriately encapsulated within each module, by domain and application experts as a medium for review, and by users of the modules to ensure suitability.

For example, one module encapsulated the on-board computer's timing facilities and presented an abstract interface of those facilities to application programs in other modules. Access procedures on its interface let callers declare timers, define events to be signaled when a declared timer reached a specified value, load a timer with a value, start and stop a timer, and read the value of a timer. The assumptions for this module included the following:

- Avionics programs need timers that keep track of real elapsed time and that may signal when a given time interval has elapsed. They need to be able to set a timer to a starting value, start it, stop it, and read it whether it is running or not.
- The maximum timing capacity of a timer can be determined at system generation time.
- If a timer runs beyond a limit specified at runtime, it should either halt or start over.
- The worst acceptable error rate for all timers can be determined by users at system generation time. This error can be specified as a fraction of the running time.
- Any number of timers can be implemented, provided that the number is known at system generation time. There is no need to create or delete timers at runtime.

- The underlying avionics computer has timer facilities with which the access programs can be implemented. This module is the only user of those facilities.

Participants on the A-7E project felt that the careful attention to module interfaces effectively eliminated integration as a step in the life cycle of that software. This was because all of the architectural mismatch was avoided by careful specification up front, including the explicit assumptions lists that were reviewed for veracity by application and domain experts.

There are advantages to specifying different interfaces for the same component rather than specifying a single omnibus base interface. The finer control over inter-component dependencies makes certain kinds of system evolution more tractable (e.g., predicting the impact of upgrading a commercial component to a new version). Wrappers can be thought of as a repair strategy for introducing privacy. Additionally, architectural styles may provide canonical forms for the interfaces so that the number of distinct derivatives of a base interface may be relatively small in a system that is based on an architectural style that defines a small set of component types.

A *parameterized interface* is an interface whose provides and requires assumptions can be changed by changing the value of a variable before the component service is invoked. Programming languages have long possessed semantically rich parameterization techniques (e.g., Ada generics, ML polymorphism, C++ templates) that facilitate tailoring a component's interface between the time that it was designed and coded and the time its services are invoked. Commercial products frequently provide some degree of customization via product parameterization (e.g., via resource files or environment variables). Parameterized interfaces result in adaptation code that resides in two places: external to the component where the values of the parameters are set and within the component (to accommodate different parameter values).

Just as a mediator is a bridge with planning logic, a *negotiated interface* is a parameterized interface with self-repair logic. A negotiated interface may auto-parameterize itself, or it may be parameterized by an external agent. Self-configuring software can be thought of as involving negotiated interfaces, where the negotiation is a rather one-way take-it-or-leave-it dialogue between component-building software and a host platform. Alternatively, products such as modems and Internet packet routers routinely use protocols to establish mutually acceptable communication parameters at runtime (rather than at install-time).

Just as wrappers can be used as a repair strategy to hide interface idiosyncrasies, mediators can be used as a repair strategy to introduce negotiated interfaces into a nonnegotiating component.

15.4 Summary

Having a product line software architecture promises significant benefits both in the cost of producing a product system and in the time to market of that system. Such benefits are not easily achieved, however.

An organization must develop a strategy for keeping the product line and its member products in synchronization, it must develop a strategy and know techniques for upgrading the product line architecture by the incorporation of components produced elsewhere, and it must understand the organizational implications of having and exploiting a product line architecture. In the next chapter, we explore in depth the story of CelsiusTech as they navigated their way to a product line of shipboard software.

15.5   For Further Reading

The reader wanting to learn more about component-based systems and mismatch should see the paper by Garlan, Allen, and Ockerbloom [Garlan 95], who coined the term *architectual mismatch*.

Parnas provided a broad notion of an interface between components that is just as applicable today as it was in 1971 [Parnas 71].

15.6   Discussion Questions

1. Some writers draw a distinction between a *product line* (a set of products that together address a certain market segment or mission) and a *product family* (a set of products built from a common set of software assets). Under this distinction, a product line need not be a product family if the products are build independently of each other. In this chapter we have been describing a product line built as a product family. Can you describe a product line that is not a product family? Can you describe a product family that is not a product line?

2. Suppose a company builds two similar systems using a large set of common assets, including a common architecture. Clearly these two systems form a product line. Suppose the two systems share only an architecture but no components. Are they still a product line? Suppose they share only a single component. What then? Suppose that all they share is the same operating system and programming language runtime libraries. Are they a product line then? Suppose that the shared asset between them is the same team of developers. What about then?

16

CelsiusTech
A Case Study in Product
Line Development

with Lisa Brownsword

> *By reducing the amount of programmers' unscheduled improvisations,*
> *the design team was able to recognize in full the benefits*
> *of reuse and portability.*
> — Bjorn Kallberg, Senior Scientist
> CelsiusTech Systems AB (1996)

This chapter relates the experience of CelsiusTech AB, a Swedish naval defense contractor, that has successfully adopted a product line approach to building complex software-intensive systems. Their product line is called Ship System 2000 (SS2000) and consists of approximately a dozen shipboard command-and-control systems for Scandinavian, Middle Eastern, and South Pacific navies.

This case study illustrates the entire architecture business cycle (ABC), but especially shows how the existence of a product line architecture led CelsiusTech to new business opportunities. Figure 16.1 shows the roles of the ABC stakeholders in the case of the CelsiusTech experience.

16.1 Relationship to the Architecture Business Cycle

CelsiusTech is one of Sweden's leading suppliers of command-and-control systems. They are part of Sweden's largest, and one of Europe's leading, defense industry groups, which also includes Bofors, Kockums, FFV Aerotech, and Telub.

Note: Lisa Brownsword is a member of the technical staff at the Software Engineering Institute, Carnegie Mellon University.

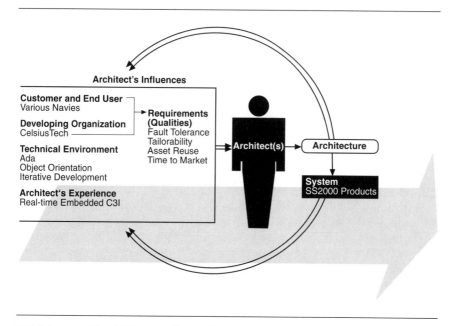

FIGURE 16.1 The ABC as applied to CelsiusTech.

CelsiusTech is composed of three companies: CelsiusTech Systems (advanced software systems), CelsiusTech Electronics (defense electronics), and CelsiusTech IT (information technology systems). CelsiusTech has approximately 2,000 employees and annual sales of $300 million U.S. dollars. Their main site is near Stockholm, Sweden, with subsidiaries located in Singapore, New Zealand, and Australia.

To understand how the ABC affected CelsiusTech, it is crucial to first understand their business and technical climate.

CELSIUSTECH COMPANY BACKGROUND

This study focuses on CelsiusTech Systems (CelsiusTech for short in this book). Their areas of expertise include command, control, and communication (C3) systems, fire control systems,[1] and electronic warfare systems for navy, army, and air force applications. The current organization has undergone several changes in ownership and name since 1985 (see Figure 16.2). Originally Philips Elektronikindustrier AB, the division, was sold to Bofors Electronics AB in 1989 and reorganized into NobelTech AB in 1991. It was purchased by CelsiusTech in 1993.

---

[1] The term *fire control* refers to the ability to fire a gun at a moving target, from a platform that is not only itself moving with 6 degrees of freedom but that is flexing as well.

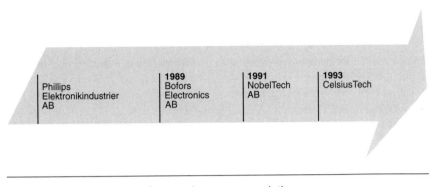

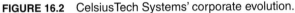

| Phillips Elektronikindustrier AB | **1989** Bofors Electronics AB | **1991** NobelTech AB | **1993** CelsiusTech |

FIGURE 16.2   CelsiusTech Systems' corporate evolution.

Although senior management changed with each transaction, most of the mid- and lower-level management and the technical staff remained, thus providing continuity and stability.

We begin by summarizing the product line for shipboard systems, its current status, and CelsiusTech's results from using their product line.

THE SHIP SYSTEM 2000 NAVAL PRODUCT LINE

CelsiusTech refers to their naval product line as the SS2000 family; internally it is also known as the Mk3 product. This product line provides an integrated system unifying all weapons systems, command-and-control, and communication functions on a warship. Typical system configurations include 1 to 1.5 million lines of Ada code distributed on a local area network (LAN) with 30 to 70 microprocessors.

A wide variety of naval systems, both surface and submarine, have been or are being built from the same product line. These include the weapon systems, command-and-control, and communications portions of the following:

- Swedish Göteborg class Coastal Corvettes (KKV) (380 tons)
- Danish SF300 class Multi-role patrol vessels (300 tons)
- Finnish Rauma class Fast Attack Craft (FAC) (200 tons)
- Australian/New Zealand ANZAC frigates (3225 tons)
- Danish Thetis class Ocean Patrol vessels (2700 tons)
- Swedish Gotland class A19 submarines (1330 tons)
- Pakistani Type 21 class frigates
- Republic of Oman patrol vessels
- Danish Niels Juel class corvettes

The last three are recently initiated projects for which production data is still emerging. The Naval Systems division has sold 55 of its Mk3 naval systems to seven different countries around the world.

Figure 16.3 shows a Multi-Role Corvette of the "Göteborg" class, which belongs to the Royal Swedish Navy, during a visit to the harbor of Stockholm. On top is the C/X-band antenna of the surveillance and target indication radar. Forward and aft of this on top of the superstructure are the two fully equipped Fire Control Radar and Optronic Directors from CelsiusTech.

Systems built from the product line vary greatly in size, function, and armaments. Each country requires different operator displays on differing hardware and presentation languages. Sensors and weapons systems, and their interfaces to the software, vary. Submarines have different requirements than surface vessels do. Computers in the product line include 68020, 68040, RS/6000, and DEC Alpha platforms. Operating systems include OS2000 (a CelsiusTech product), IBM's AIX, POSIX, Digital's Ultrix, and others. The SS2000 product line supports this range of possible systems through a single architecture, a single asset base, and a single organization.

ECONOMIES OF SCOPE: AN OVERVIEW OF CELSIUSTECH'S RESULTS

In this section we will discuss the results CelsiusTech has had building complex software-intensive systems.

Shrinking Schedules.   Figure 16.4 shows the status and schedules for recent systems under development from the CelsiusTech product line. Systems A and B were contracted for at the same time and, as we will see, caused CelsiusTech to move to a product line approach. System A is the basis of the product line. Customer project A has run almost nine years, although functional releases were running on the designated ship since late 1989. System B, the second of the two original projects, required approximately seven years to complete; it is similar to the previous nonproduct line Mk2.5 system. System B was built in parallel with system A, validating the product line. While neither system individually showed greater productivity, CelsiusTech was able to build two systems (and the product line) with roughly the same number of staff as for a single project.

Systems C and D were started after much of the product line existed, with a correspondingly shortened completion time. Systems E and F show a dramatic further schedule reduction because they are fully leveraging the product line. CelsiusTech reports that the last three ship systems are all *predictably* on schedule.

Code Reuse.   While the production schedules show time to market for a product, they do not indicate how well the systems reflect the use of a common asset base. Figure 16.5 shows the degree of commonality across the CelsiusTech naval systems. On average, 70 to 80 percent of the systems consist of components that are used verbatim (i.e., checked out of a configuration control library and inserted without code modification).

FIGURE 16.3   Swedish Multi-Role Corvette of the Göteborg class featuring a CelsiusTech command-and-control system.   Photo from Studio FJK reproduced with permission.

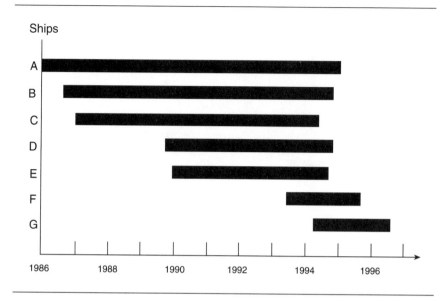

FIGURE 16.4 Product schedules.

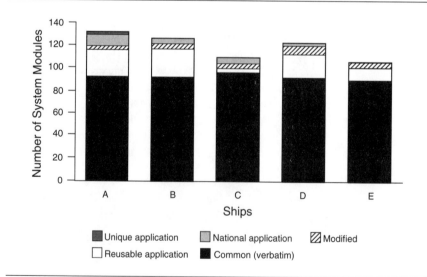

FIGURE 16.5 Reuse across customer systems.

Using Core Assets to Expand the Business Area.   CelsiusTech has expanded their business into a related area that can take advantage of the architecture and other core assets that were originally developed for naval systems. STRIC is a new air defense system for the Swedish Air Force. By embracing the abstraction that a ground station is a ship whose location doesn't happen to change very often and whose pitch and roll are constantly zero, and because of the flexibility (amenability to change) of the SS2000 architecture and product line, CelsiusTech was able to quickly build the STRIC architecture, lifting 40 percent of its components directly from the SS2000 asset base. This is a demonstration of one of the feedback links in the ABC; the existence of the SS2000 product line and architecture enabled new business opportunities.

WHAT MOTIVATED CELSIUSTECH?

To understand why CelsiusTech made the decision to develop a product line and what actions were required, it is important to know where they began. Prior to 1986, the company developed more than 100 systems in 25 different configurations ranging in size from 30,000 to 700,000 source lines of code (SLOC) in the fire control domain (see Table 16.1).

From 1975 to 1980, CelsiusTech shifted their technology base from analog to 16-bit digital systems, creating the so-called Mk2 systems. These tended to be small, real-time, and embedded systems. The company progressively expanded the functionality and their expertise with real-time applications in the course of building and delivering 17 systems.

From 1980 to 1985, customer requirements were shifting toward the integration of fire control and weapons with command-and-control systems, thus increasing the size and complexity of delivered systems. The Mk2 architecture was expanded to provide for multiple autonomous processing nodes on point-to-point links, resulting in the Mk2.5 systems. These systems were substantially larger in size, both in delivered code (up to 700,000 SLOC) and number of developers (300 engineer-years over 7 years). Conventional development approaches were used. While these had served the company well on the smaller Mk2 systems, difficulties in predictable and timely integration, cost overruns, and schedule slippage resulted. While such experiences were painful, they were important

TABLE 16.1   Systems Built by CelsiusTech Prior to 1985

	1970–1980: Mk2 Systems	1980–1985: Mk2.5 Systems
Kind of system	Real-time embedded fire control; assembly language and RTL/2	Real-time embedded C3; RTL/2
Size	30–100K SLOC	700K SLOC; 300 engineer-years over 7 years
Platforms	Analog and, 16-bit digital systems	Multiprocessors, minicomputers, point-to-point links

lessons for CelsiusTech. The company gained useful experience in the elementary distribution of real-time processes onto autonomous links and in the use of a high-level programming language (in this case, RTL/2, a Pascal-like real-time language).

In 1985, a defining event for CelsiusTech (then Philips) occurred. The company was awarded two major contracts simultaneously—one for the Swedish Navy and one for the Danish Navy. Both ships' requirements indicated the need for systems larger and more sophisticated than the previous Mk2.5 systems, which had suffered from schedule and budget difficulties. The need to build two even larger systems, let alone in parallel, presented management and senior technical staff with a severe dilemma. Clearly, the continuation of the development technologies and practices applied on the Mk2.5 system would not be sufficient to produce the new systems with any reasonable certainty of schedule, cost, and required functionality. Staffing requirements alone would have been prohibitive.

This situation provided the genesis of a new business strategy: recognizing the potential *business* opportunity of selling and building a series, or family, of related systems rather than some number of specific systems. Thus began the SS2000 product line. Another business driver was the recognition of a 20- to 30-year life span for naval systems. During that time, changes in threat requirements and technology advances would have to be addressed. The more flexible and extendable the product line, the greater the business opportunities. These business drivers or requirements forged the technical strategy.

The technical strategy would need to provide a flexible and robust set of building blocks to populate the product line from which new systems could be assembled with relative ease. As new system requirements arose, new building blocks could be added to the product line to sustain the business viability of the strategic decision.

In defining the technical strategy, an assessment of the Mk2.5 technology infrastructure indicated serious limitations. A strategic decision was made to create a new generation of system (the Mk3) that would include new hardware and software and a new supporting development approach. These would serve as the infrastructure for new systems development for the next decade or two.

EVERYTHING WAS NEW

CelsiusTech's decision to convert their business strategy to a product line approach coincided with a time of high technology flux. This meant that to implement the technical strategy for the SS2000 product line, virtually all aspects of the hardware, software, and development support changed. The hardware shifted from VAX/VMS minicomputers to Motorola 68000-series microcomputers. Whereas the Mk2.5 systems consisted of a small number of processors on point-to-point links, the SS2000 products have a large number of highly distributed processors with fault-tolerant requirements. Their software life-cycle approach shifted from RTL/2-based, structured analysis/design, and waterfall development processes to Ada83 with more object-based and iterative development processes.

Prior to 1986 **Previous Technical Infrastructure**	1986 **New Technical Infrastructure**
• Minicomputers	• Microcomputers
• Few processors on point-to-point links	• Many processors on commercial LAN
• No fault tolerance	• Fault tolerant, redundant
• RTL/2	• Ada83
• Waterfall life cycle, early attempts at incremental development	• Prototyping, iterative, incremental development
• Structured analysis/design	• Domain analysis, object-based analysis/design
• Locally developed support tools	• Rational development environment

FIGURE 16.6   Changing technical infrastructures.

Development support migrated from custom, locally created and maintained development tools to a large, commercially supplied environment. The major technical differences are summarized in Figure 16.6.

ANALYSIS OF THE BUSINESS CONTEXT

The CelsiusTech experience reveals several factors that played an important role in the establishment of the SS2000 product line. Some were advantages; some were inhibitors. They include the following.

Ownership Changes.   While it is routine to buy, sell, and restructure companies, the impact on an organization attempting to adopt significantly different business and technical strategies could be potentially devastating. Typically, management changes associated with company ownership transactions are sufficient to stop any transition or improvement efforts underway. That this did not happen at CelsiusTech could be attributed either to strong and far-sighted top management or to top management preoccupation with the other issues associated with ownership changes. Since CelsiusTech changed hands several times during this period, the latter explanation is more likely. It is clear that middle management had a strong commitment to the conversion to a product line and were allowed to proceed on their course unfettered by top management, who might otherwise have been hesitant to approve the necessary upfront investments to achieve the product line. Normally a reorganization disrupts the entire organization. In the CelsiusTech case, the effects of the reorganizations and changes of ownership were buffered by middle management.

Necessity Is the Mother of Invention.   The award of two major naval contracts in 1986, ostensibly a reason for celebration, was regarded as a crisis by CelsiusTech. They immediately realized that they had neither the technical means nor the personnel resources to pursue two large development efforts, each pioneering new technologies and application areas, simultaneously. Since all CelsiusTech contracts are fixed-price, large-scale failure meant large-scale disaster, and previous less-challenging systems had been over budget, past schedule, hard to integrate, and impossible to predict. CelsiusTech was driven to the product line approach by circumstances; they were compelled to attempt it because their company's viability was clearly at stake. The fact that this period was also one of major technological change made it much more difficult to separate the costs associated with the product line changes from those associated with adopting a new generation of technology.

Riding a Wave of Technology Changes.   In 1986, all the chosen technologies indicated were immature with limited use in large, industrial settings. Large, real-time, distributed systems making extensive use of Ada tasks and generics were envisioned but at the time were unprecedented. Object-based development for Ada was still a theoretical discussion. Thus from 1986 to 1989, CelsiusTech was coping with the following:

- The maturation of technologies, such as Ada and object technology
- The maturation of supporting technology, such as networking and distribution
- The maturation of infrastructure technology, such as development environments and tools to assist in the automation of the development processes
- The learning curve of the company, both technical and managerial, in the use of new technologies and processes inherent in the product line approach
- The learning curve of their customers, who did not fully understand the contractual, technical, and business approaches of product lines
- The management of requirements across several customers

These maturation issues significantly increased the time required to create the product line. Another organization making the same development paradigm shift today would, we believe, be in a much less tenuous position. Microcomputers, networks, portable operating systems, open systems standards, object-based development methods, Ada (or other programming languages appropriate to the domain and platforms), performance engineering, distributed systems technology, real-time operating systems, real-time analysis tools, large-project support environments, and large-project process assistants are all either mature or at least usable and readily available. CelsiusTech estimates that up to one third of their initial technology investment was spent building assets that can now be purchased commercially.

ORGANIZATIONAL STRUCTURE

CelsiusTech's organizational structure and practices have not remained constant over the past ten years but have instead migrated through several distinct structures. The kind of knowledge and skills required of the staff also have changed during the past ten years.

Previous Project Organization. The previous naval command-and-control system (Mk2.5) development efforts were headed by a project manager who used the services of various functional areas, such as weapons or C3, to develop major segments of system capability. Figure 16.7 shows the organizational structure used for the Mk2.5 project. Each functional area (command-and-control, tracking, etc.) was led by a project manager who had direct authority for staff resources and for all system-development activities through release to system integration.

CelsiusTech found that this compartmentalized arrangement fostered a mode of development characterized by the following:

- Assignment of major segments of the system to their respective functional areas as part of system analysis.

- Requirements and interfaces allocated and described in documents with limited communication across functional area boundaries resulting in individual interpretations of requirements and interfaces throughout design, implementation, and test.

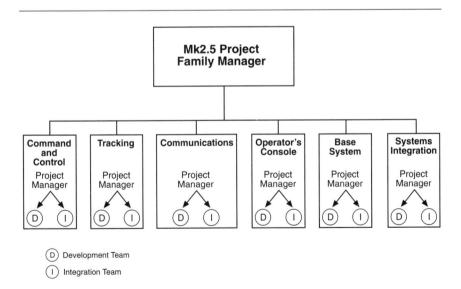

FIGURE 16.7   Mk2.5 project organization, 1980–1985.

- Interface incompatibilities typically not discovered until system integration, resulting in time wasted assigning responsibility and a protracted, difficult integration and installation
- Functional area managers with little understanding of the other segments of the systems.
- Functional area managers with limited incentives to work together as a team to resolve program level issues typical of any large system development.

SS2000 Organization, Late 1986 to 1991. With the advent of the SS2000 product line in late 1986, a number of organizational changes from the Mk2.5 project organization were put into place. Figure 16.8 shows the organizational structure CelsiusTech used from late 1986 until 1991 for the creation of the product line. A general program manager was designated to lead the program. He was responsible for both the creation of the product line and the delivery of customer systems built from the product line. CelsiusTech sought to remedy the problems associated with the compartmentalized structure of the past by creating a strong management team focused on the development of the product line as a company asset, rather than on "empire building." To this end, functional area managers now reported directly to the general program manager. Developers were assigned to functional areas—weapons, C3, or human-computer interface (HCI), common services (used by the functional areas), or the interface to the various hardware and operating systems (called the Base System).

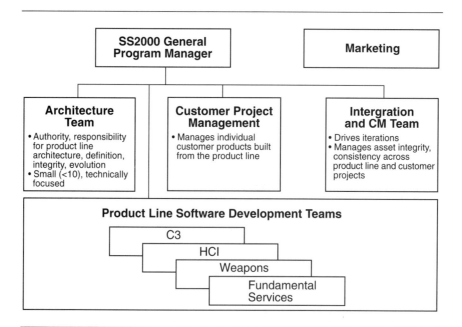

FIGURE 16.8 SS2000 organization, 1987–1991.

A small, technically focused architecture team with total ownership and control of the architecture was created. The architecture team reported directly to the general program manager. CelsiusTech determined that the success of a product line hinged on a stable yet flexible architecture, requiring visibility and authority from the highest levels of management. In this way, CelsiusTech was reorganizing itself to take advantage of the ABC: Architecture had to be at the heart of their new approach, and it in turn changed important aspects of the organization.

CelsiusTech identified the coordinated definition and management of multiple releases as central to the creation of a product line and determined that high-level management visibility was essential. To better support their release management, CelsiusTech combined the software-system integration and configuration management activities into a new group, reporting directly to the general program manager. Both the architecture team and the integration–configuration management group were novel approaches for CelsiusTech and were instrumental in the creation of the SS2000 product line.

The architecture team was responsible for the development of the initial architecture and continued ownership and control of the product line architecture. This ensured design consistency and design interpretation across *all* functional areas. Specifically, the architecture team had responsibility and authority for the following:

- Creation of the product line concepts and principles
- Identification of layers and their exported interfaces
- Interface definition, integrity, and controlled evolution
- Allocation of system functions to layers
- Identification of common mechanisms or services
- Definition, prototyping, and enforcement of common mechanisms such as error handling and interprocess communication protocols
- Communication to the project staff of the product line concepts and principles

The first iteration of the architecture was produced by two senior engineers, who had deep domain experience, over a concentrated two-week period. It remains as the framework for the existing product line. The first iteration included the organizing concepts, layer definition, identification of approximately 125 system functions (out of the current 200 or so), their allocation to specified layers, and the principal mechanisms for distribution and communication. After completion of the first iteration, the architecture team was expanded to include the lead designers from each of the functional areas. The full architecture team, comprising ten senior engineers, continued to expand and refine the architecture. This was in sharp contrast to the past, when functional area leaders had autonomy for the design and interfaces for their respective areas.

The combined integration and configuration management team was responsible for the following:

- Development of test strategies, plans, and tests cases beyond unit test
- Coordination of all test runs

- Development of incremental build schedules (in conjunction with the architecture team)
- Integration and release of valid subsystems
- Configuration management of development and release libraries
- Creation of the software delivery medium

SS2000 Organization 1992 to 1994. From 1992 to 1994, CelsiusTech's emphasis increasingly shifted from the *development* of the architecture and product line components to the *composition* of new customer systems from the product line. This trend increased the size and responsibilities of the customer project management group. CelsiusTech modified their organizational structure to assign the development staff to one of the following:

- Component Projects that develop, integrate, and manage product line components. The production of components was distributed across Component Project areas consisting of the functional areas (weapons, C3, and HCI), common services, and the operating system and network components. Component project managers were rotated regularly, providing middle management with a broader understanding of the product line. The components are provided to the Customer Projects.
- Customer Projects that are responsible for all financial, scheduling and planning, and requirements analysis through system integration/test/delivery for their customer's product. Each customer system built from the product line is assigned a project manager, who is responsible for all interactions and negotiations with the customer.

SS2000 Organization Since 1994. As CelsiusTech has completed the basic product line and gained further experience using it, they have moved to the identification of more efficient ways to produce systems and evolve the product line to take advantage of newer technology and changing customer mission needs. This is a feedback effect of the ABC, where the architecture has caused the organization to continually reinvent itself. This resulted in the organizational structure shown in Figure 16.9.

Each major application domain (naval and air defense) became its own business unit with its own manager. Each business unit has a marketing group, proposal group, customer projects, and systems definition group. The business unit is responsible for its software components and its customer project managers. Each business unit's operations are guided by a set of consistent plans: Marketing, Product, and Technical–Architecture. The marketing group is responsible for the Marketing Plan that assesses the opportunities and value of each market segment. The Product Plan describes the products the business unit sells and is owned by the proposal group. The Product Plan implements the Marketing Plan. The system definition group is responsible for the Technical–Architecture Plan for their business unit. The Technical–Architecture Plan in turn implements the Product Plan, outlining the direction for evolution of the business unit's architecture.

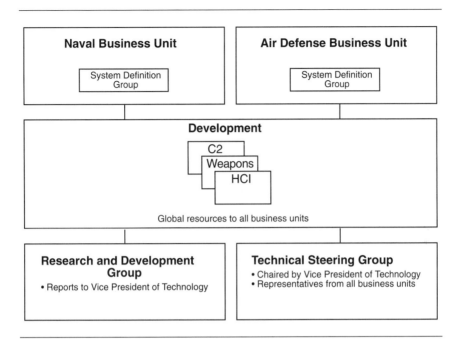

FIGURE 16.9   SS2000 organization since 1994.

New project proposals take into account the business unit's Product Plan and Technical–Architecture Plan. This approach keeps the projects aligned with the product line.

Components are supplied by the Development Group. Any customer-specific tailoring or development is managed from the business unit customer project using development resources matrixed from the Development Group. The business unit's Systems Definition Group is responsible for the architecture. They own and control the evolution of the architecture and major interfaces and mechanisms. For the Naval Business Unit, the Systems Definition Group is a small group (typically six members) of senior engineers with extensive knowledge of the naval product line. The group remains responsible for overall arbitration of customer requirements and their impact on the product line.

The Naval Business Unit has fostered a SS2000 Product Line Users Group to serve as a forum for shared customer experiences with the product line approach and to provide direction setting for future product line evolution. The Users Group includes representatives from all SS2000 customers worldwide.

The Development Group provides developer resources to all business units. Integration, configuration management, and quality assurance resources are also a part of the Development Group and matrixed to the business units as required. To further optimize the creation of new systems from a product line, a Basic SS2000 Configuration Project was recently formed. The goal is the creation of a basic, preintegrated core configuration of approximately 500K SLOC, complete with documentation and test cases that would form the nucleus of a new customer system.

The Technical Steering Group (TSG) is responsible for identifying, evaluating, and piloting potential new technology beneficial to any of CelsiusTech's business areas. The TSG is headed by the Vice President of Technology and staffed by senior technical personnel from the naval and air defense business units, Development Group, and the R&D Group. The TSG also ensures that each Systems Definition Group creates and evolves its architecture and technology plan.

Staffing Characteristics—Late 1986 to 1991. As shown in Figure 16.10, the project staffing levels ranged from 20 to 30 initially up to a peak of over 200, with an average of 150. During the early stages of the program while the product line concepts and architecture were being defined, CelsiusTech found the staff levels were too high. This caused confusion among the developers because concepts and approaches were in a state of flux.

Technical Skills and Knowledge—Late 1986 to 1991. The architecture team was responsible for the creation of the framework that defines the product line. Team members needed solid domain and customer knowledge. This knowledge was combined with engineering skills and an ability to think broadly to find relevant common mechanisms or product line components. Communication and teaming skills were also mandatory.

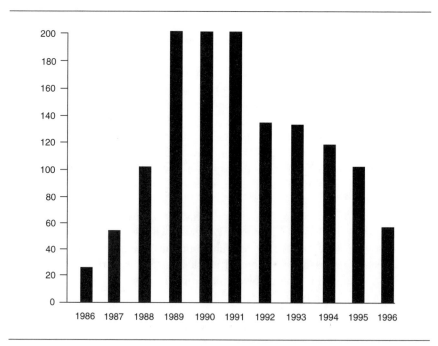

FIGURE 16.10 Approximate software staff profile.

Developers must understand the framework, building codes, and how their respective components should fit. During the formative period of the product line, the development staff required skills in the use of Ada, object-based design, and their software development environment, including the target testbed. In addition, broad areas of knowledge were required: product line concepts, SS2000 architecture and mechanisms, creation of reusable components, incremental integration, and at least one functional area domain.

Management Skills and Knowledge—Late 1986 to 1991.   With much of the necessary technology immature, the management team (and senior technical staff) was operating, to large degree, on faith in the achievement of a shared ultimate capability. A key focus of their responsibilities included "selling" the business need and the desired future state to their teams.

Organizations attempting to install immature technology encounter resistance as the inevitable problems with the technologies arise. Key to sustaining the early phases of such installations is strong, solutions-oriented managers. For example, the general program manager focused on finding solutions rather than finding fault with the various immature technologies, their suppliers, or the development team. Managed experimentation was encouraged, not penalized. Technical innovations were supported. The general program manager thus became a role model for other managers to follow.

Managers in the formative years of the product line required strong knowledge of product line concepts and the business motivation for the product line. In addition, they needed strong skills in the areas of planning, communication, and innovative problem solving.

Management also had to cope with the inevitable discontent and resistance associated with the installation of a new business paradigm and attendant technology. Substantial effort was made to help personnel understand the new business strategy and rationale. People who did not subscribe to or could not grasp the product line approach either left the company or found assignments on maintenance or other projects. This caused loss of domain knowledge that took time to redevelop.

Staffing Characteristics—1992 to 1994.   During the end of 1991 four customer systems were underway. Sufficient numbers of reusable components not only existed but had been delivered as part of the original two systems. The core of the product line was maturing rapidly. Rather than building all new components, systems were now being composed from existing product line components on an increasingly routine basis. Designers were needed less and were reassigned to other projects within the company. With the increase in parallel customer projects, more integrators were needed, although the average of three to five integrators per customer system remained steady. During this period, the number of management staff did not decrease due to the increasing number of projects.

Technical Skills and Knowledge—1992 to 1994.   With greater emphasis on the *composition* of systems from the product line, developers needed stronger domain and SS2000 knowledge than during the creation of the product line. The use of Ada, object technology, and their development environment had become more routine. The integration group focus turned to the integration and release management of many parallel systems. Increasing emphasis was placed on reusing test plans and data sets across customer systems.

The architecture team needed to maintain a solid knowledge of the product line and factor in the growing set of current and approaching customer mission needs. Communication skills with customer project managers (for negotiation of multiple customer needs) and developers (desiring to optimize major interfaces and mechanisms) continued to be extremely important. Engineering skill to balance new needs yet preserve the overall architectural integrity were vital for team members.

Management Skills and Knowledge—1992 to 1994. Less emphasis on technology maturation and training was required of management as more of the product line was available. With a larger set of customer systems existing, the coordination of changing customer requirements across multiple customers emerged as a major management focus and priority. Requirements negotiation involved not only customers but also other customer project managers and the product line architecture team. Customer project managers required increasing skill in negotiation and knowledge of the existing and anticipated future directions of the product line.

Staffing Characteristics—1994 Onward. From 1994 onward, the staffing profile has continued to change. As the product line and its use have further matured, CelsiusTech has used fewer designers, developers, and integrators for the two most recent customer systems. Even fewer designers are needed, potentially moving between business units. The downward trend is most notable in the area of integration. For the two newest customer systems, CelsiusTech has budgeted for an integration staff of one or two per system. Continuing system composition optimizations, such as the Basic SS2000 Configuration project, are expected to further reduce the development-related staff levels. With the continued increase in parallel customer projects, the number of management staff remains constant.

Technical Skills and Knowledge—1994 Onward. Developers continue to need strong domain and SS2000 product line knowledge with the emphasis on composing systems rather than building them.

The architecture team now must maintain a solid knowledge of the product line, current and approaching customer mission needs, and advances in relevant technology. This knowledge must then be balanced with engineering skill as they continually evolve the architecture and its major interfaces and mechanisms. For example, CelsiusTech is currently in the process of upgrading their user-interface technology to exploit the X-Windowing System and Motif. The architecture team has been involved in technical evaluations, prototype development of new interfaces (both for the external user and for application developers), and assessing the impact on the product line of the new technologies.

Management Skills and Knowledge—1994 Onward. Management continues to focus on the coordination of changing customer requirements across an increasing set of customers. Negotiation skills remain vital for customer project managers. Managers must also retain current knowledge of the existing product line and must increasingly be aware of anticipated future directions for it.

16.2   Requirements and Qualities

To derive new products efficiently from an organizational repository, the products must be structured similarly so that they share components. As we discussed in Chapter 15, this means there must be a standard set of components, with agreements about the responsibility, behavior, performance, interface, locality of function, communication and coordination mechanisms, and other properties of each component. This familywide structure, the components it comprises, and the properties about each component that are constant across all members of the product line constitute the architecture for the family.

As we have seen, the primary purpose of an architecture is to facilitate the building of a system that meets its behavioral and quality requirements. The architecture for each SS2000 product line member is no exception. However, the SS2000 architecture carries the additional burden of application to an entire class of systems, not just an individual one. Requirements for such an architecture include the ability to replace components with ones tailored to a particular system without disrupting the rest of the architecture.

OPERATING ENVIRONMENT AND PHYSICAL ARCHITECTURE

The requirements of modern shipboard systems influence design solutions in profound ways. Sensors and weapons systems are deployed all over the ship; crew members interact with the system via a multitude of separately housed workstations. The HCI must be highly tuned to facilitate rapid information flow and command acceptance and must be tailored to the operational mission of the vessel and the cultural idiosyncrasies of its crew. The likelihood of component failure dictates a fault-tolerant design.

Figure 16.11 illustrates a typical physical architecture for the system. A redundant LAN is the communications backbone for the system, connecting from 30 to 70 different processors that cooperate to perform the system's work. Nodes on the LAN can total around 30; a *node* is the end of a communication run and may correspond to a crew station, a weapons platform, or a sensor suite, all located in various parts of the ship and widely dispersed. A node may host up to six processors. The LAN is currently a dual Ethernet. Device-interface modules send and receive data to and from the system's peripherals, primarily sensors, and the weapons systems being controlled.

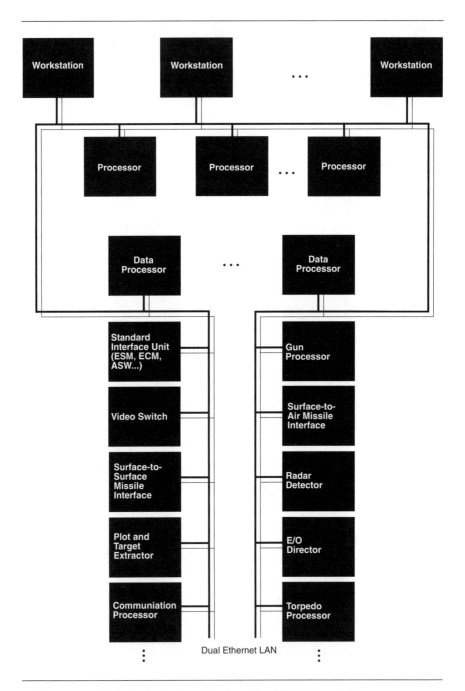

FIGURE 16.11 Typical physical architecture of a SS2000 product.

16.3   Architectural Approach

We describe the architecture using several structures. We use the process structure so that we can explain how distribution was accomplished. We also use the module structure as a basis for discussing the layering of SS2000. A different use of the module structure lets us discuss how different classes of functionality are accomplished. Finally, we discuss some of the techniques CelsiusTech uses that are specific to the maintenance and use of a product line.

MEETING REQUIREMENTS FOR DISTRIBUTION AND PRODUCT LINE SUPPORT

Each CPU on the physical architecture runs a set of Ada programs; each Ada program runs on at most one processor. A program may consist of several Ada tasks. Systems in the SS2000 product line can consist of up to 300 separate Ada programs.

The requirement to run on a distributed computing platform has broad implications for the software architecture. Distributed systems raise issues of deadlock avoidance, communication protocols, fault tolerance in the case of a failed processor or communications link, network management and saturation avoidance, and performance concerns for coordination among tasks. When the group of developers we interviewed were asked to explain the architecture, their first response was that it was distributed. A number of conventions are used to support the distribution. These respond to both the distributed requirements of the architecture as well as its product line aspects. The tasks and intercomponent conventions include the following:

- Communication among components is by the passing of strongly typed messages. The abstract data type and the manipulating programs are provided by the component passing the message. Strong typing allows for compile-time elimination of whole classes of errors. The message as the primary interface mechanism between components allows components to be written independently of each other's (changeable) implementation details with respect to representation of data.

- Interprocess communication protocol is the protocol for data transport between Ada applications that supports location independence. This protocol allows communication between applications irregardless of their residence on particular processors. This "anonymity of processor assignment" allows processes to be migrated across processors, for preruntime performance tuning and runtime reconfiguration as an approach to fault tolerance, with no accompanying change in source code.

- Ada task facilities are used to implement the threading model.

A producer of a datum does its job without knowledge of who the consumer of that datum is. Data maintenance and update are conceptually separate from data usage. The designers used a blackboard style to accomplish this. The main consumer of the data is the HCI component. The component that contains the repository is called the common object manager (COOB). Figure 16.12 illustrates the role of the COOB at runtime. We show not only the data flow that uses the common object manager but also those data flows that bypass the COOB for reasons of performance. Track information (the positional history of a target), carried in a large data structure, is passed directly between producer and consumer. Trackball information, because of its very high update frequency, also bypasses the COOB. Data-producing conventions include the following:

- Data are only sent when altered. This prevents unnecessary message traffic from entering the network.

- Data are presented as object-oriented abstractions in order to insulate programs from changing implementations. Strong typing allows compile-detection of variable misuse errors.

- Components own the data they alter and supply access procedures that act as monitors. This eliminates race conditions because each datum is accessed directly only by the component that owns it.

- Data are accessible to all interested parties at all nodes in a system. Assignment to a particular node does not affect the data to which a component has access.

- Data are distributed so the response time to a retrieval request is short.

- Data are kept consistent within the system, over the long term. Short-term inconsistencies are tolerable.

Network-related conventions include the following:

- Network load is kept low by design—that is, considerable design effort goes into managing the data flow on the network, ensuring that only essential information is transmitted.

- Data channels are error resistant. Applications resolve errors internally so far as possible.

- It is acceptable for an application to "miss" an occasional data update. For instance, because ship's position changes in a continuous fashion, a position update may be missed and interpolated from surrounding updates.

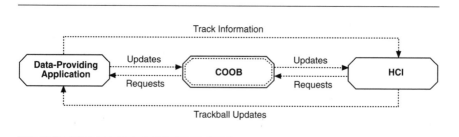

FIGURE 16.12   Using (and bypassing) the COOB.

Miscellaneous conventions include the following:

- Heavy use is made of Ada generics, for reusability.
- Ada standard exception protocols are used.

Many of these conventions (particularly those regarding abstract data types, IPC, message passing, and data ownership) allow a component to be written independently of many changeable aspects over which it has no control. In other words, the components are more generic and hence more directly usable in different systems.

THE MODULE STRUCTURE

The module structure shows that SS2000 is *layered;* this structure is as follows:

- The grouping of the components is based roughly on the type of information they encapsulate. Components that must be modified if hardware platform, underlying LAN, or internode communication protocols are changed all form a layer. Components that implement functionality common to all members of the family form another layer. Finally, components specific to a particular customer product form a layer.
- The layers are ordered, with hardware-dependent layers at one end of the relation and application-specific layers at the other.
- The layering is "proper." That is, interactions among layers are restricted. A component residing in one layer can only access components in its own or the next lower layer.

In SS2000, the bottom layer is known as Base System 2000; it provides an interface between the operating system, hardware, and network on the one hand and application programs on the other. To an applications programmer, Base System 2000 provides a programming interface with which they can perform intercomponent communication and interaction without being sensitive to the particular underlying computing platforms, network topologies, allocation of functions to processors, etc. The abstraction unit operation presents a virtual machine to the application programmer.

Layering is a central design principle that is well promulgated throughout CelsiusTech's development organizations. The layers serve as a device to help explain the product line philosophy for insulating the system from changes in the computing environment and for rapidly producing new members of the product line. This is an example of the use of the module structure as a training device. Base System 2000 is maintained by an organization devoted solely to it; hence, its contents comprise a specific, well-defined layer. This demonstrates, yet again, the use of a module structure to define organizational units, as we discussed in Chapter 13. Figure 16.13 illustrates the architectural layers of SS2000.

The primary organizational concept behind all layered systems is that elements closer to the bottom are more likely to be applied unchanged across all members of the product line. Elements at or near the top—for example, software

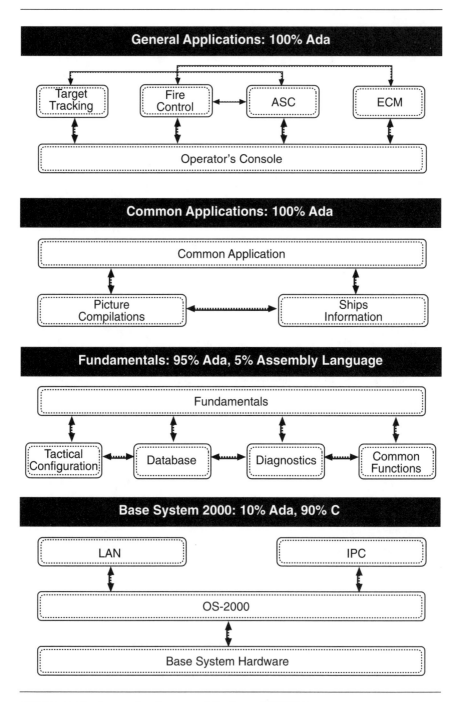

FIGURE 16.13 Layered software architecture of SS2000.

implementing customer-specific requirements—are less likely to be generic. There-fore, reusability is enhanced when an element uses only those elements that fall at its level or below it in the layered view of the system. Otherwise, when a component is used in a new customer product, it may find that a higher-level component that it relied on did not transfer with it, and so this otherwise reusable component will have to be rewritten.

SYSTEM FUNCTIONS AND SYSTEM FUNCTION GROUPS

System functions provide a different use of the module structure. Several types of components exist in the SS2000 architecture. Each serves a particular purpose. Functional requirements are embodied in *system functions*. A system function is a collection of software that implements a logically connected set of requirements. A system function is composed of a number of Ada code units. A *system function group* comprises a set of system functions and forms the basic work assignment for a development team. SS2000 consists of about 30 system function groups, each comprising up to 20 or so system functions. System function groups are clustered around major functional areas, including the following:

- Command, control, and communications
- Weapons control
- Fundamentals, meaning facilities for intrasystem communication and inter-facing with the computing environment
- Human-computer interface

Figure 16.14 illustrates the relationship between the various kinds of components.

System function groups may (and do) contain system functions of more than one layer. They correspond to larger pieces of functionality that are more appro-priately developed by a large team. For example, a separate software require-ments specification is written for each system function group.

System functions and system function groups, not the Ada code units, are the basic units of test and integration for the product line. This is a crucial point. It allows a new member of the product line to be treated as the composition of a few dozen high-quality, high-confidence components, which interact with each other in controlled, predictable ways, as opposed to thousands of small units that must be regression tested with each new change. Assembly of large components and obviating the need to retest at the lowest level of granularity for each new instantiation of the system are a critical key to making reuse work.

ARCHITECTURE WAS THE FOUNDATION

Although this case study emphasizes that technical solutions to a product line are insufficient without taking into account business, organizational, and process considerations as well, it remains a fact that the architecture for SS2000 provided

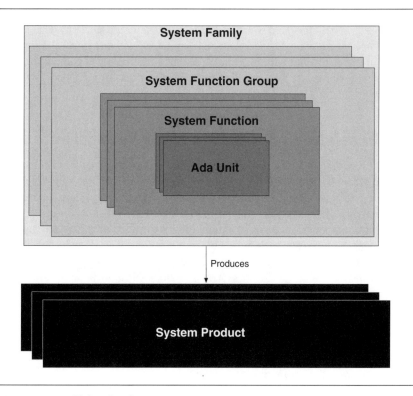

FIGURE 16.14 Units of software components.

the means for achieving a product line. Toward this end, abstraction and layering were vital. Abstraction allowed components to be created that encapsulated changeable decisions within the boundaries of their interfaces. When the component is used in multiple products, the changeable decisions are instantiated whenever possible by parameterization. When the components may change across time as new requirements are accommodated, the changeable decisions held inside the module ensure that wholesale changes to the asset base are not needed.

The size and complexity of this architecture and the components that populate it make clear that a thorough understanding of the application domain is required if a system is to be partitioned into modules that (1) can be developed independently, (2) are appropriate for a product line whose products are as widely varied as those in SS2000, and (3) can accommodate future evolution with ease. In the case of CelsiusTech, the initial domain analysis was informal and reflected years of previous work on shipboard computer systems; the domain models were manifested in the expertise of the architects. Once CelsiusTech realized the importance of domain understanding in the evolution of their systems (around 1989), they performed a more formal domain analysis to capture commonalities and variabilities of shipboard systems.

MAINTAINING THE COMPONENT BASE AS NEW
SYSTEMS ARE PRODUCED

As we discussed, the enduring product at CelsiusTech is not an individual ship system for a specific customer, or even the set of systems deployed so far. Rather, the central task is viewed as maintaining the *product line itself*. Maintaining the product line means maintaining the reusable components in such a way that any previous member of the product line can be regenerated (they change and evolve and grow, after all, as their requirements change) and future members can be built. In a sense, maintaining the product line means maintaining a *capability*, the capability to produce products from the assets. Maintaining this capability means keeping reusable components up to date and generic. No product is allowed to evolve in isolation from the product line. This is one approach to solving the problem, which we identified in Chapter 15, of keeping the evolution of the product line synchronized with the evolution of the variants.

Not every component is used in every member of the product line. Crypto-logic and human interface requirements differ so widely across nationalities, for instance, that it makes more sense to build components that are used in a few systems. In a sense, this yields product lines within the major product line: a Swedish set of products, a Danish set of products, and so on. Some components are used but once; however, even these are maintained as product line assets, designed and built to be configurable and flexible, in case a new product is developed that can make use of them.

Externally, CelsiusTech builds ship systems. Internally, they evolve and grow a common asset base that provides the capability to turn out ship systems. This mentality—which is what it is—might sound subtle, but it manifests itself in the configuration control policies, the organization of the enterprise, and the way that new products are marketed.

MAINTAINING LARGE PREINTEGRATED CHUNKS

In the classic literature on software reuse repositories, the unit of reuse is typically either a small fine-grained component (such as an Ada package, a subroutine, or an object) or a large-scale independently executing subsystem (such as a tool or a commercial stand-alone product). In the former case, the small components must be assembled, integrated, configured, and tested after checking out; in the latter case, the subsystems are typically not very configurable or flexible.

CelsiusTech took an intermediate approach. Their unit of reuse is a system function, a thread of related functionality that comprises elements from different layers in the architecture. System functions are preintegrated—that is, the components they comprise have been assembled, compiled together, tested individually, and tested as a unit. When the system function is checked out of the asset repository, it is ready for use. In this way, CelsiusTech is not only reusing components, they are also reusing the integration, component test, and unit test effort that would otherwise have to be repeated for each application.

PARAMETERIZED COMPONENTS

Although components are reused with no change in code in most cases, they are not always reused entirely without change. Many of the components are written with symbolic values in place of absolute quantities that may change from customer system to customer system. For example, a computation within some component may be a function of how many processors there are; however, the number need not be known when the component is written. Therefore, that component may be written with the number of processors as a symbolic value, a parameter. The value of the parameter is bound as the system is integrated; the component works correctly at runtime but can be used without code change in another version of the system that features a different number of processors.

Parameters are a simple, effective, and time-honored means to achieve component reuse. However, in practice, they tend to multiply at an alarming rate. Almost any component can be made more generic via parameterization. The components for SS2000 currently feature 3,000 to 5,000 parameters that must be individually tuned for each customer system built from the product line. CelsiusTech currently has no methodological approach to ensure that parameters do not conflict with each other; that is, there is no formal way to tell that a certain combination of parameter values, when instantiated into a running system, will not lead to some sort of illegal operating state.

The fact that there are so many parameters undermines some of the benefits gained from treating large system functions and system function groups as the basic units of test and integration. As parameters are tuned for a new version of the system, they in fact produce a version of the system that has never before been tested. Each combination of parameter values may theoretically take the system into operating states that have never before been experienced, let alone exhaustively tested.

The multitude of configuration parameters raises an issue that may well need serious attention. Formal models for parameter interaction (that would identify legal and illegal configurations) would solve the problem but might be too powerful a solution for the problem. Only a small proportion of the possible parameter combinations will ever occur. However, there is a danger that unwillingness to "try out" a new parameter combination could inhibit exploiting the built-in flexibility (configurability) of the components.

In practice, the multitude of parameters seems to be mostly a bookkeeping worry; there has never been any experience with incorrect operation that could be traced back solely to a set of parameter specifications. Often, a large component is imported with its parameter set left unchanged from its previous utilization.

16.4 Summary

Since 1986, CelsiusTech has evolved from a defense contractor providing custom engineered point solutions to essentially a vendor of commercial-off-the-shelf naval systems. They found that the old ways of organizational structure and management were insufficient to support the emerging business model. CelsiusTech found that achieving and sustaining an effective product line was not simply a matter of the right software and system architecture, development environment, hardware, or network. Organizational structure, management practices, and staffing characteristics were also dramatically affected.

CelsiusTech's organizational changes to create the product line were heavily influenced by their lessons learned from the Mk2.5 integration and management difficulties, emerging understanding of the vital nature of architecture to a product line, and awareness of the risks involved with the introduction of new technology.

The architecture served as the foundation of the approach, both technically and culturally. In some sense, the architecture became the tangible thing whose creation and instantiation was the goal of all of the component work. Because of its importance, the architecture was highly visible. A small elite architecture team had the authority as well as the responsibility for the product line architecture. As a consequence, the architecture achieved the "conceptual integrity" cited by Brooks as the key to any quality software venture.

Defining the architecture was only the beginning of achieving a foundation for a long-term development effort. Validation through prototyping and early use was essential. When deficiencies were uncovered, the architecture had to evolve in a smooth, controlled manner throughout initial development and beyond. To manage this natural evolution, CelsiusTech's integration and architecture teams worked together to prevent any designer or design team from changing critical interfaces without explicit approval of the architecture team.

This approach had the full support of project management and worked because of the authority vested in the architecture team. The architecture team was a centralized design authority that could not be circumvented. Conceptual integrity was thus maintained.

The organization that is used to create a product line is different from that needed to sustain and evolve a product line. Management needs to plan for changing personnel, management, training, and organizational needs. Architects with extensive domain knowledge and engineering skill are vital to the creation of viable product lines. Domain experts remain in demand as new products are envisioned and evolution of the product line is managed.

Impact of product line development on an organization is orders of magnitude greater than even transition-intensive technologies such as Ada or object technology. Everything potentially changes: management, organizational roles and responsibilities, training, personnel skills and experience, and development processes. These changes are indicative of managing a project from a product line perspective versus managing a single project. Not only are program managers concerned with meeting today's customers needs, but they are also looking longer term at tomorrow's needs. This is a different program management model than that typically practiced in today's public and private organizations.

The development of the product line, its parallel use on several initial customer products, and significant new technology caused much upheaval for the management and development staff. The visionary management of the initial SS2000 general project manager was instrumental in these formative years of the product line approach. In the mid-1980s, developing a product line for as large and varied a domain with life-critical reliability and real-time performance was untried.

Management provided incentives for long-term strategies by supporting technical innovations. They encouraged experimentation in management style. Throughout all the upper management chaos in the initial years, the middle management stayed focused on the goal. While this may sound like a small thing, these visionaries were vital to the success of the organization adopting completely new business and technical approaches.

CelsiusTech's turnaround from one-at-a-time systems to a product line involved education and training on the part of management and technicians. It also required reeducating the company's customers about what they could expect from the product line approach. All of these are what we mean by ABC phase 4: Completing the cycle.

16.5 For Further Reading

CelsiusTech maintains a home page (http://world.celsiustech.se/indexE.html) in English that can be used to get an overview of the company.

Two reports are available for further reading about CelsiusTech's conversion to a product line. One is from the Software Engineering Institute [Brownsword 96] and is the basis for this chapter. The other [Cederling 92] is a thesis from Sweden's Linkoping University, which is also available.

16.6 Discussion Questions

1. Could the CelsiusTech architecture have been used for the air-traffic system of Chapter 11? Could CelsiusTech have used that architecture? What are the essential differences?

2. CelsiusTech changed management structures several times during its development of the SS2000. Consider the implications of these decisions, given our recommendation in Chapter 13 that product structure should mirror the project structure.

17

Communitywide Reuse
of Architectural Assets

with Patricia Oberndorf

> *The nice thing about standards is that there are so many to choose from.*
> — Anonymous

In Chapter 15, we saw how an architecture could be reused within an organization and made the basis of a product line. A portion of the product line is a collection of components that are included in variants. In that discussion, we did not distinguish those components that were created to reflect *community* standards (whether formal or informal). In this chapter we discuss two different manifestations of community standards. The first is informal and is the use of *reference architectures*. The second is formal and is the development of *open systems*.

Both reflect the business issues and terminology associated with an enterprise's desire to position itself to use preexisting components or to influence the standards process to have a standard reflect an organization's goals. This is the perspective of the consumer of preexisting components, not the producer. Thus, this chapter is designed to enable an architect to become an educated consumer and to influence, indirectly, the products produced by other organizations.

17.1 Reference Architectures

One consequence of the maturation of a domain is that more and more systems are built within that field and by different organizations (consider how many Web-based systems have been built in the past three years). These systems then

Note: Patricia Oberndorf is a member of the technical staff at the Software Engineering Institute, Carnegie Mellon University.

become a portion of the technical environment that influences the development of any system. During this maturation process, pressure grows for more abstract representations of the system. Figure 17.1 shows the abstract representations for a domain as an indication of the domain's maturity (although all domains do not necessarily pass through every stage).

The stages in Figure 17.1 are presented as reflecting the increased maturity of the domain. The sequence can be seen to be correct by working backward along the sequence. That is, if there is an application generator for a domain, certainly the generation of particular components in that domain must be possible. If there is a generator for particular components, there must be a reference architecture that allows for the inclusion of those components. Finally, a reference architecture includes a division of functionality (the reference model) as one of its attributes.

In this section, we explore how reference architectures—architectural assets that are shared and reused across organizations—evolve. We give some examples of mature fields and then revisit the area of user-interface software reference models that we discussed in Chapter 6 to show what happens as a domain matures.

MATURE DOMAINS

Compilers, database management systems, operating systems, and network communication systems, to name a few, have standard well-documented architectures. Sometimes—as is the case with compilers—the architecture is "standard" in the sense that architects designing one of these systems would not spend time inventing its architecture. Rather, they would consult an authoritative source such as a textbook, adopt the solution they found there, and press on. Other times the architectures are standard in the more formal sense that a standards body has issued a formal definition for the architecture. Operating systems and network communications systems both have formally approved standards. Database management systems have an informally standardized architecture that describes how functionality is divided and gives a formal standard that pertains to query languages.

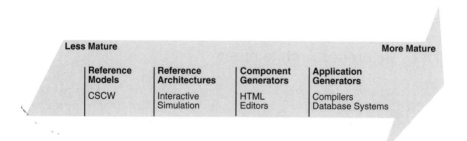

FIGURE 17.1   Levels of maturity of selected domains.

The existence of standard designs and sets of design decisions, whether formal or informal, is a sign of a mature domain. A mature domain is one in which a wealth of cumulative experience has been brought to bear to obviate design decisions for future members of the domain.

Some domains do not have standard architectures, but they do have standard ways to partition functionality. For example, computer-aided software engineering (CASE) environments always include compilers, debuggers, editors, and configuration management systems. This division is not an architecture because the precise separation and interaction between the components is not specified and can vary from system to system.

After a critical mass of systems (and system developers) exists, reference architectures begin to develop. Several forces act to encourage the generation of reference architectures as follows:

- If the systems are being developed in the research community, the researchers' need for more abstract explanations of commonality and differences among their systems will drive them to the development of a reference architecture.

- If there are external users or customers of these systems, they need a principled basis for comparison among the systems other than just features that the systems provide.

- An abstract explanation of a domain such as a reference architecture is useful for teaching novices how to program new applications in that domain.

- If there is a large user community for these similar systems, they want to be able to interchange components from different systems and to interoperate among the systems. Both of these forces lead to a reference architecture, perhaps as a first step toward formal standardization.

- A business case can be made to produce component or application generators once a reference architecture exists. This leads to pressure to define a reference architecture.

A common thread through all of these forces is the notion of a community of developers for systems in a single domain. These developers either spontaneously or under market or governmental/regulatory pressures get together to define the reference architecture. And this community has the expertise to discuss the issues associated with a reference architecture. The users of such systems can apply pressure that causes members of the community to come together, but without a community of developers, reference architectures will not appear. This leads to an expanded concept of the architecture business cycle (ABC) shown in Figure 17.2. Multiple developing organizations contribute to an architecture that then results in multiple systems being constructed across those organizations (and others).

A formal standard software architecture will prescribe a set of components with defined interfaces among them. If the domain is one with sufficiently powerful market forces, component vendors will arise to produce particular components, for example, databases, user-interface widgets, telecommunication packages, and so forth.

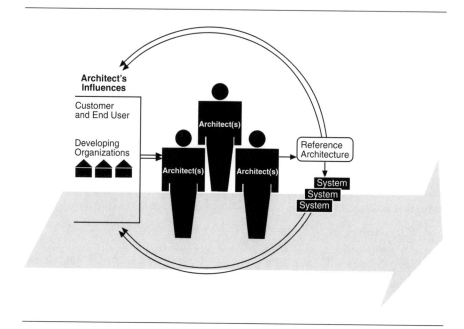

FIGURE 17.2 ABC with a community of developers.

Now let us reexamine the user-interface reference models introduced in Chapter 6 from the point of view of maturity of the domain and how community activities affected these reference models. Figure 17.3 shows the historical development of the user-interface reference models and associated systems.

The reference models of the top row of Figure 17.3 (model view controller, or MVC, and presentation, abstraction, control, or PAC) are the result of single research groups. MVC was developed by the group that developed Smalltalk and PAC, by researchers at the University of Grenoble. On the other hand, the reference models on the bottom row (Seeheim and Arch/Slinky) were both developed by groups. Seeheim was the result of a workshop sponsored by a professional society and Arch/Slinky was the result of an unaffiliated group of user-interface tool builders. Thus, in terms of the forces that encourage the generation of reference architectures, we see the ones that are developer but not customer oriented (single researcher, groups of researchers, groups of developers).

User-interface reference models continue to change and evolve because the domain of user interfaces itself continues to change and evolve. In 1983 when the initial reference models appeared, bit-mapped terminals were rare and mechanisms were needed to manage these terminals. Today, multimedia and collaborative systems are common. If the domain had been frozen when the initial reference models appeared, the reference models would not have been suitable for today's systems. The appearance of a commonly accepted, static reference model such as exists in the database domain is an indicator that the foundations of that domain are firm and unlikely to change radically for some time.

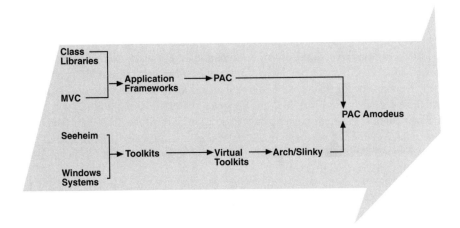

FIGURE 17.3   Evolution of user-interface architectures and artifacts.

STAGES OF REUSE

So far, we have been discussing the evolution of reusable architectures. The goal of reuse, of course, is to have a collection of reusable components that can be used together in a wide variety of systems. In this section, we briefly explore the stages that lead to reusable components.

Figure 17.4 shows the stages of reuse. Reusable architectures are the first stage and have been discussed extensively in Chapter 15. Having a reusable architecture is a precondition to successfully developing reusable components, although as we have seen in the user-interface example, the architecture does not need to be a system architecture; it could be limited to covering a small portion of

Reusable Architectures	Domain-Specific Languages	Reusable Components
Provides structure and coordination model used through multiple systems	Provides executive and basic primitive concepts used through multiple systems	Provides components used through multiple systems

FIGURE 17.4   Stages of reuse.

a system, such as the connection between a user interface and the underlying application that the interface exposes to the user.

The next stage in reuse maturity is to have a domain-specific language, discussed in Chapter 13. Such languages have been available in specialized domains for decades. For example, in the compiler domain the LEX and YACC languages have been widely used to create the lexical and syntactic analysis portions of a compiler.

Domain-specific languages add two elements to reusable architectures: (1) They implicitly define primitives that are important to the domain, and (2) they typically include some runtime support for the primitives of the language. Thus, for example, a statistical language might have a primitive for performing an analysis of variance. This routine becomes a portion of the runtime library and is used every time the language is used.

The final stage in the evolution is the development of reusable components. These components will often be primitives of the domain-specific language or have been specified in the reusable architecture.

What we have offered in this section is the proposition that a domain-specific language could provide an intermediate stage for reuse between a reusable architecture and reusable components. Such a stage is not necessary, but it provides an intermediate goal for those organizations attempting to develop reusable components. We now turn our attention to the public aspects of reusing communitywide architectural assets.

17.2   Open Systems

Open system is a buzzword that is used both to describe a system that is open to inclusion of many products from many sources, and to describe a state of being. The state-of-being usage carries with it an image of easy plug and play between components and products that were not necessarily originally designed to work together.

Specifically, an open system has interface specifications that are:

1. Fully defined

2. Available to the public

3. Maintained according to group consensus

Not only must the specifications be fully defined, but they must also be available to the public. The component's interface specifications cannot be available only to a select group of people who have some special interest. Anyone is free to obtain a copy of the specifications (perhaps at the cost of duplication and distribution, perhaps even at the cost of a small license fee) and is also free to produce and sell implementations of that specification. Finally, for a system to be truly open it is important for the component's interface specifications to be of interest to a wide range of parties and not exclusively under the control of any single vendor.

To this end, the definition includes the idea that maintenance of the specifications is by group consensus. Taken together, these criteria come close to requiring that the interface specifications be formal standards. But in practice a variety of consensus-based specifications are found, in addition to formal standards. We will discuss the formal standardization process in a subsequent section.

This definition is operational. That is, it defines a test that can be applied to a system at any time. In contrast, most other popular definitions of open systems identify desirable system qualities that open systems are expected to display, such as portability, interoperability, and scalability. These qualities are, as we have discussed, unmeasurable in the abstract and so do not form the basis of a useful definition.

We can also see how this definition supports the vision of what people hope to achieve with open systems. The phrase *plug and play* brings to mind such things as children's interlocking building blocks, which can be used to build things that the makers of the individual pieces never dreamed of. Well-defined, consistently enforced, common interface standards among the pieces are the key.

In addition to the open system, which is an end product, we also define an *open system architecture*, which will be the vehicle for carrying the open system goal to fruition. Not surprisingly, an open system architecture is the architecture of a system, where the interface specifications of the architecture are fully defined, available to the public, and maintained according to group consensus. The key to applying the concept of open systems is to first highlight the role of interfaces in a system and then to define these interfaces using standard specifications.

The attractions envisioned from the use of open systems are similar to those enumerated for product line-based systems in Chapter 15, but their community-oriented and market-based nature brings extra benefits, as follows:

- *Reduced reliance on proprietary products.* Open systems will allow system buyers to obtain components from a variety of sources, thus minimizing the power that any one vendor has over the system being constructed.

- *More competition leading to lower cost.* When true plug and play is achieved, it will mean that there are choices in the marketplace for suppliers of system components, and such competition has historically meant reduced costs to the buyers.

- *Better-tested products.* The products purchased will be better tested because there will be more users working with them find the problems.

As we noted in the similar discussion in Chapter 15, there are also the following concerns involving the use of open systems:

- *Failure to meet performance requirements, environment requirements, and so on.* Commercially available products or components that have not been engineered to work well together may not be able to meet the demands of real-time, secure, fault-tolerant systems. And vendors, sadly, cannot be relied on to provide meaningful, impartial performance characterizations of their products.

- *Conformance and certification problems.* Since plug and play implies some sort of adherence to interface agreements, it is important to be able to establish conformance, but this can be difficult.

- *Support problems.* Reliance on commercial sources of support may cause difficulties, especially when sorting out the claims of several vendors regarding the source of an incompatibility between components.

- *Continued investment.* It is often necessary to keep up with component upgrades, each of which may require additional work to keep it working in the system, as well as to test it.

- *Need for new management style.* The management techniques required for managing a system built from existing components are different from the management techniques for managing a system built from scratch.

BUILDING AN OPEN SYSTEM

The degree to which an organization wishes its systems to contain formally standardized components is a business decision that is treated as any other business decision when specifying the qualities that a system is to exhibit. When one sees the term "open system" used as the description for a system, it means that the quality of *evolvability* has been given high priority by the system's creators, and that the use of formally standardized components has been chosen as the technique to achieve that evolvability.

An *open systems approach* is a business strategy for creating more evolvable systems by capitalizing on the following three key elements:

1. A systems vision

2. A common (open systems) architecture

3. The use of standards and standards-based implementations

The systems vision captures what you want to achieve when the system under construction is finished. It is the overall driver of the business strategy and open systems approach. It offers the opportunity to take advantage of what others have done.

To create an open systems architecture, an organization must be keenly aware of the marketplace, the trends in the marketplace, and the degree and mechanisms that the organization can use to influence those trends. For example, an organization that wishes to have influence over the mechanisms by which systems interoperate might choose to adopt the Common Object Request Broker Architecture (CORBA) and join the Object Management Group (OMG). They also might choose to adopt OLE or ActiveX and attempt to influence Microsoft in some fashion. Both of these are strategies that could be adopted, and the one that an organization chooses to adopt will depend on its sense of the trends of the marketplace and the manner in which it might have the most influence.

17.3 The Process of Engineering an Open System

The first element in engineering an open system deals with requirements. It is important to understand the "openness" requirements in addition to all the requirements that are normally considered. Part of this understanding of the requirements will be to come to terms with their relative priorities. Some requirements are more stringent than others and cannot be compromised. Others are "requirements" perhaps only because "that's the way we've always done it." Later in the open systems approach, when selecting standards and implementations, it will be important to be able to distinguish requirements by these differences. Choices and trade-offs cannot be made, as they must, if all requirements are created equal. It is not realistic to expect a set of commercially developed, consensus-based interface standards to meet all of your requirements. To stay in the commercial marketplace, as opposed to reverting to the build-your-own approach, some requirements will have to be relaxed.

The second element in an open systems approach is the development of a reference model for the class of systems envisioned. In this usage, a reference model is a conceptual tool that is developed as the requirements (and the application domain) are better understood. The requirements and the reference model have an influence on each other. One goal of the reference model is to make a baseline for the current system (if there is one) in the sense of capturing the functions or services of the system. Similarly, it can capture the proposed functions or services for a new system. It also assists in understanding a system's current state of openness. Another goal of a reference model is to promote the development of common concepts and terminology among the team working on the system.

To undertake the standards activities, you must evaluate and select your standards and establish liaisons through which you can track the progress of the standards and perhaps even contribute to their development or evolution. The selection of standards should be documented in a *profile*: a set of one or more base standards. The profile is your means of identifying which standards you have chosen and also of clearly documenting how you expect those standards to cooperate and be coordinated because many of them will not have been developed by the same organization and will not necessarily be designed to work together well. We discuss profiles more fully in a subsequent section.

The implementation activities mirror the standards activities, including evaluation and selection of implementations that are consistent with the standards in your profile. These component implementations must also be acquired, which may involve buying them, modifying something you buy, or building them yourself. One critical consideration during component selection is to verify the conformance of the implementations to the interface standards and the profile: If the component implementations do not adhere to the interface standards, the system is not open.

When integrating and testing the system, it may be necessary to customize some component implementations but do so reluctantly and carefully. You are likely to find yourself integrating implementations from a number of sources, so your techniques and approaches may differ accordingly. The discussion of mismatch in Chapter 15 also applies to components derived from community standards. Also, testing does not go away with open systems. It may be true that other users have already put some of the implementations through their paces and surfaced some of the bugs. But the use of each implementation in your system will be different enough from anyone else's that testing cannot be eliminated.

Finally, you will be ready to deploy and support your system. The support process may be quite different from what you have done in the past because it may involve the coordination of multiple vendors. To the extent that your system now involves standards and implementations provided by outside sources, you will find that coordination of system changes and upgrades is a whole new challenge. You may not have control over when a vendor updates a component implementation or decides to discontinue support for a product you have used, and when standards change, you will have to decide how and when to incorporate that change in your architecture and system.

There are two important observations to make about this outline of the process of engineering an open system. The first is that these are not discrete, sequential steps. In particular there are close ties and interdependencies among the decisions that are made regarding architecture, standards, and implementation. For example, one could decide on one architectural approach, only to find out that the standards and implementations that are available do not fit well with it. This could lead to a decision to change the architecture. Further, a standard could be selected only to find out that the available implementations do not meet some other requirement, leading to a decision to use a different standard. Finally, a standards-based implementation could be selected only to find that other problems interfere with its ability to be used as part of the system, possibly affecting the choice of standard or even an architectural decision.

This brings us to the second important observation: A sound open systems approach is a basis for continuing evolution of the system. In part this is necessitated by the continual upgrade of available standards and implementations (and the accompanying abandonment of old versions of implementations as new ones are created or vendors decide to leave a certain product area). But it is also driven by continuing new investments in technology that express themselves as new standards and products. You will want and need to take advantage of these new opportunities as they emerge, and your open systems architecture and open systems approach will provide the basis on which you can do this with discipline and success. We will see this process in action in the next chapter, where we discuss the creation and evolution of the meteorological and oceanographic (METOC) system.

17.4   Standards

To appreciate the importance of standards, consider the role of standards in other industries and in everyday life. Most of us are familiar with the changes that industrialization brought to the manufacture of just about everything. One of the prominent examples was Henry Ford's introduction of the assembly line, a concept that was heavily dependent on standardization. The advantages of this approach continue to make themselves known to us every time we walk into an auto parts store to get a part we need, regardless of the make and model of our car. It is also apparent when we buy clothing or shoes or contemplate how nationwide railway systems can exist (see sidebar on the next page). Throughout history there are also examples of what can happen when standards have not been introduced, such as the tragic outcome when flames engulfed neighborhoods in Baltimore, but the city could not make use of the help offered from neighboring fire companies because the fireplug hose connections were not compatible.

The examples suggest that we too can enjoy some of the benefits of increased standardization, such as greater availability of suitable products, more vendor competition, and affordable prices. But to do so will require a greater understanding of standards and the standards world.

CATEGORIES OF STANDARDS

Standards may be categorized in a number of ways, and that there is great diversity in the standards that are available. Careful consideration must be given to the needs of the system and the variety of available standards in order to choose the ones that will be most effective for a given set of circumstances.

Accreditation.   One categorization of interest is whether a standard is accredited or nonaccredited. Accredited standards typically are approved by official national or international bodies that define and disseminate standards for the public. Some are created by standards groups of professional or technical organizations that achieve recognition (i.e., accreditation) from their respective national or international bodies.

Nonaccredited standards are generally created by suppliers or users, using a consensus method. The purpose of such groups is usually to define and disseminate standards that are for the benefit of their particular group. Examples of these organizations include some industry groups, some user groups, and most vendor consortia, such as the OMG discussed in Chapter 8.

Achieving accreditation is usually dependent on the nature of the consensus process used by the group. Most accredited organizations have a broad base of participation, with an emphasis on wide consensus. The features of the consensus process used are central to accreditation. There are typically many approvals that are required, for example, from subcommittee to the highest board.

We can contrast the accredited consensus process with the processes in operation with consortia. The typical consortium determines membership based on vendors, not individuals. The consensus process itself is generally quite different, often relying on proposals submitted by consortium members, based on a solicitation developed by the consortium. From these proposals a winner is selected, to which the whole consortium agrees to conform. Consensus is often reached through compromises between competing proposals.

Another consensus process might be called the "private" one. In this situation, a few vendors band together for mutual benefit, perhaps recognizing that it would be to their mutual advantage if their products interacted better. Membership is typically by private invitation or agreement. An example here is the X consortium.

Finally, another consensus process worth considering is that which results in de facto standards (see sidebar below). In this case there is a single vendor or source for the specification, and part of the "consensus" process is the vendor's internal design and marketing processes. However, the "voting" takes place in the marketplace, as buyers pull out their wallets and purchase the product that embodies the specification. Microsoft and IBM have defined de facto standards for years.

Where Do Standards Come From?

An interesting discussion flowed around the Usenet a couple of years ago about how the U.S. railroad gauge standard became set at the strange sounding figure of 4 feet, 8 1/2 inches. The discussion has implications for standards in any technology area.

It turns out that the standard was set for two reasons: backward compatibility with legacy systems and the experience of the architects of the railroads. To be precise, the early creators of the U.S. rail system were trained in Great Britain and had British tools and rolling stock. Of course, this just pushes the question down one level. Why did the British use this strange gauge?

As the story goes, the British built their railroads using this gauge for precisely the same two reasons of legacy compatibility and architect's experience: The trams (which existed before the railroads) used this gauge, and the builders of the new railroad were converted tram builders, initially using tram-building tools.

Of course, trams did not appear without their historical baggage. Early trams were modeled after wagons and so the early tram builders used the same jigs and the same tools that they had previously used for building wagons. But this still begs the original question: Why, then, did wagons use a wheel spacing of 4 feet, 8 1/2 inches?

They used it because they were constrained by *their* environment, the environment that had been created by the technology of the day. More plainly, the wagon builders used this spacing because any other spacing would have caused their wheels to break because the ruts on the roads in Great Britain at the time were this distance apart.

The roads were another kind of technological legacy, a standard that constrained innovation and determined this important feature of the wagons. This time, however, the legacy came from Rome. The earliest long-distance roads in Great Britain were built by the Romans, in the first four centuries A.D. And, of course, the Romans built these roads the size that they did because this was the size that fit their war chariots. So, the gauge of trains in the United States today is attributable to the design of Roman war chariots built two millenia earlier.

But it doesn't end here.

The spacing of wheels on the Roman war chariot was, in turn, dictated by the width of the yoke that attached the chariot to the horse. The yoke was made this width to keep the wheel ruts clear of the horse that was pulling the chariot. So, the gauge of a modern rail car in the United States, it can be reasonably assumed, was determined by following a set of standards, each of which were dictated by a combination of technical factors, constraints from legacy systems, and the experience of the architects. These factors, when combined, mean that the gauge of a rail car was determined by the width of the standard Roman warhorse's derriere.

Although this sounds silly, consider the consequences of ignoring the constraints of existing standards. When Napoleon attacked Russia, his armies made much slower progress than anticipated once they reached eastern Europe because the ruts on the roads there were not to Roman gauge. Because they made slower time than planned, they got caught in the Russian winter. We all know what happened after that.

— RNK

Goal.   Another distinction that can be made between standards involves the goal for which the standard is written. Some standards are product or quality standards. That is, they define a particular product. Examples of these include VCR or refrigerator standards. A second goal category are control standards, which address a societal concern or achieve a social end. These are most often generated by governments and are equated with regulations. Examples of these are auto safety regulations or standards for medical devices. The third goal standards might address is interoperability. These standards provide accepted rules of behavior that facilitate interaction. Among these are computer interface and electronic data exchange standards. Most of the interface standards we address in this chapter fall in this last group, but it is important to be aware of the other groups.

Source.   The third category is concerned with where a standard comes from. Standards may be generated and approved by governments, professional societies, trade associations, or vendor consortia. They may also be de facto standards, or they may come from an organization internally.

Type of Specification.   There are various types of standards in computing systems. Examples are application programming interfaces, service descriptions, protocols, and data or interchange formats.

Functionality.   Standards may address any number of classes of functionality. Some may address classes of services, such as operating systems, networks, backplane buses, or data exchange. Others may address classes of attributes, such as security, fault tolerance, or safety.

FORMAL STANDARDS ORGANIZATIONS

Familiarity with the standards community can help in working with standards and taking full advantage of them. As we shall see, the size and diversity found in the standards world contributes directly to some of the challenges faced in taking an open systems approach.

The international standards community that has the most effect on information technology standards is rooted in the International Standards Organization (ISO) and International Electrotechnical Commission (IEC), as shown in Figure 17.5. Both are internationally accredited standardization bodies in which membership is by nation. In the early 1990s they joined forces in the form of the Joint Technical Committee 1 (JTC1) and have since been cooperating on a number of information technology standardization efforts.

Within each nation there is typically a variety of standards bodies. In the United States, for example, the American National Standards Institute (ANSI) is the officially recognized national standards body and primary link with the international standardization community. Such bodies coordinate standardization activities within their own country. In addition, ANSI accredits other organizations, such as the Institute of Electrical and Electronics Engineers (IEEE) and maintains relationships with government bodies that have interests in standardization, such as the National Institute of Standards and Technology (NIST).

As shown in Figure 17.5, there are various avenues through which nonaccredited organizations such as consortia and industry associations may contribute to the development of national and international standards.

Each of these national standards bodies in turn organizes by committees and subcommittees until finally one gets down to the groups of technically oriented participants who actually write specifications and propose standards and standardization activities. Much of this infrastructure is echoed at the international level as well.

One source of frustration with accredited standards today is how long it takes to see a specification achieve that status. Recalling the earlier discussion of the accredited consensus process and understanding all the layers of its application that might be involved, it is not hard to understand why formal, accredited standardization, especially through to the international level, takes so long and at the same time produces a variety of standards that are not necessarily coordinated with one another.

STANDARDS AND THE MARKETPLACE

Besides the accredited standards community, there is another important force at work in determining the results of pursuing an open systems approach, and that is

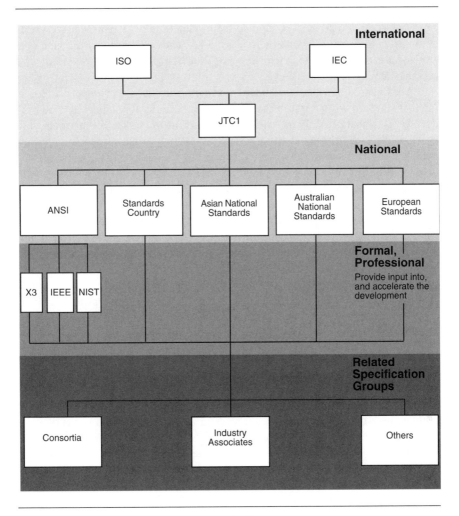

FIGURE 17.5   Relationships among standards groups.

the marketplace. In today's marketplace, individual vendors sell products that do not necessarily implement any standards. Without the clues that standards give to vendors about the probable needs of the user community, they are relying primarily on their own sense of what the users need. Users, on the other hand, let what is available in the marketplace determine what they choose to buy or have to make for themselves. In this situation, it can also be difficult for the users to tell which products are competitors and therefore are alternatives to be considered.

In a standards-driven marketplace vendors and users work together to define the standards. The ideal then is that the vendors commit to the standards by creating and bringing to market conforming products, while the users commit to the standards by using them to guide their purchases. The result should be a robust marketplace in which vendors can add their value to their standards-based products with confidence, knowing there is a market, and users can take an open systems approach with confidence, knowing that the vendors are providing the products they need.

The creation of a formal standard does not guarantee that products embodying that standard will appear in the marketplace. Waiting for standards to be produced will almost certainly increase a product's time to market. Furthermore, it is possible that a formal standard, produced by a small group of people, is either outdated or irrelevant to the vendors. Numerous examples exist of formal standards that are not available for purchase in a component. So both sides of the standards-driven marketplace (the standard and the marketplace) must be given consideration when an organization is adopting a business strategy.

One other aspect of the business strategy involving standards is suggested by the quotation with which we began this chapter. When designing a system, wanting to conform to a standard in a particular area will not guarantee interoperability because of the proliferation of standards. There are so far, for example, seven different standards governing interchange formats among different portions of a speech-recognition system. Each one of these standards makes different assumptions about how the task of speech recognition is to be decomposed. Thus, wanting to conform to a speech standard complicates, instead of simplifying, the architect's task.

SELECTING AND PROFILING STANDARDS

So far we have talked vaguely about using standards but not much about how you decide which ones to use or how to put them together to suit the needs of your particular system. The art of choosing your standards starts with market research. Surveying the available technology doesn't mean just collecting glossy product brochures. The market research needed is a thorough investigation of the standards that are available as well as the products that (claim to) conform to those standards. It means paying careful attention to key features of standards beyond just the functionality they represent. For example, you need to know how mature a standard is, whether there are multiple product sources, and what kind of market acceptance each standard and its conformant products enjoy. You also want to know about each standard's "pedigree" and the quality of the specification as well as the existence of accompanying conformance test capabilities.

To select the standards to use, you might want to categorize them. This will help to distinguish among alternatives. If there are a large number of alternatives for a given interface, you might want to start with a set of broad criteria to decide which candidates are of value to evaluate in detail. You will need to establish an evaluation method, which includes the detailed criteria you will use, who the evaluators will be, how many evaluators will look at each aspect of the standards, how each evaluation criterion will be scored, and how the evaluators' scores will be collected and reduced to some sort of overall score for each candidate standard. Keep in mind that this selection process goes hand in hand (i.e., is iterative) with the selection of the corresponding implementations and refinements to the architecture that is your open systems goal.

You will quickly find that there are more standards out there than any system would ever want to use at the same time, so you need a way not only to select which ones you will use but also to combine them to suit your needs. You will need to choose some of the available standards and put them together so they cooperate to help achieve your system goals, a process that we call *profiling,* which is defined as follows [IEEE 93]:

> A profile is a set of one or more standards, and, where applicable, the identification of chosen classes, subsets, options, and parameters of those standards, necessary for accomplishing a particular function.

Profiles are documents, like standards. They are logically complete, can be conformed with, and should also identify and document gaps in functionality. Profiles are valuable because they provide a clear method of communicating your set of standards and the relationships among them. They are necessary because a set of standards may not be compatible or complementary: In addition to gaps, there may be overlaps and places where coordination points need to be specified.

CONFORMANCE

Our definition of open systems emphasized not only that the interface specifications needed to be standards but also that the component implementations needed to properly implement those standards. This raises the question of conformance: Conformance is an action or behavior in correspondence with current customs, rules, or styles. In our case, the rules are the specifications documented in the standards.

Conformance deals with the fidelity with which an implementation meets the standard. Since interfaces are by definition between two components, both sides of the interface must conform to the standard (i.e., use it and implement it properly), or the interface will fail to support the system and the openness of the system will ultimately be diminished. Note, however, that conformance does not mean or guarantee interoperability, unless you have specifically chosen standards that are intended to provide interoperability. Nor does conformance say anything about performance or other qualities of the implementations that are not typically specified by interface standards.

There are various means of assessing conformance, the most reliable of which is a conformance test suite administered by a qualified third party. In selecting among conformance test alternatives, you will be concerned with the quality of the test suite, which may be affected by the quality or tightness of the standard specification itself.

Why Standards Aren't Enough

Standards can play an important role in getting systems to work together—but only if they're the right standards. Standards that allow too much latitude or fail to cover areas of importance will not help and in fact may hinder development because they impose constraints that serve no useful purpose. The following article, from *Government Computer News* (April 1, 1996), makes this point clear:

Mishmash at work (DOD systems in Bosnia are not interoperable)

Once again, the Defense Department is proving to itself that standards, especially vague or all-inclusive ones, don't necessarily buy you interoperability. 'Joint interoperability' may be this decade's mantra, but old service rivalries and ill-conceived standards efforts keep interoperability an elusive goal. This point is being driven home every day in Bosnia, where dozens of systems built to the much-touted Technical Architecture for Information Management (TAFIM) promulgated by the Defense Information Systems Agency (DISA) just won't talk to one another. Field reports depict users forced to deal with side-by-side systems running different applications in a place where space is at a premium. As Rear Adm. John Gauss, the interoperability chief at DISA, put it, "We have built a bunch of state-of-the-art, open-systems, TAFIM-compliant stovepipes." Ouch! That's a stinging admission of how far short TAFIM has fallen of its goals. The operations in Bosnia simply have given stark form to what has been known for some time in DISA and throughout the IRM staffs of the services. TAFIM, although laudable in its goals, is just too broad a set of standards to be meaningful. That's why Gauss and DISA, to their credit, are pushing the Defense Information Infrastructure Common Operating Environment, or DII COE. It will narrow down the TAFIM to far stricter standards that really will provide application interoperability. But you can't just blame DISA. The TAFIM mirrors the half-hearted attempts by the Unix community to achieve interoperability over the years. The vendors talk a good game, but they prefer to sell proprietary operating systems, regardless of the number of "ix" or "ux" suffixes they can dream up. Too, the major Unix database management system vendors work like the devil to prevent compatibility with competitors. TAFIM attempts to acknowledge the requirement that the government be open to all competitors. No doubt some vendors will howl when the final COE is spelled out by DISA and their products are found to be non-compliant. In that event, DISA should stick to its guns. All these systems are supposed to support the warfighters, as Pentagon brass and the vendor community are fond of saying. Well, the fact that those in Bosnia are slowed by a systems mishmash ought to give a fresh kick to the COE effort.

— PCC

WHAT STANDARDS DON'T DO

All this sounds good, but we must also consider the limitations and even some liabilities of using standards (see preceding sidebar). We have already alluded to the elaborate care with which accredited standards are generated and approved, resulting in their reputation for glacial speed. The difficulty this creates for an open systems approach is accented in today's environment of technology advances every 18 to 24 months. A standard revision cycle of 5 to 10 years can't keep up. In addition, it is possible for accredited standards to get so out of touch with what's important in the marketplace that even though they have been approved for use, no products that conform with them are ever made available to users.

This is why you see many people talking more seriously about consortium standards and making use of de facto standards. While these alternatives are attractive in terms of speed and availability of products, they lack some of the positive qualities of the accredited standards, such as stability and broad consensus-based control. The risk of using accredited standards is that they will not respond fast enough and there may be few products available. The risk of using consortium, private, or de facto standards is that they will be less stable and more susceptible to the whims of market forces and will have a more limited consensus base. Another possibility with standards, whether they are accredited or not, is that they may not address all of your needs or concerns. For example, there are still few effective interface standards to use in building systems with security requirements.

Standards and the standards world for software and electronics have a long way to go to achieve the kind of smooth operation noted in other industries. But they are a step in the right direction, and they are the basis for the advantages sought in the pursuit of open systems.

17.5   Summary

The use of formally standardized components is an engineering decision that influences an architecture just as do many other factors. Most organizations would prefer to use a component that conforms to a standard as long as that component provides utility and conforms to the architecture for the system under construction.

The community-based architecture world is not a simple one, as we have seen. There are many different communities, each with its own agenda. Some communities will produce reference models. Others will concentrate on standards. Still others will be concerned with various types of generators.

In this chapter, we attempted to survey the world of community-based architecture to give a feeling for the maturity of various types of architectures that arise in this world and to give the formal standards process some structure. This is all in the hope of making an architect better able to navigate and generate recommendations about the applicability and appropriateness of various architectural-based concepts.

17.6 For Further Reading

A standards profile is essential for keeping track of which standards your system uses and how the components reflecting those standards will work together. This is sometimes called a *technical architecture*. An example of a technical architecture widely used in the government is TAFIM [TAFIM 94].

The reader interested in finding out more about open systems is referred to *http://www.sei.cmu.edu/technology/dynamic_systems/open_systems*. The POSIX standard and a discussion of profiling are available from IEEE [IEEE 93].

17.7 Discussion Questions

1. Standards are all around us; our technological world wouldn't exist without them. Look around the room you're in right now and see how many standards you can find reflected in the objects you see. Think about standards of physical size (e.g., staples in a stapler, light bulbs in a light socket, etc.), electrical interfaces (voltage between appliance and wall socket), weight, and so forth that let different suppliers manufacture parts for things and have them all work together. Where have these made life easier? Can you think of any ways that they have made life harder? Have they impeded progress or stifled competition or ingenuity?

2. Describe some software standards that you wish existed, but do not.

18

The Meteorological Anchor Desk System

A Case Study in Building a Web-Based System from Off-the-Shelf Components

with Rob Veltre and Nelson Weiderman

> *Of course, a component is another system. The nature of a system is such that at almost any granularity it looks the same—it is a system. . . . The goal is to build a system which is necessarily made up of other systems.*
> — Richard P. Gabriel

In this chapter we examine a system called the Meteorological and Oceanographic (METOC) Anchor Desk System, a network-based collaborative information-gathering and decision-aiding system used by the U.S. military. This case study is an illustration of a system built almost entirely from preexisting large-grained components and of the Evolutionary Development method that promoted this kind of construction.

The METOC Anchor Desk System is a decentralized help desk for meteorological and environmental information. It is designed for crisis situations but also has utility during normal operations. The users of the METOC Anchor Desk (during crisis) are the meteorological officers of the various U.S. military services in

---

Note: Rob Veltre is a project scientist at the School of Computer Science, Carnegie Mellon University.

Nelson Weiderman is a member of the technical staff at the Software Engineering Institute, Carnegie Mellon University.

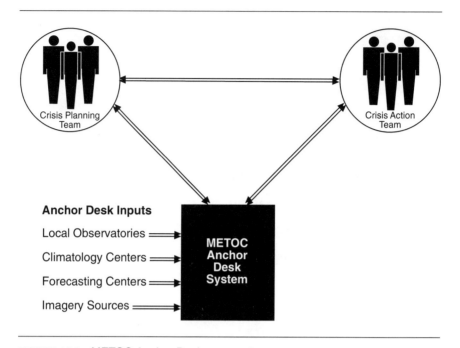

FIGURE 18.1   METOC Anchor Desks concept.

the Pacific Theater Headquarters in Hawaii. They provide support to the crisis planning and action teams that are established by the Pacific Theater Commander in Chief in response to a specific crisis.

Figure 18.1 shows the sources of information for the METOC Anchor Desk and the two different teams involved. While the METOC Anchor Desk is illustrated as a single box in the figure, it is really a globally decentralized system rather than a localized physical entity. The types of crises that are envisioned are both military (during conflict) and civilian (natural disaster relief, drug enforcement, and local law enforcement). During normal operations the same meteorological officers use the METOC Anchor Desk to generate information for their respective commanders.

For example, Figure 18.2 shows a satellite image of a set of dangerous weather systems that developed off the southeast coast of the United States in August of 1996: Hurricane Edouard, Hurricane Fran, and Tropical Storm Gustav. One purpose of the METOC Anchor Desk is to make this kind of information available on a timely basis to crisis response teams.

FIGURE 18.2   Weather systems threatening the eastern United States, August 1996.   NOAA image. Reproduced with permission.

18.1   Relationship to the Architecture Business Cycle

This case study is situated in the architecture business cycle (ABC) as shown in Figure 18.3. The system was developed using a methodology called Evolutionary Development. This method emphasizes early prototyping and customer feedback. In terms of the ABC, the Evolutionary Development method represents a fine-grained feedback from the system to the developing organization, which occurs while the system is undergoing development instead of after it has been released.

This case study differs from others in the book in that the METOC Anchor Desk System was constructed by an organization primarily interested in the process of software development rather than the products of that development. As such, we will not explore the business issues relevant to the developer.

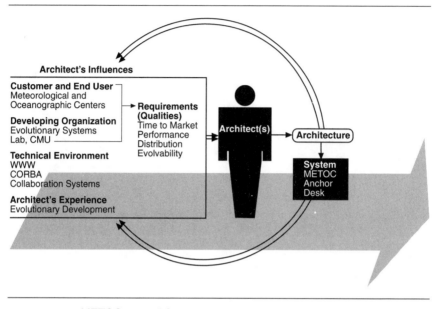

FIGURE 18.3 METOC and ABC.

18.2 Requirements and Qualities

The METOC Anchor Desk is realized as a distributed, virtual organization over-laid on top of existing METOC organizations. These organizations have a long history of operation and have joint procedures that are established and work well. The METOC Anchor Desk System does not attempt to change those procedures. Rather, it attempts to make the existing organization more efficient in executing the procedures. Also, it adds capabilities that improve the timeliness, accuracy, and effectiveness of the decision making under the existing procedures. Because the participants are geographically distributed, collaboration technology such as desktop audio/video, shared whiteboard, and shared applications plays a promi-nent role in providing improved decision-making abilities.

From a user's point of view, the mission of the METOC Anchor Desk is to do the following:

- Provide environmental decision support to both planners and action team commanders
- Assemble and integrate environmental information
- Assimilate and interpret data for the commanders

The following resources that can be brought to bear on the user's planning problems:

- Robust support for distributed collaborative planning

- A hypermedia web of environmental products and crisis management procedures
- Environmental METOC decision aids
- Legacy tools from earlier METOC systems

METOC ANCHOR DESK INPUTS AND OUTPUTS

Typical inputs to the METOC Anchor Desk could include any kind of request for environmental support or tailored meteorological products during any phase of a crisis, from situation development through execution. For example, during situation development, the METOC Anchor Desk may be asked to develop an environmental profile of the situation area, including climatological analysis. Situation analysis can be based on historical data, current satellite photographs, wind strength and direction, wave heights, cloud cover, barometric readings, and so on. The result of the analysis is provided in the form of a forecast of various weather conditions. Such information is useful during the course of action development, evaluation, and execution planning because the provisioning of personnel and the preparation of equipment are directly influenced by the weather considerations.

As another example, the METOC Anchor Desk may be asked to respond rapidly to emergent situations, such as providing quick turnaround surf forecasts for a previously unplanned amphibious landing. The anchor desk may also be asked to put up a classified Web server with environmental products tailored to the operation, thereby providing on-demand access to relevant environmental information.

Currently, requests for support can occur in either of two forms, as follows:

1. Person to person, either in person, by telephone, by video conference, by collaborative planning tools, or through some combination of the above
2. Via the World Wide Web (WWW), either through the use of forms or routine access to environmental product Web pages

TOOLS FOR COLLABORATION AND COMMUNICATION

Anchor desks are intended to enhance, not replace, person-to-person communication. The METOC Anchor Desk System's video-conferencing and collaboration tools permit people who are geographically remote from one another to collaborate about a common task. High-bandwidth networks permit the transmission of live video and audio.

While video conferencing includes video and audio communication, much more than that is required for true collaboration. Visual imagery and hypermedia provide much higher communication bandwidth and cognition than linear text alone. To collaborate remotely with the same effectiveness as one would in the same room, users simultaneously share documents, maps, and diagrams and write on them and modify them in real time in a manner such that all the participants can see the results. For the METOC Anchor Desk System, the shared whiteboard gives all the participants in the conference the ability to do the following with each of the participants seeing the same whiteboard image on a local screen:

- Load a graphic image (maps, satellite image, or forecasts) from a separate file such as a GIF or TIFF format image
- Point to items of interest (with a unique cursor for each participant)
- Draw on the image using MacDraw or similar drawing programs
- Switch whiteboard pages
- Scan and digitize a paper image for display

A screen showing several windows of a video conference session is shown in Figure 18.4. In the foreground are two participants in the collaboration and in the background is a weather depiction on a shared whiteboard.

In addition, a file transfer tool (to send text or binary files from one participant to another), a screen capture tool (to capture a user-designated area of the screen), and a "chat" tool (for participants to type messages to each other in the event that the audio fails) are provided. One of the most effective independent tools is called Shared-X. This tool works in workstation environments supporting the X-Windowing System. It gives a participant in a conference the ability to delegate to a remote participant control of a local computer process. This is particularly useful when the remote participant may be more knowledgeable about a product or problem than the local participant.

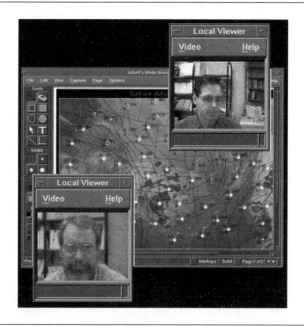

FIGURE 18.4   A METOC video conference.

HYPERTEXT APPLICATION

The second type of interaction mode is person-to-hypertext over the WWW. The Web is used by the METOC Anchor Desk System to do the following:

- Store daily weather products such as specialized weather depictions, forecasts, and satellite images
- Help train people in standard operating procedures
- Help organize the weather products of the different service components associated with a crisis task force
- Download images from the Web that can be cut and pasted into computer presentation tools, such as PowerPoint
- Enter data so that observations from the field can be made available immediately by hypertext

METOC ANCHOR DESK SCENARIO

This section describes one of the METOC Anchor Desk scenarios that has been used in actual practice. This scenario will serve to make the concepts more concrete and will guide the discussion of the architecture and design of the METOC Anchor Desk System in later sections. We describe the situation and how the system might be used to respond.

A hurricane is approaching the Hawaiian Islands. In accordance with military procedures, there are sets of activities that occur when an extreme weather event is expected. During the normal course of events, there may be from 6 to 30 briefings of the commanding authority for each service. The weather officers of each service are all concerned with different aspects of the weather and can provide different insights. Normally, the senior weather officers of each service will collaborate before and after each briefing to their commanders, and these collaborations are done through the auspices of the METOC Anchor Desk.

During a collaboration, the following and other products available on the Web, might be called up for viewing at any time:

- East Pacific satellite image
- Close-up satellite image of the hurricane
- National Weather Service buoy data
- Latest U.S. Air Force reconnaissance plane reports
- Thirty-six-hour forecast
- PowerPoint slides of briefings by each service to their commanders

Not only are these products available to the METOC officers, but they are also available for retrieval directly by staff of the commander. In-place service personnel can, through video conferencing and a shared whiteboard, discuss their interpretations of the weather data and their probabilities. Computer forecast models can be run and their results shared immediately.

18.3 Architectural Approach

The METOC Anchor Desk project made extensive use of three different emerging technologies. It uses the WWW (described as its own case study in Chapter 7), Common Object Request Broker Architecture, or CORBA (also described as a separate case study in Chapter 8), and collaboration systems.

The architecture of the METOC Anchor Desk System is not novel. In fact, that was one of its strengths; it created almost nothing from scratch. So, to truly understand the architectural solution, we must first understand the method that led to it: the Evolutionary Development Method. One of the principle tenets of this method is that architectures should be created through assembly of tailorable large-grained hardware and software components.

The code that was written for the system included Web authoring code (and scripts to generate it), high-level scripts, adaptation code (to modify components to suit its purposes), and conventional software (to provide weather objects to other servers). The system software components that were assembled were designed to work together on a variety of different computers.

The key architectural drivers behind the METOC project and the solutions adopted are shown in Table 18.1.

EVOLUTIONARY DEVELOPMENT METHOD

Evolutionary Development is applicable to development environments in which there is an authoritative and clearly defined user community where direct interaction with developers is possible. For reasons we shall see, it would not be effective in environments where there are users shielded from developers by layers of bureaucracy or in the development of shrink-wrapped systems where the user community is large and amorphous. The five paragraphs that follow describe the basic principles of Evolutionary Development.

Requirements and System Evolution Through Scenarios. Effective communication requires shared experience and shared vocabulary. Once an initial

TABLE 18.1 How the METOC Anchor Desk System Achieves Its Quality Goals

Goal	How Achieved
Short time to initial demonstrable capability	Heavy use of off-the-shelf components
Developer productivity	Only writing tailoring/glue code
Interchangeable parts and interoperability	Loose coupling through use of CORBA and WWW/HTML
Portability	Use of portable commercial products and emulators

shared vocabulary has been developed, developers and users can begin to communicate about the problem to be solved and the technological options available. First, the user describes a scenario in terms of the current solution and begins to appreciate the possibilities of the new technology. Much later, and after some hands-on experience with story boards and prototypes, the user is able to articulate that scenario in terms of a new technology. Then the discussions broaden so that when the technology is described, the user may reflect on new ways that the technology can be employed in the context of any number of user situations. The system evolves along with the scenarios. As the system is incrementally developed, the scenarios become more detailed. Mistakes in the scenarios and in the system are found at the earliest possible time.

Continuous End-User Involvement with Continuous Recalibration.   One of the biggest problems in the development of large systems is that the system requirements are defined once at the beginning, and without consulting the users again or revisiting the requirements, the developers take a long time to build the system. Two things inevitably happen. First the user's needs change over time. Second, the user's perceived needs as originally expressed turn out not to be the real needs in the context of new technology when the system is delivered. The job of systems builders is to accommodate those factors in a meaningful way. Unfortunately, user involvement is often defined in terms of more frequent and more intense design reviews with customer representatives who are not actual users.

Evolutionary Development facilitates effective user involvement, including hands-on experience with a real product or prototype. By getting frequent user feedback on products or prototypes, change is accommodated by accepting the need for rework and minimizing its effect. When an errant path is pursued, or when a user need changes, it is immediately obvious to the developer and the cost of the change is minimized. The advantage of the user-centered approach is that there is no requirement to specify every detail before moving on to the next stage of implementation. Instead, we use feedback from one iteration to feed the directions for the next iteration. This continuous recalibration minimizes the effect of the many mistakes that are *inevitable* in trying to specify the requirements of a system.

Architectures Based on Assembly and Integration.   Object technology and client-server architectures are on the verge of making prototyping and reuse work for real systems by providing an architectural infrastructure into which separately developed components can be plugged. The individual pieces of technology need to know less and less about one another to work together.

Sensible and Manageable Documentation.   The cost driver of large systems is often its documentation. Various standards required by government organizations require voluminous documentation on all phases of a multiphase development. (A possibly apocryphal story holds that the newest U.S. Air Force cargo plane is incapable of carrying all of the documentation produced during its development.)

Not only is this documentation expensive to produce in the first place, but it is even more expensive to maintain: A small user enhancement or change in operating environment can cause a ripple of changes through requirements, design, testing, maintenance, and training documentation.

The evolutionary approach reduces the initial documentation requirements and obviates much of the need to change the documentation because the inevitable blind alleys are followed to less depth. No detailed requirements document is written because the evolving system best defines the detailed requirements. In its place is a document that covers the concept of operations and scenarios of usage to set the scope of the work. Architecture, design, and training documents are still required. Test documentation is simplified because it is done incrementally with each delivery rather than trying to plan the testing for the entire system before the system is known. The user scenarios, when complete, can be the basis for much of the requirements, testing, maintenance, and training documentation.

Rework.   Evolutionary Development is a powerful method to solve the problems it attacks but it is not a panacea. Rework is an important element of Evolutionary Development. Every iteration results in refined requirements and corrections to components that embody incorrect assumptions. This holds for the documentation as well as for the system itself. The key to making the process effective is to only go into depth on portions that are agreed on. This not only results in avoiding time going down blind alleys but also reduces the rework involved in tuning the portions of the system that are going to be completed in depth. Assumptions about the underlying infrastructure are revisited during every iteration. For portions of the infrastructure that are themselves going quickly through the ABC, rework needs to be done to accommodate new releases. We will see in a subsequent section how new releases of the WWW software required accommodations in the METOC Anchor Desk System.

18.4   Architectural Solution

This section describes the METOC architecture. Like all architectures, it was a response to specific quality requirements, which we begin by describing.

KEY ARCHITECTURAL DRIVERS

The architectural drivers of the system are derived from the goals of both the customer and the user. We identify the following in order of importance to the developers. Some of the drivers are hard requirements, as indicated by (H) in the list, that were levied by the customer for business reasons.

- Short time to initial demonstrable capability (H)
- Evolvability

- User productivity (H)
- Developer productivity
- Platform heterogeneity
- Interchangeable parts (hardware and software)
- Geographical distribution (H)
- Interoperability, with legacy tools, decision aids, and other anchor desks (H)

Short time to initial demonstrable capability is fundamental to the Evolutionary Development concept. Prototypes must be put in the hands of users to help define the requirements and to establish a working relationship between the user and the developer. We link short time to initial demonstrable capability with initial operational capability and evolvability. Initial operational capability is limited in its functionality by design.

A second driver is productivity on the part of the developer. A small team was attempting to provide a great deal of capability to the users. In any user-centered development, it is necessary to keep the user engaged by providing a stream of capability increments based on feedback from demonstrations. There was not time for long analysis–design–implement–test–demonstrate cycles. Unless they could show that they could produce something useful quickly and unless they could continue to produce increments quickly, the developers would have lost the attention and commitment of the user.

Platform heterogeneity was a driving factor because of legacy systems. There are three kinds of machines in the user environment: UNIX workstations, Macintoshes, and PCs. The architecture had to accommodate this mix of computing equipment either by making software run on all three or by emulating one machine on another. It would have been unrealistic to assume that the user community would adopt a single platform.

The need for interchangeable parts is closely coupled to the evolvability driver. Tight coupling of components makes a system rigid and inflexible. Loose coupling makes a system changeable and flexible. Adding functionality to system components or improving performance of system components without changing the architecture was a goal. Less important was maintainability. Because the system was built primarily from off-the-shelf components, there was little that was maintainable by the development team. Rather, the component parts would be maintained and upgraded by the original developers of those parts.

Geographical distribution of the users drove the architecture as well. The Pacific theater of operations covers a large portion of the world and users may be in every section of that theater and in other theaters around the globe.

Finally, interoperability was a driving factor. The METOC Anchor Desk System must interoperate with legacy tools, decision aids, and other anchor desks. With regard to legacy tools, weather reporting and forecasting capabilities have been developed over many years, mostly on mainframe computers. The METOC Anchor Desk System uses these legacy tools. The decision aids and other anchor desks, on the other hand, are relatively new.

It is also instructive to list some of the notable nondrivers of the architecture. In particular, there was little consideration given to most of the typical runtime drivers of performance, reliability, safety, security, correctness, availability, or resource constraints. The reason that these were not architectural drivers was not because they were considered unimportant but because they were not under direct control of the developer. These runtime factors are largely dependent on the platform dependent components used to construct the system. For example, the safety, security, and correctness of the video-conferencing software is critical to the safety, security, and correctness of the overall system.

Certainly, the platform dependent components must be selected so as to make the system viable, but they are not drivers of the architecture. The interchangeable parts driver ensures that the system is not burdened with unacceptable components. Many times during the development, changes were made from one hardware component to another or from one software component to another to improve the system relative to one or more of these nondriving influences.

ARCHITECTURAL COMPONENTS

The small size of the development group and the need for delivering early initial capability dictated assembling the system from already-available components. In some cases this meant buying commercial software and in other cases using public domain software or shareware. The major categories of components were the following:

- Computers—UNIX workstations and PCs, including laptops
- Networks
- Video-conferencing software
- Emulators
- Web browsers
- Collaboration software
- Utility software

Computing resources included workstations and personal computers. Both categories are in widespread use in the METOC community and are accommodated in the system architecture. The workstations are all UNIX compatible machines and are primarily Sun Sparcs and Hewlett Packard TAC-3s. The PCs are both Macintoshes and IBM compatibles. Specialized hardware boards may be required on the computers to capture video images from a camera and display them on the screen.

The *network structure* is a four-tiered structure that is illustrated in Figure 18.5. At the weather center there is a 10-Mbit/second local area network (LAN). This is connected by a fiber-optic bridge to another 10-Mbit/second Operations Support System LAN for local use in Pearl Harbor. These LANs are connected to

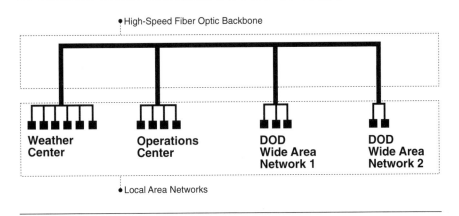

FIGURE 18.5   METOC network architecture.

preexisting Department of Defense wide area networks by T1 (1.54-Mbit/second) satellite links.The network architecture must not only provide the necessary connectivity, but there must also be enough bandwidth to carry out the communication and collaboration functions.

The *video-conferencing software* permits geographically distributed operators to carry on an audio/video conference and to collaborate over graphic and textual data.

Emulators are programs that run on UNIX machines to simulate Macintosh and PCs. Emulators, among other things, allow a UNIX computer to read and write Mac or PC disks.

Web-browser software permits users to easily access linked information on networks of computers. The browser presents information that contains links to other pages on different systems that can be invoked with a mouse click. These browsers support a wide variety of graphics formats and also permit the invocation of local computing resources, such as viewers and audio playback utilities.

Collaboration software is special-purpose software that allows two or more users to collaborate over an application.

Utility software is a catchall that includes a variety of functions—graphics scanning, graphics conversion, audio and video recording, fax software, and so on.

DESIGN OF THE METOC ANCHOR DESK SYSTEM

The overall structure of the METOC Anchor Desk organization is shown in Figure 18.6. This figure illustrates three major components, the major participants and suppliers (identified in the rectangular boxes), and the planning cells (shown in the circles). It illustrates the distributed, interconnected nature of the architecture, which is motivated by the need for the system to be geographically distributed.

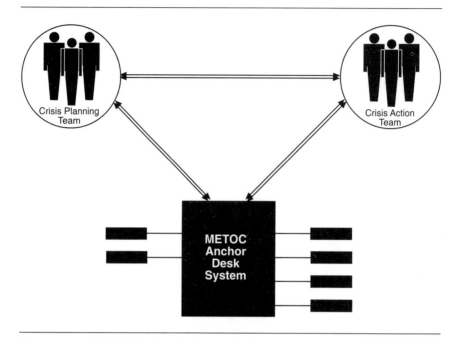

FIGURE 18.6   METOC Anchor Desk organization.

The key design decision of the METOC Anchor Desk System is not to disturb the legacy organization and the legacy systems that are in place and work well. The idea is to enhance, not to replace. From this decision come the derived requirements that address the specific computers and tools, how they are tied together into a global network, how the information space is structured, and how applications are distributed.

The design is concerned with the integration of the architectural components described in the previous section. Most of the integration is achieved by loose coupling. The integration among video-conferencing software, Web browsers, emulators, collaboration software, and utility software is primarily through UNIX files.

For integration among other tools in the project, an object request broker (ORB) approach is taken. To be effective, the system had to interface both with newly developed tactical decision aids and with legacy METOC applications. ORB interfaces were developed by other project teams for capabilities such as map and data servers. It was important not to have to reinvent component parts to provide capabilities. This design characteristic served the following architectural drivers: short time to initial demonstrable capability, developer productivity, interchangeable parts, and interoperability.

As a consequence of this design decision, there was little code that had to be written. Scripts were written for utility operations, and adaptations were made so that software could run on a variety of hardware. Decision aids were written to be compliant to ORB-based standards.

The idealized version of the METOC architecture is shown in Figure 18.7. Here we use the orchestra metaphor, suggesting a loose connection between the conductors (director and choreographer) providing direction and the orchestra (gathering, serving, and analysis objects) performing according to the direction. This can also be thought of as a client-server architecture but with more insulation and flexibility between the client and server. In Figure 18.7 the clients are illustrated on the top and the servers on the bottom. The ORB is the substrate or mechanism used for interfacing the client and server. The services listed include storage and retrieval of the raw environmental data, data gathering, data analysis, data visualization, and mapping. We distinguish between conductor- and orchestra-level roles in describing this architecture.

One conductor-level role is the director. The director presents end users with a palette of available decision aids (tools) and permits selection from the palette. It maintains a registry of tools that form the universe from which palettes can be chosen for each user. Finally, it allows new tools to register themselves at runtime. New tools can then be made available to end users without recompilation.

Another conductor-level role is the choreographer. This role insulates the director from knowledge of elements at the orchestra level. Each of the choreographers has knowledge of one subset of the orchestra-level objects that are required to service one particular tool. By providing this level of indirection, the runtime extensibility of the director is enhanced and the localization of knowledge (to the choreographers) reduces complexity.

At the orchestra level, the data server provides direct access to environmental data. It insulates data-gathering objects from knowledge of underlying database management systems. The data gatherer knows how to gather and filter specific kinds of environmental data for a particular tool or class of tools. The

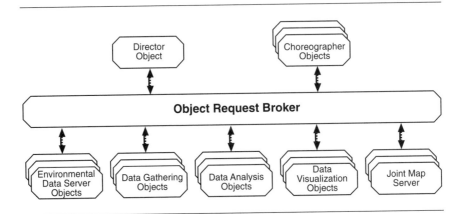

FIGURE 18.7   METOC Anchor Desk System architecture.

data analysis service acts on gathered and filtered data to produce some analytical output for downstream processing. The visualizer renders the result of data gathering and analysis. Several visualizers may operate on the same data to produce alternative visualizations. The map server is utilized by some of the visualization objects to render the weather over a map. This map may show geopolitical boundaries, topographical features, or landmarks such as roads and airports.

In this architecture, a new tool may be introduced quite simply by adding a new choreographer object and, if required, new services such as an analysis or a visualization. This produces a great deal of flexibility and supports the short time to market and developer productivity drivers.

Another characteristic of the design was the choice of both commercial off-the-shelf products and public domain products that operated across many different platforms. In many cases more than one product would be necessary for a single function. The architectural driver in this case was the multiplatform requirement. For example, an early decision was made to use a commercial product, Communique, for video conferencing. This decision was made, in part, because Communique was supported on UNIX workstations and PCs. An alternative public domain product was only available on Sun systems. After the public domain product was adapted for HP machines, it became an alternate choice for implementing video conferencing for better integration with other project products. Netscape replaced Mosaic as the Web browser during the development due to its greater functionality.

RESULTING IMPLEMENTATION

The resulting implementation of the METOC Anchor Desk System is shown in Figure 18.8. In this version of the system, software runs on HP machines, a Sun, a desktop PC, and a portable PC. All the machines are running video-conferencing software, Web browsers, and frame grabbers. The HPs and Suns run collaboration software. Where required, these machines run Mac and PC emulators and decision aid tools.

The implementation started by using a commercial video-conferencing product to demonstrate the concepts and gather performance data but later switched to public domain software for compatibility with other projects in the program. The shareware did not work on HP platforms and had a limited shared whiteboard capability. The developers made source code changes to make the video-conferencing software run on the HPs and improved the whiteboard.

The Theater-Level Analysis, Replanning and Graphical Execution Toolbox (TARGET) is an integrated set of planning tools for supporting joint operations. It is designed to support distributed collaborative planning. One of the functions provided to TARGET by the METOC Collaboration System is the ability to place weather information in TARGET folders. To accomplish this, the developers wrote scripts in Tcl/Tk to automatically grab a screen window as a GIF image and then to ship it off to TARGET.

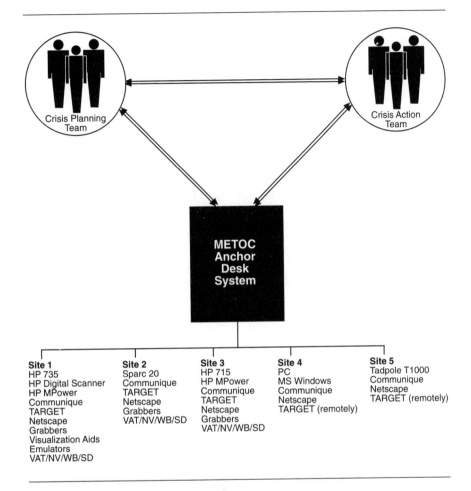

FIGURE 18.8   A METOC implementation.

The METOC Anchor Desk System permits collaboration using legacy tools as illustrated in Figure 18.9. From an appropriately equipped terminal it is possible to view and operate on a variety of objects that previously required three computers. In the METOC system, these operations can take place in separate windows on the same machine by using public domain and commercially available emulators.

In addition, many legacy systems use Macintoshes and PCs. Macs are used mostly for presentations, while PCs are used for various decision aids, general data processing, and file transfer. MacCIDSS and PowerPoint are examples of two of the Mac applications, and Optimal Track Ship Routing and Enroute Weather Forecast are two of the PC applications. With Mac and PC emulators on the same machine as the video-conferencing tools, it becomes easy to do analysis

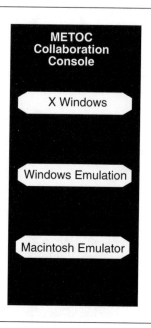

FIGURE 18.9   Tools for collaboration.

and then paste the results onto a whiteboard and share it with the conference. Conversely, when someone else shares a result, it is possible to grab it from the whiteboard and paste it into a PowerPoint presentation.

Figure 18.10 illustrates the kind of data that is available from the World Wide Web and the parties that access and supply that data. Two important decisions about using the Web are what information is to be stored and how it is to be presented. The structure of the information in the Web remains relatively constant from day to day, but the data is perishable and changes by the minute.

Considerable effort was spent designing and writing dozens of Web pages using HyperText Markup Language (HTML). Tcl/Tk scripts automate the moving of data from an "incoming" area on disk to the Web pages so that creating a new set of data in the Web is a simple one-line operation for a METOC user. This ease of use is central to getting the user to welcome the adoption of the new technology.

One of the collateral uses of the Web is as a repository for METOC procedures. The METOC operations floor is a beehive of activity 24 hours a day. There are satellite images arriving, forecasts being written, advisories being sent out by fax, etc. Hundreds of operating procedures appear in notebooks taking several feet of shelf space. Many of these procedures can better be represented in Web pages. Each step in a procedure may have links to more detailed instructions, illustrations, audio and video clips, and even to tools to be used when performing the step.

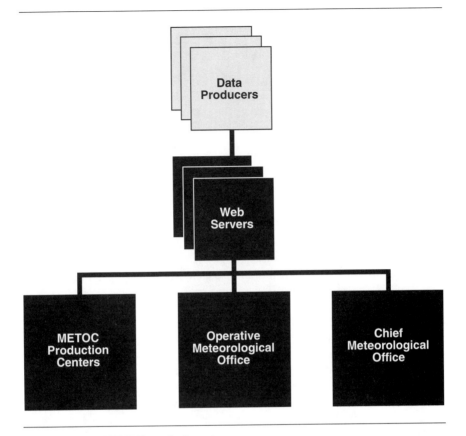

FIGURE 18.10 METOC products web.

As an example of a collaborative decision-aiding application that can run using the METOC Anchor Desk System, the developers implemented a weather specialist that plugs into a legacy map server. This weather specialist overlays pressure, wind, precipitation, cloud cover, and temperature on a given geographical area displayed by the map server.

The map server has several subservers (specialists) that it communicates with to draw maps. The map server uses a C++ Specialist class that was specialized to handle weather displays. CORBA allows the weather specialist object to register the weather specialist with the ORB. The specialist then waits for client requests. When the map server gets a request to show weather, it asks the ORB for a weather specialist object. Then it asks for the needed information from the object and displays it.

Thus, weather functionality was added to a weather-ignorant map server; the weather software needed no map-specific details other than coordinates. Furthermore, the map server did not have to know anything about weather and only provided

TABLE 18.2 Lines of Source Code Written for the METOC Anchor Desk System

Weather Specialist	C++	3000
GrabWindow script	Tcl	25
GrabWindow script	C	350
SendImageToTarget script	Expect	92
SendImageToTarget script	C	50
METOC Product Web	HTML	1215
METOC Product Web	Tcl	403
METOC Procedures Web	HTML	10014
METOC Developers Web	HTML	5154
Total lines of code		20303

an interface written in CORBA's Interface Description Language. This loose coupling of the implementation components through the use of object technology facilitated the implementation in terms of the productivity and interoperability drivers.

Table 18.2 gives the approximate number of lines of source code that were written by the developers, as opposed to represented in an off-the-shelf product, and the language used. Note the large number of languages and the small number of lines of code. There are five languages represented—hypertext, scripting, and general-purpose languages—and each is chosen for a specific task. The figures for HTML are not good indicators of effort since many of the lines in those instances are data giving textual information and are copied from other sources. Not represented in this table is any effort involved with creating graphic images.

Another item of note is the knowledge and background required to produce the code. C, C++, and Tcl were written by software engineers. HTML was written by graphic designers who were either undergraduates or recent graduates. Thus, the bulk of the code was written using preexisting text or with relatively inexperienced personnel. On the other hand, the creation of graphical images is not enumerated in the table, and this requires a type of skill not usually found in software engineers.

18.5 Summary

In Chapter 8 we saw object request brokers from the point of view of the developers of the ORBs. In this chapter we have described a system constructed on top of an ORB from the perspective of a user of the ORB technology. This case study provides evidence that many of the claims of Chapter 15 and Chapter 17 about the ability to integrate legacy systems and incorporate systems on diverse platforms are achievable in practice.

In Chapter 13 we presented architecture as the foundation for component-based system development. The architecture forms a skeleton into which separate but cooperating components are plugged. This case study provides evidence that component-based development using off-the-shelf pieces can succeed, be economical, and still satisfy the system's requirements.

Finally, Chapter 7 presented the World Wide Web and a unique set of motivating requirements that led to its design. This case study illustrates how those features of the Web were put to use as the backbone of a widely distributed decision-making system. When the project began in 1993, Web technology was still relatively immature. However, it was the best available to meet the project goals, so the developers earnestly adopted it and began the process of making that technology suit an operational military context. This involved designing and deploying mission-critical Web pages of environmental information. This work continues today because the Web pages are constantly evolving to meet new needs and deliver new functionality.

Since 1992, Web technology has changed significantly. Some of these changes affected the appearance of Web pages that the METOC developers designed. For example, the advent of tables in Netscape significantly improved the ability to present tabular information. Prior to tables, a complex scheme of transparent in-line GIF images was used to attain modest control over horizontal and vertical white space. Tables provide a much more robust and flexible palette from which to design and implement. Initially, the developers adapted earlier pages to use simple tables. As understanding of tables grew, they dealt with new issues of page layout and implementation that had not existed previously.

Adaptation, experimentation, demonstration, and evolution are recurring themes in this project, and all are made possible by the robust architecture and the loose coupling among the components that it provides.

18.6 Discussion Questions

1. How dependent is the Evolutionary Development method on the existence of technologies such as CORBA and the WWW? Could it exist in the absence of such technologies? Or, more generally, what are the ramifications of the technical environment on the ways in which the ABC is realized?

2. In Chapter 13, we discussed building domain-specific languages as an approach to architecture-based development. How does this approach and the Evolutionary Development method relate to each other?

3. What architectural styles do you recognize in the METOC architecture?

19

Software Architecture
in the Future

I know no way of judging of the future but by the past.
— Patrick Henry

You can never plan the future by the past.
— Edmund Burke

The history of programming can be viewed as a succession of ever-increasing facilities for expressing complex functionality. In the beginning, assembly language offered the most elementary of abstractions: exactly where in physical memory things resided (realitive to the address in some base register) and the machine code necessary to perform primitive arithmetic and move operations. Even programs rendered in this primitive environment exhibited architectures: Components were blocks of code connected by physical proximity to one another or knitted together by branching statements or perhaps subroutines whose connectors were of the branch-and-return construction. Early programming languages institutionalized these constructs; connectors were the semicolon, the Go To statement, and the parameterized function call. The 1960s were the decade of the subroutine.

The 1970s saw a concern with the structuring of programs to achieve qualities beyond correct function. Data-flow analysis, entity-relation diagrams, information-hiding, and other principles or techniques formed the bases of myriad design methodologies, each of which led to the creation of subroutines or collections of subroutines whose functionality could be rationalized in terms of developmental qualities. These components were usually called modules. The connectors remained the same, but some module-based programming languages became available to enhance the programmer's ability to create these things. Abstractions embedded in these components became more sophisticated and substantial, and for the first time reusable components were packaged in a way that their inner workings could theoretically be ignored. The 1970s were the decade of the module.

In the 80s, module-based programming languages, information-hiding, and associated methodologies crystallized into the concept of objects. Objects are now the components du jour, with inheritance adding a new kind of (nonruntime) connector. And now standard object-based architectures, in the form of frameworks, are appearing on the scene. Objects have given us a standard vocabulary for components and have led to new infrastructures—such as Common Object Request Broker Architecture, or CORBA—for wiring collections of them together. Abstractions have grown more powerful along the way; we now have computing platforms in our homes that let us treat complex entities such as spreadsheet, document, graphical image, audio clip, and database as interchangeable black-box objects that can be inserted blithely into instances of each other.

Architecture places the emphasis above individual components and concentrates on the arrangement of the components and their interaction, and it is this kind of abstraction, away from the individual components, that makes such breath-taking interoperability possible.

This, then, is where we are today. There is no reason to think that the trend to larger and more powerful abstractions won't continue. Already there are early *generators* for systems as complex and demanding as database management and avionics, and a generator for a domain is the first sign that the spiral of programming language power for that domain is about to start another upward cycle. *Systems of systems* is another phrase that is starting to appear more commonly, suggesting emphasis on system interoperability and signaling another jump in abstraction power.

In this chapter, we will revisit the topics covered in the book. Heeding Patrick Henry, we will try to extrapolate this into a vision of architecture in the future. Heeding Edmund Burke, our vision will be not so much predictive as much as hopeful: We will examine areas of software architecture where things are not as we would wish and point out areas where the research community has some work to do.

We'll begin by recapping what we learned about the architecture business cycle (ABC).

19.1   The Architecture Business Cycle Revisited

In Chapter 1, we introduced the ABC as the unifying theme of the book. We have been exemplifying and elaborating this cycle throughout this book and have tried to convey some of the principles of architectural creation, representation, evaluation, and development along the way. We have also emphasized that although the roots of software architecture as a research area are deep, the field itself is relatively new and immature. If the field is to have stamina, there must be areas of research that create a more mature field, with results that can be transitioned into practice.

Now we are prepared to discuss different kinds of ABCs, as follows:

- The original one, in which a single organization creates a single architecture for a single system
- One in which a business creates not just a single system from an architecture but an entire product line of systems that are related because they share a common architecture and a common asset base
- One in which, through a communitywide effort, a standard architecture or reference model is created from which large numbers of systems flow
- One in which the architecture becomes so pervasive that the developing organization effectively becomes the world, as in the case of the World Wide Web (WWW)

Each of these ABCs contains the same elements as the original: customers, developers, a technical environment, an existing experience base, a set of requirements to be achieved, an architect or architects, an architecture or architectures, and a system or systems. Different versions of the ABC result from the business environment, the size of the market, and the goals being pursued.

In the future, we believe that software cost models will exist that will incorporate all these versions of the ABC. In particular, models will take into account the upfront cost that architecture-based development, especially product line development, usually entails. And they will also be able to predict the quantitative benefits that architectures yield.

19.2 Architecture and Legacy Systems

Dealing with existing, or legacy, systems is problematic. Existing systems run the gamut from well designed and documented to poorly designed and undocumented. The original architects and developers may no longer be employees of the organization. As a consequence, the development of techniques to determine (in many cases to *rediscover*) the architecture of such systems is the first critical research area we identify.

The architectural problem in legacy systems involves making intelligent changes to a system in which an organization has a large investment. This problem has several subparts: determining the existing architecture of a legacy system, determining the goal state of a reengineered architecture, and developing a strategy to migrate the system to this new architecture, presumably one better suited to a new environment. This migration might be through reengineering of parts of the system, wrapping of existing parts to work within a new infrastructure, or completely replacing the existing system. We now elaborate on these areas.

ARCHITECTURE ARCHAEOLOGY AND CONFORMANCE

There are three problems that motivate the need for architectural archaeology; they are as follows:

1. Many systems have no documented architecture at all. (*All* systems have an architecture, but frequently it is not explicitly known or recorded by the developers but evolves in an ad hoc fashion.)

2. In systems that have some architectural documentation, the architecture is represented in such a way that the relationship between the documentation and the actual system, particularly its source code, is unclear.

3. In systems that *do* have properly documented architectures, the architectural representations are frequently out of phase with the actual system due to maintenance of the system without a similar effort to maintain the architectural representation.

Because of these issues, we have a serious problem in assessing architectural conformance, and if we cannot assess architectural conformance, what good is having an architecture? How do we know that what was designed is what was built?

In addition, when a system enters the maintenance portion of its life cycle, it may sustain modifications that alter its architecture. Hence, a second problem arises: How do we know that maintenance operations are not eroding the architecture, breaking down abstractions, bridging layers, compromising information hiding, and so forth?

These problems have two underlying causes. The first is that a system has many runtime relationships, its data flows, its control flows, its code structure, and so on. All must be maintained. The second and more serious problem is that the architecture represented in a system's documentation may not coincide with *any* of these structures. It frequently describes some ad hoc combination of runtime structures.

Representative of solutions to the reconstruction problem currently being pursued is a tool called *Dali*. Developed at the Software Engineering Institute, Dali is an open workbench for architectural extraction and conformance. The approach with Dali is to make the reconstruction of an architecture an iterative, interpretive process that relies on the knowledge and skills of someone who is at least somewhat familiar with the system being studied. In Dali we can quickly move from the "white noise" of information that is an extracted source model to an architectural representation, as shown in Figure 19.1. Along the path from source artifacts to architecture we are alerted to places where the as-built architecture diverges from what was designed.

ARCHITECTURAL REENGINEERING

Once the existing architecture of a system is known, either through existing documentation, human archaeology, tool-assisted means, or a combination of these, a designer can contemplate if and how the architecture should evolve: what new

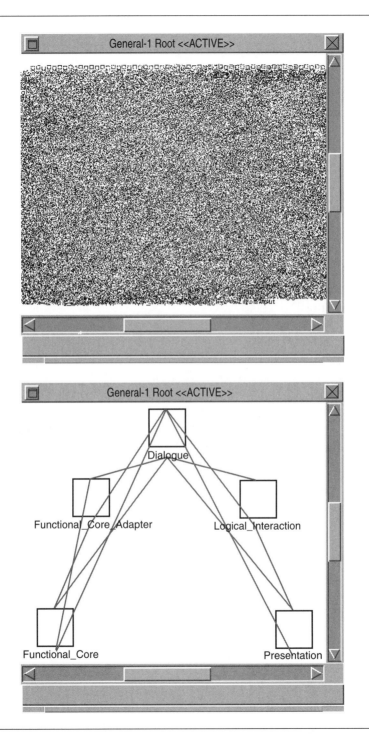

FIGURE 19.1 Two views of the same system: extracted source code artifacts and the architecture.

technologies it should incorporate, what new style or styles it should be organized around, what new patterns it might encompass, and how regular the architecture is.

Architectures must incorporate new technologies or be relegated to technological backwaters. Enormous numbers of products are currently becoming Web
aware, CORBA compliant, distributed, or internationalized. For the incorporation
of new technologies, an architect is wise to consider the availability of off-the-shelf
software, the existence of standards, and the number and stability of vendors building those technologies. If an architecture's complexity is not *continually* managed
and tamed, it will become an impediment to future enhancements.

For the incorporation of new styles or patterns, the architect must be aware
of existing styles and patterns, their uses, their benefits and drawbacks, and their
interactions. An architecture's complexity can also be managed by making it
more regular, reducing its pattern-based complexity. Thus, for regularization of
an architecture, an architect must have the means to automatically find areas of
structural similarity within the architecture. These areas are then the likely targets
for reengineering.

ARCHITECTURE MIGRATION TECHNOLOGY

Given an architecture and a set of proposed changes, there will be changes that it
was designed to support and changes that are outside its scope. For the out-of-scope
changes, technology is needed that will provide disciplined ways to migrate an
architecture. Not only must a target architecture, which will meet anticipated requirements, be defined but a migration strategy to this architecture must be created.

On one level, this may require a business reorganization so that technical
foci are matched with organizational changes. For example, if a product is to
have a WWW interface added, there may be a need to have a corporate Web
group that specializes in this technology rather than allocating part of the integration task to each developer.

An understanding about closeness of fit is also needed to handle the case
where components are almost, but not quite, compatible with each other, and
strategies, such as those we outlined in Chapter 15, for handling component mismatch must be promoted and standardized.

19.3   Achieving an Architecture

Every one of this book's case studies focused on achieving particular quality
attributes. The particular qualities were different for the various case studies, but
each system began with an explicit recognition on the part of the architect of the
qualities they were attempting to achieve. Qualities do not arise, unbidden, from
an architecture; they must be planned for.

Achieving an architecture in a reliable, repeatable manner from a precise statement of the quality requirements is a key open research area. The problem has several components, which are as follows:

- Having meaningful and quantifiable definitions of the various qualities
- Creating or selecting an architecture based on a set of functional and quality requirements
- Understanding and measuring the trade-offs involved in any architectural decision

UNDERSTANDING QUALITY ATTRIBUTES

Current understanding of the meaning of quality in software is confused. As a start, we can define quality as *fitness for use* but, once we ask what that means, we have problems with many of the attributes. We discussed some of the problems with such terms as *modifiability* in our discussion of the software architecture analysis method (SAAM) in Chapter 9. The problem with understanding the meaning of a quality attribute is especially acute with respect to developmental qualities.

The fundamental problem with understanding developmental qualities is the lack of suitable models for discussing them. Performance is an example of a quality where mature analysis models already exist and where, as a consequence, early architectural performance evaluations are possible. Performance can be discussed, analyzed, and measured in terms of resource availability and resource consumption. Resource consumption can be characterized in terms of arrivals of resource requests. This is based on a model of the computer system as a collection of resources and connections among these resources. This abstract model is suitable for discussing any computer system, or network of systems.

Developing models that enable the discussion of developmental qualities in the abstract is an important open question. Static models, such as constructive cost modeling (COCOMO) or function point modeling, attempt to estimate development time, but these are based on measurements of external phenomena rather than on an abstract understanding of the development process.

Once qualities can be discussed in terms of an abstract model, systems can be analyzed to determine their quality attribute values. Techniques such as SAAM are based on evaluating an architecture based on its suitability at a specific set of points in the space of qualities and assuming that the architecture is similarly suitable in regions around those points. These points are represented by scenarios. SAAM is the best we can do in the absence of quantitative models for quality attributes such as modifiability.

Current research at the Software Engineering Institute is concentrating on defining abstract models for all quality attributes and on defining fulcrum points among these models. *Fulcrum points* are measurable properties of a system that affect two (or more) quality attributes. For example, the amount of jitter (variance of arrival times) along a communication path can obviously affect a system's performance, but it can also affect a system's security and its reliability. It can affect the system's security in that the smaller the jitter, the less time there is for an intruder to modify the contents of the communication undetected. Jitter can affect the system's reliability because if it is too great, the jitter becomes indistinguishable from a component failure. Thus, jitter is a fulcrum for these quality attributes. Identifying fulcrum points, and describing how to analyze software architectures with respect to them, is an exciting new area of research.

THE EFFECT OF PATTERNS ON SOFTWARE ARCHITECTURE

Being able to analyze and build a system with a regular set of building blocks aids human comprehension of complex systems and hence aids both development and maintenance. The regular set of building blocks represents common patterns of usage. Simply put, patterns allow humans to understand complex systems in larger conceptual chunks, thus reducing the cognitive burden.

Research on encouraging the use of patterns in software architecture is proceeding along two fronts: description and tool support. The description work is an area of intense activity in the object-oriented design patterns community. As for tool support, Figure 19.2 shows interactive architecture pattern recognition (IAPR), an experimental system for finding user-specified software patterns in an architecture. IAPR aids in architectural exploration and measurement by attempting to match architectural patterns to an architecture. As a diagnostic tool, IAPR provides a significant new architectural complexity metric for designing systems. A system can be measured according to its pattern coverage: the proportion of an architecture that can be covered by patterns and the number of patterns it takes to cover an architecture. These are complementary measures of the system's regularity and hence its architectural complexity.

CREATING OR SELECTING AN ARCHITECTURE

Technologies to support the creation or selection of an architecture for a system exist along a continuum, as shown in Figure 19.3. At one end are ad hoc techniques in which experienced, talented designers conjure up an architecture in a largely unrepeatable fashion. Farther up the spectrum lie reuse techniques, from previously used architectures to architectures populated with reusable components, to architectures populated with components that can be tailored and parameterized. Architectures based on frameworks, such as MacApp (a development environment for Macintosh application programs) or CORBA, lie in this region. They offer differing levels of plug-in-and-run completeness and application independence, but both provide their own architectural reference models and support those models with executable software components.

At the high end of the spectrum lie partial and pure application generators. An *application generator* is a program that incorporates knowledge about the relevant application domain and, given as its input a set of requirements for a particular

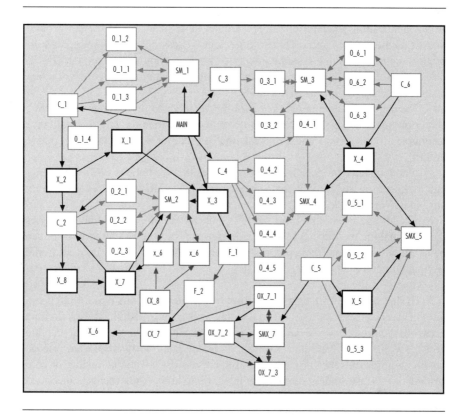

FIGURE 19.2   Software patterns automatically recognized by IAPR.

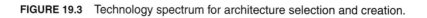

FIGURE 19.3   Technology spectrum for architecture selection and creation.

member of that domain, generates software that implements that domain member. A pure application generator produces a turnkey system and renders moot the question of architecture to the user of the generator. Less encompassing generators produce components that must be integrated into the eventual system; the UNIX-based parser generator YACC is an example, and the many fourth-generation languages centered on databases are another.

The major outstanding research areas in creating and selecting an architecture center on quantitative architectural evaluation (rather than the largely qualitative techniques, both formal and informal, that we use presently) and prescriptive design.

When we have models of quality attributes that we believe in, we can annotate architectural styles with their prototypical behavior with respect to quality attributes. We can talk about performance styles (such as priority-based preemptive scheduling) or modifiability styles (such as layering) or reliability styles (such as analytic redundancy) and then discuss the ways in which these styles can be composed and what their potential fulcrum points are. In this way, an initial architecture could be generated for a new system out of composed attribute-specific styles.

To support this effort, experience must be gained in building reusable architectures in particular style families. Central to this work is understanding the relationship between requirements and architecture; specifically, this means understanding how a system is "driven" into a certain architectural style family. What role do quality requirements, performance requirements, or organizational history or constraints play? Case studies can provide insight into how requirements and context interact with each other to produce an architecture.

As case studies are promulgated, the following results can be expected:

- *Agreement will emerge as to a taxonomy of systems' problem spaces.* A gross taxonomy exists today. Does a system have hard real-time deadlines or not? Is it required to be distributed or not? Is it acceptable if the system fails once a day or once a year? These and other coarse-grained discriminators that currently exist fundamentally affect the type of system fielded and will evolve to more sophisticated and fine-grained characterizations of the problem space in the future.

- *Agreement will emerge as to a taxonomy of systems' context space.* What are the organizational influences on architecture? What effect does the prior experience of senior designers have? In what direction is the marketplace moving? What are the emerging standards or "winning" technologies? As these and other influences emerge and are systematically captured, business case strategies can be built based on an organization's technical background, infrastructure, and capability.

- *Agreement will emerge as to a taxonomy of systems' solution spaces.* The work in architectural styles and solution viewpoints represents early promising work, as do taxonomies of coordination mechanisms. Work on finding, capturing, formalizing, and exploiting design patterns and on identifying supporting technology for pattern-based development also represents an important approach that is young but growing in importance.

In theory, case study work could result in the production of design guidebooks, like those found in other engineering disciplines and which seem to be emerging in the software engineering community; the flurry of activity in the design patterns community is one example of this.

The goal here is to produce systematic, reliable design guidance: assistance in asking appropriate architecture-determining questions about requirements and being directed to architectures or architectural decisions that plausibly solve the problem, including an understanding of the trade-offs incurred in any decision.

APPLICATION GENERATOR TECHNOLOGY

To produce a pure application generator for a domain, an alphabet of primitive components must be built to be combinable in flexible, arbitrary ways. Component identification, component composition, and mapping to a given physical architecture are the driving problems.

Component identification is currently ad hoc. The codification of this part of the process, by marrying domain analysis methods with architecture component identification, should produce a dramatic improvement in our ability to build generators for domains for which such a possibility was only recently unthinkable. For example, the existence of parser generators, optimization generators, program flow graph generators, and the like renders it unthinkable to build a compiler from scratch today. Similarly, it may soon be the case that nobody will ever build from scratch an avionics program, a database management system, a military command center, or a software engineering environment because of the existence of generators to produce application-standard components attached to an application-standard architectural framework. Certainly few people today think of building their own user-interface tool set or telecommunications software. Promising generator work includes the construction of generator generators, generators with user-level interfaces (including graphical specification languages), and generators that allow a declarative specification of the target computing environment.

19.4   From Architecture to System

Many of the case studies emphasized the reduction of the testing and integration phases of the life cycle as a result of the architecture that was developed. The CelsiusTech, Structural Modeling, and A-7E case studies all reported substantially reduced testing and integration time as a result of their architectural practices. Integration and interoperability are the main motivations for the WWW, the meteorological and oceanographic (METOC), and the CORBA case studies.

Once an architecture has been specified, there are still many open areas for research. We need proven, documented ways to both communicate the architecture and then to ensure that the system is developed in conformance with the architecture.

A system's architecture serves many stakeholders, and it must be communicated to each of them. For example, no matter how components and component configurations are chosen, that architectural choice becomes the foundation for the developing organization's work-breakdown structure, team assignments, unit test plans, integration test plans, project schedule, and maintenance and evolution plans. The architecture provides the medium for interteam cooperation and communication. It serves as the basis for early modeling, evaluation, and prediction of performance, schedulability, feasibility, and resource allocation.

Communicating an architecture to a stakeholder becomes a matter of representing it in an unambiguous, understandable form that contains the specific information appropriate to that stakeholder. While development of architecture definition languages (ADLs) is proceeding apace—there are at least two dozen languages capable of, if not developed explicitly for, representing architectural information; less attention is being paid to the areas described in the following sections.

INFRASTRUCTURES TO SUPPORT ADL DEVELOPMENT

Most ADLs share a set of common concepts. Building tools to support an ADL involves solving a common set of problems. Development of an ADL development environment would facilitate the rapid production of ADLs and supporting tools, thus allowing good ideas to come to market faster. This, however, requires broad community-based agreement on the functional decomposition of an ADL. The creation of such a decomposition is a communitywide domain engineering task.

INTEGRATION OF ADL INFORMATION WITH OTHER LIFE-CYCLE PRODUCTS

As ADLs mature, they will take a more prominent role in the litany of life-cycle products, such as detailed design documents, test cases, and so on. Encouragement should be given to early consideration of the relationship that an architecture description (and the tool to create it) will bring to bear on these other documents and the tools that produce and maintain them, including the following:

- What test cases might be generated for a system based on a description of its components and interconnection mechanisms?
- What kinds of executable code can be automatically generated?
- How can traceability of architecture to requirements be established?
- How can architectural patterns, like design patterns, be rapidly imported into the architecture?

This work could culminate in the complete integration of architecture descriptions into the development environment, giving rise to a sort of "architectorium." This can be thought of as an exploration environment in which architectures are drafted and validated via mapping to requirements, their implications explored via analysis or rapid prototyping, alternatives suggested in an expert-systemlike fashion, and project infrastructures necessary for development are generated.

PRACTICAL VERIFICATION STRATEGIES

A number of environments, such as ObjecTime (presented in Chapter 12), exist in which an architecture can be used to generate a simulation of the system. However, simulation is inherently a weak validation tool in that it only presents a single execution of the system at a time. Like testing, it can only show the presence rather than absence of faults. More powerful are verifiers or theorem provers that are able to compare a desired safety assertion against all possible executions of a program at once. Current generation verifiers are limited in power because they suffer from state explosion problems, rendering them useful only for small problems or subsets of actual systems. Given an architecture, in the form of components, connections, functionality, reliability and performance information about the components, and built-in semantic knowledge about connector types, a verifier could assure developers that performance requirements, deadline satisfaction, availability, resource utilization constraints, and security and invariant safety conditions were all achievable or point out places in the architecture where they were not.

19.5   Summary

Where are the study and practices of software architecture going? Our clairvoyance is no more powerful than anyone else's, but with apologies to Edmund Burke, we will indulge in some predictions. Besides more powerful abstractions and more sophisticated component building blocks for systems, we have two primary predictions for the future where architecture is concerned.

First, the trend toward enterprise development of product lines will continue and blossom. Flexibility—always the key to software's success—is now the watchword in most marketing circles. Making a product flexible to meet the demands of a single customer or small group of customers is seen as the way to grow the customer base and increase market share. And an enterprise-standard architecture for software systems is the key to such flexibility, as we saw in the product line case study. We predict that successful organizations will have one or more carefully developed architectures among their core capital assets and use these architectures to produce (or generate) different versions of their mainline products to effectively and aggressively address different market segments.

Second, from the study of architecture will emerge a relatively small (under 50) set of primary architecture styles that will allow the next generation of systems to be built. Designers will be expected to choose from a standard set of architectures and will be encouraged (coerced) to do so by sophisticated architecture-level automated support tools. New architectures will probably appear as new currently uncontemplated applications for computers emerge, but these will be the exception. For most of the applications most of the time, a standard set of architectures will emerge and become embraced by the community, an architectural version of Knuth's *Fundamental Algorithms.* By limiting ourselves to this workable set of standard architectures, system interoperability will be made as easy as component integration is being made today through the use of standard interfaces. Systems of systems will be constructed with approximately the effort it takes to build systems of components now.

Both predictions, then, are for architecture standardization: the first within an enterprise and the second across the community. Should these come to pass, the study of architecture may in fact subside as an area of intense investigation, having served its purpose by providing us with the enduring models of system building.

Fred Brooks was once asked what made his book, *The Mythical Man-Month,* so timeless. He replied that it was not a book about computers but rather a book about people. Software engineering is like that. Dave Parnas says that the difference between programming and software engineering is that programming is all you need for single-person, single-version software, but if you expect other people to ever look at your system (or you expect to look at it yourself later on), you need to accommodate those people by using the discipline of software engineering. Architecture is like that, also. If all we cared about was getting the right answer, a trivial monolithic architecture would always suffice. Architecture is brought to bear when the people issues are exposed: making the system perform well, letting teams work cooperatively to build it, helping the maintainers succeed, letting all the stakeholders understand it.

With this in mind, then, we can offer our final prediction. Architecture will continue to be important as long as people are involved in the design and development of software.

19.6 For Further Reading

For further reading about software architecture in general, readers are encouraged to visit the Software Engineering Institute's Web site on architecture: *http://www.sei.cmu.edu/technology/architecture.* This site includes a large bibliography on a wide range of topics germane to software architecture.

For a general background in the area of reverse engineering, see Tilley and Smith [Tilley 96]. For a detailed description of the Dali workbench for architectural reconstruction, see Kazman and Carriere [Kazman 97]. Other discussions of the architecture archaeology process can be found in papers by Murphy, Notkin, and Sullivan [Murphy 95] and Yeh, Harris, and Chase [Yeh 97]. For interesting approaches to the area of architectural migration, consult DeLine, Zelesnik, and Shaw [DeLine 97], and the article by Griswold and Notkin [Griswold 93].

A number of application-specific domain taxonomies have emerged recently, such as Jackson's work on problem frames [Jackson 94] and Landwehr's taxonomy of computer program security flaws [Landwehr 94].

Finally, work in design patterns and architectural patterns are becoming widely publicized. Some representatives can be found in Gamma et al. [Gamma 95], Pree [Pree 95], and Shaw [Shaw 96*b*].

Acronyms

AAS advanced automation system, the name given to the planned complete overhaul of the United States air traffic control system

ABC architecture business cycle

ADL architecture description language

ADT abstract data type

AMODEUS Assessing Means of Design Expression for Users and Systems

ANSI American National Standards Institute

API application program interface

ATC air traffic control

BCN backup communications network

BNF Backus-Naur form

CASE computer-aided software engineering

CDE common desktop environment

CERN European Laboratory for Particle Physics

CGI common gateway interface

CIP controller interface processing, an application within Display Management of the ISSS

COCOMO constructive cost modeling

COI common input–output services, an application within Common System Services of the ISSS

CORBA Common Object Request Broker Architecture

COSE common operating system environment

COTS commercial off-the-shelf, referring to software or other components that can be readily purchased

CSCI computer software configuration item, a component of software

CSCW Computer Supported Cooperative Work

DBMS database management systems

DIF dynamic invocation interface

EDARC enhanced direct access radar channel within the ISSS

EFC EDARC format conversion, an application within Display Management

EIS EDARC interface software, an application within Common System Services

ESI EDARC system interface

ESIP ESI processor

FAA Federal Aviation Administration, the customer for ISSS

FAR Federal Acquisition Regulations

FDM fight data management, an application within Display Management for the ISSS

FG functional group, an application that is not fault tolerant (i.e., is not an operational unit) for the ISSS

FTP File Transfer Protocol

GIOP general inter-ORB protocol

GMS global monitor support, an application within Common System Services of the ISSS

GUI graphical user interface

HCI human-computer interface

HCIS Host computer interface software, an application within Common System Services of the ISSS

HCS Host Computer System, the central ATC computer.

HFC Host format conversion, an application within Display Management of the ISSS

HTML HyperText Markup Language

HTTP HyperText Transfer Protocol

IAPR interactive architecture pattern recognition

IDL Interface Definition Language

IMS inertial measurement system

IEEE Institute of Electrical and Electronics Engineers

IP Internet protocol

ISO International Standards Organization

ISSS Initial Sector Suite System, the system intended to be installed in the en route air traffic control centers, and the subject of the case study in Chapter 11

ISV independent software vendor

KSLOC thousands of source lines of code, a standard measure of a computer program's static size

KWIC   keyword in context

LAN   local area network

LCN   local communications network

LGSM   local/group SMMM, an application within Common System Services

LUI   LCN interface unit

M&C   monitor and control, a type of console in ISSS

MEFT   manage external facility time, an application within Common System Services for the ISSS

METOC   Meteorological and Oceanographic

MIFT   manage internal facility time, an application within Common System Services for the ISSS

MVC   model view controller

NASM   national airspace system modification, one of the CSCIs of ISSS

NISL   network interface sublayer within the ISSS

NIST   National Institute of Standards and Technology

NNTP   Network New Transfer Protocol

OLE   object linking and embedding

OMA   object management architecture

OMG   Object Management Group

ORB   object request broker

PAC   presentation, abstraction, control

PAS   primary address space, the copy of an application that does actual work for the ISSS; see also SAS

PCTE   portable common tools environment

PDF   Portable Document Format

PICS   platform for Internet context solution

PMS   prepare messages, an application within Common System Services for the ISSS

RCS   Revision Control System

RID   restart interim display, an application within Display Management for the ISSS

RISC   reduced instruction set chip

RMI   remote method invocation

ROOM   real-time object-oriented modeling

RPC   remote procedure call

SAAM   software architecture analysis method

SAR system analysis and recording, a function of ISSS; also an application within the recording, analysis, and playback function

SAS secondary address space, a backup copy of an application ready to take over if the corresponding PAS fails within the ISSS

SEI Software Engineering Institute

SIMD single instruction, multiple data

SITS simulation and test support, an appliation within Common System Services for the ISSS

SLOC source lines of code

SMMM system monitor and mode management

TAFIM Technical Architecture for Information Management

TARGET Theater-Level Analysis, Replanning and Graphical Execution Toolbox

TCA Terminal Control Area

URL Uniform Resource Locator

WAIS Wide Area Information Service

WIMP window, icon, mouse, pointer

WWW World Wide Web

References

[Abowd 93b] Abowd, G., Bass, L., Howard, L., and Northrop, L., "Structural Modeling: An O-O Framework and Development Process for Flight Simulators." Software Engineering Institute, Carnegie Mellon University, Technical Report CMU-SEI-93-14, 1993.

[Abowd 95] Abowd, G., Allen, R., and Garlan, D., "Formalizing Style to Understand Descriptions of Software Architecture," *ACM Transactions on Software Engineering and Methodology*, 4(4):319–364, 1995.

[Abowd 96] Abowd, G., Bass, L., Clements, P., Kazman, R., Northrop, L., and Zaremski, A., "Recommended Best Industrial Practice for Software Architecture Evaluation." Software Engineering Insitiute, Carnegie Mellon University, Technical Report CMU/SEI-96-TR-025, 1996.

[Alexander 77] Alexander, C., Ishikawa, S., Silverstein, M., Jacobson, M., Fiksdahl-King, I., and Angel, S., *A Pattern Language.* New York: Oxford University Press, 1977.

[Alexander 78] Alexander, C., *The Timeless Way of Building.* New York: Oxford University Press, 1978.

[Andrews 91] Andrews, G., "Paradigms for Process Interaction in Distributed Programs." *ACM Computing Surveys*, 23(1):49–90, 1991.

[ASCYW 94] Air Force Aeronautical Systems Command, *Structural Modeling Handbook,* November 1994.

[AT&T 93] AT&T, "Best Current Practices: Software Architecture Validation," Internal Report. Copyright 1991, 1993, AT&T.

[Berners-Lee 96a] Berners-Lee, T., *WWW Journal,* 3, 1996—*http://www.w3.org/pub/WWW/Journal.*

[Berners-Lee 96b] Berners-Lee, T., "WWW: Past, Present, Future." *IEEE Computer,* October:69–78, 1996.

[Binder 94] Binder, R., "Design for Testability in Object-Oriented Systems." *CACM,* 37(9):87–101, 1994.

[Boehm 95] Boehm, B., "Engineering Context [for Software Architecture]." First International Workshop on Architecture for Software Systems, Seattle, April 1995.

[Booch 93] Booch, G., *Object-Oriented Design with Applications, Second Edition.* Redwood City, CA: Benjamin-Cummings Publishing Company, 1994.

[Britton 81] Britton, K., and Parnas, D., A-7E Software Module Guide. NRL Memorandum Report 4702, December 1981.

[Brooks 69] Brooks, F., and Iverson, K., *Automatic Data Processing (System/360 Edition)*, p. 250. New York: Wiley, 1969.

[Brooks 75] Brooks, F., *The Mythical Man-Month—Essays on Software Engineering.* Reading, MA: Addison-Wesley, 1975.

[Brooks 95] Brooks, F., *The Mythical Man-Month—Essays on Software Engineering (20th Anniversary Edition).* Reading, MA: Addison-Wesley, 1995.

[Brown 95a] Brown, A., Carney, D., and Clements, P., "A Case Study in Assessing the Maintainability of a Large, Software-Intensive System." *Proceedings of the International Symposium on Software Engineering of Computer Based Systems,* pp. 240–250. Tucson: IEEE Computer Society, March 1995.

[Brown 95b] Brown, A., Carney, D., Clements, P., Meyers, C., Smith, D., Weiderman, N., and Wood, W., "Assessing the Quality of Large, Software Intensive Systems: A Case Study." *Proceedings of the European Conference on Software Engineering,* pp. 384–404, September 1995.

[Brownsword 96] Brownsword, L., and Clements, P., "A Case Study in Successful Product Line Development." Software Engineering Institute, Carnegie Mellon University, Technical Report CMU/SEI 96-TR-016, 1996.

[Buschmann 96] Buschmann, F., Meunier, R., Rohnert, H., Sommerlad, P., and Stal, M., *Pattern-Oriented Software Architecture: A System of Patterns.* New York: Wiley, 1996.

[Bush 45] Bush, V., "As We May Think." *Atlantic Monthly,* 176:101–108, July 1945.

[CACM 88] *Communications of the ACM,* HyperText Systems Special Issue, July 1988.

[Cederling 92] Cederling, U., "Industrial Software Development—A Case Study" (Thesis No. 348). Linkoping, Sweden: Linkoping University, 1992.

[Chastek, 96] Chastek, G., and Brownsword, L., "A Case Study in Structural Modeling." Software Engineering Institute, Carnegie Mellon University, Technical Report CMU/SEI-96-TR-35, ESC-TR-96-035, December 1996.

[Clements 96] Clements, P., "A Survey of Architecture Description Languages," *Proceedings Eighth International Workshop on Software Specification and Design,* Paderborn, Germany, 1996.

[Conway 68] Conway, M., "How Do Committees Invent?" *Datamation,* 14(4):28–31, 1968.

[Coutaz 87] Coutaz, J., "PAC, An Implementation Model for Dialog Design," *Proceedings of Interact '87,* pp. 431–436. Stuttgart, September 1987.

[Cusumano 97] Cusumano, M., and Selby, R., "How Microsoft Builds Software." *CACM,* 40(6):53–61, 1997.

[Davis 04] Davis, G. E. *A Handbook of Chemical Engineering* (illustrated with working examples and numerous drawings from actual installations), 2nd ed. Manchester, England: Davis Bros., 1904.

[DeLine 97] DeLine, R., Zelesnik, G., and Shaw, M., "Lessons on Converting Batch Systems to Support Interaction," *Proceedings of ICSE,* 19:95–204, 1997.

[Deng 95] Deng, R. H., Bhengle, S., Wang, W., et. al., "Integrating Security in CORBA-Based Object Architectures." *Proceedings of the IEEE Symposium on Security and Privacy,* May 8–10, pp 50–61. Los Alamitos, CA: IEEE Computer Society Press, 1995.

[Dewan 95] Dewan, P., "Multiuser Architectures." *Engineering for Human-Computer Interaction,* pp. 247–269. London: Chapman & Hall, 1995.

[Dijkstra 68] Dijkstra, E. W., "The Structure of the 'T.H.E.' Multiprogramming System." *CACM*, 18(8):453–457, 1968.

[Ellis 96] Ellis, W., Rayford, D., Millard, R., et al., "Toward a Recommended Practice for Architectural Description." *Proceedings of the Second International Conference on Engineering of Comples Computer Systems*, pp. 408–413. Montreal, 1996.

[Fogarty 67] Fogarty, L., "Survey of Flight Simulation Computation Methods." *Third International Simulation and Training Conference*, April:36–40, 1967.

[Furter 80] Furter, W. (Ed.), *History of Chemical Engineering*. Washington D.C.: American Chemical Society, 1980.

[Gabriel 96] Gabriel, R., *Patterns of Software*. New York: Oxford University Press, 1996.

[Gamma 95] Gamma, E., Helm, R., Johnson, R., and Vlissides, J., *Design Patterns, Elements of Reusable Object-Oriented Software*. Reading, MA: Addison-Wesley, 1995.

[Garlan 95] Garlan, D. Allen, R., and Ockerbloom, J., "Architectural Mismatch: Why Reuse Is So Hard." *IEEE Software,* 12(6):17–26, 1995.

[Gibbs 94] Gibbs, W., "Software's Chronic Crisis." *Scientific American*, September:86–95, 1994.

[Gray 97] Gray, M. Further information available from the author at mkgray@mit.edu.

[Griswold 93] Griswold, W., and Notkin, D., "Automated Assistance for Program Restructuring." *Transactions on Software Engineering and Methodology,* 2(3):228–269, 1993.

[Hager 89] Hager, J. A., "Software Cost Reduction Methods in Practice." *IEEE Transactions on Software Engineering,* 15:1638–1644, 1989.

[Hager 91] Hager, J. A., "Software Cost Reduction Methods in Practice: A Post-Mortem Analysis." *Journal of Systems Software,* 14:67–77, 1991.

[Hamilton 96]. Hamilton, M., "Java and the Shift to Net-Centric Computing." *IEEE Computer,* 29(8):31–39, 1996.

[Harel 88] Harel, D., Lachover, H., Naamad, A., Pnueli, A., Politi, M., Sherman, R., and Shtul-Trauring, A., "STATEMATE: A Working Environment for the Development of Complex Reactive Systems." *Proceedings of the 10th International Conference on Software Engineering,* Singapore, April 1988.

[IEEE 93] Institute of Electrical and Electronic Engineers, "Draft Guide for Information Technology—Portable Operating System Interface (POSIX)—The Open Systems Environment," P1003.0/D16 (also known as POSIX.0). Portable Applications Standards Committee of the IEEE Computer Society, August 1993.

[IEEE 95] Special Issue on Software Architecture, *IEEE Transactions on Software Engineering*, 21(4), April 1995.

[ISO/IEC 91] International Organization for Standardization and International Electrotechnical Commission, "Information Technology—Software Product Evaluation—Quality Characteristics and Guidelines for Their Use." ISO/IEC 9216: 1991(E).

[Iverson 89] Iverson, K., "Notation as a Tool of Thought" (ACM Turing Award lecture). In R. L. Ashenhurst (Ed.), *ACM Turing Award Lectures: The First Twenty Years—1966–1985*, ACM Anthology Series. Reading, MA: ACM Press/Addison-Wesley, 1989.

[Jackson 94] Jackson, M., "Problems, Methods, and Specialization." *IEEE Software,* 11(6):57–62, 1994.

[Jacobson 92] Jacobson, I., Christerson, M., Jonsson, P., and Overgaard, G., *Object-Oriented Software Engineering: A Use Case Driven Approach.* Reading, MA: Addison-Wesley, 1992.

[Jahanian 94] Jahanian, F., and Mok, A., "Modechart: A Specification Language for Real-Time Systems." *IEEE Transactions on Software Engineering,* 20(12): 933–947, 1994.

[Jell 95] Jell, T., and Stal, M., "Comparing, Contrasting and Interweaving CORBA and OLE," *Proceedings of OBJECT EXPO Europe,* September 25–29. Newdigate, UK: SIGS Publications, 1995.

[Kazman 97] Kazman, R., and Carrière, J., "Playing Detective: Reconstructing Software Architecture from Available Evidence." Software Engineering Institute, Carnegie Mellon University, Technical Report CMU/SEI-97-TR-10, 1997.

[Klein 93] Klein, M. H., Ralya, T., Pollack, B., Obenza, R., and Harbour, M. G., *A Practitioner's Handbook for Real-Time Analysis: Guide to Rate Monotonic Analysis for Real-Time Systems.* Boston: Kluwer Academic Publishers, 1993.

[Krasner 88] Krasner, G., and Pope, S., "A Cookbook for Using Model-View-Controller User Interface Paradigm in Smalltalk-8." *Journal of Object Oriented Programming,* 1(3):26–49, 1988.

[Kruchten 95] Kruchten, P., "The 4+1 View Model of Architecture." *IEEE Software,* 12(6):42–50, 1995.

[Lai 97] Lai, R., and Weiss, D., *A Formal Model of the FAST Process.* Reading, MA: Addison-Wesley, 1997.

[Landwehr 94] Landwehr, C., Bull, A., McDermott, J., and Choi, W., "A Taxonomy of Computer Program Security Flaws." *ACM Computing Surveys,* 26(3):211–254, 1994.

[Lee 88] Lee, K., Rissman, M., D'Ippolito, R., Plinta, C., and Van Scoy, R., *An OOD Paradigm for Flight Simulators,* 2nd ed. Software Engineering Institute, Carnegie Mellon University Technical Report CMU/SEI-88-TR-30, 1988.

[Lindstrom 93] Lindstrom, D., "Five Ways to Destroy a Development Project." *IEEE Software,* 10(5):55–58, 1993.

[Luckham 95] Luckham, D., and Vera, J., "An Event-Based Architecture Definition Language." *IEEE Transactions on Software Engineering,* 21(9):717–734, 1995.

[Marsman 85] Marsman, A., "Flexible and High Quality Software on a Multi Processor Computer System Controlling a Research Flight Simulator." *AGARD Conference Proceedings No. 408: Flight Simulation,* 9(1):9–11, 1985.

[Medvidovic 96] Medvidovic, N., "A Classification and Comparison Framework for Software Architecture Description Languages." Department of Information and Computer Science, University of California, Irvine, Technical Report UCI-ICS-97-02, February 1996.

[Morris 93] Morris, C., and Ferguson, C., "How Architecture Wins Technology Wars." *Harvard Business Review,* 71(March–April):86–96, 1993.

[Murphy 95] Murphy, G., Notkin, D., and Sullivan, K., "Software Reflexion Models: Bridging the Gap Between Source and High-Level Models." *Proceedings of the Third ACM SIGSOFT Symposium on the Foundations of Software Engineering (FSE '95),* Washington, D.C., October 1995.

[Murphy 96] Murphy, G., Notkin, D., and Lam, E., "An Empirical Study of Static Call Graph Extractors." *Proceedings of the Eighteenth International Conference on Software Engineering*. Tucson: IEEE Computer Society Press, March 1996.

[Newton 92] Newton, P., and Browne, J., "The CODE 2.0 Graphical Parallel Programming Language." *Proceedings of the ACM International Conference on Supercomputing,* Washington, D.C., July 1992.

[Nigay 91] Nigay, L., and Coutaz, J., "Building User Interfaces, Organizing Software Agents." *Proceedings of ESPRIT '91*, Brussels, November 1991.

[Parnas 71] Parnas, D., "Information Distribution Aspects of Design Methodology," *Proceedings of the 1971 IFIP Congress*. Amsterdam: North Holland Publishing, 1971.

[Parnas 72] Parnas, D., "On the Criteria for Decomposing Systems into Modules." *CACM*, 15(12):1053–1058, 1972.

[Parnas 74] Parnas, D., "On a 'Buzzword': Hierarchical Structure." *Proceedings of the IFIP Congress,* 74:336–390, 1974.

[Parnas 76] Parnas, D., "On the Design and Development of Program Families." *IEEE Transactions on Software Engineering*, SE-2(1):1–9, 1976.

[Parnas 79] Parnas, D., "Designing Software for Ease of Extension and Contraction." *IEEE Transactions on Software Engineering*, SE-5(2):128–137, 1979.

[Parnas 85a] Parnas, D., Clements, P., and Weiss, D., "The Modular Structure of Complex Systems." *Proceedings of the Seventh International Conference on Software Engineering,* pp. 408–417. March 1984. Reprinted in *IEEE Transactions on Software Engineering,* SE-11:259–266, 1985.

[Parnas 85b] Parnas, D., and Weiss, D., "Active Design Reviews: Principles and Practices." *Proceedings of the Eighth International Conference on Software Engineering,* pp. 132–136. 1985.

[Perry 66] Perry, D., Warton, L., and Welbourn, C., "A Flight Simulator for Research into Aircraft Handling Characteristics." Aeronautical Research Council Reports and Memoranda No. 3566, London, 1966.

[Pfaff 85] Pfaff, G. E., (Ed.), *User Interface Systems* (Eurographics Seminars). New York: Springer-Verlag, 1985.

[Pree 95] Pree, W., *Design Patterns for Object-Oriented Software Development.* Reading, MA: Addison-Wesley, 1995.

[Rissman 90] Rissman, M., D'Ippolito, R., Lee, K., and Stewart, J., "Definition of Engineering Requirements for AFECO—Lessons from Flight Simulators." Software Engineering Institute, Carnegie Mellon University, Technical Report CMU/SEI-90-TR-25, 1990.

[Roy 95] Roy, M., and Ewald, A., "Distributed Object Interoperability." *Object Magazine,* 5(1):18, 1995.

[Shaw 96a] Shaw M., and Garlan, D., *Software Architecture: Perspectives on an Emerging Discipline.* Englewood Cliffs, NJ: Prentice Hall, 1996.

[Shaw 96b] Shaw, M., "Some Patterns for Software Architechture." In J. Vlissides, J. Coplien, and N. Kerth (Eds.), *Pattern Languages of Program Design*, 2, pp. 255–269. Reading, MA: Addison-Wesley, 1996.

[Shaw 97] Shaw, M., and Clements, P., "A Field Guide to Boxology: Preliminary Classification of Architectural Styles for Software Systems." *Proceedings of COMPSAC,* Washington, D.C., August 1997.

[Smith 90] Smith, C. U., *Performance Engineering of Software Systems.* The SEI Series in Software Engineering, Reading, MA: Addison-Wesley, 1990.

[Smith 93] Smith, C. U., and Williams, L. G., "Software Performance Engineering: A Case Study Including Performance Comparison with Design Alternatives." *IEEE Transactions on Software Engineering*, 19(7):720–741, 1993.

[Soni 95] Soni, D., Nord, R., and Hofmeister, C., "Software Architecture in Industrial Applications." *Proceedings of the International Conference on Software Engineering*, 196–210. Seatttle, April 1995.

[TAFIM] U.S. Department of Defense. *Technical Architecture Framework for Information Management* (TAFIM), Vols. 1–8, Version 2.0. DISA Center for Architecture (10701 Parkridge Blvd., Reston, VA 22091-4398), June 30, 1994.

[Tilley 96] Tilley, S., and Smith, D., "Coming Attractions in Program Understanding," Software Engineering Institute, Carnegie Mellon University, Technical Report CMU/SEI-TR-96-019, December 1996.

[UIMS 92] UIMS Tool Developers Workshop, "A Metamodel for the Runtime Architecture of an Interactive System." *SIGCHI Bulletin*, 24(1):32–37, 1992.

[Vestal 93] Vestal, S., *A Cursory Overview and Comparison of Four Architectural Description Languages.* Honeywell Technical Report, February 1993.

[Watson 96] Watson, A., "The OMG after CORBA 2." *Object Magazine,* 6(1):58–60, 1996.

[Wirth 89] Wirth, N., "Programming Language Design to Computer Construction" (ACM Turing Award lecture). In R. L. Ashenhurst (Ed.), *ACM Turing Award Lectures: The First Twenty Years—1966–1985*, ACM Anthology Series. Reading, MA: ACM Press/Addison-Wesley, 1989.

[Witt 94] Witt, B. I., Baker, F. T., and Merritt, E. W., *Software Architecture and Design.* New York: Van Nostrand Reinhold, 1994.

[Yeh 97] Yeh, A., Harris, D., and Chase, M., "Manipulating Recovered Software Architecture Views." *Proceedings of ICSE,* 19:184–194, 1997.

Bibliography

[Abowd 93a] Abowd, G., Allen, R., and Garlan, D., "Using Style to Give Meaning to Software Architecture." *Proceedings of SIGSOFT '93, Software Engineering Notes,* 118(3):9–20, 1993.

[Arango 89] Arango, G., and Prieto-Diaz, R., "Domain Analysis: Concepts and Research Directions." In R. Prieto-Diaz and G. Arango (Eds.), *Domain Analysis: Acquisition of Reusable Information for Software Construction,* pp. 9–26. Tucson: IEEE Computer Society Press, May 1989.

[Binns 93] Binns, P., Englehart, M., Jackson, M., and Vestal, S., "Domain-Specific Software Architectures for Guidance, Navigation, and Control." Honeywell Technology Center, 1993.

[Birman 93] Birman, K., "The Process Group Approach to Reliable Distributed Computing," *CACM,* 36(12):37–53, 1993.

[Boehm 96] Boehm, B., "Identifying Quality-Requirement Conflicts," *IEEE Software,* March:25–36, 1996.

[Budgen 93] Budgen, D., *Software Design.* Reading, MA: Addison-Wesley, 1993.

[Cagan 90] Cagan, M., "The HP SoftBench Environment: An Architecture for a New Generation of Software Tools." *Hewlett-Packard Journal,* June:36–47, 1990.

[Clements 85] Clements, P., Parnas, D., and Weiss, D., "The Modular Structure of Complex Programs." *IEEE Transactions on Software Engineering,* SE-11(3):259–266, 1985.

[Clements 86] Clements, P., and Parnas, D., "A Rational Design Process: How and Why to Fake It." *IEEE Transactions on Software Engineering,* SE-12(2):251–257, 1986.

[Cline 96] Cline, M., "The Pros and Cons of Adopting and Applying Design Patterns in the Real World." *CACM,* 39(10):47–49, 1996.

[Constantine 79] Constantine, L., and Yourdon, E., *Structured Design.* Englewood Cliffs, NJ: Prentice Hall, 1979.

[Crispen 93] Crispen, R., Freemon, B., King, K., and Tucker, W., "DARTS: A Domain Architecture for Reuse in Training Systems." *Proceedings of the Fifteenth I/ITSEC,* pp. 659–668. November 1993.

[Cusumano 95] Cusumano, M., and Selby, R., *Microsoft Secrets.* New York: Free Press, 1995.

[Edwards 94] Edwards, S., Heym, W., Long, T., Sitarman, M., and Weide, B., "Specifying Components in RESOLVE." *Software Engineering Notes,* 19(4):29–51, 1994.

[Fernandez 93] Fernandez, J., *A Taxonomy of Coordination Mechanisms Used in Real-Time Software Based on Domain Analysis.* Software Engineering Institute, Carnegie Mellon University, Technical Report CMU/SEI-93-TR-34, ESC-TR-93-321, December 1993.

[Ganger 94] Ganger, G., Worthington, B., Hou, R., and Patt, Y., "Disk Arrays: High-Performance, High-Reliability Storage Systems." *IEEE Computer*, 27(3):30–36, 1994.

[Garlan 92] Garlan, D., Kaiser, G., and Notkin, D., "Using Tool Abstraction to Compose Systems." *IEEE Computer*, 25(6):30–38, 1992.

[Garlan 93] Garlan, D., and Shaw, M., "An Introduction to Software Architecture." In Ambriola and Torura (Eds.), *Advances in Software Engineering and Knowledge Engineering,* Vol. I, Singapore: World Scientific Publishing Company, 1993.

[Garlan 94] Garlan, D., Allen, R., and Ockerbloom, J., "Exploiting Style in Architectural Design Environments." *Proceedings of SIGSOFT '94: Foundations of Software Engineering,* pp. 175–188. ACM Press, December 1994.

[Green 85] Green, M., "Report on Dialogue Specification Tools." in G. Pfaff (Ed.), *User Interface Management Systems,* pp. 9–20. New York: Springer-Verlag, 1985.

[Hartman 95] Hartman, J., and Chandrasekaran, B., "Functional Representation and Understanding of Software: Technology and Application." *Proceedings of the 1995 Dual-Use Technologies and Applications Conference,* Utica, New York, 1995.

[Hauser 88] Hauser, J., and Clausing, D., "The House of Quality." *Harvard Business Review*, 32(5):63–73, 1988.

[Jazayeri 95] Jazayeri, M., "Component Programming—A Fresh Look at Software Components." Technical University of Vienna, Technical Report TUV-1841-95-01, 1995.

[Johnson 89] Johnson, J., "The Xerox Star: A Retrospective." *IEEE Computer*, 22(9):11–28, 1989.

[Kazman 94] Kazman, R., Bass, L., Abowd, G., and Webb, M., "SAAM: A Method for Analyzing the Properties of Software Architectures," *Proceedings of ICSE-16*, pp. 81–90. Sorrento, Italy, May 1994.

[Kazman 96] Kazman, R., Abowd, G., Bass, L., and Clements, P., "Scenario-Based Analysis of Software Architecture." *IEEE Software*, 13(6):47–56, 1996.

[Knuth 73] Knuth, D., *Fundamental Algorithms.* Reading, MA: Addison-Wesley, 1973.

[Kontio 96] Kontio, J., "A Case Study in Applying a Systematic Method for COTS Selection." *Proceedings of the International Conference on Software Engineering,* Berlin, 1996.

[Lane 90] Lane, T., "A Design Space and Design Rules for User Interface Software Architecture," Software Engineering Institute, Carnegie Mellon University, Technical Report CMU/SEI-90-TR-22, 1990.

[Luqi 93] Luqi, Shing, M., Barnes, P., and Hughes, G., "Prototyping Hard Real-Time Ada Systems in a Classroom Environment." *Proceedings of the Seventh Annual Ada Software Engineering Education and Training (ASEET) Symposium,* pp. 12–14. Monterey, January 1993.

[McConnell 96] McConnell, S., "Missing in Action: Information Hiding." *IEEE Software*, 127–128, 1996.

[Meyers 96] Meyers, B. C., and Oberndorf, P. A., "Open Systems: The Promises and the Pitfalls." Software Engineering Institute course, 1996.

[OMG 90] Object Management Group and X/Open, "The Common Object Request Broker: Architecture and Specification." OMG Document No. 91.12.1 (revision 1.1). Framingham, MA: OMG, 1990.

[Palsberg 95] Palsberg, J., Xiao, C., and Lieberherr, K., "Efficient Implementation of Adaptive Software (Summary of Demeter Theory)." Northeastern University, Boston, January 10, 1995.

[Paulk 88] Paulk, M., Curtis, B., Chrissis, M. B., et al., "Capability Maturity Model for Software." Software Engineering Institute, Carnegie Mellon University, Technical Report CMU/SEI-91-TR-24, 1988.

[Perry 92] Perry, D. E., and Wolf, A. L., "Foundations for the Study of Software Architecture." *Software Engineering Notes, ACM SIGSOFT*, 17(4):40–52, 1992.

[Rochkind 92] Rochkind, M., "An Extensible Virtual Toolkit (XVT) for Portable GUI Applications." *Digest of Papers, COMPCON Spring 1992,* pp. 485–494. San Francisco, February 1992.

[Rumbaugh 91] Rumbaugh, J., Blaha, M., *et al., Object-Oriented Modeling and Design.* Englewood Cliffs, NJ: Prentice Hall, 1991.

[Scheifler 86] Scheifler, R., and Gettys, J., "The X Window System." *ACM Transactions on Graphics,* 5(2): 79–109.

[Schwanke 94] Schwanke, R., "Industrial Software Architecture with Gestalt." Siemens Corporate Research Technical Report, Princeton, NJ, 1994.

[Selic 94] Selic, B., Gullekson, B., and Ward, P., *Real-Time Object-Oriented Modeling.* New York: Wiley, 1994.

[Shaw 90] Shaw M., "Prospects for an Engineering Discipline of Software." *IEEE Software,* 7(6):15–24, 1990.

[Shaw 94] Shaw, M., "Procedure Calls Are the Assembly Language of Software Interconnection; Connectors Deserve First-Class Status," Software Engineering Institute, Carnegie Mellon University, Technical Report CMU/SEI 94-TR-02, January 1994.

[Shaw 95] Shaw, M., DeLine, R., Klein, D., Ross, T., Young, D., and Zelesnik G., "Abstractions for Software Architectures and Tools to Support Them." *IEEE Transactions on Software Engineering,* 24(4):314–335, 1995.

[Simon 81] Simon, H., *The Sciences of the Artificial.* Cambridge, MA: MIT Press, 1981.

[Terry 94] Terry, A., Hayes-Roth, R., Erman, L., Coleman, N., Devito, M., Papanagopoulos, G., and Hayes-Roth, B., "Overview of Teknowledge's DSSA Program." *ACM SIGSOFT Software Engineering Notes,* 19(4):68–76, 1994.

[Tracz 93] Tracz, W., "LILEANNA: A Parameterized Programming Language." *Proceedings of the Second International Workshop on Software Reuse,* March 1993.

[Trevor 94] Trevor, J., Rodden, T., and Mariani, J., "The Use of Adapters to Support Cooperative Sharing." *Proceedings of the 1994 Conference on Computer Supported Cooperative Work,* pp. 219–230.

[Wasserman 89] Wasserman, A., "Tool Integration in Software Engineering Environments." In F. Long (Ed.), *Software Engineering Environments* (Lecture Notes in Computer Science No. 467). New York: Springer-Verlag, 1989.

[Woods 96] Woods, S., and Yang, Q., "The Program Understanding Problem: Analysis and a Heuristic Approach." *Proceedings of ICSE* 18:6–15, 1996.

Index

The SEI Series in Software Engineering

Introduction to the Team Software Process[SM]
by Watts S. Humphrey
0-201-47719-X • 2000 • Hardcover • 496 pages

Watts Humphrey provides software engineers with precisely the teamwork training and practice they need. While presenting a quick and comprehensive perspective of what team software development is all about, the book provides practitioners and students in any projects-based software engineering environment with a practical and realistic teamworking experience. The Team Software Process (TSP) is built on and requires knowledge of the author's influential Personal Software Process (PSP), which details how programmers can (and should) manage time and achieve quality in their own work. The TSP shows how to apply similar engineering discipline to the full range of team software tasks, leading ultimately to greater productivity.

Introduction to the Personal Software Process[SM]
by Watts S. Humphrey
0-201-54809-7 • 1997 • Paperback • 304 pages

This workbook provides a hands-on introduction to the basic discipline of software engineering. Designed as a programming course supplement to integrate the PSP into a university curriculum, the book may also be adapted for use by industrial groups or for self-improvement. By applying the book's exercises, you can learn to manage your time effectively and to monitor the quality of your work.

A Discipline for Software Engineering
by Watts S. Humphrey
0-201-54610-8 • 1995 • Hardcover • 816 pages

This book scales down successful methods developed by the author to a personal level for managers and organizations to evaluate and improve their software capabilities. The author's concern here is to help individual software practitioners develop the skills and habits they need to plan, track, and analyze large and complex projects and to develop high-quality products.

Managing the Software Process
by Watts S. Humphrey
0-201-18095-2 • 1989 • Hardcover • 512 pages

This landmark book introduces the author's methods, now commonly practiced in industry, for improving software development and mainte-nance processes. Emphasizing the basic principles and priorities of the software process, the book's sections are organized in a natural way to guide organizations through needed improvement activities.

The SEI Series in Software Engineering

Managing Technical People
Innovation, Teamwork, and the Software Process
by Watts S. Humphrey
0-201-54597-7 • 1997 • Paperback • 352 pages

This insightful book—drawing on the author's extensive experience as a senior manager of software development at IBM—describes proven techniques for managing technical professionals. The author shows specifically how to identify, motivate, and organize innovative people, while tying leadership practices to improvements in the software process.

The Capability Maturity Model
Guidelines for Improving the Software Process
by Carnegie Mellon University/Software Engineering Institute
0-201-54664-7 • 1995 • Hardcover • 464 pages

This book provides a description and technical overview of the Capability Maturity Model (CMM), with guidelines for improving software process management. The CMM provides software professionals in government and industry with the ability to identify, adopt, and use sound management and technical practices for delivering quality software on time and within budget.

Managing Risk
Methods for Software Systems Development
by Elaine M. Hall
0-201-25592-8 • 1998 • Hardcover • 400 pages

Written for busy professionals charged with delivering high-quality products on time and within budget, this book is a comprehensive guide that describes a success formula for managing software risk. The book is divided into five parts that describe a risk management road map designed to take you from crisis to control of your software project.

Software Architecture in Practice
by Len Bass, Paul Clements, and Rick Kazman
0-201-19930-0 • 1998 • Hardcover • 480 pages

This book introduces the concepts and practice of software architecture—what a system is designed to do and how its components are meant to interact with each other. It covers not only essential technical topics for specifying and validating a system, but also emphasizes the importance of the business context in which large systems are designed. Enhancing both technical and organizational discussions, key points are illuminated by substantial case studies undertaken by the authors and the Software Engineering Institute.